RETRIEVED RICHES: SOCIAL INVESTIGATION IN
BRITAIN 1840–1914

out as a wedge into this bar & round it are ranged the other bars. next below the public bar is the womens bar. below that the Select bar. This finishes the front part of the house.

[drawing labels: East India Dock Road, Entrance, Entrance, Entrance, Entrance, Jug & bottle bar, Entrance, Womens bar, Select, Stairs to Hotel, Public Bar, Bar for beer Spirits, Pumps & taps, Saloon bar, Ale pumps, Bar pumps & taps, Stool, Empty barrel, Door, Womens bar, Select bar, Entrance, Entrance, Door, Fire, West India Dock Road]

[Ground Plan of G. E. Hotel]

back of the serving bar is a door through leading from the — Saloon bar which is quite apart from to the front of the house×

Frontispiece A pen and ink ground plan of the Great Eastern Hotel, West India Dock Road, entered into George Duckworth's record of his walk around the area. Note the separate bars for women and also the jug and bottle bar well away from the rest of the public house. This was where children would purchase alcoholic beverages for their parents. (Booth Collection, B352, p.33)

Retrieved riches: social investigation in Britain 1840–1914

Edited by David Englander and Rosemary O'Day

Ashgate

Aldershot • Brookfield USA • Singapore • Sydney

© David Englander and Rosemary O'Day

Published by
Ashgate Publishing
Gower House
Croft Road
Aldershot
Hants GU11 3HR
England

Ashgate Publishing Company
Old Post Road
Brookfield
Vermont 05036
USA

Reprinted 1998

British Library Cataloguing-in-Publication Data

Retrieved Riches: Social Investigation in Britain, 1840–1914
     I. Englander, David II. O'Day, Rosemary
     300.72041

Library of Congress Cataloging-in-Publication Data

Retrieved Riches: Social Investigation in Britian, 1840–1914/edited by
     David Englander and Rosemary O'Day
     Includes bibliographical references and index.
     ISBN 1–85928–118–4. – ISBN 1–85928–229–6 (pbk.)
     1. Sociology – Great Britain – History. 2. Booth, Charles,
     1840–1916. I. Englander, David, 1949–   II.   O'Day,
     Rosemary, HM22.G7R48   1995
     301'.0941–dc20   5–7265 CIP

ISBN 1 85928 118 4 hard covers
     1 85928 229 6 paperback

Printed in Great Britain at the University Press, Cambridge

Contents

List of figures, maps and tables   vii

List of abbreviations   viii

List of contributors   ix

Preface   xi

Introduction
David Englander and Rosemary O'Day   1

Part I: Social and economic thought

1   Social facts, social theory and social change: the ideas of
     Booth in relation to those of Beatrice Webb, Octavia Hill
     and Helen Bosanquet
     Jane Lewis   49

2   Between civic virtue and Social Darwinism: the concept of
     the residuum
     José Harris   67

3   Charles Booth as an under-consumptionist economist
     Alon Kadish   89

Part II: Methods of social inquiry

4   Comparisons and contrasts: Henry Mayhew and Charles
     Booth as social investigators
     David Englander   105

5   Interviews and investigations: Charles Booth and the
     making of the Religious Influences survey
     Rosemary O'Day   143

6   Women and social investigation: Clara Collet and Beatrice
     Potter
     Rosemary O'Day   165

7   Paradigms of poverty: a rehabilitation of B.S. Rowntree
     J.H. Veit-Wilson   201

Part III: Retrieved Riches: using the Booth archive

8   Charles Booth and the social geography of education in
        late nineteenth-century London
        William Marsden   *241* Yes.

9   Working-class religion in late Victorian London: Booth's
        'Religious Influences' revisited
        Hugh McLeod   *265*

10   Booth's Jews: the presentation of Jews and Judaism in *Life
        and Labour of the People in London*
        David Englander   *289*

11   Representations of metropolis: descriptions of the social
        environment in *Life and Labour*
        David Reeder   *323* Yes

12   Women in Victorian religion
        Rosemary O'Day   *339*

13   Gambling, 'the fancy', and Booth's role and reputation as
        a social investigator
        Mark Clapson   *365* Yes

Select bibliography   *381*

Index   *402*

List of figures, maps and tables

Figures

Frontispiece   Plan of the Great Eastern Hotel, West India Dock Road, according to George Duckworth. (By kind permission of the British Library of Political and Economic Science)   *ii*

3.1   George Duckworth's walk through the Parish of St John, Whitechapel, March 1898. (By kind permission of the British Library of Political and Economic Science)   88

11.1   George Duckworth's walk through Cartwright Street, East Smithfield, March 1898. (By kind permission of the British Library of Political and Economic Science)   322

Maps

8.1   Bermondsey, 1875: Board school fees and social area differentiation (after Booth)   244

8.2   St George's-in-the-East: selected Board school catchment zones and social area differentiation in the 1890s (after Booth)   252

8.3   Hampstead and environs, 1890s: social area differentiation (simplification of Booth's map)   253

8.4   London: distribution of persons engaged in education, 1891 (after Booth)   257

Tables

7.1   Population statistics and percentages in poverty, York, 1899   210

7.2   Population statistics and percentages in poverty, York, 1936, and comparisons with 1899   221

7.3   Rowntree's 1950 poverty line and Townsend's 1969 deprivation standard compared with National Assistance or supplementary benefit scales   229

8.1   Six classes and three grades of elementary schools   247

List of abbreviations

BAAS	British Association for the Advancement of Science
BLPES	British Library of Political and Economic Science
BWD	Beatrice Webb's Diary
CBC	Charles Booth Centre
COS	Charity Organization Society
GLCRO	Greater London Record Office
Industry	Charles Booth, *Life and Labour of the People in London*, Industry Series, 5 vols (London: Macmillan,1902)
LL&LP	*London Labour and the London Poor*
MCS	*Morning Chronicle Survey*
MSS	Manchester Statistical Society
NAPSS	National Association for the Promotion of Social Science
Poverty	Charles Booth, *Life and Labour of the People in London*, Poverty Series, 4 vols (London: Macmillan, 1902)
RC	Royal Commission
Religious Influences	Charles Booth, *Life and Labour of the People in London*, Religious Influences Series, 6 vols (London: 1902)
RSS	Royal Statistical Society
SBV	School Board Visitor
SC	Select Committee
SDF	Social Democratic Federation
VCH	Victoria County History

List of contributors

Mark Clapson is Lecturer in History at the University of Luton.

David Englander is Senior Lecturer in European Humanities Studies and Co-Director of the Charles Booth Centre at the Open University.

José Harris is Fellow and Tutor in History at St Catherine's College, Oxford.

Alon Kadish has been on the faculty of the Hebrew University of Jerusalem and the University of Manchester and is Deputy Editor of the *New Dictionary of National Biography*.

Jane Lewis is Professor in the Department of Social Administration at the London School of Economics.

William Marsden is Professor in the School of Education, University of Liverpool.

Hugh McLeod is Professor in the Faculty of Theology, University of Birmingham.

Rosemary O'Day is Senior Lecturer in History and Co-Director of the Charles Booth Centre at the Open University.

David Reeder is Fellow at the Centre for Urban Studies, University of Leicester.

J.H. Veit-Wilson is Professor Emeritus of the University of Northumbria and Guest Member of the Research Staff of the Department of Social Policy, University of Newcastle.

Preface

The editors have many debts to acknowledge. We have great pleasure in thanking the Faculty of Arts at the Open University for its support (both moral and financial) and the Women in the Humanities Seminar therein for listening patiently to several of the essays at an early stage, and offering encouragement and constructive criticism. It is equally gratifying to acknowledge the contribution of the Charles Booth Centre to the successful fruition of the project. The essays themselves came largely from members and associates of the Centre. Many drew their inspiration from a conference organized by the CBC in April 1989, which was opened by Dr John Stevenson and which included papers from Mark Clapson, David Englander, José Harris, Jane Lewis, Hugh McLeod, Lawrence Marlow, Bill Marsden, David Reeder and Raphael Samuel. Our heartfelt thanks are due, once again, to Dr Angela Raspin and Ms Sue Donnolly of the British Library of Political and Economic Science, for their time and expertise. Dr Judith Ford, Research Fellow at the Centre, was unstinting in her work on the volume. Dr John Stevenson commented on the final draft, for which we are most grateful. Denise Powers (secretary to the CBC) and Wendy Clark helped to produce an initial typescript of the entire volume. We owe an especial debt to Kate Clements, without whose able and generous assistance this book could not have appeared.

We thank *History*, *Victorian Studies* and the *Journal of Social Policy*, for permission to republish chapters 5, 6, 10 and 7, which appeared either in whole or in part of their pages as follows:

> Rosemary O'Day, 'Interviews and investigation: Charles Booth and the making of the Religious Influences Survey', *History*, 74 (1989), pp.361–77; Rosemary O'Day, 'Before the Webbs: Beatrice Potter's early investigations for Charles Booth's Inquiry', *History*, 78 (1993), pp.218–42; David Englander, 'Booth's Jews: the presentation of Jews and Judaism in *Life and Labour of the People in London*', *Victorian Studies*, 32 (1989), pp.551–71; J.H. Veit-Wilson, 'Paradigms of poverty: a rehabilitation of B.S. Rowntree', *Journal of Social Policy*, 15 (1986), pp.69–99.

Last but not least, the editors thank their two young sons, Daniel and Matthew, and apologize for giving them so much cause to say: 'You're not working on that book again?' At least next time it will be a different book!

We dedicate this book to our nieces and nephews: Helen, Charlotte and Alexander Brander of Maidstone; Richard, Martin and Timothy Poole of Stoke-on-Trent; and Mandy Brookes of Manchester.

Introduction

David Englander and Rosemary O'Day

'The majority of Englishmen', John Stuart Mill observed, '... have no life but in their work.' Mill, writing in 1857, thought that the absence of a taste for amusement and pleasure in repose was evidence of a deficient sensibility and want of cultivation.[1] What for Mill was an expression of a disagreeable materialism, however, was for the wage-earning classes the very fabric of their existence. Those who knew about the realities of industrial life knew better. Work supplied the organizing insight of *London Labour and the London Poor* and of *Life and Labour of the People in London.* Its omnipresence in the titles of these inquiries reflects its salience in the everyday experience of the metropolitan masses. Whether useful and fulfilling or alienating and oppressive, work was more than an act of production; it was the central feature of people's lives. The work that supplied their subsistence and identity was also the principal cause of their poverty. That poverty, and the way it was conceptualized, measured and understood in social theory and social action, provides one of the main themes of this volume. Our concern is with the process of social investigation as it occurred in the Victorian and Edwardian periods, and its intellectual and ideological underpinnings. This is a subject altogether wider than that of the history of the social survey or of the origins of British sociology, with which it is sometimes still confused. Our aim is to restore social inquiry to its true context, to view it not as a critique or defence of current welfare practices, but to retrieve meanings, values, assumptions and beliefs which might help to set such issues in historical perspective.

This volume has grown out of the work of the Charles Booth Research Centre for the Study of Social Investigation at the Open University. In April 1989, one hundred scholars and students gathered together at Walton Hall to discuss the work of Charles Booth. Out of this conference emerged several of the essays included in this book (chapters 1, 2, 3, 8, 9, 10, 11 and 13). Members of the Centre then pursued several new areas of research, which formed the basis of further essays included here (chapters 4, 5, 6, 12 and the Introduction). The book also contains a reprint of the seminal essay on Rowntree by J. Veit-Wilson.

The book is divided into three parts. Part I examines the context of social and economic thought in which Booth and his contemporaries worked. Part II treats more microscopically the methodologies employed by Booth and his team, Mayhew and Rowntree. Part III shows some ways in which scholars can use the 'retrieved riches' from the Booth archive to add detail and depth to our picture of the life and labour of the late Victorian metropolis.

Three studies – those by Henry Mayhew, Charles Booth and Seebohm Rowntree – lay at the heart of social investigation in the Victorian period. The pivotal text here is *Life and Labour of the People in London*. Charles Booth's monumental study, with its scientific estimates of poverty, its methodological rigour and precision, and its innovation in quantification, emerged out of a specific tradition of social inquiry, the key features of which need to be defined. Yet to locate such a work intellectually and ideologically demands that we should do more than explore earlier attempts at social investigation. Until very recently scholars have too easily accepted the idea that Booth rejected contemporary social theories and engaged in a form of 'mindless' empirical investigation. They have also concentrated, almost to the exclusion of all other aspects of his work, upon the Poverty Series. It is important, therefore, to see how Booth's life-work related to the wider intellectual scene and also to see the Poverty Series as but a part, albeit a prominent part, of this work.

In this introduction we seek to place Booth's massive undertaking within its complex context – indicating what he owed to existing traditions of social inquiry and social theory, but also how and why he sometimes parted company with these established ways and developed fresh approaches to analysing the 'social problem', approaches which were often inextricably linked with the methodologies he chose to employ in its investigation.

Traditions of social inquiry

It is appropriate in an introduction to this subject to say something of the tradition of social investigation which the Victorians inherited. Charles Booth, while he came to social investigation via rather different routes from many others, none the less placed his inquiry within the ambience of the venerable Royal Statistical Society. He read the work of other investigators and, if he maintained a critical stance, was aware of the methodologies and ideologies pursued by others. Earlier social investigation, however indirectly, did inform his thought and work. And methods of investigation which we might regard as peculiar to the late nineteenth century turn out upon closer examination to have been pioneered long before and, in some cases, to have become part of the very fabric of English social thought and action.

The collection of accurate and comparable information about whole societies enabled the English to construct databases for the purposes of taxation, military preparedness and the enforcement of religious orthodoxy. The Domesday Book of 1086 is the best known but by no means the only example of such a dataset. In this the unit of 'record' was the village, and information collected related to the 'fields' of men, villeins, cottars, serfs, freemen and socmen. The data was collected for purposes of taxation. Other 'taxation' databases included the Poll Tax returns of 1377, the Hearth-Tax returns of 1662–90 and the preliminary surveys for the Marriage Duties of 1685–1706.[2]

An appreciation of the reality of social, demographic and economic change was apparent in the updating of existing datasets. For example, 'extents' or surveys were frequently made after about 1250 to bring the information in the Domesday Book up to date.[3]

Censuses or enumerations of the population have, of course, an ancient history. They had no role in modern Europe, however, until the late seventeenth and early eighteenth centuries (when they were still often closely connected to the purpose of taxation) and the first country to introduce a regular census was Sweden in 1749. A bill to introduce a census to Britain in 1753 was defeated. One MP stated, 'I hold this project to be totally subversive of the last remains of English liberty'.[4] (The suspicion of the census as an unwarrantable invasion of the privacy of the individual and as a potential instrument of government against the interests of the individual remains to this day, and permeated the attitude of many Victorian social investigators.) It was not until 1801 that the first British census was made. It was able to draw upon the experience of Canada and America. The work of the census office and the possibility that the official census might be used as a massive data collecting agency was to intrigue the Victorian reformers, Booth included. Indeed, Booth was to regard some of his work as a pilot scheme for what the census might do in the future.

Ecclesiastical census-taking had an earlier British pedigree. One thinks of the count of 'houslings' in the 1547 Chantry Certificates, of that of households in 1563, of that of communicants in 1603 and so on. These and other later religious censuses were designed to further policies of the enforcement of orthodoxy and so they enumerated (variously) communicants, households, conformists, males. They were in some cases notoriously unreliable as a guide either to the size of the general population or to the extent of conformity/nonconformity. Nevertheless, they represent an important stage in the organization of data collection. And they established the view that the head of the household is an appropriate 'voice' for information about the composition and behaviour of the household.

There was a long-standing tradition, especially in the industrial north, of private census taking. Liverpool (Charles Booth's place of origin) had such a census every decade from 1700 to 1770. There were private censuses for eighteenth-century Manchester, Salford, Bolton and towns near Manchester.[5] An Edinburgh minister of religion, Alexander Webster, initiated a census of the Scottish parishes and analysed the results in 1755.[6]

The use of statistical data for social and economic purposes was promoted most notably from the seventeenth century onwards. The early political arithmeticians included John Graunt and William Petty, authors of *Observations on the London Bills of Mortality* (1662). Petty, a doctor and public servant who was a surveyor and a geographer as well as a political economist and statistician, believed that the end of politics was to 'preserve the subject in peace and plenty' and that this purpose could only be achieved through an accurate knowledge of 'the lands and hands of the territory'. His profound belief that social facts could best be ascertained through quantitative measurement and that inductive reasoning required a basis of statistical data was shared by Gregory King, Charles Davenant and others. All were preoccupied with the importance of the balance of trade in ensuring the nation's wealth. But increasingly political arithmeticians were convinced also of the importance of ensuring the nation's health and of the significance of the problem of poverty. The link between the problems of poverty, employment and national prosperity was established. And the key to the solution of such problems was seen to lie in empirically derived statistics and not in abstract speculation.[7] The links between social investigation and social action were already to the fore in the work of the early political arithmeticians.

During the eighteenth century, however, statistics served another purpose. They fuelled debate and panic about the population question. Initially, this was a fear of underpopulation; by the end of the eighteenth century it was a fear about overpopulation and its social and political consequences. Speculative calculations triumphed over the urge to collect accurate data of actual behaviours.[8] Yet there was a continuing conviction in some circles that empirically derived data would enable action and amelioration of social and economic problems. For example, John Rickman pressed for the introduction of a national population census as a direct response to the crisis of the disastrous harvest of 1800. Only an accurate headcount would enable the government to assess the demand for food. Rickman pioneered methods of deriving statistics for the pre-census period using records of vital registration.

Historians have identified the existence of a statistical movement in early to mid Victorian Britain, in some sense distinct from the tradition of the political arithmeticians and economists.[9] Certainly the period saw the foundation of several statistical societies, including the most lasting and famous, the Manchester Statistical Society (founded 1833) and the Royal or London Statistical Society (founded 1834), and also those of Birmingham (1835), Bristol and Glasgow (1836), Liverpool, Leeds and Ulster (1838). Important though the development of these statistical societies was, it must not be allowed to obscure the already well-established tradition of the 'blue book'. Royal and parliamentary commissions, using question and answer techniques to ascertain and amass information about specific social and economic phenomena, date back to the eighteenth century. Between 1832 and 1846 there were over 100 royal commissions. In the early nineteenth century the voluminous blue books presented the evidence given before such commissions by large numbers of interested parties. The assumption behind the collection and publication of such data was that it would make informed decisions possible and lead to eventual solution of the problems considered. The Benthamite reasoning behind them was clear.[10] Whereas the prejudices of the commissioners undoubtedly affected their presentation of the evidence, there should be no suggestion that they deliberately rigged the evidence. The assumption was that the 'facts' spoke for themselves. It is important to note, however, that there was considerable overlap in personnel between the early nineteenth-century government commissions and the work of the private statistical societies – William Farr, Edwin Chadwick, James Phillips Kay, Poulett Thompson and so on.

In 1851 the government also sponsored Horace Mann's census of religion as a pilot for the inclusion of religious questions in the decennial national census. Mann's census counted those who attended church on a particular Sunday. Arguments in parliament precluded further official censuses of this type and as a result the taking of religious counts was handed over to the denominations themselves. The non-comparability of the data and the amount of guesswork involved in estimating the size of the denominations meant that these unofficial censuses provided only a rough 'guide' to the attendance of members of the Christian churches at places of worship.

In the late Victorian period two religious censuses of London were attempted – William Roberston Nicoll's for the *British Weekly* in 1886 and Richard Mudie-Smith's survey for George Cadbury's *Daily News* in 1901.[11] While Charles Booth systematically collected data about church, chapel and mission attendance for the period 1897 to 1901, he deliberately eschewed making his Religious Influences series a census of church attendance.[12]

The so-called statistical movement in Britain deliberately encouraged another development – the involvement of commercial interests in the advancement of social inquiry. At the second meeting of the British Association for the Advancement of Science, held in Oxford in 1832, Charles Babbage made a blatant appeal for such money to support the pursuit of science:

> ... attention should be paid to the object of bringing theoretical science in contact with the practical knowledge on which the wealth of the country depends ... I trust we may be enabled to cultivate with the commercial interests of the country that close acquaintance which I am confident will be highly advantageous to our more abstract pursuits.[13]

To the third meeting of the BAAS at Cambridge came the Belgian mathematician Adolphe Quetelet who had been involved in the design of the Belgian census in the 1820s. Quetelet was notable for his belief that it was possible to discern laws of social physics from the physical characteristics of populations. He perceived correlationships between the physical attributes of a people and, for instance, rates of crime, marriage, suicide and disorder. Babbage used the opportunity 'to contact all the members who took an interest in statistical researches in order to form a statistical section'. The clique who formed the new statistical section of the BAAS included Thomas Malthus, Quetelet, Richard Jones, Charles Babbage, W.H. Sykes and John Elliot Drinkwater.[14] Some of these men were deductive political economists of the classical school but others, especially Richard Jones, Professor of Political Economy at King's College, London, espoused 'massive data-collection' techniques for the purpose of a science of society. When he became Professor in 1833 he expressed the hope that 'a statistical society will be added to those which are advancing the scientific knowledge of England' and bemoaned the neglect in England of systematized statistical inquiry. Arising out of his initiative at the Cambridge meeting of the BAAS a permanent London Statistical Section of the Association was established. Then on 15 March 1834 the Statistical Society of London was formed and 250 individuals were sent prospectuses prior to the first meeting in May 1834.

The statistical societies turned again in favour of the principles of political arithmetic, to a reassertion of Petty's belief that ideas should follow facts. The Council of the Statistical Society of London in 1838 wrote:

> It is indeed truly said that the spirit of the present age has an evident tendency to confront the figures of speech with the figures of arithmetic; it being impossible not to observe a growing distrust of mere hypothetical theory and a priori assumption, and the appearance of a general conviction that, in the business of social science, principles are valid for application only inasmuch as they are legitimate induction from facts, accurately observed and methodically classified ...

Before we rush into the assumption that these societies were peopled by statisticians in the modern sense of the term it is as well to consider their composition. The membership of the statistical societies was very closely associated with social and political reform. A strong thread of philanthropy ran through it. William Langton, founder member of the Manchester Statistical Society, had been involved with the Provident Society in Liverpool which undertook organized visiting of the poor in order to inculcate habits of 'sobriety, cleanliness, forethought and method', and now was involved not only in the secretaryship of the Statistical Society but in founding a Manchester and Salford Provident Society, the Manchester Athenaeum, the Manchester Society for the Promotion of National Education, the Chetham Society and Owens College, Manchester. James Phillips Kay (later Sir James Kay-Shuttleworth), another secretary of the Society, was secretary to the Manchester Board of Health and also Physician to Knott Mill Hospital, before moving on to the national stage as secretary of the Committee of Council for Education. Samuel Gregg, the son of a cotton spinner, had built up a model village for workers on the Owenite model at Lower House Mill, Bollington in 1832. His brother, William Rathbone Gregg, was a vehement opponent of both the Corn Laws and slavery. The first president of the society, Benjamin Heywood, stood square in a tradition of moral and social involvement. As T.S. Ashton observed, the membership of the MSS was largely identical to that of the District Provident Society.[15] The MSS owed its origin, in the words of its first report:

> ... to a strong desire felt by its projectors to assist in promoting the progress of social improvement in the manufacturing population by which they are surrounded. Its members are not associated merely for the purpose of collecting facts concerning the condition of the inhabitants of this district, as its name might seem to imply, but the first resolution entered on its minutes pronounces it to be 'a Society for the discussion of subjects of political and social

economy, and for the promotion of statistical inquiries, to the total exclusion of party politics.[16]

Early concerns included the effects of education upon criminality, the provision of public swimming baths, the work of dispensaries, and the educational provision in Manchester. Kay's report on the dispensaries concluded with a reiteration of the view that the poor were often responsible for their own degradation and that the work of those above them lay in helping them to correct their behaviour:

> We must make it evident that in the exercise of moral restraint, and by industry, sobriety, a peaceful demeanour, an economical management of their resources, and a far-sighted provision for the day of calamity from which few are exempt, they may escape the misery into which imprudent marriages, insobriety, irregularity, turbulence, infrugality and improvidence plunge men gifted by nature with every quality necessary to procure happiness.[17]

It is against this background of a certain 'attitude' to the problem of poverty in the urban areas of Britain that the statistical inquiries undertaken by the societies should be set. The inquiries undertaken by the MSS were inspired and guided by Poulett Thompson, the Radical Vice-President of the Board of Trade, who opined that there was little chance of the government engaging in a national statistical collecting exercise and saw the amateur societies' work as in some sense supplying this deficiency. The MSS should begin by classifying the population of Manchester and identifying access to the necessaries of life. The MSS set up seven committees of inquiry which delved into such matters as the circulation of immoral and irreligious publications, conditions in the factories, the use of steam power, and the state of education.

For the purposes of this volume, the most interesting aspect of the work of the MSS might seem to be its pioneering house-to-house survey of the Police Divisions of St Michael's and New Cross in 1834, set up to explore the fate of the hand-loom weavers. Certainly, as we shall see in a moment, this was an intriguing development but it must be set in the wider context of the MSS's total programme of inquiry if we are to see the significance of it in the history of social investigation.

The inquiry into St Michael's and New Cross was privately funded by Benjamin Heywood and the conduct of the inquiry was supervised by the District Provident Society, William Langton and Dr Kay. An agent, Mr Henderson, took a list of questions door to door during May and June 1834, producing information on almost half the houses in the divisions.[18] The results of the inquiry were read to the

MSS but were also given a wider circulation in, for example, the *Manchester Guardian* and the *Courier*. This inquiry led to the extension of the method to Manchester, Salford, Ashton, Bury, Dukinfield, and Stalybridge. Four paid agents in 1834–36 collected information door to door which became the basis of detailed reports. The inquiry cost £175. W.R. Gregg read the resulting 'Report on the Condition of Working Classes in an Extensive Manufacturing District' to the Statistical Section of the British Association at Liverpool in 1837. The introduction of the comparative method, with all its attendant problems, and the need to define precisely the meaning of such descriptive terms as 'comfortable', 'not comfortable', 'middling', 'well furnished', 'ill furnished' and so on should be noted. The list of questions was modified as the work progressed and agents were given rough indices of the meaning of the various terms. For example, 'well furnished' meant possession of 'a table and chairs, a clock, a chest of drawers, and a fair stock of necessary utensils'. Attempts were made to check the completeness and accuracy of returns from independent sources and double-checking. Whatever their defects, these surveys, brought together with the independent results of inquiries into the state of education in Liverpool (1835–36), a house-to-house survey of Hull in 1839 and a survey of an agricultural area of Rutland (again in 1839), permitted informed debate about inferiority of conditions in the older areas of Manchester and Liverpool compared to the newer industrial North and East, and the responsibility of the manufacturing system itself for the problems faced by the workers. House-to-house inquiry methods became an accepted part of social investigation in the mid century. For example, in 1838–39, a study of educational facilities in Pendleton, Salford, was based upon such a survey.[19] The comparative method was also pursued in the study of education.[20] These were methods used throughout the century. One thinks, for example, of the inquiries in Deansgate, Peter Street and Ancoats in 1864 and into Gaythorn and Knott Mill in 1868 which provided fuel for the drive for public educational provision.[21]

To the extent that these surveys were designed and supervised by committees, they did represent innovation in social inquiry. They were nevertheless part of the tradition of private enterprise. Side by side with the work of the committees, individuals (often members of the societies themselves) engaged in smaller scale investigations. Benjamin Heywood investigated Irlams-o'-th'-Height (1835); Edward Stanley produced detailed statistics for the parish of Alderley (1836), and James Heywood inquired into housing and conditions in Miles Platting (1837). Stanley counted literates and illiterates, ownership of Bibles and Prayerbooks, occupations, stock and implements, religious attendances – thus demonstrating that holistic approach to the 'welfare of the people' which is easy to miss if we concentrate purely upon poverty and definitions thereof.

David Elesh has noted a shift of emphasis in the interests of the Statistical Society of Manchester after 1841. Instead of engaging in original inquiry, papers were secondary analyses of existing statistics. Members also became more involved in discussions of general questions of political economy. Education remained to the fore but 'papers on working conditions, criminality, vital statistics, and religion steadily diminish in number'.[22] He suggests that the failure of the MSS to continue its earlier tradition of empirical research and, indeed, to institutionalize it, was a result of political divisions among the membership; diversion of interest, money and manpower to other causes (for instance, the Anti-Corn Law League); the establishment and development of government collection of statistics, especially through the Royal Commissions; the co-option of members, notably Kay-Shuttleworth, to undertake government work; and the overriding motivation of social reform, to which the work of statistical collection was subordinate and consequential.

Because of the involvement of so many of the late nineteenth-century social investigators in its activities, a knowledge of the early years of the Royal Statistical Society is imperative. Its initial prospectus, when it was the Statistical Society of London, was adamant that the 'first and most essential rule of its conduct [was] to exclude all *opinions*'. At its first meeting in May 1834 it divided its interests into four – political, economical, moral and intellectual. The Statistical Department of the Board of Trade would advise it of the appropriate topics to investigate. This done, a year would be spent in which subcommittees would devise schedules of questions. The resultant questionnaires, it was hoped, would be circulated and collected by new local societies.[23] Yet in the early years this commitment was not realized. George Richardson Porter attempted to launch through the society a major national investigation into savings banks. He persuaded the council to approve a questionnaire, but the project floundered when it became impossible to find people willing to distribute them. In 1836 a select committee inspired by Holt Mackenzie began to devise a new statistical account of London, using existing information and collecting new data, and to prepare it for publication. This, too, collapsed.[24] Papers presented to the society were slight. Attendance at meetings was poor.

A new commitment to social reform was apparent in the work of the revitalized society under the leadership of Porter and Rawson Rawson. There was, however, a continuing commitment to 'objectively' collected data and eschewing of twisting the 'facts' to suit the purposes of the reformer. Committees were set up to collect criminal and educational statistics. The survey of various London parishes was undertaken by a paid agent, supervised by a committee dominated by Porter and B.F. Duppa, and resulted in publication between 1838 and 1843. William Farr, physician and medical statistician, contributed greatly to the development of vital statistics, clearly seeing public health as a major social issue which was directly related to the lives of the working classes. A committee dedicated to studying the statistics of life turned its attention to the methodology of the forthcoming 1841 Census. As Cullen points out, this committee brought together the work of the government's own statisticians and that of the best men outside the government. As such it was to set a pattern for the work of Victorian social inquiry. It consulted with Quetelet; collected data on foreign censuses; and examined closely the industrial census of Coventry made by Joseph Fletcher for the Royal Commission on Hand-Loom Weavers. It suggested a full census. Its apparent success in influencing House of Commons' amendments to the government census bill led the society to repeat its activities before later censuses. Another committee was set up in May 1838 to inquire into the condition of the working classes and employed two agents to survey the parishes of St Margaret's and St John's Westminster. The inquiry revealed the exorbitant rents which landlords were obtaining for substandard accommodation, and the committee recommended the establishment of philanthropic building companies who would provide adequate housing at modest rents while taking a profit.[25]

Interestingly, these and other large-scale surveys undertaken by the Society of London stretched its finances to the limit. The survey of the poor of St George's in the East between 1844 and 1846 had to be financed by a donation from Henry Hallam. Once again, the close interplay between the work of the societies and individuals with money is revealed.

The links between empirical social research and the movement for solution of social problems were many. In the second half of the century, however, its force was to some extent weakened by the rise of ameliorism. From its foundation in 1857 the National Association for the Promotion of Social Science harnessed the energies of many of the people involved in social investigation to achieve reform and to pressure MPs to introduce and pass legislation to this end. The task of collecting statistics, it urged, belonged to the state and should be undertaken by the state. There was a good deal of self-interest to be served: many of the members of the NAPSS were government servants. Yet, first and foremost, the NAPSS (1857–86) stressed individual responsibility for the conditions of the people and removed the emphasis from the need for large-scale empirical inquiry. Reform must begin not with society but with the individual. The NAPSS's activities led directly into the work of the Charity Organization Society rather than the work of the late Victorian social investigators.

Charles Booth

Born in Liverpool into a public-spirited commercial family who were Liberal in politics and Unitarian in religion, Booth was involved in communal controversies from an early age. Earnest, serious and civic-minded, he combined the development of his shipping line with an active commitment to franchise reform, popular education and social betterment. The slums of mid-Victorian Liverpool provided ample scope for an aroused social conscience. Booth, though, was no ordinary philanthropist.[26] He rejected charity as a cure and Christianity as a creed. Positivism, the Religion of Humanity, presented a more satisfying foundation for a rational faith. Positive Philosophy, as espoused by his cousins, Albert, Henry and Caroline Crompton, offered the young, the intellectually curious and those of unsettled faith a humanist religion and a new ethic of personal social obligation. 'The peculiarity of infidelity in this age,' he wrote in 1870, 'is that it is more religious that faith – it is no longer a wild insurrection against authority – it is a fresh growth of man's whole nature and casts off the old forms as a necessity of progress.'[27] The crisis of authority had a material as well as a spiritual dimension and Positivists were as much preoccupied with the 'social question' as with any other.[28] Booth, like so many of his generation, was repelled by the crass materialism of the age and the selfishness it encouraged. 'The race for wealth is run by a few only and the prizes fall to those who are already rich,' he wrote.

> The leaders in this fatal competition, blind to all else, are willing to sacrifice everything to the production of wealth and even talk of the laws which govern this struggle as though they were the only guides to human life ... I would not undervalue the motive of this race, or the effect it has had in developing the resources of the world and the power of the workers, nor do I say that it can be dispensed with. But I do say that it now needs checking and that it is only in its subordination to public welfare that we can look for that social improvement which we need.

Positivism had its share of drawing-room radicals, idealists and dreamers. But it also had a hard edge. Henry Crompton, an able and engaging lawyer, was, for example, among that group of intellectuals who enjoyed a special relationship with the trade union movement during the 1860s and 70s.[29] Booth, as a large employer of port labour, was hardly unaware of working people and their wants. His personal relations with trade unionists, though, would bear closer scrutiny. It is possible that the Crompton connection, which quickened his social conscience, also played some part in widening his social contacts. His attempts to interest trade unionists in arbitration and conciliation procedures, though they proved unavailing, did introduce him to the more thoughtful and intelligent working men as did the Trades Hall which he also helped to found. The sectarianism that destroyed his attempts to introduce free secular education into Liverpool's schools, however, convinced him that 'Humanity' could be better served by means other than politics.[30]

Unaffected by the religiosity of his cousins, Booth nevertheless shared their conviction that personal actions should benefit others. So strong was this conviction that he at times anguished over the 'surplus' income that he had accumulated. 'My expenditure is £1000 – my income is £2000 – and the question I wish to consider is "what is it right or wise to do with the surplus"', he wrote. 'I and my household spend £150 a year on food … I will suppose that half the cost of all we eat is made up of the costs of ill remunerated labour and that the wages of these men might be doubled with advantage. My food would then cost 50 per cent more than it does – instead of £150 I should pay £225 and be glad to do it.' Booth continued in like vein to describe his expenditure on dress and other commodities and to acknowledge that he owed a debt of £500 – half of his entire expenditure – to the workers. He worried about the best course of action. 'I would rather, if it could be so, that £500 should go towards equalising the lot of poor and rich – Can I do anything whatever towards this? If not, what must I do instead?' Indiscriminate charity, he felt, did more harm than good. Rapid change, too, was disruptive. 'If the labouring poor are to have a share of the comforts of life,' he concluded, 'they must get it by their own strength and patience and then only step by step if any good is to come out of the change. This debt I admit must be claimed by them before it can be paid by me – the arrears can never be claimed at all.' What have we here – a conventional COS rejection of money doles? No, Booth, as a businessman, goes on to scout the possibilities of trade policies to provide more work and more wages for the labouring poor. He reflected that, while there might in consequence be some 'revolution in employment' and the distribution of wealth, 'the revolution would not be so great as that caused by the expenditure of so large an income being taken from the few rich and given to the many poor'.[31] Booth, though he had yet to unburden himself of the

Malthusian constraints on economic and social progress, was uneasily aware that poverty might be connected with the unequal distribution of income as much as with the want of character. The under-consumptionist strand in his thought, explored by Alon Kadish below, was present, albeit in protean form, before the studies of poverty and old age gave it a wider field for action. The service of Humanity which he had entered in his twenties was still the dominant influence upon his outlook as he stood on the threshold of middle age. As late as 5 August 1883 he penned a passionate credal statement beginning with the assertion 'I am a Positivist'.[32]

By this time Booth had removed to London where the advantages of family wealth and connection gave ready access to that band of moralists, philanthropists and members of the professional classes who dominated public debate on the social question. Booth, who as a follower of Comte, believed that social action should be grounded in the scientific study of the laws of society, found himself both moved and fascinated by the lives of the working poor. On a business trip to the United States, for example, he was struck by the housing conditions of the glove workers of Gloversville. But it was upon the East End of London that his sights fixed. His wife Mary may well have acted as the range-finder. The daughter of Charles Zachary Macaulay, a distinguished public servant, her uncles included the historian Thomas Babington Macaulay and Sir Charles Trevelyan, the reformer of the civil service who was also a founder of the Charity Organization Society. Her mother, Mary Potter, was the daughter of a MP who founded the *Manchester Guardian* and the brother of Richard Potter, a railway director, who promoted numerous companies and fathered Beatrice Webb. Booth's interest may well have been more sharply focused by his wife who met the Barnetts in the East End in 1878 and told Charles that she was stirred 'to help in all this misery'.[33] Her cousins, Kate, Teresa and Beatrice Potter, who were working in Whitechapel, may likewise have contributed to the quickening of interest, which expressed itself in Booth's immersion in the lives of the working people (staying in the East End of London and visiting working men's clubs). Cripps in later life recalled that, in the early years of his marriage to Teresa Potter, 'on more than one occasion we met at his [Booth's] house, a party from the East End of London, in order to talk over the unsatisfactory social conditions...'. Here was brought home to them the day-to-day implications of existence on or just above the poverty line: 'workman from the East End told me how much he appreciated a supper at which there was sufficient for all the guests, so that there was no need to grab and scramble for the food'.[34] The onset of economic depression, mass unemployment and social unrest gave these interests a new urgency. Such anxieties as he possessed, however, found release in social inquiry rather than in social work. In later life Mary Booth attributed his concern about the problem of the poor to personal connections with the amelioristic world of the COS (through Barnett and Hill). The ideological differences, however, were considerable. Booth's most consistent antagonists were drawn from the COS who considered his methods of social research suspect and his conclusions dangerous. Booth did not share their conviction that the poor were entirely responsible for their own lot. With characteristic independence of mind he attempted to find out for himself what it was like to be poor. His talks with Barnett and Hill and with others confirmed his belief that what was required were facts – an accurate description of the condition of the people throughout London – which would provide the basis for social diagnosis and social action.

Socialism gave the social question a new aspect. The Booths were quick to recognize its importance. Charles engaged the Democratic Federation; Mary read Marx. In itself this was not remarkable. The path from positivism to socialism was well-trodden during the 1880s. The travellers, one suspects, were generally drawn from the *nouvelle couche sociale*. The insecurities that drove them in that direction, however, exerted no comparable pull upon the more socially assured Booths. The latter, though, were not unaffected by their encounter with socialism.

In the Booth papers in the Senate House Library there exists a verbatim record of a 'discussion on socialism' held between Booth, Beatrice Potter's brother-in-law, Alfred Cripps (later Lord Parmoor), John E. Williams (1854–1917) and James Macdonald.[35] Internal evidence seems to suggest that the meeting belonged to 1882 or 1883 when both Williams and Macdonald were involved with the Democratic Federation. Mary Booth later commented that Booth was attending meetings of the SDF at about the same time that he staged this 'symposium'. Williams, born in Holloway, north London, and raised in the workhouse, was a passionate Fenian and close friend and associate of H.M. Hyndman and of James Macdonald of the [Social] Democratic Federation. (At the time of the discussions it was still the Democratic Federation, changing its title in 1884.) Shortly after this Williams and Macdonald formed a window-cleaning company. James Macdonald was by trade a tailor. By any measure, 'rugged and rough-hewn' Jack and even James Macdonald, that ladies' tailor and 'socialist of a moderate type',[36] must have been ill at ease in the genteel surroundings of the Booths' South Kensington townhouse.

Over three long evenings the four men sat there discussing the socialist approach to Britain's social problems.

There has been a long-standing historical debate about the nature of Booth's indebtedness (if any) to H.M. Hyndman. Was Booth provoked into organizing his survey of the condition of the people in Tower Hamlets by what he considered to be Hyndman's exaggerated claim that more than 25 per cent of the people were living below the subsistence line? Was he galvanized into action by Hyndman's insistence that his assertion rested upon the firm foundation of a house-to-house survey?[37] In the light of this controversy, the twenty-four ledger-size pages of notes on Booth's meeting with two of Hyndman's closest associates are exceptionally precious and worthy of detailed comment. We have here not only a rare glimpse of a debate between capitalist and socialist but also a clue to the development of Booth's thought. The report, in Booth's distinctive hand, indicates a carefully orchestrated discussion of four areas: (i) how the employing class earn their money; (ii) how the employed class earn their money; (iii) how the employing class spend their money and (iv) how the employed class spend theirs. When this discussion was completed there was to be consideration of 'positive schemes of socialism'. Each speaker was to have his say uninterrupted. Booth opened the proceedings.

The meeting was designed to improve mutual understanding. Booth explained the position of the capitalist; Cripps the perspective of the lawyer and landowner; Macdonald that of the craftsman; and Williams that of the labourer. When Booth contended that employers 'earned their money by doing work as necessary as that done by the employed class, and that no scheme of socialism could succeed that did not provide for this work' he 'instanced and described his own business and some others'.[38] Macdonald 'referring to his own trade [tailor] ... said the men knew much better than the master what man would make a good foreman'.[39] Cripps was 'a lawyer and had started with a good education but what money he had, he had earned'.[40] 'Mr Williams said he knew exactly what his present employer made out of him. He was working for a window-cleaning company who paid him so much a day and charged so much a window; and so the more windows he cleaned, after a certain number, the more profit they made out of him. He thought it could not be denied that all profit was unpaid wages, and said that if he had capital he should think it wrong to take profit, as he considered it robbery. Referring to a remark of Mr Cripps, he did not see why houses built for the working classes should pay 3 per cent or any interest.'[41] When he summed up this part of the discussion, Booth discounted the argument put forward by the men that general educational improvements would facilitate the choice of superior men for positions of management. He referred to the operation of 'some sort of natural selection'; 'those firemen who rose to be engineers [on his ships] were picked men of exceptional intelligence and capacity and determination – ready to sacrifice present ease in order to improve themselves and their position'.[42] A debate about the value of expensive advertising ensued. The first evening concluded with Macdonald's eloquent denunciation of the 'class' system which dictated that unless the workers pandered to the needs of the capitalists they could not exist at all. Collectivism was, to his mind, the only 'road out of the present disorder'.

On the next night Jack Williams opened a discussion of the earnings of the employed and a development of the view 'that profit consisted of unpaid wages and was robbery'. Cripps rejoined that 'it began with work – one man spent less than another, and so acquired capital', thus revealing his ignorance both of the actualities of the lives and conditions of the poor and also of any contemporary theories. He used the example of a tailor to elaborate upon his point. [43] Macdonald protested. 'As to capitalism he could not admit that it was to any great extent the result of thrift. There was no thrift among the rich and they got more rich by other means; using, and only partly paying for, the labour of others.' The present system was nothing but wasteful. Now man could make goods and produce food so cheaply, the onus should be upon the rich to ensure fair distribution of these commodities and not to maximize profit and competition between man and man. Booth leapt in, using his knowledge of big business, to try to explain that quite a small rise in wages could threaten the viability of a company.[44] Wages were taken from profit and not profit from wages.[45] 'Profit was the fund from which all remuneration came.' And it was the intelligence emanating from the employing class which converted raw materials into profitable goods. Booth sought to explain that the law of wages 'as regards the worker was simply "what he could get". It was for him a question of possible alternatives. If he had no alternative but starvation he would get only "starvation wages".' Thus it was not necessary for all businesses to be co-operative for co-operation to affect positively the bargaining position of the worker; similarly, emigration had simply to act as a safety valve to remove surplus labour from the country, to raise the chances of remaining workers to attain a suitable level of remuneration.[46] In the course of the evening Macdonald referred to the anomalies arising out of the present organization of work: 'there were many unemployed poor, and so [he] thought the working hours might be greatly reduced; and for those now in work the hours were too long at certain times, balanced by their being no work at all at other times; all of which better organisation would avoid...'[47]

Socialist schemes for the correction of the system were the subject for the third meeting of the conference. Macdonald was charged with explaining why such changes were necessary. He justified the desire for a better system 'by a description of the evils of the present system – the degradation and hopeless condition of the mass of the workers; who became less and less men, and more and more parts of a machine, without freedom, and without leisure, and without a future'. Although it might be true that 'they could dress better and have comforts and even luxuries which their grandparents had not' they had gained relatively less 'in proportion to other classes. At best they had nothing to spare and at worst they had nothing at all; most of them had no security and however willing to work, might find it impossible to work or to get anything in exchange for their labour.'[48] When asked what remedy socialists would propose, Macdonald confessed that, 'if six socialists were in one room they would each have their own plan'. What must be done was 'to get rid of a bad system' and then choose the best replacement. Booth countered by reference to Hyndman's denial that his aim was bureaucratic state socialism.[49] What then was it to be? Macdonald spoke for himself. He wanted a national board of trade to control the operation of each trade – wages, working conditions and hours, prices. Wages would be paid to all, with freedom to spend them as the individual wished, but employing others at a profit would be strictly forbidden. This situation would evolve as part of a long-term strategy. Williams described a grandiose plan for public housing financed from a graduated income tax. Once the problem of housing the poor had been solved, the taxes would be used to acquire the railways and the means of production. There was much discussion of the Octavia Hill approach to housing the poor and of the preoccupation or otherwise of the employer class with the miserable plight of the people.[50] Williams 'thought the great majority of the rich thought and cared nothing about the condition of the poor'.[51] Macdonald, however, believed 'they did begin not to like it and they might well feel the condition of things a danger as well as a bother to them'.[52] The discussion ranged widely over the virtues of nationalization and the implications of the introduction of labour-saving machinery. Macdonald argued for gradual, historical evolution to achieve a replacement of the system which crushed men's best instincts and allowed 'only those of the tiger, the wolf, and the fox' full play.

The report ends with summaries of the opposing sides – the individualist and the collective remedies for social ills.

These encounters with Macdonald and Williams brought Booth face to face with the socialist analysis of the current problems of society. Whereas historians have argued for and against the view that Booth's statistical view of London's *Life and Labour* owed its origin to Hyndman's putative house-to-house survey and his insistence on a high estimate of the incidence of poverty among the workers of London, in truth Booth was searching for something else – an understanding of the problem of poverty, which led him to discuss the views of those who believed that the poor were responsible for their own plight as well as of those like Williams, Macdonald and Hyndman, who believed that the system and not the individual was at fault. At this time Booth was introduced to the realities of the work place as well as to the housing conditions of the poor. How, said Macdonald, could the poor live better if they had no work? How, said Williams, could they improve themselves if they were given starvation wages and no access to education? The possibility that there were structural explanations for poverty and not simply moral ones had to be explored. It was no accident that the Poverty Series was not a house-to-house survey, charting the living conditions of the poor, but rather originally an examination of the nexus between the 'Conditions and Occupations' of the inhabitants of the East End of London. The design of Booth's inquiry (Poverty, Industry and Religious Influences) indicates that he was always motivated not purely by a desire to describe how the poor lived but by a need to discover why they lived like this. He was searching for verifiable data but of a much less basic variety than has sometimes been implied. His close association with working men in the East End in the 1878–84 period should be seen as crucial to the development of his ideas and inquiry. This was an association which did not end. While he rejected socialism and collectivist solutions, he was sensitized to the picture of the world which they painted. Into his enterprise he took perspectives revealed to him by these men: the concept of the relative deprivation of the poor, for example, crops up in the first volume of the Poverty Series: 'The contrast with that to which men have been accustomed is doubtless the principal factor in sensations of well or ill being, content or discontent; but we have also to take account of the relation of the present life, whatever it may be, to the ideal or expectation.'[53]

To interpret the life of either an individual or a class, he emphasized, one must 'lay open its memories and understand its hopes'.[54] He and his associates drew considerably upon a pool of friendly trades unionists among the working men for information and assistance.[55] The same James Macdonald who participated in the symposium on socialism contributed a section on the West End tailoring trade to the Poverty Series, and helped Beatrice Potter considerably in her work on the East End trade.[56]

Booth, if not prompted by Hyndman to undertake his inquiry, unquestionably felt the need to clarify his thinking in consequence of his encounter with socialism. Two charges were particularly troubling. The proposition that profits were unpaid wages and its corollary that capitalists were thieves, struck at his self-image as one who was personally responsible and socially useful. In the writings of the American economist F.A. Walker, and above all in his rent theory of profits, Booth found the most able expression of the arguments he was working towards. The recognition of entrepreneurial gains as rents of ability supplied a new rationale for the privileged position which Comte prescribed for industrial management.[57] Socialism, however, left Booth unconvinced as much on sociological as on theoretical grounds. The issue was not the extent of poverty; rather it was the socialists' claim to represent the labouring class and the poor that required refutation. Were it true, such a union might conceivably have constituted a formidable threat to the capitalist system. In April 1888 Booth told the Political Economy Club that 'there is at present in England a genuine, though to some extent unconscious, conflict of interest between different sections tending to take the shape of a conflict between class and class, which it is the duty of statesmen to consider and deal with before it becomes more acute'.[58] The most dangerous of these conflicts, he believed, lay in the class antagonisms mobilized around Protectionism. The analogous strategy pursued by the socialists was potentially just as dangerous. 'The interests of labour,' Booth wrote, 'are not the same as the interests of the poor. Hence just as Protection would step more readily into the field of practical politics with us if it could weld together the interests of labour in agriculture and manufacture, so would socialism if it could combine the interests of poverty and labour.'[59] Booth was confident that no such combination could be effected. His researches, even at this stage, were sufficiently advanced to dismiss the likelihood of any such union.

'The force of labour,' he wrote, 'considered as a class consists in the amount of its earnings, the regularity and value of its work. The force of the poor considered as a class consists in their poverty, in the irregularity of their work and the smallness of their earnings. The socialists like to treat these forces and interests as questions of numbers, but this plan is delusive and would be so even with manhood suffrage. There is no uniformity of interest and can be no uniformity of aim, any more than there is uniformity of social position, amongst the millions who fill up the ranks of poverty and labour.'[60]

The confusion of the interests of the poor with the interests of the workers, Booth concluded, meant that it was the taxpayer rather than the capitalist who was likely to be the victim of socialism. The almost summary dismissal of socialism reflected Booth's already considerable understanding of the sources of differentiation and the extent of overlapping or cross-cutting cleavages within the labouring classes and the poor.

The milieu of the inquiry

The nature of Charles Booth's associations has become more apparent of late. His world, and therefore that of his inquiry, crossed those of Toynbee Hall, of the Royal Statistical Society, of the Charity Organization Society, of the Royal Economic Society and so on. It is important to highlight these connections but also to resist the corollary that Booth's Inquiry was, in some sense, the child of Toynbee Hall or the Royal Statistical Society or the Royal Economic Society. It was not.

The Toynbee Hall Settlement was a work station for Charles Booth's survey. After Samuel Barnett's initial reservations about Booth's projected investigation into the condition and occupations of the people of Tower Hamlets in 1886, he proved a good friend to Booth's inquiry. Barnett was responsible for introducing Booth and his associates or 'secretaries' to East End officials, businessmen, clergy and tradesmen who could provide him with information. It was from Toynbee that Booth drew many of his collaborators – not only known associates such as Ernest Aves and Hubert Llewellyn Smith but also men such as Henry Woodd Nevinson, Clem Edwards, E.W. Brooks, Percival Burt Allen, Fred Maddison and Harry Lewis, who now emerge as actively involved in collecting material for Booth. As Rosemary O'Day indicates in 'Before the Webbs', Beatrice Potter, who was herself on good terms with Barnett and very much involved in rent collecting and philanthropic visiting in Toynbee's housing project at Katharine Buildings, examined the Toynbee 'case book' in her search for information about the 'sweating system'.[61] At about this time she observed that she 'secured one of the Toynbee men to work for me'.[62] It seems highly probable that this was Ernest Aves; for David Schloss, who eventually assumed responsibility for the Booth inquiry into the Boot and Shoe trades of the East End, made use of a notebook of boot and shoe interviews kept by Ernest Aves in autumn 1887, and there is one mention of a meeting between Aves and Potter in connection with this inquiry.[63] William Beveridge remembered Beatrice Potter working on her Docks study for Booth at Toynbee.[64] Other of Booth's associates who were not residents of Toynbee took the Inquiry into the ambience of the settlement. Henry Higgs, E.W.

Brooks and Clara Collet lectured there. George Arkell and Jesse Argyle read papers.[65] Booth's collaborators attended (and perhaps inspired) conferences on subjects highly relevant to the Booth investigation – Women's Work and Wages in 1887 and Working Men's Budgets as well as Industry in 1891.[66] The Toynbee Economic Club, founded in November 1890, had Clara Collet as one of its Vice-Presidents and, for example, from 1896 to 1898, was dominated by the work of Booth's associates, especially Ernest Aves, G.H. Duckworth and Jesse Argyle.[67] The work undertaken on working men's budgets seems to have fed into the parallel publication by the Junior Economic Club on that subject in 1896.[68]

Some evidence has recently emerged which indicates that an even closer and more institutionalized connection between the Booth Inquiry and Toynbee Hall was mooted. From its inception Toynbee had engaged in investigation or social observation of its own. On 27 June 1885 James Bonar was paid £30 to produce a report on the condition of shopworkers in the East End tailoring trade. Unfortunately, according to the Minutes of August 1885, Bonar was unable to do the work. And when Ernest Aves became a resident in 1886, 'he was accordingly started on one street in St Jude's parish, and sent out to visit unknown people and ascertain facts'. But with the introduction of Alfred Marshall to the Trustees of the Settlement in March 1887 and the prominence on the Board of men to the fore in the Economic Club and the Royal Statistical Society (notably H.S. Foxwell, A.H.D. Acland and A. Milner) collaboration with Booth was promoted.[69] In May 1888 the Toynbee Minute Book reads:

> … some discussion took place as to the advisibility of appointing
> another gentleman to undertake an inquiry either into the history
> and prospects of co-operation in East London or into the
> employment of the people in connection with the work of Mr
> Booth. It was decided to postpone a final decision on this subject
> to the next meeting of the trustees which was fixed for Monday
> June 5th.[70]

Later in the summer, on 18 June, Acland and Milner reported that 'the idea of employing an inquirer in connection with the work of Mr Booth … was abandoned in consequence of Mr Booth's declaration that he would not be able to avail himself of such assistance at the present time'.[71] But by July a greater degree of co-ordination of the efforts of Booth and Toynbee Hall again seemed on the cards. Hubert Llewellyn Smith wrote to Acland in somewhat of a quandary. He had been appointed by the Toynbee Trustees in autumn 1887 to study the movement of industrial population 'from Trade to

Trade and Place to Place' in Bradford and district. This was as yet incomplete. Now Charles Booth had asked him 'to make an investigation in London during the coming autumn in connection with his great inquiry', 'making a similar inquiry for East London with the view of writing a chapter on the subject'. The problem was that Booth wanted the chapter by 31 December 1888. Accordingly Smith was writing to ask the Trustees' permission to delay his report for them and undertake the work for Booth. 'I would point out that the postponement of my general report will be but slight, as in any case I wish to make some London enquiries before writing, and it will of course be more complete in many respects when I write it, as I can work in all the materials I collect for Mr Booth. The two inquiries will thus supplement one another.'[72]

The Royal Statistical Society connection was also of vital importance and our understanding of the way in which this society worked alongside government and individual members should throw Booth's work into a fresh light. In 1885 Booth became an active member of the RSS and an heir to its traditions. Unfortunately there seems to be no hard evidence about why he joined the society at that time although he was nominated by Leonard Courtney and seconded by Leone Levi, and this was the natural forum for his views.[73] As we have seen above, his own route to social inquiry was an idiosyncratic one and he feared the reception which the society might give him. Already on 12 November 1885 he had formally proposed his paper on 'Changes in Occupations 1831–1881' and in early 1886 he sent his paper to the Society who submitted it to two referees, Dr Robert Lawson and N.A. Humphreys.[74] In March Mary Booth wrote to her cousin Beatrice Potter that Charles had 'this morning received the reports of the referees...'. 'One man likes the paper; the other doesn't like it at all; and is very cutting in his criticisms; especially of the hypothetical apportionment of "dependants" to the different occupations. However, they [the Statistical Society] are going to let him read his paper – he first making certain omissions of the more hypothetical calculations.' 'I think Charlie is satisfied on the whole', she mused: 'he had expected objections; – and knew that his criticism on the way in which the census department does its work must create a certain soreness'. 'He feels confident that the paper has value in it', she continued, 'and it is plain that the statisticians think the same.' His amateur status was, however, a problem. 'There may be some disposition to snub a youthful pretender who presumes to find fault with the experts.'[75] Several pieces of his work were in the first instance presented as papers for the society and he received criticism, sometimes blistering, from its members. Many found both his ideas and his methodologies difficult to stomach. At least two of the members to whom he was closest, Alfred Marshall and Arthur Acland, were also closely connected to Toynbee Hall. But he also drew upon, directly and indirectly, the expertise of Leone Levi, Richard Valpy and Graham Balfour. Balfour, sometime President of the Royal Statistical Society, actively participated as an associate in the Inquiry. Balfour followed Booth's methodology in his study of Battersea – recording information supplied by the School Board Visitors in notebooks which were available to Booth in early 1890. Perhaps their influence would have continued; in the event all three died before the Industry Series was well under way. From 1892 to 1894 Booth was president of the society. He drew into the Society several of his associates – Cripps, Collet, Argyle, Schloss, Grosvenor.[76] The RSS rented part of its premises in Adelphi Terrace, The Strand, to Booth in 1892, to which he moved the headquarters of his Inquiry from 2 Talbot Court.[77] In his capacity as President Booth led a delegation to the President of the Board of Trade asking for the creation of a permanent statistical organization.[78] The establishment in 1893 of the Labour Department as an outgrowth of the Labour Statistical Bureau (founded in 1886) owed much to the Royal Statistical Society's long campaign and Booth's support, together with the presence of A.J. Mundella, a Fellow of the Royal Statistical Society, as President of the Board of Trade. Immediately Booth's associates were employed. Booth had also attempted a pilot study to demonstrate how important statistics could and should be collected by the Board of Trade. As a member of a committee set up to advise the Registrar General he had urged the inclusion in the census of 'some simple facts by which the position and manner of life of each family could be measured'.[79] Accordingly, in the Census of 1891 the Registrar General ordered his officers to record the number of rooms occupied by each householder living in four rooms or less and the number of servants employed in houses of five rooms or more. Booth met each of the registrars of the metropolitan sub-districts more than once to discuss the practicalities of this decision and was convinced that the enumerators (some 3000 plus) did their work conscientiously and well.[80] These statistics were used by Booth.[81] In the remainder of the series he demonstrated what other information could usefully be collected for the Board of Trade at 'the epoch of any numerical census' – material on apprenticeships, trade organization, family constitution and so on. 'With a little preconcerted arrangement, so that the information gathered by the Registrar General might lend itself easily to much further investigation, the work I have attempted might, I venture to suggest, be taken up by the Board of Trade with the certainty of a far larger measure of success.'[82]

Such a social-industrial census, coupled with the numerical, should be quinquennial. The close relations between the Registrar General's Office and the Board of Trade and the Royal Statistical Society (which had, as we have seen, a long history) ensured Booth a forum and partial success. There is no suggestion in our minds that Booth's initial inquiry was purely the result of RSS influence. Nevertheless, the RSS was keen to embrace Booth's work and to mould it in its own image.

The place of other clubs and societies, notably the Charity Organization Society, the Junior Economic Club and the British or Royal Economic Society, in the order of things is more shadowy. It has been possible to build up a partial picture of Booth's activities. Booth and his associates had connections with the Charity Organization Society although he was never a member. Octavia Hill contributed to the Inquiry and, despite her opposition to Booth's Old Age Pensions schemes, remained a friend to the last. Mary Booth, in particular, developed a friendship with Miss Hill. C.S. Loch and Booth also disagreed fundamentally over the issues of Old Age Pensions and Pauperism but the lines of communication were open and frequently busy, especially in the 1880s, before Booth published the Poverty Series.[83] Beatrice Potter had been a member of the COS; Clara Collet remained a member from 1888 to 1906. Booth's daughter Imogen became secretary of the Hoxton branch of the COS. Once Booth declared his hand and suggested structural explanations for poverty, however, the COS was inevitably opposed to his line of thinking.

Clara Collet was a founder member of the Junior Economic Club which provided another important forum for discussion of and work on economic issues. In mid June 1890 Collet suggested to Henry Higgs the formation of a club of young economists who had trained under Professor Foxwell in London, and on 27 June at a meeting of the Denison Club at University College she founded the Junior Economic Club. It had a committee of nine (which included other of Booth's associates who were not products of London University – Ernest Aves and Llewellyn Smith – as well as Clara Collet and Henry Higgs who were) and a score of members. By the time of its first meeting on the second Tuesday of October 1890 it may have had fifty members in all, all carefully vetted by the committee and approved as trained economists. Its meetings took several forms: discussions of major works (for example, Alfred Marshall came to the club to discuss his work);[84] later in 1890 Sidney Webb informed Beatrice that 'the economic club had an evening over Industrial Democracy', with short papers on it. This was at Miss Collet's suggestion, 'in order to make the members read it';[85] considerations of chosen themes and questions in some detail (the first chosen was 'The Consumption of Wealth', which was to be examined under several heads including 'Curves of Demand', 'Theory of Utility', 'Standard of Comfort' and 'Luxury'); original investigation leading to publicaton (it was probably the Junior Economic Club that published a work on family budgets edited by Booth, Aves and Higgs in 1896). On 9 December 1890 Charles Booth, John Burnett and Alfred Marshall were invited to a meeting of the club to discuss family statistics. Charles and Mary Booth went 'To Economic Club in the evening' of 23 June 1893 to hear 'keen discussion between the Webbs and the Co-op men' on Co-operation, Production and Distribution.[86] It was clearly in the Junior Economic Club that Booth's ideas and work were discussed and to some extent developed. And it is evident that several of Booth's leading associates were in touch with the mainstream economic thought of the period. The Junior Economic Club is easily confused with the British or Royal Economic Society (also founded in autumn 1890) and even more easily confused with the Toynbee Economic Club, formed in November 1890 with Clara Collet as one of its vice-presidents and with monthly meetings on the second Tuesday of each month.

Charles Booth belonged to the intellectual aristocracy described elsewhere by Noel Annan. Potter, Courtney, Grosvenor, Cripps, Duckworth, Howard, Harrison and Edgeworth, all members of that aristocracy, were his friends and associates. The Potter-Courtney-Cripps connection was especially important to him in the mid to late 1880s.[87] But Booth also had connections with members of the first and second elevens of the intellectual world – Alfred Marshall, Hubert Llewellyn Smith, Sidney Webb, Ernest Aves, David Schloss, Clara Collet, Henry Higgs – and introduced some of them through his own person to the intellectual aristocracy. They were people who did not come from a background of wealth or high society, although they were in some cases to become connected by marriage to such a world – Marshall's wife was Mary Paley; Ernest Aves married Eva Maitland; Llewellyn Smith almost married Booth's daughter; Sidney Webb married Beatrice Potter. They were civil servants, university teachers with lively, sometimes original, minds, scholarly interests and great public spiritedness. They were drawn into the milieu of the intellectual aristocracy by these very attributes. This milieu included the great societies of the day – the Economic Club, the British or Royal Economic Society, the Royal Statistical Society – but it also took in the British Museum Reading Room, the University Settlements, the dinner table, the house party, even the Booths' breakfast table.

The team

Social investigation was frequently team work. Mayhew used a small team; so did Rowntree. In most cases, however, members of these teams_were dogsbodies – collectors of data, amanuenses. Booth, unusually, used a large team of university-educated men and women in the course of his investigation. Beatrice Potter, despite her lack of university education, brought her individual brand of sparkling intelligence to the inquiry. These men and women contributed to the inquiry much more than the data they collected on Booth's behalf. They contributed ideas. They had a formative influence on parts of the survey. They authored specific sections of the published work. Booth described himself as the 'editor' of the four-volume edition of *Life and Labour* and his associates as 'several able contributors'.[88] Of course, it was Booth who initiated and controlled their work but, none the less, his assistants were 'associates'. Even his devoted 'secretaries', Jesse Argyle and George Arkell, served an apprenticeship in investigation which fitted them to fulfil the role of investigators themselves. No fewer than thirty-four people were employed at some time. Not all had an equal importance in the inquiry. Here we concentrate upon the most prominent contributors.

When Booth began his work on Tower Hamlets in 1886 it was with Jesse Argyle and Maurice Eden Paul as his chief assistants. Paul was a medical student at one of the London teaching hospitals (probably the London Hospital) and possibly a student lodger at Toynbee Hall. While he continued to be actively involved in the philanthropic management of an East End 'model dwellings' throughout the 1880s, he apparently ceased to work for Booth after 1886. It is from his correspondence with Beatrice Potter that much early information about the conduct of the Poverty survey derives.[89]

Jesse Argyle was originally one of the Booth Steamship Company clerks and became Booth's secretary in 1884. Argyle was a cockney with a good knowledge of the East End. The first we hear of him is when Booth seconded him to work for the Mansion House Inquiry into unemployment in August 1885. During the summer of 1886 he was offered as a research assistant to Beatrice Potter. But from September 1886 he worked fulltime on Mr Charles Booth's Inquiry. He was responsible for organizing the office of the Inquiry, first at Talbot Square and then at Adelphi Terrace, The Strand. He and Booth met with the School Board Visitors to draw up and test 'a principle of classification of their information' to employ in the interviews with school board visitors. The interview notebooks in the Booth Collection show Argyle as an active and perceptive interviewer. He was made responsible for the investigation into poverty in Walthamstow and special districts of West and North London and wrote the findings up for the published book. He wrote an essay on Silk Manufacture for the fourth volume. Later he was to make a considerable contribution to the Industry Series. His contribution has been largely overlooked: in 1892 his nomination as a Fellow of the Royal Statistical Society was accepted.[90] That he was fully involved in the inquiry as a social investigator and not purely as a secretary is suggested by his involvement in the Toynbee Economic Club in the mid 1890s. On 31 March 1896 he lectured on 'The Attractiveness of London to Provincial Labour'.[91] In the later years he co-operated with Mary Booth to prepare the survey for publication and to undertake proofreading and correction. It was during this time that his worth was truly appreciated by Mary Booth.

Booth also enlisted the help of several others in connection with the streets survey. Foremost was Graham Balfour who was a fellow member of and sometime President of the Royal Statistical Society. He was responsible for the Battersea inquiry, which he wrote up for the published work. The central London streets survey was undertaken by a committee of six: E.C. Grey, R.A. Valpy, H.G. Willink, W.C. Lefroy, Margaret Tillard and Booth himself. All these inquiries employed assistants. For instance, Clara Collet interviewed school board visitors for Balfour. Collet was to become quite a prominent member of Booth's team.

The Poverty Series also included a number of special subject inquiries, most of which were undertaken by associates. Beatrice Potter, who wrote the essays on the Docks, the Tailoring Trade and the Jewish Community, has received the most attention from scholars because of her later eminence.[92] Clara Collet (1860–1948) was much less showy and less adept at self-advertisement, but had an excellent mind and possessed a flair for solid research and analysis which was coupled with tremendous concern for the lot of working women. Her chapters on women's work and girls' education repay a careful reading. Our knowledge of the conduct of both Potter's and Collet's work, however, points to the crucial role played by George Arkell and, to a lesser extent, Jesse Argyle in the organization of their research into their special subjects. Similarly, David Schloss's investigation into the Boot and Shoe Industry was underpinned by the painstaking preparatory work done by Argyle in addition to his interviewing of informants.

Other contributors to the Poverty Series included Octavia Hill, James Macdonald, Mary Tabor and Stephen Fox. Octavia Hill (1838–1912) was not, of course, an employee of Booth but she was a natural choice as a contributor on 'Model Dwellings' and their influence upon the character of the poor. Her model dwelling schemes had had a profound influence upon the provision of housing in the East End and upon legislation. It is worth noting, however, that it was George Arkell and not Octavia Hill who provided most of the material on blocks of dwellings included in the Poverty Series. James MacDonald, as has been noted, was a tailor and trade unionist with whom Booth had a long-standing connection by the end of the 1880s. He served as an informant for Potter's inquiry into the Wholesale Clothing Trade and his own observations concerning the West End tailoring trade were published in the Poverty Series. William Marsden draws attention to the contribution of Mary Tabor to the education chapters of the Poverty Series in his essay below. Stephen N. Fox contributed a chapter on tobacco workers to the same series. He seems to have been a resident of Toynbee Hall.[93] He helped Beatrice Potter with her work on the Jewish Community,[94] and he may have participated in the Bootmaking inquiry.[95] He went on to contribute to the Industry Series and was one of the team of workers who gathered together at the Savoy Hotel to celebrate the conclusion of the Inquiry in 1904.

Key contributors to the Poverty Series were Ernest Aves and Hubert Llewellyn Smith. Ernest Aves (1857–1917) was a Cambridge-educated resident (and later sub-warden) of Toynbee Hall. In all probability he became associated with the Inquiry when he was seconded to assist Beatrice Potter with her inquiry into sweating, for which his knowledge of St Jude's parish well-equipped him. His work on the furniture trades of the East End, which he summarized in the printed work, survives in the Booth Collection (A6, 7 and 8).[96] He spent three years researching and writing up the Building Trades for the later Industry Series, was consulted at all stages of the survey and was responsible for such attempts as there were to draw comparisons and formulate conclusions. Although he appears as Booth's assistant on the title page of the final volume of the Industry Series, he wrote the lion's share of the text and might reasonably have claimed it as his own.[97] His contribution to the Religious Influences Series was enormous. The surviving correspondence underlines his role as resident critic, at times regarded as a thorn in the side by other members of the 'team' but regarded with great respect and affection by Booth himself.[98] Those scholars who can decipher his spidery handwriting find his researches penetrating. He was, without doubt, the single most important influence upon the organization of the research and analysis of the data, next to Booth himself. Aves had a reputation in his own day as a man of progressive outlook, who supported actively the extension of democratic association among producers and consumers, welcomed the New Unionism, supported the men in the 1889 Dock Strike, became the first president of the Trafalgar Branch of the Dock, Wharf, Riverside and General Labourers Union, was a leading figure in the anti-sweating agitation and tirelessly expounded the virtues of the co-operative ideal. In the Edwardian period he was a Special Commissioner on wage boards and compulsory arbitration in the Antipodes and also Chairman of the British and Irish trade boards. Like most of Booth's key associates, Aves exemplified the commitment to social action.

Hubert Llewellyn Smith (1864–1945) was like-minded. He became a lecturer at Toynbee Hall after a brilliant undergraduate career at Oxford and London. Perhaps he came to know Booth through membership of the Royal Statistical Society.[99] The New Unionism found in him an able defender. As co-author of *The Story of the Dockers' Strike* (1890) he stood for all that was best in late Victorian social radicalism. His association with Booth's inquiry was curtailed when in 1892 he became Commissioner of Labour in the Labour Department of the Board of Trade where he had ample opportunity to demonstrate his 'constructive practical mind'.[100] He later became Permanent Secretary to the Board of Trade (1907–19) and Chief Economic Adviser to the Government (1919–67). Here was no mere research assistant. His later work on the *New Survey of London Life and Labour* (1928–35) illustrated his commitment to Booth's endeavour as well as his relative ignorance of Booth's earlier methodology.

George Herbert Duckworth (1868–1934) was also of singular importance to the Booth inquiry. He joined Mr Charles Booth's Inquiry soon after leaving Cambridge and researched considerably for the Industry Series. His role on the Religious Influences Series is even better documented. Well-placed socially (he married Lady Margaret Herbert, daughter of the Earl of Carnarvon) and educated at Eton and Cambridge, Duckworth was a man of distinguished presence who, despite his love of good living, was curious about and responsive to the problems of Londoners. Booth said that he had 'a quick eye observant of details, a cool counsel, judgement, plenty of determination and conciliatory manners' and anyone who has had the pleasure of reading his reports to Booth and his interviews will find themselves concurring with this assessment. As with so many of Booth's 'team' he became a distinguished public servant.

Another important contributor to the Industry Series was Esmé Howard (1863–1939), an aristocratic friend of George Duckworth, drawn into the inquiry not by need but by interest in social questions. His work included surveys of Musical Instrument, Fishing Tackle and

Toy manufacture; the Glass and Earthenware industry; the Chemicals Industry; the manufacture of brushes and combs; and dyeing and cleaning. But for him social investigation was an interlude, albeit an interesting one, in a career devoted to the diplomatic service. Unlike Aves, Fox, Duckworth, Collet, Schloss and others, Howard made no mark for himself as a thinker and writer on economic and social questions.

Equally influential was A.L. Baxter (*b.*1860), a University College, London graduate and a barrister. Baxter had been unable to assist in the Industry Series but joined a select team on the religious influences survey in 1897. His interviews for the series were frequently models of the genre.[101] In the last years of the inquiry, Baxter lent invaluable aid to Mary Booth in revising the Industry Series and finalizing the Religious Influences Series for the new edition of 1902–03. He spent long hours at Adelphi Terrace assisting Jesse Argyle in correcting the proofs. He was responsible for providing an abstract of all seventeen volumes.[102]

It is difficult to establish the precise nature and extent of the contribution to the inquiry of Mary, Booth's wife, but it seems to have been considerable. The family later asserted that the two styles detected 'in the book' by the Simeys, 'one more direct and one more literary' were 'Father's and Mother's of course'.[103] George Booth told the Simeys, 'with regard to written contributions by my Mother and others, we are all conscious of many contributions from my Mother'.[104] If in the early years she saw the inquiry as her husband's hobby, it was not long before she saw it in a more serious light.[105] Mary read widely both with and for Booth – Marx and Webb, James and Rowntree, Barnett and Price. She, and sometimes their eldest daughter 'Dodo', attended meetings with him. In 1887, for example, the two heard his address at the Royal Statistical Society, and in 1893 Mary accompanied Charles to a discussion between the Webbs and the Co-operative Men at the Economic Club. Her letters to Beatrice Potter in the 1880s suggest that Mary was at least fully aware of the state of the inquiry; in March 1893 it was she and Jesse Argyle who saw 'the Pauper' through proof and press;[106] she interviewed people on occasion for Booth and held a press reception on the publication of at least one of his works.[107] But her work in relation to the Religious Influences series is by far the best documented. She played a major critical role during the authorship of the series and was left holding the Star Volume baby when Booth absented himself in 1903.[108]

Retrieved riches

When Samuel Barnett received his copy of *Life and Labour of the People in London* in 1903 he wrote to Booth: 'The value of your gift to London is not only in the facts you have provided but in the start you have given to another way of considering the poor.'[109] Barnett's meaning, however, is far from clear, at least to modern scholars who remain at odds over the nature and significance of Booth's ideas and methods. How, for example, does *Life and Labour of the People in London* connect with *London Labour and the London Poor*? The tendency at present is to emphasize their dissimilarities. Booth, by comparison with Mayhew, is said to have been more limited in his understanding by the preconceptions and prejudices of his class. 'Basically,' writes Eileen Yeo, 'Booth was a middle-class moralist who saw any departure from middle-class norms as social disorganization and immorality.' Gertrude Himmelfarb, by contrast, is equally convinced that Mayhew is the inferior of the two. Booth, she tells us, is worthy of greater attention because he 'significantly defined and explicated the social problem, whereas Mayhew merely popularized and dramatized it'.[110] The clash of opinion is in large measure driven by partisan considerations. Himmelfarb, who has an abiding hatred of collectivism in general and considers the welfare state an egregious error, tends to view Victorian Britain from the peculiar perspective of late twentieth-century American conservatism. She is particularly hostile to left-wing historians whose commitment to a privileged concept of class and class consciousness leaves neither space nor sympathy for the exploration of the work of social theorists and philanthropists of the middle classes. Her mission is to do for the public-spirited and socially aware bourgeois of late Victorian England what E.P. Thompson did for the maligned and misunderstood workers of an earlier period. She sets out to explore the movement away from individualism in terms of the growth of the moral imagination of the middle classes and the development of a larger and more generous sensibility towards the labouring poor. Mayhew, who might reasonably have been included as a fair specimen of the compassionate middle classes, receives a battering, less, one suspects, because of what he wrote and more because of the way in which he has been taken up and lionized by those whose politics Himmelfarb abhors. The Mayhew that emerges from the right/left crossfire is an isolated erratic genius who has no coherent class connection, no clear identity and no firm location in social research or in social theory. David Englander finds neither approach satisfactory. In chapter 4 he presents a reassessment of Mayhew in comparison with Booth. Mayhew is seen to have been more influenced by liberal social theory than previously acknowledged and more directly affected by degenerationist concerns about criminality and social order. His extraordinary insights into the world of the labouring classes and the poor are not, however, considered unique. Booth, it is argued, was his equal both in curiosity and understanding. The Booth survey, like the Mayhew survey, was firmly grounded in the class anxieties of Victorian England. *Life and Labour of the People in London*, though acclaimed for its innovatory approach to the measurement of poverty, was as much concerned with the values, beliefs and interests of the proletariat as with the enumeration of its privations. Booth, conscious of the influences on which poverty depends and on those which depend on it, was equally interested in the institutions which might have had a direct bearing on the situation of the workers in the metropolis. A more historically informed reading of the Booth inquiry, it is suggested, might help to remove certain of the misunderstandings that have arisen. 'Wondrous and complicated misery' was how Thackeray described Mayhew's revelations of labour and poverty. The poverty, waste and despair described by Booth and Rowntree was equally arresting and equally baffling.

Mayhew's ideas never assumed programmatic form. Apart from proposals for more comprehensive industrial training and sundry schemes for emigration, education and mutual aid, he had no coherent social reform strategy. The most distinctive feature of Booth's thought, by contrast, lay in its system and in its belief in social action through social engineering. Booth, as Jane Lewis shows in the opening chapter of this book, had no sympathy with the street-door philanthropy of Octavia Hill or the casework approach of the Charity Organization Society and 'tended to move from aggregate analysis to faith in reform from above'. His preference for administrative action, whether to remove pensioners from the poor law or the unfit from the daily struggle for existence, reflected the habits of a businessman engaged in large-scale international trade as well as someone with an acute awareness of the scale and pressing nature of the social problem. But it also reflected a firm commitment to the principles of 1834.

At the core of Booth's thinking lay an unswerving belief not in the particular formulations of political economy but in a hedonistic theory of psychological action which was consistent with positivism but not with socialism which, Booth insisted, was a denial of human nature. From this perspective questions of individualism and collectivism were beside the point. Booth's advocacy of non-contributory old age pensions, Alon Kadish reminds us (chapter 3), was to improve the efficiency of the Poor Law!

Mayhew's poor resisted precise classification and enumeration. No consistent categories were developed to estimate the relative size of the population in poverty. In these respects Booth was far more systematic. Booth's strength, however, lay not in the originality of his social theory but in the possession of tremendous energy and synthetic skills of a very high order. In respect of his perception and understanding of poverty, Booth had more in common with Mayhew than is sometimes allowed. The residuum and its repression, once considered the centrepiece of the social strategies of the 1880s, is now recognized as less of an innovation than was previously imagined. Foreshadowed in Mayhew's depiction of social and cultural degeneration, it became an organizing concept of the mid-Victorian debate on the political integration of the working classes and, as José Harris shows, never lost the connection with character and citizenship thereafter. Examining the origins and development of residualist thinking, her contribution in chapter 2 highlights the ways in which the leakage of evolutionist terminology into the language of social reform in the last quarter of the nineteenth century, concealed underlying continuities with an earlier period.

Mayhew and Rowntree, though not usually bracketed together, do have one thing in common. Neither preserved for posterity the materials collected for their respective survey inquiries. Booth was different. His private papers and notebooks which are readily available for scholarly inspection enable us to see how he proceeded and what he was trying to achieve. Rosemary O'Day's discussion of 'Interviews and Investigations' in the religious influences series (chapter 5) fits in part into the framework of the history of interviewing as a tool and, specifically, as part of Booth's developing methodology, and, in part, into an examination of the nature and purpose of the Religious Influences Series itself – what was Booth trying to do? The essay describes Booth's interviewing practices as they developed between 1886 and 1902–03 and as he communicated them to his team of associates. Both data derived from the interview reports themselves and data external to them is exploited. O'Day highlights Booth's awareness of some of the problems of interviewing – bias of the interviewees; non-comparability of data; non-cooperation from informants – and the solutions which he determined upon. Booth believed that the bias of individuals could be ironed out if a sufficiently large cohort were involved; a similar approach was taken to the problem of non-cooperation. Careful attention was paid to structuring the schedules which were used, the interviews and the interview reports. The voluminous notes which resulted from this method of investigation contrasted with the brevity of the poverty notebooks and posed very considerable problems of manageability and analysis. O'Day argues that the form of the interview reports (and the information sought after and collected) indicate that initially Booth was interested in a considered assessment of the nature of the individual ministries in which the informants were involved. Why he drew back from printing such an assessment is the subject for debate elsewhere.[111] The essay suggests both the importance of the interview material for any modern portrait of religion in late Victorian London and the caveats which should be observed in their use.

Chapter 6 'Women and Social Investigation: Clara Collet and Beatrice Potter' explores two issues: what did social inquiry offer to two of Booth's female associates, and what did they, in their turn, offer to social inquiry. A wide variety of archival sources is explored to show how both women came to become Booth's associates in his great inquiry, comparing their attitudes to their femininity and individuality, and to social investigation as a suitable occupation. Collet emerges as the feminist who found her own identity through work on women's work. Her complex emotional development and her concerns about her own physical attractiveness and the intellectual status of women are viewed alongside the work which she did to further women's living and working conditions. Potter, no less troubled by the issue of her womanhood and not a feminist in any conventional sense, deliberately eschewed work on women for Booth and maintained her suitability to study what were considered 'male' subjects. As such the essay fits into a growing literature concerning the colonization of philanthropic and investigative work by women on both sides of the Atlantic in the Victorian and Edwardian eras. The essay also considers in some detail the actual contribution made by both women to Booth's Poverty Series, concentrating on Potter's work on the docks, tailoring and Jews, and Collet's on women workers. Potter underwent an apprenticeship in a form of social investigation which she almost immediately rejected while Collet was to build considerably upon the methodologies she learnt in Booth's employ in her later career in the civil service and as an independent investigator.

Booth invented the poverty line; Rowntree perfected it. Such, in summary form, is the received wisdom with respect to the development of social research and social policy. Rowntree's incorporation of nutritional science to measure poverty in terms of the ability to meet a minimum standard of physiological health and efficiency, and his distinction between primary and secondary poverty, are said to place him head and shoulders above the arbitrary, uncertain and class-bound prejudices of the Booth standard. John Brown tells us that Rowntree deliberately eschewed 'unfavourable judgements on those living in poverty' while Booth was riddled with unconscious moral assumptions. Peter Hennock is likewise persuaded that

Rowntree's work is superior in theory and method.[112] Both views are in need of revision. An attempt is made in chapter 4 to place Booth's relativistic concept of poverty in proper perspective, to see it, not from the standpoint of some abstract value-free social science, but as contemporaries saw it. Rowntree is the subject of a thorough-going reassessment in chapter 7. John Veit-Wilson, in a controversial contribution, argues that Rowntree's concept of poverty has been seriously misunderstood by historians and social scientists.[113] Rowntree, he points out, is widely regarded as having originated in 1901 the 'scientific' definition of poverty as the minimum income level required for physical subsistence, and is often quoted as defining 'secondary poverty' above this income level as mismanagement. Critics of this approach confuse Rowntree's use of concepts with his discussion of causes, and they overlook Rowntree's own explanation that his concept of poverty was relativistic life-style, and that his distinction between primary and secondary poverty was a heuristic device to convince individualists that the life-style of the poor was at least in part caused by low income and not by improvidence. Townsend's major life work in defining and measuring poverty as relative deprivation is usually presented as overthrowing Rowntree's paradigm. Veit-Wilson's contribution shows that Rowntree's early views and methods have been widely misunderstood by later authors, and it argues that the evidence necessitates a reconsideration of Rowntree's position, which would show Townsend's achievement as a paradigmatic shift not from absolutist to relativist models of poverty but from relativistic models based on standards prescribed by expert observers to relativistic models based on standards derived from the whole population by social surveys.[114]

The historian of the future, wrote Mary Booth, 'if he dives into the mass of notebooks from which the pages of *Life and Labour* were gleaned, will find himself repaid by revelations more vividly true and lifelike than have found their way into the book'.[115] Contributors to Part III substantiate this claim through a series of essays which, in different ways, explore the Booth archive and its possibilities for further historical inquiry. In chapter 8, William Marsden pinpoints the importance of the educational component in Booth's survey. According to Marsden, Booth, like so many contemporaries, viewed education as a potential rescue agency.[116] For the historian of education one of the chief values of the Poverty Series is that it was based on data at street, district and metropolitan levels provided by the school board visitors and teachers at the very time when the London School Boards had come of age. The Industry Series, on the other hand, dealt with teaching as a 'trade'. Last, but not least, the Religious

Influences Series extended the territorial coverage of the Poverty Series, identified ecological change which had occurred during the 1890s, and made judgements, especially about the influence exercised by church and school upon the manners and morals of the urban population. The essay examines the Booth survey as an unparalleled source for investigation into the varieties of urban educational provision, identifying, in particular, territorial variations, hierarchical gradation of schooling, studies of individual schools and their social catchments, the mismatch between the residence patterns of teachers and the location of the schools in which they taught, and the attitudes of teachers to their work and to that of the London School Board. It summarizes many of the conclusions presented by Booth's team. Dr Marsden's essay provides an accessible and illuminating introduction to a much neglected aspect of Booth's work.

Hugh McLeod (chapter 9) revisits Booth's Religious Influences Series to examine the way in which the voluminous archive for this series reveals the religious outlook of Booth and his associates and the manner in which it might be used to provide a 'more adequate religious history of working-class London'. He pays tribute to Booth's humane and broadly sympathetic attitude when dealing with individuals, but underlines several of the weaknesses of his religious overview: the resort to hostile stereotypes when describing groups – Roman Catholics as drunken and habitual beggars, for example; the underrating of religiosity in working-class districts and the overrating of religiosity in middle-class areas, in defiance of much of his own evidence; the assumption of a male perspective; hostility to philanthropic efforts by the churches. The essay summarizes the use of Booth's analysis made by three authors – Jeffrey Cox, McLeod himself and Alan Bartlett. The essay explores the outlook of the interviewing team as evidenced by the interviews themselves. McLeod offers an important discussion of the tendency of part of Booth's team to disregard the value of a religious contribution to social progress in favour of a dependency upon secular agencies. Booth, with his belief in the civilizing influence of religion, is here set against Aves and Baxter. McLeod suggests that this difference in approach was partly a generational one and partly associated with rejection of Christianity. McLeod also demonstrates how Booth's materials, while offering little direct evidence of the religious views of working-class people, may be used to produce a more rounded portrait of London working-class religion. A balanced picture, giving due weight to secularist and diffusive as well as organized religious elements, and to female as well as male perspectives, must be achieved. Oral sources allow us to give proper weight to the religiosity of the church-going minority of

London's working class. The contribution of church-going to the divide between rough and respectable is stressed. McLeod also argues for a comparative religious history of London which discusses Judaism alongside Christianity.

McLeod's theme is developed in chapter 10 where the considerable information acquired by the Booth Inquiry upon ethnic and religious minorities provides material for a fresh assessment of the Jewish community in London. David Englander's discussion seeks to illuminate the situation of the immigrant settlers in East London, and to reveal the ideological framework with which the images and impressions of the newcomers were perceived and structured. It shows, too, how the problems posed by alien immigration limited the angle of vision, so that questions concerning spirituality or inter-group relations were raised, but not pursued.

Rosemary O'Day (chapter 12), accepting that Booth's printed survey of religious influences neglects the female perspective, shows that the archive provides much of the data necessary to correct this deficiency. Her essay indicates both the strengths and the weaknesses of the archival data. Booth and his, by this time, all-male team of associates – Arkell, Argyle, Baxter, Duckworth and Aves – relied almost exclusively on male testimony for their information on women, and they inherited the perspectives of their male informants in this as in so much else. The stereotypes that Booth drew upon in the printed works (to which McLeod, Reeder and Clapson make reference) often came to him via the secretaries' reports which were frequently digests of the declared opinions of the interviewees. But the archive can be used to display the attitudes of late Victorian ministers to women, both as church and chapel workers and as potential and actual congregations. Their approach was by no means entirely negative. The material on women as sustainers of religiosity within the family is especially revealing. The archive also contains the substantive evidence necessary to document the contribution of women as congregation, as carers and as members and organizers of clubs. Jeffrey Cox's thesis which explains the crisis of the churches in terms of the encroachment of the state upon the accepted social role of the churches can be stood upon its head. As urban parishes grew in size and the ratio of minister to flock worsened, any pretence which the Christian churches could make to fulfil a truly pastoral role rested upon the work of women. Booth's information was collected at the moment of transition: dependence upon women workers was identified, but so was the problem of finding women able and willing to do the work. The state or someone else had to step in to fill the vacuum.

Popular culture forms the subject of chapter 13. Mark Clapson presents an original assessment of the place of gambling in the Booth survey. The essay offers fascinating insights into the development of 'the Fancy' in late Victorian London through the medium of Booth's investigations. Dog-fancying, bird breeding and fancying, street betting on horses, are all brought vividly to life and placed geographically and socially. Clapson explains the sources which Booth consulted and the use he made of them – policemen, school board visitors, clergymen, missionary workers. He draws attention to Booth's definition of an undifferentiated 'sporting set' belonging to Class A which serviced the demands of Class B for unedifying and unrespectable entertainments and acted as a drag on its economic well-being, and places this approach within the context of the thought of middle-class reformers such as Beatrice Potter. He shows that Booth saw gambling as a symptom rather than as a cause of poverty – as a part of the 'culture of poverty'. In the Religious Influences Series it was identified as an impediment to the civilizing influences of church and charity. Clapson shows how Booth's approach to gambling was related to his position as a social reformer.

Dr David Reeder (chapter 11) takes as his starting point the view that Booth's survey is important to us less for its statistical analysis than for the descriptive account of London that it offers. He explains the place of social mapping in Booth's total survey and concludes that, as Booth became more and more absorbed in describing highly differentiated localities, the 'representation of London's social geography seemed to become almost an end in itself'. The methods of Booth's social reportage are given due prominence. Reeder demonstrates that Booth's social map was linked inextricably to his theory of urban change – it is 'represented in the survey volumes as an outcome of tendencies in the development of the metropolis which operated with the force almost of natural laws'. Reeder highlights the different features of this theory – the clustering of people in neighbourhoods similar to themselves in wealth and social standing; the operation of a law of successive migration; the pressure on living space which led to overcrowding in the poorer outer suburbs; the relationship between London's natural features – for example, hills and commons – and its manmade features – railways and alleys – and flows of people; and the precise nature of social deterioration at different social levels. The essay looks in detail at Booth's analysis of the cultural patterns discernible in working-class London. It argues that, despite Booth's division of the working-class population into five classes, his description accepts the established polarity between rough and respectable arguing chiefly about the contribution of Classes C and D to this pattern. While Booth brought out admirably the diversity of London society, he also reinforced existing stereotypes of working-class behaviour. This is a point on which both Clapson and McLeod agree.

No single volume can hope to encompass a subject as wide as the history of social investigation which touches upon so many of the major themes of social history and social policy. Our aims have been more modest. The contributors to this volume, all of them leading authorities in the field, have been concerned to identify the salient features of the investigative process, to locate it firmly within its contemporary context, to suggest new interpretations, present new directions for research and generally to raise issues that open up rather than close down further inquiry. We hope that it conveys our own continuing fascination for the subject and that it will communicate to a new generation of scholars the enthusiasm which brought the contributors together on a day in April in 1989 to celebrate and study the work of Charles Booth.

Notes

1   Mill, John Stuart (1921), *Principles of Political Economy* (4th edn. 1857) Ashley, W. J. (ed.), London, p.105.

2   Thirsk, Joan (1959), 'Sources of Information of Population, 1500–1760', 1 and 2, *Amateur Historian*, 4, 4 and 5, Summer and Autumn, pp.129–33; 182–5.

3   Hollingsworth, T.H. (1969), *Historical Demography*, Hodder and Stoughton, p.112.

4   Census of 1881, *General Report*, 4, p.1.

5   Percivall, T. (1774, 1775, 1776), 'Observations on the State of Population in Manchester and other adjacent places', *Philosophical Transactions of the Royal Society*, 64, 65 and 66.

6   Youngson, A. (1961), 'Alexander Webster and his Account of the Number of People in Scotland in the year 1755', *Population Studies*, 15; Kyd, J.G. (1952), *Scottish Population Statistics Including Webster's Analysis of Population, 1755*, Edinburgh Scottish History Society, 3rd Series, 43.

7   See Charles Wilson's excellent discussion of 'Political Arithmetic and Social Welfare' in *England's Apprenticeship, 1603–1763*, (1965), Longman, especially pp.226-32.

8   See Malthus, Thomas (1798), *Essay on Population*.

9   Cullen, Michael J. (1975), *The Statistical Movement in Early Victorian Britain, The Foundations of Empirical Social Research*, Hassocks, Sussex: Harvester Press. Cf. Harrison, Brian (1982), *Peaceable Kingdom: Stability and Change in Modern Britain*, Oxford University Press, pp.260–308.

10   Yeo, Eileen (1992), 'The Social Survey in Social Perspective, 1830–1930', in Bulmer, M. *et al.* (eds), *The Social Survey in Historical Perspective*, Cambridge University Press, p.52.

11   The latter was published by Mudie-Smith, Richard (1904), as *The Religious Life of London*. See Chadwick, Owen (1980), *The Victorian Church*, Part 2, London, A & C Black, 2nd Edition, pp.218–38, for information on amateur religious censuses and their findings.

12   See O'Day, R. and Englander, D. (1993), *Mr Charles Booth's Inquiry*, Hambledon, pp.170–2 for suggestions about Booth's reasoning in this regard.

13   'Proceedings of the Second Meeting of the British Association for the Advancement of Science', *Trans BAAS*, I, 1831–2, p.107; cited in Cullen, *Statistical Movement*, p.78.

14   Cullen, *Statistical Movement*, p.79.

15   Ashton, T.S. (1977), *Economic and Social Investigations in Manchester, 1833–1933*, Harvester Press, (reprint of book of 1934), pp.4–12.

16   Ashton, *Economic and Social Investigations*, p.13.

17   Phillips Kay, James (Dr) (1834), 'Defects in the Constitution of Dispensaries'.

18   Elesh, David (1972), 'The Manchester Statistical Society: A Case Study of Discontinuity in the History of Empirical Social Research' in Oberschall, Anthony (ed.), *The Establishment of Empirical Sociology, Studies in Continuity, Discontinuity, and Institutionalization*, New York, Harper and Row, p.52, reprints the form of inquiry.

19   Ashton, *Economic and Social Investigations*, p.29.

20   *Ibid.*, p.32.

21   *Ibid.*, p.63.

22   Elesh, David, 'The Manchester Statistical Society', pp.39–41.

23   Cullen, *Statistical Movement*, pp.85–6.

24   *Ibid.*, p.90.

25   *Ibid.*, p.102.

26   For this see Norman-Butler, Belinda (1972), *Victorian Aspirations: The Life and Labour of Charles and Mary Booth*, Allen and Unwin, pp.37–8; for further comment on Mary's poor relations with the Booth family, see *Victorian Aspirations*, p.43.

27   'Positivism' (1870?) MS 797/II/25/2.

28   *Ibid.*

29   The classic study of this special relationship is 'The Positivists: A Study of Labour's Intellectuals' in Harrison, Royden (1965), *Before the Socialists: Studies in Labour and Politics, 1861–1881*, Routledge and Kegan Paul.

30   Simey, T.S. and M.B. (1960), *Charles Booth, Social Scientist*, Oxford University Press, pp.43–8.

31   MS 797/II/26/15.

32   MS 797/II/26/15 (vii).

33   Norman-Butler, *Victorian Aspirations*, p.52.

34   Parmoor, Lord (1936), *A Retrospect*, William Heinemann, pp.37–8.

35   MS 797/II/27/7.

36   BLPES, Passfield 7.1.8 fo.56.

37   Simey, T.S. and Simey, M. (1960), *Charles Booth Social Scientis*; Rubinstein, David (1968), 'Booth and Hyndman', *Bulletin of the Society for the Study of Labour History*, 16, pp.22–4; Hennock, E.P. (1976), 'Poverty and Social Theory in England: The Experience of the Eighteen-Eighties', *Social History*, 1, pp.70–2; O'Day, R. and Englander, D. (1993), *Mr Charles Booth's Inquiry*, pp.30–1; Hyndman, H.M. (1911), *Record of an Adventurous Life*, Macmillan, p.331.

38   MS 797/II/ 27/7/1.

39   *Ibid.,* p.2.

40   *Ibid.*, p.4.

41   *Ibid.*, pp.4–5; a reference to so-called 5 Per Cent Philanthropy.

42   *Ibid.*, p.5.

43   *Ibid.*, pp.9–10.

44   *Ibid.*, p.11.

45   *Ibid.*, p.12.

46   *Ibid.*, p.13.

47   *Ibid.*, p.15.

48   *Ibid.*, p.16.

49   *Ibid.*, p.17.

50   It should be noted that this discussion was taking place when Samuel Barnett was becoming involved with model housing developments in the East End. Cripps' wife, Theresa Potter, and his sister-in-law Beatrice, were both intimately involved with both Octavia Hill's and Barnett's ventures and provided a direct link with Booth.

51   *Ibid.*, p.19.

52   *Ibid.,* p.19.

53   *Poverty*, 1, p.173.

54   See O'Day and Englander (1993), *Mr Charles Booth's Inquiry*, pp.54–6.

55   Passfield VII.I.8 *passim*.

56   *Poverty*, 3, pp.142–9; Passfield VII.I.8 fo.56.

57   See O'Day and Englander, *Mr Charles Booth's Inquiry*, pp.146–58.

58   MS 797/II/29/2/ fo.13; this paper occurs in two forms in the archive – this, which is a copy of the paper as delivered in April 1888, and another rough draft.

59   *Ibid.*, fo.18.

60   *Ibid.,* fos 18–19.

61   O'Day, Rosemary (1993), 'Before the Webbs: Beatrice Potter's Early Investigations for Charles Booth's Inquiry', *History*, 78, pp.228–30; Passfield, MS Diary, 6 October 1887.

62   Passfield, MS Diary, 14 October 1887.

63   Schloss Collection; see O'Day and Englander, *Mr Charles Booth's Inquiry*, p.94.

64   William Beveridge to *The Times*, 1960.

65   University of Warwick, Modern Records Centre, Collet MS29/3/13/5/16–17; 20/8/1/55–110.

66   Collet MS 29/3/13/5/16–17; GLCRO A/TOY/22/6/1.

67   See *Toynbee Record*, 8 (June 1896), p.110; *Toynbee Record*, 10 (December 1897), p.104; *Toynbee Record*, 10 (April 1898), p.104.

68   O'Day and Englander, *Mr Charles Booth's Inquiry*, p.15.

69   A/TOY/1/1, Toynbee Minute Book, 26 March 1887.

70   A/TOY/1/1, Toynbee Minute Book, 7 May 1888.

71   A/TOY/1/1, 18 June 1888.

72   A/TOY/2/50, 30 July 1888, H. Llewellyn Smith to A.H.D. Acland.

73   Obituary of Charles Booth, *Journal of the Royal Statistical Society*, 1917.

74   Minute Book of the Royal Statistical Society, 12 November 1885, p.508 and 11 February 1886, p.521.

75   Passfield, II (i) ii 6 Mary Booth to Beatrice Potter, 13 March 1886.

76   Cripps, Collet and Argyle became fellows in 1892 during Booth's Presidency; Smith, Grosvenor and Schloss joined between 1888 and 1891.

77   It is worth noting that the Royal Economic Society also had its offices at Adelphi Terrace. The close physical relations between the two royal societies, the registrar general's office and Booth's inquiry strengthened their intellectual relationship. University of London Library, Foxwell Papers.

78   Minute Book of the Royal Statistical Society, 1890–1909.

79   *Industry*, 1, p.16.

80   *Industry*, 1, p.12.

81   *Industry*, 1, *passim* and especially pp.13 ff.

82   *Industry*, 5, p.65.

83   Nevertheless Booth was to select C.S. Loch as one of his four vice-presidents when he became President of the Royal Statistical Society. See Minute Book of the Royal Statistical Society.

84   See 'Obituary of Henry Higgs', *Economic Journal* (1940), p.561.

85   Mackenzie, Norman (1978) (ed.), *The Letters of Sidney and Beatrice Webb*, 2, Cambridge University Press, p.363, Sidney to Beatrice Webb, 16 June 1890.

86   Mary Booth's Diary, 23 June 1893.

87   Courtney, who had married Kate Potter in 1883, presented Booth to the Royal Statistical Society in 1885; Cripps was a close associate

throughout the period 1881 to 1893, when Theresa Potter, his wife, died and Cripps became an MP.

88   Booth, Charles (1888), 'Conditions and Occupations of the People of East London and Hackney, 1887', *Journal of the Royal Statistical Society*, 51, p.339.

89   Passfield 2 (1) 2, 8; for further detail see O'Day, and Englander, *Mr Charles Booth's Inquiry*, pp.38–48.

90   Minute Book of the Royal Statistical Society, 1890–1909, 10 November 1892, Jesse Argyle (private secretary) of 74 Lordship Road, Stoke Newington, was made a fellow.

91   *The Toynbee Record* (1896), 8, no.6, 6 March 1896.

92   O'Day, R. (1993), 'Before the Webbs: Beatrice Potter's Early Investigations for Charles Booth', *History*, 78, pp.218–42.

93   Simey, *Charles Booth*, p.101.

94   Passfield, MS Diary, November 1888.

95   O'Day and Englander, *Mr Charles Booth's Inquiry*, p.95.

96   Booth Collection, A6, 7 and 8.

97   Simey and Simey, *Charles Booth*, pp.123–24; Parliamentary Papers (91895), Select Committee on Distress from Want of Employment: Minutes of Evidence [365] PP.1895 (9) qq.10,874–11,004; Booth Correspondence, MS 797 I/3935, Charles Booth to Ernest Aves, 12 June 1903.

98   See O'Day and Englander, *Mr Charles Booth's Inquiry,* pp.173–87 for a detailed discussion of Aves's contribution.

99   Minute Book of the Royal Statistical Society, 15 November 1888, H. Llewellyn Smith approved as fellow.

100   BLPES, Beveridge Collection 9a, 110.

101   For example, B169, fo.45, Interview of Reverend Charles Neil, Vicar of St Matthias, Poplar.

102   O'Day and Englander, *Mr Charles Booth's Inquiry*, pp.181, 185.

103   Booth Correspondence, MS 797 I/3030, Meg Booth Ritchie, daughter of Charles Booth, to George Booth, son of Charles Booth, 22 January 1956.

104   Booth Correspondence, MS 797 I/2402 (2), George Booth, Charles Booth's son to Margaret Simey, 23 January 1956.

105   Passfield, 2 (1) 2, 6, Mary Booth to Beatrice Potter, 1887.

106   Norman-Butler, *Victorian Aspirations*, p.121.

107   Norman-Butler, *Victorian Aspirations*, p.110. In January 1892, Mary interviewed J.A. Spender, author of *The State v. Pensions in Old Age*; Mary entertained the Press to lunch in May 1890 to launch the second volume of the Poverty Series, Norman-Butler, *Victorian Aspirations*, p.120.

108   For a detailed account see O'Day and Englander, *Mr Charles Booth's Inquiry*, pp.161–98.

109   MS 797/I/47, Samuel Barnett to Charles Booth, 27 March 1903.

110   Yeo, Eileen, 'Mayhew as a Social Investigator', in Thompson, E.P. and Yeo, Eileen (eds), *The Unknown Mayhew*, Penguin, p.108; Himmelfarb, Gertrude (1991), *Poverty and Compassion: The Moral Imagination of the Late Victorians*, Alfred Knopf, p.18.

111   See O'Day, and Englander, *Mr Charles Booth's Inquiry*, pp.161–98 and O'Day, R. (1988), 'The Men from the Ministry' in Parsons, G. (ed.), *Religion in Victorian Britain*, 2, Manchester University Press, pp.259–79.

112   Brown, John (1968), 'Charles Booth and Labour Colonies,' *Economic History Review,* 2nd Series, 21, p. 352; Hennock, E.P. (1976), 'Poverty and Social Theory in England', *Social History,* 1, p.91.

113   The debate provoked by this item may be followed in the exchanges between Peter Townsend, Hugh MClachlan and the author in *Journal of Social Policy*, 15 (1986), pp.497–507.

114   The implications for contemporary social policy are developed in Veit-Wilson, J.H. (1987), 'Consensual Approaches to Poverty Lines and Social Security', *Journal of Social Policy,* 16, pp.183–211.

115   Booth, Mary (1918), *Charles Booth, A Memoir,* Macmillan, p.105.

116   Osborne Jay, however, was much more cautious. See Jay, Osborne (1893), *The Social Problem: Its Possible Solution*, pp.16–29.

Part I Social and economic thought

1 Social facts, social theory and social change: the ideas of Booth in relation to those of Beatrice Webb, Octavia Hill and Helen Bosanquet

Jane Lewis

Biographers of Booth have lamented the fact that he left no record of the processes by which he arrived at his conclusions, or it may be added, of the place social investigation occupied in his universe of social and political ideas.[1] Aside from Mary Booth's *Memoir*, Beatrice Webb's diary and letters provide virtually the only source through which to explore the wider issues of the relationship between social facts and social theory, as well as the more closely defined but crucial issue as to the choice of methods of social investigation and, in particular, the relationship between qualitative and quantitative methods. Beyond this, Booth's ideas about the ways of achieving social change and his attitude towards the poor also come into focus only when situated more broadly in relation to those of his contemporaries – something that this paper attempts in a speculative and limited fashion.

Booth is usually portrayed as representative of the empirical strand in British sociology that was for the most part divorced from social theory.[2] But it is doubtful as to whether such firm compartmentalization has served the historical record well. Even someone like Octavia Hill, who despised the gathering of social facts, deplored 'windy talk' and focused her attention firmly on social work with individuals, nevertheless worked to a firm set of principles. The value of McBriar's and of the recent contributions of Vincent and Plant have been to show the extent to which, among certain pillars of the Charity Organization Society such as Helen and Bernard Bosanquet, there was a well-worked out and explicit set of ideas about social problems which made social work integral to their solution.[3] The struggle between the social theories of the Fabian Webbs and the Idealist Bosanquets reached its apogee in the work of the Royal Commission on the Poor Laws, on which Octavia Hill and Charles Booth also sat.

It is not my intention to turn Booth into a social theorist but in so far as he, like Hill, Webb and Bosanquet, was motivated by concern about the problem of poverty rather than by research for its own sake, his ideas about the nature of his work and about its relationship to social change warrant as much attention as the social survey techniques he developed. Peter Hennock's careful analysis of his survey has already shown that the categories Booth used were derived from ideas about the nature of social progress that were already well-established and which stressed the progressive incorporation of the respectable poor within one nation.[4] But in terms of his view of the mechanisms of social change, Booth's biographers have tended to succumb to the rather unhelpful label of 'individualism'. While the individualist/collectivist dichotomy has provided the main organizing framework for historians of political ideas in the late nineteenth and early twentieth centuries,[5] more recent work has questioned its usefulness and pointed to the way in which a commitment to social action transcended political differences.[6] The truth of this is immediately apparent when the widely differing political ideas of Charles Booth, Octavia Hill, Helen Bosanquet and Beatrice Webb are considered. In the case of Booth, it is in any case hard to affix any rigid label to someone who made old age pensions his *cause célèbre*, but who, as a member of the Royal Commission on the Poor Laws, was firmly in favour of returning to the principles of 1834.

While Booth did not write explicitly about social investigation, its methods, or its relationship to social theory and to social change, it is possible to situate his ideas more firmly in regard to those of others interested in social problems and social action whom he was close to and worked with. The most obvious candidate is Beatrice Webb, who was the cousin of Booth's wife Mary Macaulay and who was very close to both throughout the 1880s until her marriage to Sidney Webb, of whom Mary Booth particularly disapproved.[7] Another is Octavia Hill, whom the Booths met for the first time at the end of the 1880s and who remained a firm friend, despite her opposition to old age pensions. Both women, together with Helen Bosanquet, became colleagues on the Royal Commission on the Poor Laws, from which Booth resigned in 1908.

Octavia Hill believed that only 'patient detailed' personal social work would achieve social change. Undoubtedly it was her emphasis on the importance of changing individual habits that Booth responded to; they also shared a commitment to the principles of the 1834 Poor Law. Helen Bosanquet and Beatrice Webb were both like Booth in terms of their commitment to social investigation, although they were radically opposed to each other in their views as to the relationship between social facts and social theory. Helen Bosanquet propounded a coherent theory of social change that relied, not unlike Octavia Hill, on modifying individual character (by means of personal social work) and strengthening family responsibility for its members' welfare, while Beatrice Webb derived her prescriptions for systemic change from the social facts. From his letters to Beatrice Webb in the mid 1880s, it seems that Booth never resolved the matter of the relationship between facts and theory. In terms of his views about social change, he shared Octavia Hill and Helen Bosanquet's conviction that individual habits and character had to be modified for change to be lasting. But unlike them he did not believe that this inevitably meant the use of large-scale individual social work. Indeed, Booth lacked the faith of Hill and Bosanquet in the poor. Like Beatrice Webb, he tended to move from aggregate analysis to faith in reform from above.

Social investigation as a means to social change

Octavia Hill saw no possibility of achieving social change other than by slow, patient work with individuals: 'my only notion of reform is that of living side by side with people, till all that one believes becomes clear to them'.[8] Changing 'machinery' as Octavia Hill put it, could not achieve lasting social change. For Hill, the individual work of personal service was crucial to the realization of her Christian obligation to serve others. Only 'infinitesimally small actions' by the rich could produce a change in the character and hence in the behaviour and circumstances of the poor.[9] She believed that face to face interaction was necessary to change habits and character. In 1889, she reminded her fellow workers that irrespective of what action was taken in future on issues such as the provision of school meals by the state, 'for you and me there remain much the same great duties, love, thought, justice, liberality, simplicity, hope, understanding, for ever, still human heart depends on human heart for sympathy and still the old duties of neighbourliness continue'.[10]

According to Hill, the objectives of those working with the poor should be to know, love and befriend rather than a 'lady bountiful' desire to help and give alms. The path of true liberalism lay in having the patience to wait until by dint of careful teaching the people chose the 'right way'.[11] She denied any desire to impose the will of social workers (lady visitors and rent collectors) on the poor, but nevertheless urged her fellow workers to act as 'QUEENS as well as FRIENDS' in their domains.[12]

The numbers she and her fellow workers could thoroughly know were inevitably small. But, anticipating criticism of the scale of her work, she demanded only whether the mass of people was not 'made up of small knots', claiming proudly that 'my people are numbered, not merely counted, but known, man woman and child.[13] While the problem of poverty would thus only be solved by small armies of social workers working to change the habits of the poor, Octavia Hill refused to contemplate any means of compelling 'right action' on the part of the rich. Each one had the Christian duty of searching his or her conscience, of 'trying to see and do right' and of being judged in the sight of God. She was sustained in the small scale of her enterprise, much to her mentor Ruskin's impatience, by the optimistic faith that God would not allow right action to fail, and that eventually good example would secure change on a broader scale.[14]

During the mid 1880s, Beatrice Potter moved away from this world of social work towards that of social investigation as a more promising means of tackling the problem of poverty. In the chapter of her autobiography which is devoted to the Charity Organization Society and written more with the benefit of hindsight than any other in the book, she acknowledged the value of the principles on which the COS was founded: patient and persistent personal service, the acceptance of personal responsibility for the consequences of charitable assistance and the application of scientific method to each case.[15] But increasingly Beatrice experienced difficulty in applying COS principles to applicants for relief, and frustration both at the small scale of the work and at the lack of interest shown by philanthropists in examining the problem beyond the level of the individual case.

In 1883 she found it difficult to put COS ideas about charitable relief into practice in the case of an opium eater, his wife and three children. She pondered in her diary: 'One is tempted to a feeling of righteous indignation against the man, but did he make himself? And is he not on the whole more pitiable?'[16] Nevertheless, on this occasion, it seems that she toed the COS line and refused the family relief: when in 1886, a fellow worker reflected in her turn on the difficulty of applying COS principles in hard cases, she recalled Beatrice's account of her response to the opium addict as a model of good practice.[17] At this point in her career, Beatrice Potter, like Octavia Hill and Booth, felt no temptation towards old-fashioned alms-giving. Rather, in the manner of the good Spencerian she then was, she worried lest no matter how it was practised, charitable relief would favour the weak to the detriment of the strong.

However, she became critical of the distinction the COS made between those deserving and those undeserving of charitable help (the undeserving being those of poor character, such as the drunkard or the opium eater).[18] She noted that the deserving were often people whom it was impossible to help effectively. Helen Bosanquet's efforts in 1893 to drop this distinction in favour of deciding merely whether the applicant was 'helpable' – defined in terms of whether he or she was likely to be able to attain self-support – did nothing to obviate Beatrice Potter's point that many of those in poverty through ill fortune might still not qualify for assistance.[19] Beatrice found difficulty in seeing how such principles could be 'made consistent with the duty persistently inculcated [by the COS] of personal friendship with the poor'.[20] This perception of a double tension at the level of principle and practice was acute. Even workers who did not question the principles of scientific charity, experienced conflicts in their practice, especially when confronted by 'hard cases'.

Beatrice Potter's experience of rent collecting was similarly depressing. By 1885, she felt that her efforts and those of her fellow workers were 'an utter failure'.[21] She recorded in her autobiography Octavia Hill's condemnation (in evidence to the Royal Commission on the Housing of the Working Classes) of reformers who wanted to do too much at once by moving the poor out of damp, one-room cellars into ideal homes, and noted that the dreary buildings in which she collected rents were the outcome of these ideas. With their blocked sinks and lack of privacy, they housed tenants whom Beatrice regarded as a degenerate and hopeless mass.[22] Where Octavia Hill and Helen Bosanquet saw hopeful possibilities for developing friendly relations, Beatrice Potter saw brutality and decay and despaired of social work producing social change. Booth suffered a similar disillusionment with philanthropy during the late 1860s, albeit, given the gendered nature of philanthropic work, his efforts in Liverpool involved municipal politics and education rather than visiting and rent collection. He too despaired of philanthropy as a means of effecting change in what he came to regard as a brutalized and corrupted working class.[23]

Beatrice Potter was additionally shocked at the lack of interest on the part of leading women social workers in record keeping and in rigorously examining the nature of their work above and beyond the fate of individuals. After a visit to Emma Cons, Octavia Hill's lieutenant, she recorded her dismay at the fact that Cons kept no records about her tenants and made no 'attempt to theorise about her work'.[24] Similarly, Octavia Hill was contemptuous of record keeping and told Beatrice that there was too much talking when all that was needed was hard, detailed work.[25] Beatrice was quite clear, even at this early stage, as to the kind of information she wanted about her tenants: number of children per family, their occupations, income, race, place of birth, religion, whether of London stock, or recipients of charity.[26] She was already beginning to make a connection between her observations that many of the Katharine's Buildings tenants were in-migrants to the capital and the problem of casual labour at the docks. Her first published articles arising out of her work for Booth posited a causal connection between the existence of a pool of migrant labour and casual employment. It was in this context that Beatrice found work on Booth's survey more intellectually satisfying, providing as it did the opportunity to investigate the circumstances not just of the individual case, but of locating the problems of individuals on a wider canvass, classifying them and deriving from them principles and proposals for solutions that stretched beyond the individual.

(i) Fact and theory

Beatrice spent considerable time in the late 1880s thinking about how she might attempt the task of social investigation. She recorded in her autobiography that Herbert Spencer had been the first to teach her the value of facts, even though later she came to deplore the way in which he used them.[27] She abhorred the way in which Spencer deduced 'social laws from the laws of another science' and then proceeded to select facts to illustrate the laws he propounded. In 1885, she wrote: 'He irritates me by trying to palm off illustrations as data; by transcribing biological laws into the terms of social tacts, and then reasoning from them as social laws.'[28] When a year later, Canon Barnett, founder of the Toynbee Hall Settlement, stated that it was his belief that ideas had more influence than facts (because ideas influenced the development of character which was in turn the key to social change), Beatrice noted that she believed in ideas, but in ideas following facts.[29] She went on to plan an article on 'Social Diagnosis' to show how far social action had been influenced by fact. She believed that the historical record could be made to show how social sentiment had been formed by descriptions of social facts, which in turn had given rise to political action. Ironically this was an argument which owed as much to conviction as to evidence. Both Mary and Charles Booth commented favourably on her paper. Taking up the relationship between facts and theory, Booth characteristically felt his way forward, rather than opting for Beatrice's laborious struggle to situate her ideas within the existing social and economic literature, and his thinking was considerably less coherent than hers. He began a letter to Beatrice on the subject stating a position that appeared very close to Beatrice's own:

> A framework can be built out of a big theory and facts and statistics run in to fit it. But what I want to see instead is a large statistical framework which is built to receive accumulations of

facts out of which at last is evolved the theory and the law and the basis of more intelligent action.

In other words, theory properly followed fact. But he went on later in the same letter:

As to deductive and inductive methods, I seem to need both eternally and never could separate them in my mind nor decide which moved first. No induction is possible (I should say) without preceding deduction. If induction does not promptly lead to fresh deduction it is barren and if deduction be not very humble and modest leaning on induction past and demanding increasing inductive proof for every step it makes forward it will assuredly go wrong. I think Political Economy needs badly to step back just now – we have had too many hasty deductions and too much cutting out of complicating considerations – which we never cut out in nature ... by ... the deductive method. I here mean having or finding a theory and looking for the facts; and induction ... getting the facts and looking for a theory or law.[30]

There is no evidence that Booth ever resolved or even showed further interest in pursuing the problem of the relationship between fact and theory. Indeed it may be argued that his policy prescriptions reflect in part these rather muddled views expressed in 1886. For while his commitment to old age pensions arose from his analysis of his data on poverty, his equally strong commitment to the principles of the 1834 Poor Law owed more to an *a priori* set of beliefs as to the demoralizing nature of poor relief and the importance of independence and self-maintenance that he shared with pillars of the COS such as Octavia Hill.

Booth showed a much greater preoccupation with the methods of social investigation and the different ways of collecting and verifying data. In the end Beatrice decided that his approach produced only a static snapshot which failed to reveal causality or the actual processes of birth, growth, decay and death. All it could do was provide clues through 'affiliations or concomitants [correlations], for example, between poverty and poor sanitation or infant mortality'.[31] Beatrice showed a much more realistic awareness of the limitations of the method than she did in the later, historically based studies she carried out with Sidney, where it seemed that she expected cause and effect to emerge automatically. Indeed, the relationship between fact and explanation remained elusive, as the Webbs were forced to admit in their study of trade unions, where despite their best efforts, the search for a theoretical framework proceeded deductively rather than arising inductively out of the facts. In 1894, working on the second volume of the study, Beatrice recognized that it was 'silly to suppose that facts *ever tell their own story* – it is all a matter of arranging them so that they may tell something – and the arrangement is purely a subjective process' (her italics).[32] That process of deriving an explanatory framework, of seeking a pattern in the data, was for Beatrice a largely intuitive one. By mid 1897 she recorded triumphantly in her diary that she and Sidney had '*found* our theory' (my italics) and that 'every previous part of our analysis seems to fit in perfectly, and facts which before puzzled us range themselves in their places as if "by nature"'.[33] She also acknowledged the difficulty of acting as both investigator and agitator: 'we are trying, in our humble way, to lead both lives – to keep our heads clear to see the facts – without loosing that touch of the political market which leads to efficient propaganda'.[34] The struggle became harder rather than easier. It was not waged at all by Octavia Hill, who was impatient with social investigation, or by Helen Bosanquet, who, in accordance with her Idealist beliefs, argued for the primacy of mind and motive in achieving social change, and hence for a strategy of social action that would permit the detailed individual casework necessary to build character and strengthen the 'natural' family affections, whereby stable family combined 'young and old in one strong bond of mutual helpfulness'.[35] Helen Bosanquet refused to allow that social investigators could ignore mind and motive. Theory needs must precede fact and she deplored both Beatrice Webb's contrary approach and Booth's inclination to sidestep the issue.

(ii) Methods

During her work with Booth, Beatrice became aware of the choice to be made between the collection of statistical material, whether from census data or by interview, and the qualitative data produced by social observation. In her paper on Social Diagnosis (and elaborated in an unpublished paper of 1887 on 'Personal Observation and Statistical Enquiry'), she held that investigators should 'know and realise distinguishing qualities and peculiar conditions' before they could enumerate the people possessing those qualities or living in those conditions.[36] Crucially, she felt both methods were necessary for the construction of social facts. For to establish a finding as a social fact, the investigator had to show those qualities to be characteristic of enough people. Beatrice was therefore impressed by the potential of Booth's method, of what she called 'wholesale interviews' for eliminating bias and for serving this purpose of verification.[37] Booth's own use of different methods of social investigation and his assessment of the value of qualitative and quantitative data was more intuitive. As he wrote to Beatrice:

> It is to me not so much verification – the figures or the facts may
> be correct enough in themselves – but they mislead from want of
> due proportion or from lack of colour – but it is very difficult as
> you say to state this – to make it neat enough and complete
> enough.[38]

The idea that social facts were a product of more than one
research method was important. Personal observation and interview
were particularly crucial to Beatrice's success as a social investigator.
She excelled Booth in both. Early in 1887, she provided an early
demonstration of her understanding of the importance of interview
technique. Accompanying Booth to interview a factory inspector, she
reflected that they had gained little information because Booth had
failed to show sufficient sympathy with the man's wounded vanity:
'Although I was sorry I had not been alone with him; I should have
managed him better, with softer and less direct treatment'.[39] While
Booth agreed that social investigation was not a matter of making a
choice between methods and types of data, his primary aim was
nevertheless the 'construction of a large statistical framework'. Later
on, under the influence of Sidney Webb, Beatrice was to privilege
written documentary material above the data produced by personal
observation and interview, in part because she considered the latter to
be less easily verifiable (that is, 'soft'), and in part because her
Spencerian belief in female inferiority led her to distrust those
methods in which women seemed to excel.[40] Ironically, just as
Beatrice observed that Booth's methods tended to produce a static
snapshot, so her own and Sidney's narrowing focus on more limited
sources of data and on the importance of collecting as many facts as
possible from which true patterns of development would emerge,
resulted in a more narrow administrative, top-down approach, and
tended as T.H. Marshall observed, to be divorced from consideration
of the wider social, economic and political fabric.[41] When Beatrice
ceased to observe, she also seemed to lose sight of the actors and to
become absorbed in the workings of machinery. Booth's methods also
produced a set of top-down policy prescriptions relatively divorced
from the lives of the people he spent so much time living among.

The methods of Beatrice and Sidney Webb and of Booth were
roundly criticized by Helen Bosanquet. Because mind and will were
the makings of character, both Helen and Bernard Bosanquet argued
that a science of society had therefore to be a science of mind. Helen
Bosanquet's objections to the social survey method developed by Booth
were sustained primarily by her faith that the world of facts had to
have an idea, a principle, and an order that had to be discovered first.
She was fundamentally opposed to the idea of Beatrice and Sidney that

empirical facts could be reshuffled to produce a variety of causal explanatory frameworks. She suggested that 'from the point of view of the historian, the plan is open to the grave objection that the excerpts [a reference to the Webb's famous method of taking notes which allotted each fact to a separate sheet of paper] are very effectively separated from their content'.[42] This criticism was prescient and remarkably close to that of Marshall in his 1975 introduction to the Webb's text on methods. She also criticized Booth's and Rowntree's delineation of a poverty line. Here she was by no means convinced as to the state of the 'facts' in the first place. McKibbin has pointed out that she was unable to accept Rowntree's argument that 'structural' poverty in York resulted from low wages and was independent of the character of the poor.[43] But the recent analysis of Vincent and Plant is also right to suggest that her criticisms of Booth's and Rowntree's data collection and assumptions had validity.[44] She insisted that both Booth and Rowntree's poverty lines had a 'false air of definiteness' about them.[45] She was probably right that Booth's school board visitors missed the income contributions of household members other than the male breadwinner; Margery Loane made the same point in a book she published in 1910.[46] In the manner of a true COS visitor, Helen Bosanquet maintained that the true position of a family would only be ascertained after extensive interviews with family members, neighbours and employers. She maintained that Booth and Rowntree appealed to the emotions on the basis of bad statistics, thus throwing back Beatrice Webb's charge of 'sentimental philanthropy', which was in part directed at writers like herself and their tendency to rely on the emotional power of the single illustration. But Bosanquet's point that statistical material was not necessarily value-free in the way that early practitioners, including Beatrice Webb, assumed, has been confirmed time and again by social scientists since.

Helen Bosanquet was of course convinced that her own methods were beyond reproach. Her major books began by asserting the importance of character and then used psychology (a true science of mind) to prop up a much larger moral and social theory than it had been intended to support. While her descriptions of working-class life were often both perceptive and sympathetic, the prescriptions following from her analysis relied on the imposition of a pre-existing framework of moral and social philosophy which to all intents and purposes assumed the status of 'natural law'. Beatrice Webb's criticism of Herbert Spencer's tendency to mix induction and deduction and to give hypothetical laws of behaviour the status of social facts could also have been levelled at Helen Bosanquet, who did not feel it necessary to conduct any rigorous investigation into the

causes of poverty. She felt it sufficient to set out a theory of
'progressive wants', short-circuited in some way by lack of character
development and poor habits, and then to draw on illustrations of
human behaviour derived from what Octavia Hill would have termed
'a thorough knowledge of the poor' which came from working among
them.

In terms of his ideas about the proper relationship between social
fact and theory about methods of social investigation, Charles Booth
undoubtedly had more in common with Beatrice Webb than with
Helen Bosanquet. Yet many of his solutions to the problem of poverty
were ones with which both Bosanquet and Hill could sympathize. As
Hennock's study of Booth's classification of the causes of poverty has
shown, Booth fully accepted the importance of character and habits.
He also put his faith in education, albeit via the Board School rather
than the social worker, as a remedy for social ills. Like Hill and
Bosanquet, he felt that social progress ultimately depended on 'the
deepening of the sentiment of the individual responsibility'.[47] But this
did not mean that he shared Hill's and Bosanquet's faith in the poor
individual's willingness and capacity to change his or her habit. Like
Beatrice Webb, Booth lacked sympathy with the very poor – classes A
and B in his classification. Hill and Bosanquet's idea of casework as
an opportunity to develop relationships between rich and poor based
on love and sympathy held no appeal for either Webb or Booth, who
saw in the very poor only corruption and brutality rather than affection
and hope.

Social investigation and policy prescription

Charles Booth and Beatrice Webb were committed to the idea of
careful investigation as a basis for policy prescription. Beatrice's early
articles on dock labour, which noted the movement of the docks down
the river and the changing structure of occupations, nevertheless gave
priority to the drift of unskilled labour into the city, attracted, she
believed, by the low amusements of city life.[48] Thus in 1886, Beatrice
had not reached the point where social observation led her to
conclusions that differed significantly from those of scientific charity.
Not until her article on sweated labour, also prepared for Booth and
published in 1890, did she achieve an analysis of cause that relied on
more than individual character and that therefore matched her solution
to the problem, which she believed to be municipal workshops, and, in
the short term, factory inspection and a minimum wage.

But just as faith in the COS perspective had distorted the logic of
her arguments in regard to dock labour, so later faith in a particular
form of administrative solution was allowed in large measure to dictate

the choice of 'facts' marshalled to support it. On the Royal Commission on the Poor Laws, Beatrice joined forces with Booth in the initial stage of the Commission's work in order to press for proper social investigation, but she went on to produce a Minority Report that was more a propaganda document. She wrote energetically to Sidney in May 1908:

> With seeming impartiality and moderation every work of the Report has to tell in the direction of breaking up the Poor Law, the argument has to be repeated in any conceivable form so that the reader cannot escape from it. It must be a real work of Art; we can dismiss Science. It will be High Jinks doing it and we will get to work at once.[49]

Knowing the solution they wished to promote, Beatrice set about 'discovering' the principles to underpin it and the facts to support it: 'manufacturing the heavy artillery of fact that is to drive both principles and scheme home'.[50] Helen Bosanquet was undoubtedly justified in her scathing criticism of Beatrice's reading of poor law history; it was at this point that she made her famous suggestion that some of the slips of paper the Webbs used to record individual facts must surely have fallen under the table.[51] Similarly, Booth's plan for reforming the Poor Law published two years after he had departed from the Royal Commission in 1910, owed more to his belief in the importance of a tightly administered destitution authority than to the findings of the social investigation mounted by the Royal Commission, which served substantially to modify the views of the majority of commissioners, who reacted strongly to evidence of inefficiency by boards of guardians who opted for the creation of new public assistance authorities under the control of local government.

Booth's view of the way to reform the Poor Law was thus at the furthest remove from that of Beatrice Webb, yet their approach to the problem of poverty and indeed their view of the poor had much in common. Both their solutions were above all administrative. As Hennock has observed, Booth believed that poverty would be dealt with by better organization aimed at encouraging production,[52] a strand of thinking that persisted through Beveridge's early analysis of unemployment.[53] In respect of the Poor Law, Booth wanted to see more rational areas of local administration, each with a complete set of Poor Law institutions as a means of exerting tighter control on the pauper population and of achieving greater uniformity in relief procedures. Beatrice also exhibited touching faith in the power of the right administrative structure to achieve reform. Leonard Woolf was perceptive on this score when he wrote that the Webbs believed that:

... if the machinery of society was properly constructed and controlled efficiently by intelligent people, if the functions of the various parts of the organisation were scientifically determined and the structure scientifically adapted to the function – then we should get an adequately civilized society.[54]

Booth's commitment to the principles of the 1834 Poor Law were long-standing. His data on the causes of poverty had persuaded him of the wisdom of removing a deserving group like the elderly outside the provisions of the Poor Law,[55] but he had no sympathy with the dependence of his social class B on poor relief, and would have liked to have seen them removed to labour colonies.[56] There are parallels here with the draconian measures envisaged in Beatrice Webb's Minority Report for forcing recalcitrant labour into a useful life. Like the COS, Beatrice was full of admiration for the respectable working poor; the co-operators of Bacup were to her a model working-class community full of 'moral purpose'.[57] She never developed any sympathy with the very poor 'degenerate masses' from her first horrified exposure to them as rent collector. They featured as 'loafers ... bestial content or helpless discontent on their faces'[58] in her observations of casual labour in 1886; were hovering in the background of her account of her analysis of the sweated trades, many of whose workers she felt should be removed from the labour market on grounds of inefficiency (irrespective of the effects on them and their dependants); and persisted in her views of the recalcitrant in her 1909 Minority Report.[59]

Helen Bosanquet and Octavia Hill were implacably opposed to Booth's ideas regarding old age pensioners, but more in sympathy (especially Hill) with his views on the reform of the Poor Laws. However, both demonstrated considerably more sympathy than he did with the lot of the 'residuum', and Helen Bosanquet, who substantially wrote the 'Majority Report of the Royal Commission on the Poor Laws', was much less ferocious in her prescribed treatment of the residuum than either Booth or Webb. Helen Bosanquet's concern to keep the destitute as a separate category was not inspired, as Beatrice Webb feared, by simple desire to push (in the sense of cause hardship to), but rather to promote 'the restorative treatment of individuals' through personal social work.[60] She believed that doles, including those in the form of old age pensions, would only serve to weaken both the individual's resolve to make provision for his or her old age and the family's commitment to the welfare of its dependent members.[61] Helen and Bernard Bosanquet saw the family as the place where character was developed. Homes were 'nurseries of citizenship' and state intervention could but threaten these 'natural ties' of affection and support.

The Majority Report envisaged a reformed destitution authority employing nothing less than an army of trained social workers devoted to helping families back to independence and self-maintenance. Faith in social work was firmly grounded, as it has always been, in the Bosanquets' belief in the primacy of mind and will. Changing character not machinery was the important thing, something Octavia Hill wholeheartedly agreed with. Indeed, she was lukewarm about any attempt to reform the Poor Law, maintaining that the solution to the problem of poverty depended 'not on machinery which commissions may recommend ... but on the number of faithful men and women who England can secure and inspire as faithful servants'.[62] As Vincent has noted, unlike the Webbs, the Bosanquets wanted casework recognized as a specialism in its own right. They envisaged 'every family in contact with the Poor Law [coming] under careful and friendly scrutiny with a view of its restoration to independent citizenship'.[63] Bernard Bosanquet emphasized that in dealing with the destitute 'you offer everything – the whole material and guidance of life'.[64] The social work to be done was described in terms resembling a religious crusade: 'an army of social healers to be trained and organized ... disciplined and animated with a single spirit and purpose'.[65] In practice, the possibilities for social control would doubtless have proved as chilling as Booth's or the Webbs' plans for disciplining the residuum, but this was not the intent at least. In the event, the Bosanquets plan for practising 'social therapeutics' on a grand scale would have proved as costly as the Webbs' plan for abolition of the Poor Law would have proved administratively complicated.

Octavia Hill and Arthur Downes were sufficiently in tune with Booth's ideas about reform of the Poor Laws to allow their memoranda of dissent from the Majority Report to be reprinted in the book he published setting out his ideas for Poor Law reform, but neither Octavia Hill nor Helen Bosanquet would have agreed with the wholly administrative nature of his solutions, derived, as they would have perceived it, from his preoccupation with aggregates rather than with the character and habits of individuals.

* * *

Like Beatrice Webb, Booth rejected the commitment to personal social work that characterized the work of philanthropists like Octavia Hill and Helen Bosanquet in favour of an analysis of aggregates as a necessary prerequisite for social action. At an early stage, he refused to wed himself to privileging either facts or theory. In this way he was probably more honest than Beatrice Webb who insisted on the primacy of facts, but often reached her conclusions by a series of imaginative leaps and insights that had as much or more to do with her faith in a rational bureaucratic machinery and administrative expertise than to the painstaking collection of data.

Booth remained committed to the individualist's belief in character and good habits as the way of solving the problem of poverty but, like Beatrice, he tended to lose sight of the poor themselves, not least because from early on he found it very difficult to summon up any enthusiasm for their powers of self-determination. Ways had to be found of channelling them along the right path and Booth had a more realistic appreciation than Helen Bosanquet and certainly than Octavia Hill of both the size and urgency of the problem. He was therefore doubly prepared to invoke a variety of administrative solutions, some of which involved using the power of the state, to impose social discipline, rather than opting for the much slower and as costly personal service work proposed by the Majority Report. What is nevertheless striking is the way in which Octavia Hill, Helen Bosanquet and Charles Booth, together with Beatrice Potter in the days of her early work as a social investigator, found it possible to reconcile a belief in individualism with a commitment to different forms of social action, whether social work or social investigation, and whether using volunteers or the state, or a mix of both. In the end the hegemony of ideas regarding the need for social action seems more striking than any division between individualism and collectivism.

Notes

1   Simey, T.S. and Simey, M.B. (1960), *Charles Booth Social Scientist*, Oxford University Press, p.8.

2   Abrams, P. (1968), *The Origins of British Sociology*, Chicago University Press; Bulmer, M. (ed.), (1985), *Essays on the History of British Sociological Research*, Cambridge: Cambridge University Press; Kent, R.A. (1981) *A History of British Empirical Sociology*, Aldershot : Gower.

3   McBriar, A.M. (1987), *An Edwardian Mixed Doubles. The Bosanquets versus the Webbs*, Oxford: Clarendon; Vincent, A. and Plant, R. (1984), *Philosophy, Politics and Citizenship*, Oxford: Blackwell.

4   Hennock, E.P. (1976), 'Poverty and Social Theory in England: the experience of the 1880s', *Social History* 1.

5   E.g. Barker, Rodney (1978) *Political Ideas in Modern Britain*, Methuen, 1.

6   Harris, José (1989), 'The Webbs, the COS and the Ratan Tata Foundation: Social Policy from the Perspective of 1912' , in *The Goals of Social Policy*, eds Bulmer, M., Lewis, J., Piachaud, D., Unwin Hyman.

7   Norman-Butler, Belinda (1972), *Victorian Aspirations. The Life and Labour of Charles and Mary Booth*, Allen and Unwin, pp.114–5.

8   Maurice, Emily (1928), *Octavia Hill: Early Ideals.* Allen and Unwin, p.211.

9   Hill, Octavia (1869), 'Organised Work among the Poor' , *Macmillans Magazine*, 20, May/October, p.222

10   Hill, Octavia (1889), *Letter to My Fellow Workers*, p.11, Marylebone Public Library Hill Coll. 84/5.

11   Hill, Octavia (1875), *Homes of the London Poor*, Macmillan, Preface.

12   Hill, Octavia (1874), *Letter to my Fellow Workers*, p.10, Marylebone Lib., 84/5.

13   Hill, Octavia 'Organised Work among the Poor', pp.224–5.

14   Hill, Octavia (1879), *Letter to my Fellow Workers*, p.6, Marylebone Lib. 84/5.

15   Webb, Beatrice (1979), *My Apprenticeship*, Cambridge: Cambridge University Press, p.201.

16   Beatrice Webb's Diary (hereafter BWD: references in this essay are to the typescript Diary), 20 May 1883, BLPES, f.311, TS.

17   Ella Pycroft to Beatrice Webb, 15 July 1886, BLPES, Passfield 2(i) 2, item 155.

18   Webb, *Apprenticeship*, p.202.

19   Dendy, Helen (1893), 'Thorough Charity', *Charity Organization Review*. June, pp.206–14.

20   Webb, *Apprenticeship*, p.202.

21   *Ibid.*, p.277.

22   BWD 7 November 1886, f.743, 745.

23   Simey and Simey, *Charles Booth*, pp.40–5.

24   Webb, *Apprenticeship*, p.67.

25   *Ibid.*, p.278.

26   *Ibid.*, p.273.

27   *Ibid.*, p.193.

28   *Ibid.*, p.270.

29   *Ibid.*, p.286.

30   Charles Booth to Beatrice Webb, 31 July 1886, Passfield 2 (i) 2 item 172.

31   Webb, *Apprenticeship*, pp.245, 248.

32   BWD 10 July 1894, f.1317.

33   BWD 1 May 1897, f.1488.

34   BWD 5 January 1896, f.1429.

35   Bosanquet, Bernard (1895) 'Duties of Citizenship', in *Aspects of Social Reform*, Macmillan, p.10; Bosanquet, Helen (1906) *The Family*, Macmillan, p.66.

36   'Personal Observation and Statistical Enquiry' in Passfield 7, item 6, 25 September 1887 and reprinted in *Apprenticeship*, Appendix A pp.417–22.

37   Webb, *Apprenticeship*, p.230.

38   Booth to Webb, 31 July 1886.

39   Webb, *Apprenticeship*, p.317.

40   BWD 30 July 1893, f.1290; 28 April 1899, f.1958; Webb, Sidney and Webb, Beatrice (1897) *Industrial Democracy*, Longmans, Preface 11, 13.

41   Webb, Sidney and Webb, Beatrice (reprinted 1975), *Methods of Social Study*, Cambridge: Cambridge University Press, Introduction by T.H. Marshall, p.35.

42   Bosanquet, Helen (1910), 'The Historical Basis of English Poor Law Policy', *Economic Journal* 20, June, p.183.

43   McKibbin, R.I. (1978), 'Social Class and Social Observation in Edwardian England', *Transactions of the Royal Historical Society*, p.276.

44   Vincent and Plant, *Philosophy, Politics and Citizenship*, p.98

45   Bosanquet, Helen (1903), *The Poverty Line*, COS, p.1.

46   Loane, M. (1910), *The Queens Poor*, Edward Arnold, p.158.

47   Pfautz, H.W. (1967), *Charles Booth on the City,* Chicago University Press, p.84.

48   'A Lady' s View of the Unemployed at the East', Passfield V7II, item 4a, 18 February 1886, published in the *Pall Mall Gazette.*

49   Beatrice Webb to Sidney Webb, 2 May 1908, Mackenzie, Norman (ed.), (1978), *The Letters of Sidney and Beatrice Webb,* Cambridge University Press and the LSE, 2, p.313.

50   BWD 30 January 1908, f.2528. (See also Kidd, Alan J. (1987), 'Historians or Polemicist? How the Webbs Wrote their History of the Poor Laws', *Economic History Review,* 40, August, pp.400–17.

51   Bosanquet, Helen 'Basis of English Poor Law Policy', p.185.

52   Hennock, E.P. 'Poverty and Social Theory'.

53   Harris, J. (1972), *Unemployment and Politics. A Study in English Social Policy 1886–1914,* Oxford: Oxford University Press.

54   Greenleaf, W.H. (1983), *The British Political Tradition* 1, Methuen, p.392.

55   Booth, Charles (1899), *Old Age Pensions,* Macmillan.

56   Brown, J. (1968), 'Charles Booth and Labour Colonies, 1889–1905', *Economic History Review* 21, August.

57   Webb, *Apprenticeship,* p.151.

58   BWD 6 May 1887, f.814.

59   Potter, B. (1892), 'How Best to do away with the Sweating System', paper read at the 24th Annual Congress of Cooperative Societies, Manchester Cooperative Union Ltd; Webb, Beatrice (1896) *Women and the Factory Acts,* Fabian Tract no.67; Parliamentary Papers (1909) Report of the Royal Commission on the Poor Laws and Relief of Distress, Cd 4499, 38.

60   Bosanquet, Bernard (1909), 'The Majority Report', *Sociological Review* 2, p.117.

61   Bosanquet, Helen (1897), *The Standard of Life,* Macmillan.

62   Maurice, C. Edmund (1913), *Life of Octavia Hill,* Macmillan, p.565.

63   Vincent, A.W. (1984), 'The Poor Law Reports of 1909 and the Social Theory of the COS', *Victorian Studies* 27, pp.343–63.

64   Bosanquet, Bernard 'The Majority Report', p.112.

65   *Ibid.*

2 Between civic virtue and Social Darwinism: the concept of the residuum

José Harris

The idea of the 'residuum' has been identified by many historians as one of the key concepts in late Victorian social science, and as a vital component in the paradigmatic shift from the rationalistic hedonism of the New Poor Law era to the 'social Darwinism' of the age of imperialism. Whereas early and mid Victorians, so it has been argued, blamed social dependency on the wilful contumacy of rationally calculating individuals, later Victorians increasingly ascribed pauperism and chronic poverty to the miscalculation of people inherently unable to help themselves, because of biological and psychological degeneracy. Moreover, whereas early Victorian paupers were seen as damaging to other people simply by being a charge upon public finance, the late Victorian 'residuum' was perceived as dragging down the general standard of the race – both by competing unfairly with more efficient members, and by harming the organic tissue of the wider society. Whereas the early Victorian unemployed were seen as wilfully choosing not to work even though work was available, the late Victorian unemployed (or at least the 'casual' section of them) were viewed as being largely incapable of regular, profitable employment under conditions of modern capitalism. A framework for understanding this new phenomenon of a 'residuum' of industrial incompetents was supplied, so it is often suggested, by the social application of Darwin's theory of natural selection: the process of economic competition gave victory to those most adapted to survival, leaving a residue of the 'unfit', who survived only because 'civilization' could not bring itself to leave them to die out. It was their anachronistic survival which largely accounted for the phenomenon of mass poverty, both because the 'unfit' themselves were poor and because their undercutting of wages and availability for spasmodic work depressed the living standards of the competent and regular working class. Thus it is claimed that 'social Darwinism added a cosmic significance' to the struggle between different groups of workers, and 'biologism provided a framework for a comprehensive theory of hereditary urban degeneration'. The poor in great cities were increasingly identified as 'primitive tribes' and 'savages', separated from the civilized by an 'ineradicable hereditary gap'; and social Darwinism was invoked as a 'justification for existing social relations and as a vehicle for a belief in the inequality of race and class'.[1]

The emergence of the 'residuum' as a central theme of social debate has been specifically located by historians in the socio–economic crisis of the mid 1880s – a time when cyclical depression, agricultural collapse, migration to the cities and desperate competition for domestic and industrial space thrust the outcast poor and the respectable working class into unprecedented and dangerous proximity. Numerous popular and official studies from the 1880s onwards commented on and explored the emerging syndrome of urban degeneration, drink, early marriage, feckless procreation, hereditary disease and chronic social dependency, which characterized the 'residuum' and its various synonyms: the 'hopeless classes', 'the unfit', 'the abyss', the 'quagmire', the 'pauper Frankenstein' and the 'submerged tenth'. It was against this backcloth that Charles Booth initiated his famous survey of London, and put forward his proposals for segregating incompetent workers into industrial labour colonies – thus, it was hoped, liberating the competent majority for higher wages, self-help and upward social mobility. Booth's 'distinction between the "true working classes" and the casual residuum' was identified by Gareth Stedman Jones in his study of *Outcast London* as 'central to the crisis of the 1880s', and as reflecting the 'social attitudes of every grouping' from the Charity Organization Society to the Social Democratic Federation. The whole genre of 'residuum' writing has been portrayed by Stedman Jones, Greta Jones, Daniel Pick, Christopher Shaw and others as a prelude to Edwardian and inter-war fears about 'dysgenic' racial decline, and as anticipating more recent concerns in Britain and North America about the existence of an urban 'underclass' prone to hereditary social dependency.[2]

This paper seeks not wholly to reject these interpretations, but to supplement and recast them in rather a different light. I shall suggest that the term 'residuum' was used by late Victorian theorists and social administrators in many different ways; that practical and theoretical demarcation between the respectable and the degenerate poor long ante-dated the 1880s; that 'residuum' theories had many sources in political and social thought other than just the social application of Darwinism; and that, at least in a British context, there is very little evidence to suggest that use of the term 'residuum' automatically implied any wider commitment to an intellectual framework of societal 'natural selection' or hereditary 'degeneration'.

First, then, the use and meaning of the term 'residuum'. That the word 'residuum' and its many synonyms crop up very frequently in late Victorian and Edwardian social debate is, I think, undeniable. The term was used not just by Charles Booth, but by Beatrice Webb, Alfred Marshall, W.S. Jevons, William Beveridge and General William Booth, to name but a few; and it appears in the reports and evidence of the Royal Commission on Housing (1885), the Select Committees on Distress from Want of Employment (1894–96), the Interdepartmental Committee on Physical Deterioration (1904), the Royal Commission on the Care and Control of the Feeble Minded (1904–08) and the Royal Commission on the Poor Laws (1905–09). The widespread currency of the term accurately reflects the prevalence of evolutionary and 'organic' language in theoretical discussion of practical social problems – language that by the turn of the century had become part of the commonplace vocabulary of public social debate. As informed contemporaries were very well aware, however, there was more than one possible variant of social evolution. A strict Darwinian version modelled on the *Origin of Species* implied not simply 'evolution' (a process that had a long, pre-Darwinian, history in social thought, going back via Malthus to the eighteenth century and beyond) but 'natural selection', which meant that structures evolved through the medium of random and irreversible biological or socio-biological mutations. A literal application of 'natural selection' to society entailed no possibility of improvement for the unfit or their descendants, no escape route through better conditions or social learning, no legitimate social policies except either *laissez–faire* or sterilization and compulsory segregation.[3]

That some late Victorian and Edwardian residuum theorists in Britain held precisely those views is of course undeniable; they were strongly canvassed by sensation-seeking journalists like Arnold White, and by the coterie around Professor Karl Pearson in the sphere of university laboratories. But many more were exponents of a Spencerian, Lamarckian (or often merely eclectic) view, that organisms learned from and transmitted the lessons of their environment, that survival involved adaptation rather than mutation, that evolution was in some sense purposive, and that social improvement could therefore be secured by an appropriate programme of environmental conditioning. Evolutionists differed widely about what such a programme should actually consist of; but the view that organic progress could be deliberately fostered and degeneracy halted or reversed was common to widely disparate groups such as the Fabians and the Charity Organization Society, the Salvation Army and the Social Democratic Federation, the White Cross League and the Association of Medical Officers of Health. The proceedings of the famous Interdepartmental Committee on Physical Deterioration in

1904 (often cited as the official apogee of social Darwinian thought in Britain) clearly belonged within this other evolutionary tradition, since the vast majority of witnesses to this Committee firmly repudiated any suggestion of biologically transmitted social degeneration. And the Committee itself concluded that although there was much evidence of 'deterioration' and 'deplorable habits' among the lower sections of the working class, there was no firm evidence of irreversible 'organic' and 'racial' decline.[4]

The same point may be made about many other public inquiries of the period, including the Royal Commission on the Feeble Minded (again often cited as a stronghold of social Darwinian thought). Witnesses before this commission differed widely about the causes, extent and treatment of mental deficiency. But eugenists and environmentalists alike distinguished carefully between the 'feeble minded' (what Sir James Crichton Brown, FRS, referred to as 'the heap of social rubbish corresponding with mental defect', whose condition was perceived both as more or less hereditary and as randomly distributed throughout all social classes) and the 'residuum of the casual poor' (whose 'deterioration' was seen by theorists of both persuasions as largely reversible by wise social policies).[5] This distinction was made very precisely in the deliberations of the commission by the secretary of the Charity Organization Society, C.S. Loch (who is frequently cited as a prominent exemplar of the transition from *laissez-faire* individualism to eugenics and social Darwinism). Loch somewhat reluctantly supported eugenic intervention in the sphere of feeble mindedness, but never budged from the view that poverty and physical deterioration by themselves were the products of bad but reformable moral character.[6] The only major contributor to the commission who clearly identified mental deficiency with what he called the 'large residuum of physical and moral degenerates in the slum areas' was the Board of Education's Dr Alfred Eichholz; and, far from being a social Darwinist, Eichholz was perhaps the most extreme pro-environmentalist and anti-hereditarian publicist of the Edwardian age.[7] A few years later the Royal Commission on Venereal Disease heard conclusive evidence about the transmissability of syphilis from parent to child; but representatives on this commission appeared to be at least as alarmed about the influence of VD upon female sterility and high rates of infant mortality as about its role in creating an hereditary degenerate class. The sinister-sounding phrase 'racial decay', used by several participants in the VD enquiry, turns out on closer inspection to refer to nothing more than the prevailing decline in fertility.[8] Even the unofficial National Commission on the Birth Rate (1912–16), which was composed almost entirely of people who were worried about national racial decline, ultimately rejected the view that the poorest class was composed of hereditary biological degenerates. It is true that this inquiry commission deplored the low fertility of the highest classes and believed that 'the physical and mental inferiority of the most fertile social strata ... is indisputable'. But it concluded that

> ... the greater part of this class inferiority is probably due to bad environment, and deprecate[d] the tendency to identify the economic élite with the psycho-physical élite. The commission does not of course seek to deny the inheritance of both mental and physical characteristics ... but it cannot accept the hypothesis that the broad distinctions between social classes are but the effects of germinal variations, and is satisfied that environmental factors which cannot be sensibly modified by individuals exposed to them, however gifted, often prevent the utilization of natural talents.[9]

Even more firm in their rejection of a 'social Darwinist' perspective was the substantial body of evolutionists who claimed that physiological evolution had little or no relevance in the social sphere, and that the province of social evolution was organizational and moral; a group that included not merely reformist liberals like T.H. Huxley and L.T. Hobhouse, but hard-nosed social imperialists like Benjamin Kidd. There was a recurrent vein of anxiety in Edwardian sociology, partly inspired by Huxley's famous lecture on *Evolution and Ethics*, that the moral imperatives of social evolution *might* in the long run conflict with those of physically based natural selection.[10] But this theme was nearly always overridden by the view that natural selection itself was often harmful and inefficient – that it preserved physical characteristics that were no longer functional in complex industrial societies, and that the process of competition which deposited the residuum also damaged and dragged down the 'fit'.[11] Moreover though some residuum theorists used the term exclusively with reference to the 'very poor' (and indeed assumed that poverty was in itself a litmus test of evolutionary failure) there were others who firmly denied that it was a class-specific phenomenon. John Bright himself – who as we shall see was the original coiner of the term – claimed that there was 'a residuum in every class'; while Helen Bosanquet (one of the leading residuum theorists of the 1890s) constantly insisted that it was 'a vertical not horizontal phenomenon' ('the most trivial accident of birth or fortune may enable a true member of the Residuum to conceal himself in that section of society which Mr. Giffen characterises as the upper barbarians').[12]

Such varied perspectives may account for the fact that very few of those who used the language of the residuum supported the policies of malign neglect that such a concept seemed to entail; and those who did so, though often conspicuous for the stridency of their arguments, were often notably unsuccessful at influencing social policy. When in 1905 the young William Beveridge proposed in a paper to the Sociological Society that members of the residuum who proved to be unimprovable should be segregated in institutions and deprived of the right to marry and bear children, he found himself in a minority of one.[13] By contrast, new liberals, social imperialists, socialists, evangelicals, Board of Trade officials (including Beveridge himself in a more mature phase) and even the majority of participants in the Edwardian eugenics movement, all concurred in the view that the residuum could and should be elevated, improved, organized and regimented into conformity with the rest of society. The only significant deviation from this view can be found in the debate on mental deficiency, leading to the Mental Deficiency Act of 1913, which authorized the compulsory segregation of the feeble minded, particularly women of childbearing age. But, as noted above, even strong environmentalists and old-fashioned individualists took the view that certain forms of mental deficiency were wholly different in kind from the problems of poverty and social dereliction (though conceding that in practice there was some overlap between them). Moreover, some at least of those who used the imagery of the residuum to describe the very poor explicitly rejected the notion of irreversible racial degeneracy as both fallacious and immoral. General William Booth's *Darkest England* – a book that dealt in great detail with the residuum problem – specifically challenged and denounced 'those anti-Christian economists who hold that it is an offence against the doctrine of the survival of the fittest to try to save the weakest from going to the wall'.[14] And, from a wholly different standpoint, Helen Bosanquet's study of 'The Industrial Residuum' in 1893 clearly envisaged that the residuum could be reclaimed – by a mixture of tough social policies, neighbourly visiting, and training in citizenship and the habits of good housekeeping.[15]

Talk of the 'residuum' therefore by no means necessarily implied that the poor were viewed as the mere survivors of an inexorable Darwinian anthropology. Moreover, as was hinted at in the above quotation from General Booth, residualist thought contained other and more complex strains than the crude and obvious inheritance of social Darwinism. Classical political economy as set out by Smith and Ricardo harboured intimations of the residuum concept, in the doctrine that rational men would automatically adapt to structural innovation –

but not without the risk of long-term distress over more than one generation for those cast aside by technological change. Helen Bosanquet's study of 1893 analysed the residuum mainly within the categories of neo-classical and marginalist economics: the residuum consisted of those in all social classes for whom the pleasures of idleness bisected the pains of industry at a lower point on an indifference curve than in the case of normal people, and for whom the 'final utility' of regular work was virtually nil.[16] And, far from being alien to the philosophy of radical hedonism (as some commentators have suggested), the arch-hedonist himself, Jeremy Bentham, had uncannily foreshadowed many aspects of late nineteenth-century social-evolutionary thought in his book, *Outline of a Work entitled Pauper Management Improvement*, written in 1798. Like some residuum theorists of the 1880s Bentham had emphasized the defective 'moral sanity' of the dependent poor, their economic unproductiveness if left to their own devices, and the gulf between them and the ordinary working class; all of which in Bentham's view legitimized denial of normal civil liberties and the imposition of paternalistic controls by pauper-managers licensed by the state.[17]

Similar themes can be detected in the generation that followed Bentham: a generation that supposedly saw the apogee of rationalistic and atomistic theories of poverty. The Poor Law Amendment Act of 1834 in theory made no distinction between different grades of the able-bodied poor (all were deemed equally rational, and thus equally culpable if they lapsed into public dependence). But social debate in early and mid Victorian England makes it manifestly clear that this lack of discrimination was never wholly acceptable either to popular opinion or to more systematic social thought. As Himmelfarb and others have shown, the phemomenon if not the actual word 'residuum' was omnipresent in the writings of Henry Mayhew.[18] The transactions of the National Association for the Promotion of Social Science suggest that participants (including many strict Poor Law administrators) were only too willing to differentiate between the feckless and immoral poor and the working class, and – as early as the 1850s and 1860s – were uneasily aware of the lurking problem of urban physical degeneration.[19] Discussion of the poor physical standards of army recruits in the 1860s foreshadowed almost verbatim the much more famous debate on 'deterioration' in the aftermath of the Boer war.[20] The Charity Organization Society was founded in 1869 specifically to discriminate between the two classes of the poor and to segregate the 'hopeless' from the 'helpable'; and observers of working-class life such as Thomas Wright and James Greenwood focused attention on 'the two races of the poor' – the industrious but unfortunate poor and the depraved, semi-professional clients of misguided philanthropy.[21] Such perceptions were by no means confined to an English context. As Karl Marx wrote in 1851 in relation to France:

> the lumpen proletariat ... in all towns forms a mass quite distinct from the industrial proletariat. It is a recruiting ground for thieves and criminals of all sorts, living off the garbage of society ... vagabonds, *gens sans feu et sans aveu*, varying according to the cultural level of their particular nation.[22]

Social perception of a derelict residuum had therefore long preceded the genesis of social Darwinism and the structural crisis of the 1880s. To recapture the resonance of the term more precisely, however, something must be said about the context of ideas within which talk of the residuum had first been specifically formulated: namely the onset in gradual stages of limited local and parliamentary democracy. The term had first been used in a British context by the radical MP for Birmingham, John Bright, in the debate on the Second Reform Act of 1867; and it was used by Bright (the great promoter of popular suffrage extension) to define those who in no circumstances should be allowed to have the vote. Bright defended his line of demarcation to the House of Commons not in sociological or evolutionary terms, but in the antique political language of civic virtue and the ancient constitution. 'I believe', declared Bright,

> that the solid and ancient basis of the suffrage is that all persons who are rated to some tax ... should be admitted to the franchise. I am quite willing to admit there is one objection to that wide measure, which exists ... in almost every franchise you can establish. At this moment, in all, or nearly all boroughs, as many of us know sometimes to our sorrow, there is a small class which it would be much better for themselves if they were not enfranchised, because they have no independence whatsoever, and it would be much better for the constituency also that they should be excluded, and there is no class so much interested in having that small class excluded as the intelligent and honest working men. I call this class the residuum, which there is in almost every constituency, of almost helpless poverty and dependence.

Bright's case against the residuum was couched in terms not of their poverty *per se*, but of the age-old constitutional language of property, now transposed to the support of the independent working class. The regularly employed, rate-paying working man (possessed of a house, a wife, children, furniture, and the habit of obeying the law) was the heir of the Anglo–Saxon freeman. The residuum, by contrast, were the 'intemperate', the 'profligate', the 'naturally incapable':

> all of them in a condition of dependence, such as to give no reasonable expectation that they would be able to resist the many temptations which rich and unscrupulous men would offer them at periods of election to give their vote in a manner not only not consistent with their own opinions and consciences, if they have any, but not consistent with the representation of the town or city in which they live.[23]

The philosophy behind Bright's speech had been spelt out even more clearly a few years earlier in a lecture by James Kay Shuttleworth to the Social Science Congress. 'One thousand five hundred years have elapsed in our history, and yet the theory of our Saxon constitution is only partially realised', Shuttleworth had declared. Modern progress had slowly but surely emancipated our humblest classes from serfdom, from villeinage, from pauperism; and the question now remained of whether the English could

> proceed to fulfil the apparent destiny of our race, by completing the freedom of the mass of our countrymen, by raising them to the dignity of freemen in the power of self-control, and to the intelligent exercise of the rights of freemen by the recognition of their claim as a class to a more direct influence in our representative system.

The chief obstacle to political emancipation in Shuttleworth's view was that the residual habits of the 'ceorl' and the 'bondsman' were still ominously prevalent in English lower-class culture of the present day: 'it is to be confessed that that portion of the workmen who spend their evenings in sensual excesses have not yet become free men'.[24]

After the 1860s the well-honed imagery of the ancient constitution gradually receded in British parliamentary debate: yet the hopes and fears which it expressed remained an important thread in the agenda of public life for the next half-century. The household suffrage provisions of the 1867 Act were very deliberately designed to create a direct ratepayers' franchise, in which the imputed independence and good character of respectable working men who paid their own rates were admitted to the constitution as surrogate forms of property. Contemporaries were often confused about whom the Act let in; but all were agreed that the residuum should be left out, and that the residuum by definition did not include household ratepayers.

Yet such a balance was inherently unstable, as events were to prove. The Act provided no definition of what constituted a household, and legal decisions in the 1860s and 70s increasingly interpreted the term to include the tenancy of parts of multi-occupied dwellings. The revival of compounding in 1873 (whereby rents paid to non-resident landlords were deemed to include rates) almost accidentally extended the franchise to many inhabitants of slum tenements. The Municipal Registration Act of 1878, which aimed at tidying up the vagaries of electoral case law, redefined the concept of a 'dwelling house' to include any part of a house separately occupied as a dwelling, even where tenants shared common facilities such as privies and kitchens. Thus technical safeguards against enfranchisement of the occupants of single rooms were gradually whittled away, and the door was opened to inclusion of the poorest class within the constitution.[25]

Uneasy awareness of this new and unknown quantity within the constitutional system was an important part of the social politics of the 1880s, and of the whole debate on the residuum. Recent historians have tended to emphasize how limited and how slow was the impact of the very poor upon mass democracy until well into the twentieth century; but this was not how it appeared to many contemporaries in the 1880s. Debates on the 1884 Reform Act, which enfranchised rural householders, again invoked the model of the Anglo-Saxon freeman and gave expression to many ancient fears about the perversion of the ancient constitution by a property-less rabble.[26] In particular, the doubling of the Irish vote (that race notoriously lacking in Anglo-Saxon civic virtue) caused much alarm: Irish Home Rule and expropriation of landlords were ominously predicted as the logical consequence of emancipating a class who knew nothing of wider civic and imperial concerns. And it was seen as no accident that the 1885 Medical Relief (Disqualification Removal) Act – later described as the 'first nail in the coffin of the "new" poor law' – was an Irish-sponsored measure.[27] In the redistribution of parliamentary boundaries which accompanied the third Reform Act, concern to protect the identity of 'ancient communities' was clearly used as a cloak to protect the privileged from the onset of the masses; and the fact that redistribution largely affected urban constituencies suggests that such fears cannot have been confined merely to the rural householders newly enfranchised in 1884.

Such apprehensions, moreover, were by no means confined to conservatives. Progressive liberals who had staunchly defended the civic virtue of the working man in 1867 were by the 1880s looking with mounting dismay upon the seeping into the constitution of a feckless property-less proletariat.[28] James Bryce, for example, who in

Essays on Reform had specifically contrasted the corruption of the rich with the public spirit of the poor, two decades later was writing in highly pessimistic terms about what he saw as the trans-national phenomenon of the modern urban 'residuum'.[29] And another avant-garde theorist of 1867, Goldwin Smith, twenty years later was bemoaning the fact that 'qualifications of any real value have been swept away' and that the constitution had been invaded by those 'ignorant of all questions of state, liable to be misled by the grossest illusions, hurried away by the blindest passions, cozened by the lowest charlatans'.[30] The political writings of the Bosanquets continually harped upon the theme of the public danger of extending both voting and welfare rights, without at the same time extending the moral ethos of independent citizenship.[31] And many other contemporary sources indicate that fear of the London mob at this time stemmed far more from their supposed influence at the ballot-box than from the threat of riot and revolution. Lord Salisbury, for example, ascribed the ascendancy of radicalism in London politics to 'the votes of those who had been dispersed' after the Trafalgar Square riots of 1886–87; while Alfred Marshall's fears of the residuum were specifically linked to imminent working-class dominance of Imperial and Local Government.[32] Such alarms were doubtless in part fanciful, since difficulties of registration, receipt of poor relief, lack of a fixed address and sheer inertia doubtless disfranchised many of the very poor who might otherwise have had the vote: and right down to 1918 the parliamentary franchise remained heavily stacked in favour of the owners of property. But upper-class fears were not entirely groundless. As the recent research of John Davis has shown, the process of both registering and de-registering electors was often inaccurate and haphazard – to such an extent that electoral registers included many who were paupers, aliens, unqualified by residence, or under age. In the Old Nicol, that most deprived area of Bethnal Green where Charles Booth in the late 1880s found 80 per cent of the population living below the poverty line, no less than 40 per cent of adult males were parliamentary electors – a considerably higher proportion than in the property-owning heartlands of Kensington and Belgravia.[33]

Fear of the 'residuum' therefore long ante-dated the crisis of the 1880s, and was fuelled at least as much by traditional constitutional concerns as by newer fears about biological degeneracy. The upsurge of 'residuum' thought in the 1880s was fuelled not just by economic crisis but by popular democracy: indeed, perhaps paradoxically, the advance of democracy helped to reinforce anxieties about marginal groups, who were seen as having acquired a foothold in the structure of political power. More remains to be said, however, about the meaning and salience of residuum ideas in late Victorian sociological thought, and about the relationship of such ideas to practical social policies. In particular, what significance should be attached to the proposals of Charles Booth, Alfred Marshall, William Beveridge and many others that the residuum should be politically and economically detached from the rest of the body politic by physically confining them in institutions or in industrial labour colonies. The peculiar confluence of old and new ideas about the very poor is perhaps most clearly demonstrated by the 'residuum' theories of Charles Booth, whose studies of the people of London coloured and conditioned a whole generation of social thought about the habits and conditions of the different social classes.

Booth himself never clearly defined the concept of the residuum, but the volumes of *Life and Labour of the People in London*, together with Booth's papers to the Royal Statistical Society and his evidence to public enquiries, were all strongly imbued with residualist and evolutionary language and conceptions. The 'organic' character and 'restless innovation' of modern industrial society he saw as generating a 'heightened struggle for existence, with its ups and downs of commercial inflation and contraction ... a constant seeking after improvement, a weeding out of the incapable and a survival of the fittest'.[34] Such processes engendered upwardly spiralling standards for the vast majority, but insecurity and unemployment for the minority – and 'the unemployed as a class are a selection of the unfit'.[35] Competition precipitated 'a sort of quagmire underlying the social structure', a 'deposit of those who, from mental, moral or physical reasons, are incapable of better work', 'a large class who must be regarded as outcasts'.[36] The inhabitants of the quagmire were 'most likely to be incapable of permanent improvement ... [they] do not and cannot become self–supporting'. They were 'incapable of managing their own lives, and are thus the prey of every kind of misfortune and a great burden on the community'.[37] This was the group whom Booth classified as Class B: those who scraped a living from casual employment and charity; not habitual paupers, but the recruiting ground of pauperdom; never properly in the labour market but never wholly out of it; who dragged down and discredited the rest of the working class. Booth's proffered solution for these problems, elaborated in many forms between 1887 and 1902, was that the inhabitants of Class B (about 11 per cent of the population of London) should be removed from the normal labour market and confined in industrial homes run by agents of the state. The inmates of these homes would be 'gradually absorbed into other industries, or, if the worst comes to the worst, they pass through the workhouse and finally die. It is, no doubt, a very hard saying, but it is I believe, the only way in which improvement can be reached'. 'However slowly and kindly it may be done, it is not a pleasant process to be improved off the face of the earth, and this is the road along which we have as I think to travel.'[38]

Booth's whole approach to the residuum in the passages cited above sounds very close to what is usually thought of as a 'social Darwinist' or degenerationist position. But such a view is in fact misleading in a number of different ways. Like many social theorists of the period Booth used Darwinesque language very loosely and metaphorically, rather than in an exact scientific and literal way; and, although there is no doubt that Booth was in some sense a 'social evolutionist', I do not think that he can be seen as a 'social Darwinist' in any very precise meaning of that term. At no point in *Life and Labour* or in any of his other writings did Booth ever suggest that progress or degeneracy were the product of irreversible biological mutation. On the contrary, men and women were largely the products of experience and circumstance. Men of previously regular habits who were forced into casual work rapidly acquired a taste for it; whereas the regularization of casual work had the opposite effect; 'it tends to subdue the repugnance to regular work ... which I think goes hand in hand with the facilities for its indulgence.'[39] The cumulative effect of bad conditions on a particular individual might be so great as to be ultimately irreversible; but the process was one of degree rather than kind. Moreover, like John Bright and Helen Bosanquet (and, a decade later, Lady Florence Bell), Booth thought that the 'residuum' mentality was found at all levels of society, the only difference being that among the upper classes 'the consequences are not the same'.[40] Nor did Booth appear to believe that degeneracy was hereditary in any physiological sense. Quite the opposite, in that although he sometimes referred to a 'hereditary taint', he constantly wrote about the need to adopt policy measures to make transmission of bad characteristics from parents to children 'less hereditary' (an obviously non-Darwinian position).[41] Though he disapproved strongly of improvidence, he did not (unlike some residuum theorists such as Alfred Marshall) view early marriage and high fertility among the poor as a cumulative source of organic racial decline: 'The individuals may be past cure; I cannot tell ... but it does not in the least follow that the children will be past cure if properly educated.'[42] He constantly ascribed the physical deterioration of the 'London-born' to the downward pressure of an adverse urban and industrial environment. A very similar perspective can be found in the writings of Booth's research assistants. Though they used an explanatory and linguistic framework of evolution and decline, most of the detailed case studies published in *Life and Labour* were based on the view that inheritance was overwhelmingly social and cultural. Octavia Hill's contribution on model dwellings (which claimed that the poor could be raised from poverty by self-help and sympathetic casework), was a clear expression of the dominance of nurture over nature.[43] Beatrice Potter's study of casual labour in the docks expressed very vehemently the view that dock employment harboured a class of worthless 'parasites' who were sucking the life-blood of the regular working class; but she no less than Booth thought that parasitism and worthlessness had been artificially manufactured for generations past by chaotic industrial structure.[44]

Booth's 'residuum' or 'quagmire' was therefore a cultural phenomenon susceptible to social pressure and manipulation, rather than the product of an inexorable natural law. In essence his analysis of social inheritance amounted perhaps to little more than the truism that human beings are creatures of circumstance and that children copy the parents who bring them up. Booth's evolutionism in general was much closer to the cultural and organizational model of Herbert Spencer's *Principles of Sociology* than to the biological model of *Origin of Species*, though Booth differed markedly from Spencer in his perception of what kinds of social organization were progressive and regressive. Moreover, it may perhaps be questioned how far evolutionary thought of any kind was an indispensable feature of Booth's social thought. As mentioned earlier, evolutionary terminology was seeping into the language of social reform throughout the 1880s and 90s, but much of it may be regarded as emblematic verbiage rather than precise social science. Booth's self-appointed role was one of publicist and social reformer as well as scientific social investigator, and he necessarily exploited the fashionable rhetoric of his age. But at least as important in his analysis of social success and failure was the continuing centrality of the role of personal character and rational choice. When asked by the Select Committee on Distress from Want of Employment to single out the causes of unemployment which he regarded as most important, he unhesitatingly identified as the two crucial factors 'the condition of trade' and the 'character of labour'. These were not in Booth's view two independent variables but were inextricably bound up with each other, in that trade fluctuations acted as a kind of utilitarian 'distress meter' which unerringly weeded out the marginal man.[45] In this respect Booth's thought – and that of many other residuum theorists of the 1880s and 90s – owed more to the psychology of classical economics or to the newer political economy of marginalism than to evolutionary thought of any kind.

Booth's ultimate solution for the social problem was not forcible segregation of the residuum (there is little evidence to suggest that he ever took his own proposals seriously on this point) but that individuals at all levels, including the very poor, should make greater efforts to practise personal prudence, to develop moral character and to enhance the public good. 'Moral effort' and 'public spirit' perhaps contributed little to the systematic analysis of the problems of the outcast poor; but they bore very little relation to the theory of natural selection.

Booth's perception of the role of character, however, deserves further comment. As Stefan Collini has reminded us, 'character' occupied a 'privileged place' in mid nineteenth century social thought and was 'the favoured explanatory element in the analysis of different human fates'.[46] Charles Booth would certainly have recognized and endorsed Collini's depiction of character as 'the moral collateral which would reassure potential business associates or employers'. Moreover, Booth's personal history lends some substance to the rather sketchy claim in Collini's *Public Moralists* that Victorian ideas of character had long subterranean roots in the soil of classical and civic humanism.[47] Booth, like John Bright (and indeed like Bernard and Helen Bosanquet, Joseph Chamberlain, Alfred Marshall, William Beveridge and many others who employed a residuum model), belonged to a family and a cultural tradition that had inherited 'old dissent' and sympathy for ideals of 'republican' independence over many generations. He had been educated not at a public school or ancient university, but at a provincial unitarian academy and at Apenzell in German-speaking Switzerland, the world headquarters of the philosophy of civic virtue. All these influences predisposed Booth to judge social arrangements through the lenses of character, property, independence and cyclical decay, rather than in more clinical and positivistic terms.

Where Collini's depiction of 'character' seems remote from Booth and his associates, however, is in the suggestion that by the latter half of the nineteenth century the invocation of 'character' both as a moral ideal and as a mode of social explanation was largely confined to the inner private sphere.[48] It is true that Booth had withdrawn from active politics in the late 1860s; but over the next forty years he constantly identified himself with those in public life and in the formation of social policy who were 'most determined to insist on individual independence as the first of civic virtues'.[49] The deficiency of the very poor not just in resources and physique but in capacity for citizenship – their lack of independence and foresight, their passive psychology, their hopeless indifference to wider issues, their chronic inability to manage their own affairs – was an endemic theme throughout the volumes of *Life and Labour*. This lack of civic virtue alarmed Booth much more than racial degeneracy or capacity for violent revolution (the latter he saw in any case as non-existent among the 'submerged tenth'); and it links Booth's analysis of poverty in the 1880s and 90s very directly with John Bright's account of the character and status of the political residuum a quarter of a century before.

This same emphasis on bad citizenship as the core of the social problem may be found throughout the writings of the residuum school. Octavia Hill told the Royal Commission on the Housing of the Working Classes that instilling civic consciousness and 'public opinion' in the minds of tenement dwellers was a far more serious and urgent problem than the problem of clean air: while the works of the Bosanquets constantly harped upon the theme that the test of a good social policy was not quantitative relief of material need but active involvement of both giver and receiver in a wider civic relationship.[50] Moreover, 'character' was a crucial feature in the social philosophy of the Ethical Movement – that movement of the 1880s and 90s that attracted support from many different branches of the reformist intelligentsia, idealist and positivist, liberal, socialist and conservative. And, as Bernard Bosanquet told a meeting of the London Ethical Society in 1894, far from fading into the periphery of public debate, 'character' was now playing a more central role in official thinking about poverty and pauperism than at any time since the introduction of the New Poor Law sixty years before.[51]

The 'residuum' issue of the 1880s and 90s was therefore at least as much a political as a sociological phenomenon, and at least as much an expression of certain ancient moral and constitutional ideas as of new-fangled notions of science and social evolution. Its core concerns were defective citizenship, lack of economic and political independence and failure of the moral will, as well as – and in the eyes of many contemporary observers far more than – biological degeneracy. The term 'residuum' was invoked by both conservative and progressive theorists, by both 'individualists' and 'collectivists' – the majority of whom subscribed not to biological determinism, but to the possibility of far-reaching social, moral and physical improvement among the very poor – and who saw such improvement as closely linked with widespread inculcation of the theory and practice of citizenship. Such a perspective did not preclude the support of often quite draconian social policies, both in the form of 'personal casework' and of more obviously coercive institutional measures, such as incarceration in labour colonies or sanatoria. The tradition that emphasized fitness for citizenship sheltered many ambiguous and quasi-authoritarian positions on such issues as race, gender, function and class; and in the Edwardian period some extreme social environmentalists such as Dr Alfred Eichholz held far more authoritarian views about what should be done to the casual poor than many eugenicists and hereditarians.[52] However, as suggested above, the only area of social policy in which a strictly 'Darwinian' model obtained a serious hold in Britain was the treatment of mental deficiency; and in this case even quite strong proponents of negative eugenics were careful to differentiate the specific case of the feeble minded from the wider issues of poverty and 'physical deterioration'. Failure to notice this distinction has generated confusion among some historians, who have exaggerated the role of 'degeneracy' and other deterministic ideas in late Victorian and Edwardian attitudes towards poverty and the poor. It has led also to a failure to note some of the powerful underlying continuities between late Victorian and Edwardian ideas about poverty and the moral, economic and constitutional concerns of an earlier age.

Notes

1   Jones, Gareth Stedman (1971), *Outcast London. A Study in the Relationship between Classes in Victorian Society*, Oxford University Press, pp.10-15, 130; Jones, Greta (1980), *Social Darwinism and English Thought. The Interaction between Biological and Social Theory,* Harvester, pp.151–9.

2   Jones, Gareth Stedman, *Outcast London*; Jones, Greta, *Social Darwinism*; Pick, D. (1989), *Faces of Degeneration*, Cambridge University Press; Macnicol, John (1987), 'In Pursuit of the Underclass', *Journal of Social Policy*, 16 (3), pp.293–318; Shaw, Christopher (1987), 'Eliminating the Yahoo. Eugenics, Social Darwinism and Five Fabians', *History of Political Thought*, 8 (3), pp.521–44.

3   Darwin himself, of course, in *The Descent of Man* had alluded to the possibility of cultural as well as biological evolution and to the possibility of conscious adaptation in human societies. But it seems reasonable to identify the term 'Darwinism' with the more physiological and random model of *Origin of Species*.

4   Parliamentary Papers (1904), *Report of the Interdepartmental Committee on Physical Deterioration*, Cd.2175, esp. pp.44–6 and 92–3.

5   Parliamentary Papers (1908), *Report of the Royal Commission on the Care and Control of the Feeble-Minded*, Cd.4202, part VI, c.27, pp.179–85; and minutes of evidence, qq.961, 5982–3, 6233, 9161, 9995.

6   Loch, C.S. (1913), 'Charity Organisation and the Feeble-Minded', *Charity Organization Review*, 33, pp.6–8.

7   *RC on the Feeble-Minded*, qq.3614–5, 3657, 3691, 3757.

8   Parliamentary Papers (1916), *Report of the Royal Commission on Venereal Disease*, Cd. 8189, pp.27–34; minutes of evidence, qq.6388–6400, 6516–20, 11259–61.

9   National Birth Rate Commission (1916), *The Declining Birth Rate. Its Causes and Effects,* Chapman and Hall, pp.44–5.

10   Huxley, T.H. (1894), *Evolution and Ethics and Other Essays,* Macmillan. For echoes of such fears in more humble quarters see Reynolds, Stephen (1913), *Seems So! A Working-Class View of Politics,* Macmillan, pp.xxiv–v; and (1962), *The Journals of George Sturt 1890–1927,* 2 vols., Cambridge University Press, 25 November 1890.

11   E.g. Newman, George (1908), *The Nation's Health,* London: Beveridge, W.H., leader in *Morning Post*, 15 June 1906.

12   Hansard, Third Series, 286, 690, 24 March 1884; Dendy, H., 'The Industrial Residuum', in Bosanquet Bernard (1895), (ed.), *Aspects of the Social Problem*, Macmillan, pp.82–4, 334.

13   Beveridge, W.H. (1906), 'The Problem of the Unemployed', *Sociological Papers*, 3, pp.328–31.

14   Booth, William (1890), *In Darkest England and the Way Out*, Salvation Army, p.18.

15   Dendy, 'Residuum', pp.82–102.

16   *Ibid,* pp.85–6.

17   Himmelfarb, Gertrude (1970), 'Bentham's Utopia: the National Charity Company', *Journal of British Studies*.

18   Himmelfarb, Gertrude (1984), *The Idea of Poverty*, Faber, pp.356–62.

19   Forrest, Noah (1859), 'The Chain and Tracemakers of Cradley Heath', *Transactions of the National Association for the Promotion of Social Science*, p.654; (Dr) McCormack, Henry (1861), 'A Few Particulars Relative to our Town-Poor, especially the Irish Town-Poor', *NAPSS Transactions*, pp.613–19; Morgan, John Edward

(1865), 'The Danger of Deterioration of Race from the too Rapid Increase of Great Cities', *NAPSS Transactions*, pp.427–45.

20   Ikin, J.I. (1864), 'On the Prevalent Causes of Rejection of Recruits, Enlisted in the West Riding and Northern Districts', *NAPSS Transactions*, pp.525–31.

21   Wright, T.R. (1873), *Our New Masters*, London; Greenwood, James, 'A Night in the Workhouse', cited in Keating, P.J. (1976), *Into Unknown England 1866–1913*, pp.33–54.

22   'The Class Struggles in France 1848–50', in Marx, Karl (1973), *Surveys from Exile. Political Writings*, Volume 2, London, p.52.

23   *Hansard,* 26 March 1867, Third Series, 186, 626–42.

24   NAPSS (1859) *Transactions*, 'On the Progress of Civilisation in England', pp.122–151.

25   Davis, John (1991), 'Slums and the Vote, 1867–90', *Historical Research*, 64, 155, pp.375–8.

26   *Hansard*, 24 March 1884, Third Series, 275, 107f.; 236, 621–33, 651–3, 686–90; 27 March 1884, 971–2; 31 March 1884, 1207; 3 April 1884, 1572–3.

27   Rodgers, Brian (1955–6), 'The Medical Relief (Disqualification Removal) Act 1885', *Parliamentary Affairs*, 9, pp.188–94.

28   Harvie, Christopher (1976), *The Lights of Liberalism: University Liberals and the Challenge of Democracy 1860–1886*, Allen Lane.

29   Bryce, James (1888), *The American Commonwealth*, London, 3 vols.

30   Smith, Goldwyn, 'The Political Crisis in England' in *Essays on Questions of the Day*, (1893), London, p.98.

31   Bosanquet, Bernard (1895), 'The Duties of Citizenship' in *Aspects of the Social Problem*, Macmillan, pp.1–27.

32   PRO, CAB 41/21/3, Lord Salisbury to Queen Victoria, 12.2.1888; (1925), *Memorials of Alfred Marshall*, Pigou, A.C., London, p.373.

33   Davis, John, seminar paper given in All Souls College, Oxford, 1990. I am most grateful to Dr Davis for permission to cite his unpublished work.

34   Booth, Charles (1902), 5, London, p.74.

35   *Poverty*, 1, pp.149–50.

36   *Poverty*, p.176; *Religious Influences*, 2, p.65.

37   Parliamentary Papers (1895), *Select Committee on Distress from Want of Employment,* minutes, q.10544.

38   Parliamentary Papers (1895), *SC on Want of Employment,* q.10524; Booth, Charles (1888), 'The Condition and Occupations of the People of East London and Hackney, 1887', *Journal of the Royal Statistical Society,* 51, p.300.

39   Parliamentary Papers (1895), *SC on Distress from Want of Employment,* minutes, q.10524.

40   Parliamentary Papers (1895), *SC on Distress from Want of Employment,* minutes, qq. 10722–3.

41   *Poverty,* 1, pp.168, 173–4.

42   Parliamentary Papers (1895), *SC on Distress from Want of Employment,* minutes, q.10597, 10692–3.

43   *Poverty,* 3, pp.29–36.

44   *Poverty,* 4, pp.12–36. Exactly the same theoretical approach underpinned her account of the East London Jewish community, whom she saw as an object lesson in the 'inheritance of acquired characteristics' *Poverty,* 3, pp.166–92.

45   Parliamentary Papers (1895), *SC on Distress from Want of Employment,* minutes, qq.10518–10785, *passim.*

46   Collini, Stefan (1985), 'The Idea of "Character" in Victorian Political Thought', *Trans. Royal Hist. Soc.,* 35 pp.29–50.

47   Collini, Stefan (1991), *Public Moralists. Political Thought and Intellectual Life in Britain 1850–1930,* Oxford University Press, p.95.

48   Collini, *Public Moralists,* pp.109–11.

49   Booth, Charles (1894), *The Aged Poor in England and Wales,* Macmillan, p.8.

50   Parliamentary Papers (1884–5), *Royal Commission on the Housing of the Working Classes, Minutes of Evidence,* Cd.4402, q.8896; Bosanquet, Bernard (1899), *The Philosophical Theory of the State,* Macmillan, pp.296–334; Bosanquet, Helen (1902), *The Strength of the People,* Macmillan, pp.97–8, 121–2. For a classic statement of the link between voting rights and economic independence, see Beveridge, W.H. (1905), 'The Question of Disfranchisement', *Toynbee Record,* March, pp.100–2.

51   Bosanquet, Bernard (1895), 'Character in its Bearing on Social Causation', in *Aspects of the Social Problem,* pp.103–17.

52   See, for example, Parliamentary Papers (1908), *Royal Commission on the Care and Control of the Feeble-Minded*, minutes of evidence, q.3807.

Elizabeth St. purple as map, houses on both side of street
Queens Place. a court on the East side has 4. 2st. cott
poor but respectable, lb. North up Providence
Place 2st. better north end than S, mess, bread.
this orange peel, purple as map, into Berner St.
children just coming out of Bd school. Jewish type,
all fairly dressed some very well dressed, all clean.
well fed, booted, large majority with hats, girls & boys.
under gateway on S.E side took place one of the
'Ripper' murders, houses in St. 2 storied, purple as map,
mess. At the north end running west into Backchurch
lane is Sander's St. purple rather than lb. of map.
cleaner than the other streets. St John's Working Mens
Club in the St. John's Schools on S side (subs. 2d per
wk), clean windows & doorsteps. houses 3 st & attic
Nr E End & 3 Storied S.W end.
South down Berner St. & went through Boyd St. 2st all
foreign, many cannot speak or understand English.
only a trouble to police when ejectments are necessary
& neither side can comprehend the other. children hatless
but

3.1   George Duckworth's notes of his walk through the Berner Street area indicated the difficulties he had classifying the Jewish inhabitants of the district. The mess in the streets generally denoted poverty and 'viciousness' but these Jews, while poor, were respectable, and did not belong to the vicious semi-criminal classes, and the streets were assessed as purple. See also Chapter 10: 'Booth's Jews'. (Booth Collection, B351, p.69)

3 Charles Booth as an under-consumptionist economist

Alon Kadish

Charles Booth, ship owner and self-trained social investigator, thought little of economic theory. Having briefly toyed with Comtist Positivism[1] he appears to have adopted the Positivist position on the method of social studies whereby the accumulation of facts preceded the formulation of theory, and its emphasis on viewing economic problems within a wide social context thereby conveying the organic nature of society. Indeed, in presenting the Royal Statistical Society with his initial findings, Booth associated the delusion of inevitability, with which poverty was commonly perceived, with the deductive method of orthodox economics:

> … the wage earners are helpless to regulate or obtain the value of their work; the manufacturer or dealer can only work within the limits of competition; the rich are helpless to relieve want without stimulating its resources; the legislature is helpless because the limits of successful interference by change of law are closely circumscribed. From the suggestions of ignorance, setting at naught the nature of man and neglecting all fundamental facts of human existence.
>
> To relieve this sense of helplessness, the problem of human life must be better stated. The *a priori* reasoning of political economy, orthodox and unorthodox alike, fails from want of reality. At its base are series of assumptions very imperfectly connected with the observed facts of life. We need to begin with a true picture of the modern industrial organism.[2]

In a later statement on the nature of economic discourse one may discern, in addition to a Positivist influence, traces of Booth's Unitarian upbringing in his condemnation of economic dogmatism:

> The discussion of economic questions has in our generation acquired an eagerness and intensity of feeling usually peculiar to questions of religion. We hear the same language of orthodoxy and heresy, and use again the well-worn similes, speaking of 'bulwarks' against 'inroads' of socialism, etc. There is the same frequent use of authority, and reliance on tradition, and the written

word of the great teachers of the past. Of all which I should be glad, if it be possible, to steer clear.[3]

'[A]ny claim on abstract thought', Booth wrote to Beatrice Potter in July, 1891, 'I abandon as a childish delusion'.[4] The only role he was initially prepared to allow theory was as a classificatory aid:

> ... the intensive method of investigation should go hand in hand with the extensive. Without a full comprehension of unexpressed details, general statements are always lifeless, and often misleading; without some trustworthy generalisation – some ground plan of classification, by which, as in the drawers of a mineralogist's cabinet, details can be classified and seen in their proper place – elaboration is partly thrown away.[5]

Yet it would be a mistake to assume that Booth's work was devoid of any conscious economic analysis. At the time the study of economics was defined by subject matter rather than method. An economist was a student of economic phenomena regardless of the nature of his formal training or the lack thereof. Furthermore, economics was yet to acquire the academic status of an autonomous discipline requiring specialized training, so that despite his lack of training in, and his dislike for abstract theory, there was no reason why Booth should have avoided studying and pronouncing upon the economic aspects of, say, poverty. However, since his work was avowedly empirical, and as the theoretical influences which are discernible in his work came from outside neo-classical high theory, the economic content of his work has been largely ignored. This may have been partly because of his economic views often contradicting economic orthodoxy. Thus Alfred Marshall welcomed his work as an invaluable compendium of facts and statistics. In commenting on Booth's paper 'Enumeration and Classification of Paupers, and State Pensions for the Aged', read to the Royal Statistical Society in December 1891, Marshall stated: 'in talking to German Friends, if he wanted to prove that England could show as good studies of contemporary social history as Germany could, his first example was always taken, not from the work of leisured professional economists, but from that of the busiest of business men, Mr Charles Booth'.[6] (Although he then went on to question some of Booth's figures.)

In his evidence to the Royal Commission on the Aged Poor, taken on 5 June 1893, Marshall even supported one of Booth's main assumptions – that a higher standard of living would result in a general improvement in the condition and attitude of the working classes rather than in a reckless increase of population.[7] But when it came to his practical recommendations, Marshall advocated the extension and improvement of the existing system whereby the Boards of Guardians would be left in charge of administrating the law, while the Charity Organization Society would, ideally, screen all applicants, referring all obvious cases for outdoor and indoor relief (classes A and C) to the Guardians, and looking after, with the use of charity funds, the more problematic cases which called for closer personal supervision and greater flexibility (class B).[8] Booth's plan he thought expensive, its educational influence on the working classes (e.g. in encouraging thrift) indirect, and it was likely to become perpetual. Whereas Marshall regarded 'this problem of poverty as a mere passing evil in the progress of man upwards', his criticism of Booth reveals the latter's underlying assumption that poverty was an inherent feature of industrial society which should be contained but could not be entirely abolished.[9]

Booth's economics largely resemble those of a large non-academic and highly politicized school of thought which was also largely ignored by contemporary neo-classical theoreticians. The influences on Booth's economics may be identified through the changes in his explanations of the causes of poverty and pauperism and the economic justification of his old age pensions scheme. At first (*circa* early 1886) Booth had rejected Hyndman's and the Democratic Federation's estimate that over 25 per cent of London's workers were living under conditions of extreme poverty.[10] Such an estimate, he believed, could be reached only by confusing social categories out of ulterior motives:

> The question of those who actually suffer from poverty should be considered separately from that of the true working classes, whose desire for a larger share of wealth is of a different character. It is the plan of agitators and the way of sensational writers to confound the two in one, to talk of 'starving millions', and to tack on the thousands of the working classes to the tens or perhaps hundreds of distress ... To confound these essentially distinct problems is to make the solution of both impossible.[11]

Initially Booth adhered to the individualistic view of society in stating that unemployment was largely a result of personal inadequacy rather than of, say, a structural flaw in the market mechanism.[12] Those who truly sought employment usually found it. The residue which remained unemployed consisted of men who 'cannot keep work when they get it; lack of work is not really the disease with them, and the mere provision of it is therefore useless as a cure. The unemployed are, as a class, a selection of the unfit, and on the whole those most in want are the most unfit. This is the crux of the position'.[13] The market should not, therefore, be blamed for individuals' defects and did not require major modifications in order to deal with the problem. Even public works, according to this view, could only have a superficial effect on the numbers of the chronically unemployed.

By 1891 Booth had abandoned the strictly individualistic view of society. Personal vice, commonly associated with pauperism, was now seen by him as a characteristic of pauperism, not its cause. It was easy, he stated,

> ... to exaggerate any one of ... [the causes] at the expense of the rest. Incapacity and mental disease might be stretched to cover almost all. Vice, drink, and laziness, themselves closely bound together, fill also a great place in connection with sickness and lack of work – or we may reverse this and show how sickness and lack of work, and the consequent want of proper food, end in demoralisation of all kinds, and especially in drink.[14]

Booth still regarded some types of individual faults, such as laziness, as significant contributors to pauperism.[15] But the main causes he identified as old age, sickness, and drink.[16] Old age and sickness were neither primarily attributable to individual inadequacies nor to the operation of the market, while drink tended to aggravate rather than directly cause pauperism. Hence the standard COS argument which explained the high rate of pauperism as the result of personal vice aggravated by indiscriminate outdoor relief was untenable:

> ... doubtless all pauperism may be said to argue some fault on the part of the pauper. He might have gone less often to the public-house; have been more industrious or less lazy; with sufficient care he might have saved; he might have made friends and kept them; if his children had been well brought up they would have taken care of his old age, and so forth.
>
> If we all had equal opportunities in every respect this view might be completely true, but things being as they are; it is not tenable. The popular sentiment which accounts as misfortune the lapse into pauperism of any who up to old age have kept clear of relief, is perhaps more just.[17]

Similarly Booth now regarded poverty as primarily a result of economic causes – irregular employment, coupled with, but not caused by, irregular habits. 'I cannot overstate', he told the Royal Statistical Society in his inaugural address in November 1892,

> I cannot even adequately state, how great a blessing more regular work would bring to some of the poorest parts of London. Of all

the causes of poverty and misery, irregular work, coupled with irregular lives, is by far the greatest. A change in this would effect more than almost anything else could do for the welfare of the people.[18]

The study of poverty and pauperism could no longer be isolated from that of earning.[19]

If pauperism was largely the result of misfortune, special care should be taken in order to ensure that the scheme suggested by Booth to relieve it – state pensions of five shillings a week for anyone passed the age of sixty-five, must not hamper the operation of the market or undermine existing social norms. 'State action with regard to any pension scheme would be fatal if it in any way disturbed the basis of work and wages, discouraged thrift, or undermined even in the slightest degree self-respect, or the forces of individuality upon which morality as well as industry depends.'[20] This was especially true of working-class thrift, seen by some as a total or partial (through state supplemented pensions) means of dealing with old age pauperism. If the poor were encouraged to save for their old age, it was argued, old age pauperism would be largely eliminated.[21] Booth argued that the empirical study of the nature of working-class thrift clearly showed that it was unrealistic to expect a young working man to put aside part of his salary for his old age. Most savings, Booth discovered, were for close purposes, not out of fear of distant hardship. The main reasons for saving were entrepreneurial and for the sake of children. Furthermore, 'the possession of some wealth is an encouragement to the acquisition of more; and it is certain that nothing provides so persistent and irresistible an incentive as a prolonged experience of comfort'.[22]

Booth had found that an improved standard of living was essential for dealing effectively with some of the main immediate causes of pauperism such as drink, early marriages, and large families.[23] Thus in his general observations based on his findings Booth implied the need for a structural change in the existing system of distribution. However, in 1891 he was not yet prepared to abandon the current orthodoxy and he accordingly stressed that old age pensions would serve to strengthen thrift, i.e. individualism. They would enable a change in the distribution of wealth without a change in the system by providing 'that security necessary to a higher standard of life. A security of position which will stimulate rather than weaken the play of individuality on which progress and prosperity depends'.[24]

Booth's plan for state pensions had been preceded by the proposals of the Reverend Canon William L. Blackley for compulsory

state insurance and of J. Chamberlain for voluntary state supplemented
pensions which assumed both the moral value and the feasibility of
working-class thrift under existing conditions.[25] Booth's plan for
universal state pensions which did not require proof of the applicants'
worthiness was therefore attacked both by defenders of the COS's view
which called for tighter control of outdoor relief, and reformers in
favour of state insurance who hoped to encourage thrift.[26] The latter
warned that indiscriminate state pensions 'must produce a paralysis of
thrift, an overburdening of industry, and the degradation of the main
part of our population'.[27] What did 'state aid' mean, it was asked, 'but
that the thrifty have to provide for the unthrifty?[28] 'There is hardly a
man among our working classes', wrote another critic, 'who, being
sober and industrious and remaining single, could not put by £10
yearly between 18 and 28.'[29] Booth's scheme, some of his critics
realized, constituted a radical departure from the orthodox view of
pauperism:

> Broadly speaking, the opinions given with regard to the causes of
> old age pauperism fall under two heads, according to the answer
> given to the question: Is it possible, under existing conditions and
> with existing opportunities, for a working man not only to support
> himself and his family, with due regard to their physical and moral
> welfare, during the time when he has full wage-earning capacity,
> but also to make provision for the time when old age impairs or
> altogether destroys that capacity? To those who consider that this
> is possible, the causes of old age pauperism appear to be moral,
> and in the majority of cases preventable by the individuals
> concerned. To those, on the other hand, who consider this
> impossible, these causes seem to lie in economic and social
> conditions, which are for the most part beyond the control of the
> individuals in question.[30]

On the other hand, Booth's plan won the approval of more
radical reformers who adapted it to a different view of the operation of
industrialized economy, one based on the concepts of under-
consumption and over-production.

Despite J.A. Hobson's later claims, the explanation of recurring
economic recessions as the results of under-consumption or over-
production was quite common in popular economic thought. Orthodox
and neo-classical economists, committed to the liberal faith in the
market's natural tendency towards equilibrium, explained current
disequilibria as the result of the disturbing effects of external factors,
for example, the price of gold on world markets. Once identified and
controlled (e.g. by converting to bimetallism) the market would return

to its normal equilibrium-seeking operation. Economists (i.e. those who sought to explain economic phenomena) who were not committed to an overall theory, or who questioned the basic tenets of liberal economics, might, on the other hand, explain conditions of disequilibrium as a result of structural faults in the system and therefore endemic.

An example of the treatment of thrift from a radical under-consumptionist point of view may be found in the socialist pamphlet, *The Futility of Pecuniary Thrift as a Means to General Wellbeing* by G.A. Gaskell, published in 1890 probably in response to schemes suggesting state supplemented savings as a solution to old age pensions. Gaskell maintained that:

> ... saving money in youth for expenditure in old age does not mean that old people can in that case live on their own resources, but simply, that they live on the labour of others at the time of expenditure. The fact of saving money does not set production in motion, but the reverse. The longer it is delayed in the spending, the less brisk is trade.[31]

Thrift, discussed as an economic phenomenon, was seen as a disequilibriating and self-defeating factor:

> Increase of thrift necessarily means lessened demand for certain commodities and services. If we suppose that a large majority of the workers adopt thrifty habits, the lessened demand would result in serious complications. Very many businesses would be ruined and immense numbers of workers thrown out of work, while, to make matters worse, there would be no increased demand for other commodities not prejudicially affected. An increase of the number of unemployed would cause keener competition for work. Wages would go down all round, and the voluntary lowering of the standard of comfort by means of thrift would soon be followed by compulsory poverty and the impossibility of saving anything whatever from the diminished wages.[32]

As for thrift as a personal virtue, Gaskell stated: 'We live in a state of industrial competition wherein private interests are not the same with the public interest.'[33]

By 1892 three major works had been published expounding the theory whereby under-consumption or over-production were identified as the main causes of current economic hardship. First there came A.F. Mummery and J.A. Hobson, *The Physiology of Industry: Being an Exposure of Certain Fallacies in Existing Theories of Economics* (London, 1889), which laid down the theory and called for a simple increase in consumption through higher wages, a restriction on immigration of foreign labour to Britain, trade unions' restriction of labour competition, and so on. It was followed by H.M. Hyndman, *Commercial Crises of the Nineteenth Century* (London, 1892) which aimed at proving that the great economic crises of the century were because of an inherent fault in the capitalist system resulting in recurring gluts and consequent depressions. And finally J.M. Robertson, *The Fallacy of Saving. A Study in Economics* (London, 1892), viewing the subject from the perspective of the history of economic thought. It was the latter who pointed out the relevance of the theory of under-consumption to the discussion on old age pensions by questioning the very utility of working-class thrift. Booth, Robertson pointed out, may

> ... argue that there is no danger of a pension scheme discouraging thrift; the implication being that, with pensions, the workers will save more and not less ... But it will be the principal service a pension system can render, to encourage the workers to consume and not paralyse production by restricting their demand.[34]

Hyndman believed that 'No improvement of the capitalist system of production can change or seriously modify the bitter struggle which must go on so long as that system endures in any shape'.[35] Production and consumption could reach an equilibrium only through the intervention of government including the state, municipal councils and district assemblies.[36] Robertson suggested instead a number of measures which would improve the capitalist system's operation without disposing of it altogether. These included 'a restraint of the rate of increase of population', and raising the standard of living, i.e. the quality, and not just the quantity, of consumption, so as to draw labour away from 'the fatally easy fruitions of the mechanical manufacture of common necessaries'.[37] However, the similarities in their analysis of current economic distress, and their consequent rejection of the common view of thrift, explain the warm reception Booth's plan was accorded among new liberals and socialists. It may also explain Booth's adoption of under-consumptionist theory.

In *The Aged Poor in England and Wales*, published in 1894, Booth described pauperism as largely the result of the state of the economy in general – 'varying degrees of pauperism are mainly the result of varying degrees of poverty; and similarly ... varying rates of improvement in pauperism are to be connected with degrees of general progress and prosperity'.[38] Booth also directly challenged the feasibility and utility of working-class thrift as a means of dealing with old age pauperism:

As a rule, savings are small. It is the exception when they reach a substantial sum, and are kept together in old age. Savings are most usually amongst the unmarried, but to make, to save, to keep, and to accumulate is a rare combination – a sort of gift of character not at all common and not in every way desirable.[39]

Thrift might be theoretically or arithmetically possible but it was nevertheless unrealistic to expect young men to act contrary to their nature at 'the time of life when they naturally seek pleasure and spend their money'.[40] In his evidence to the Royal Commission on the Aged Poor (of which he was also a member) Booth was prepared to admit that some progress in the material conditions of the working classes was noticeable, but its rate was far too slow, hence the need for state intervention in the form of old age pensions to be paid by means of a graduated tax.[41] In this he was supported by the other signatories to the minority report – J. Chamberlain, C.T. Ritchie, H. Maxwell, and W.H. Hunter, and by Henry Broadhurst who submitted his own report.[42]

A fuller under-consumptionist analysis may be found in the later volumes of *Life and Labour*. In volume 5 of the second (Industry) series, Booth identified demand rather than production as the main disequilibriating factor in the modern industrial economy.[43] The constant and increasing competition between producers over customers resulted in 'great irregularity of employment' and 'had even shaken seriously the stability and hold on public opinion of orthodox economic doctrine'. The problem was further aggravated by the introduction of better means and methods of distribution of goods: 'We escape from the grip of dearth only to suffer the strange and monstrous strangulation of over-production.'[44]

Booth did not altogether abandon liberal economics. In the long run the cycles of gluts and trade depressions proved beneficial by 'weeding out the incapable, and [by allowing] a survival of the fittest',[45] resulting in more widespread supply of cheaper and better products and a rising standard of living. Nevertheless there remained the problem of the short run – 'the periodical recurrence of glutted markets and workless workers'.[46] 'It may be that in ordinary times', Booth concluded, 'no very large proportion of the population are sufferers from these evils, but whatever their numbers, or to whatever extent their misfortunes may be traceable to their own fault, we cannot unheeding pass by on the other side.'[47]

Following his study of the operation of the industrial economy in detail, Booth found it necessary to attempt a more general view in order to gain some sense of direction in offering particular suggestions for dealing with the negative effects of economic convulsions:

> ... the industrial conditions under which we live lead to poverty ...
> The immediate explanation of poverty is usually very simple: No
> savings; no opportunity of remunerative work; inadequate pay;
> inability or unwillingness to do the work that offers; reckless
> expenditure – such are the causes of which one thinks. But in
> seeking remedies it is rather for *causae causarum* that we must
> look. We ask why pay is insufficient, how it is that work cannot be
> had, by what choice the sufferer has no share of accumulated
> wealth; or we may seek to explain incapacity or to analyse sloth.
> Finally, in the attempt to reach the very root of things, we are
> driven to turn these questions another way, and to inquire why
> work should be remunerated at all; how there comes to be an
> accumulated wealth, or what claim any one in particular has to its
> enjoyment.[48]

Having initially rejected *a priori* theorizing, Booth discovered
that a mere 'itinerary of highways and byways' which 'indicates the
principal points of interest, but leaves its readers to use their own eyes
and form their own opinions on the journey they are invited to take'[49]
did not suffice. A general, if largely inductive, theory was needed,
which would provide the general principles of the operation of the
productive system in order to explain how particular schemes such as
old age pensions were socially and economically desirable. Concerning
poverty Booth's general conclusion was that:

> ... the final cure of poverty must lie either in increasing the
> serviceableness of the work done, or in securing for the less
> capable a sufficient share of that which is produced by the more
> capable members of society, or most likely in a combination of
> these two.
>
> Social remedies are all concerned with securing advantages for
> the less capable. Industrial remedies, while using both methods,
> are more particularly directed to the widening of opportunity and
> the increases of serviceableness.[50]

Old age pensions, which came under the category of social
remedies, did not undermine the operation of the market as seen from
an under-consumptionist point of view. In the final volume of *Life and
Labour*, Booth explained:

> It is the part of some not only to earn but also to spare, while the
> function of others is to earn and spend. All ought to earn, for
> earnings are the basis of the whole; but to spend is as essential as
> to spare, and that the two functions should be to a great extent
> distinct is in itself no evil.

This view which I put forward as theory, is instinctive in the people, and is reflected in their habits.[51]

In describing inequality in the consumption and accumulation of wealth as instinctive, i.e. natural, Booth indicated the limits of his economic radicalism. He had embraced the new liberalism but had not gone beyond it. The capitalist system was thought of as improvable (Robertson) rather than obsolete (Hyndman). The solutions he suggested – diminishing the size of the labour market and increasing the value of labour, aimed at improving the market's operation, not replacing it.[52] Universal old age pensions, seen by old school liberals as a threat to the capitalist system and to liberal values, was seen from the new liberal under-consumptionist position as an improvement on existing arrangements. Old age pensions, Booth explained in the final volume, were advocated

... not so much in aid of poverty as of thrift; but acting directly and indirectly in relief of both of the Poor Law and of private charity; simplifying the problems which each has to treat; and making concerted action on their part of dealing with destitution and distress more practicable and more efficacious.[53]

Notes

1   Simey, T.S. and Simey, M.B. (1960), *Charles Booth. Social Scientist*, Oxford University Press, pp.44, 48, and Norman-Butler, Belinda (1972), *Victorian Aspirations. The Life and Labour of Charles and Mary Booth*, Allen and Unwin, pp.35–6. Booth was introduced to Positivism by his cousins, Albert and Henry Crompton. For the latter's views and method see his *Industrial Conciliation* (1876), London, and Kadish, A. (1986), *Apostle Arnold. The Life and Death of Arnold Toynbee 1852–1883*, Chapel Hill, pp.98–100.

2   Booth, Charles (1887), *Condition and Occupations of the People of Tower Hamlets 1886–87*, Edward Stanford, Read to the Royal Statistical Society, May, p.6.

3   Booth, Charles (1892), *Pauperism. A Picture and Endowment of Old Age. An Argument*, Macmillan, p.71.

4   Booth, Charles and Potter, Beatrice, 15 July 1891, quoted in Norman-Butler, *Victorian Aspirations*, p.113. See also Simey and Simey, *Charles Booth*, p.77.

5   Booth, Charles (1893), 'Life and Labour of the People in London: First Results of an Inquiry based on the 1891 Census', delivered in absentia to the Royal Statistical Society, 21 November, in

Journal of the Royal Statistical Society, 56, December, p.591. Compare with Cunningham, William (1892), 'A Plea for Pure Theory', in the *Economic Review*, January.

6   *Journal of the Royal Statistical Society* (1892), 55, March, p.60. See also Price, L.L.'s (1891), reviews of various volumes of *Life and Labour* in the *Economic Journal*, 1,(3), September, and (1896) 6, (24), December.

7   Parliamentary Papers (1895), *Royal Commission on the Aged Poor. Minutes of Evidence*, London, 10,272, 10,273, and 10,384. Marshall's evidence is reproduced in Marshall, Alfred (1926), *Official Papers by Alfred Marshall*, London.

8   For a useful discussion of Marshall's views on the subject see Reisman, David (1987), *Alfred Marshall. Progress and Politics*, London, pp.207–21.

9   *Royal Commission on the Aged Poor*, 10,356. For an orthodox economist's view of the matter see the evidence of L.R. Phelps who recommended that the system be left unchanged.

10   See Hyndman, Henry Mayers (1911), *The Record of an Adventurous Life*, London, pp.330–3. According to Simey and Simey, *Charles Booth*, p.70n. the meeting between Hyndman and Booth described in Hyndman's autobiography took place in February 1886.

11   Booth (1888), 'Condition and Occupations', pp.6–7.

12   On the ideological dimension of these views see Freeden, M. (1978), *The New Liberalism. An Ideology of Social Reform*, Oxford University Press, pp.206–24.

13   Booth (1888), 'Condition and Occupations', p.53.

14   Booth, *Pauperism*, p.46. On the duality in Booth's position on poverty see McKibbin, Ross (1990), 'Class and Poverty in Edwardian England', in McKibbin, Ross (ed.), *The Ideologies of Class. Social Relations in England 1880–1950*, Oxford University Press.

15   Booth, *Pauperism*, p.47.

16   *Ibid.*, p.49.

17   *Ibid.*, p.55.

18   *Journal of the Royal Statistical Society* (1892), 55.

19   Simey and Simey, *Charles Booth*, pp.117–18, 131.

20   Booth, *Pauperism*, p.59. See also p.65.

21   See Collins, Doreen (1965), 'The introduction of old-age pensions in Great Britain', in the *Historical Journal*, 8.

22   Booth, *Pauperism*, p.71. See also his answer to his discussants in the *Journal of the Royal Statistical Society* (1892), 55, March, p.79.

23   Booth argued that the recklessness which was responsible for the high birth rate among the lower classes was also the cause of the high infant death rate. The reduction of the one would be accompanied by the diminution of the other. Booth, Charles (1893), 'Life and Labour … First Results', p.578.

24   Booth, *Pauperism*, p.77.

25   See Gilbert, Bentley B. (1966), *The Evolution of National Insurance in Great Britain. The Origins of the Welfare State*, Michael Joseph, ch.4.

26   For C.S. Loch's criticism on behalf of the COS see his comment in the *Journal of the Royal Statistical Society* (1892), 55, March, and his 'Mr Charles Booth and the Aged Poor' (1894), in the *Economic Journal*, 4 (15), September.

27   Letter by W.L. Blackley to *The Times*, 25 December 1891. See also criticism by Blackley, Courtney, Leonard, Allen, J.H. and Hendriks F. (1892), in the *Journal of the Royal Statistical Society*, 55.

28   Letter by Col. C.C. Fitzroy to *The Times*, 25 December 1891.

29   Letter by Florence Davenport-Hill to *The Times*, 2 January 1892.

30   Drage, Geoffrey (1895), *The Problem of the Aged Poor*, London, pp.287–8.

31   Gaskell, G.A. (1890), *The Futility of Pecuniary Thrift as a means of General Wellbeing*, London, p.9.

32   *Ibid.*

33   *Ibid.*, p.11.

34   Robertson, J.M. (1892), *The Fallacy of Saving. A Study in Economics*, London, p.129. See also p.128: 'The rapid extension of the vogue of this proposal [for old age pensions] within the past year or two is one of the few satisfactory symptoms in industrial politics, from the scientific point of view'.

35   Hyndman, H.M. (1892), *Commercial Crises of the Nineteenth Century*, London, p.173.

36   *Ibid.*, p.164.

37   Robertson, *The Fallacy of Saving*, pp.113–14.

38   Booth, Charles (1894), *The Aged Poor in England and Wales*, Macmillan, p.514. See also the quotation from Sir Frederick Eden in pp.328–9n.

39   Booth, *Aged Poor*, p.325.

40   Parliamentary Papers (1895), *Royal Commission on the Aged Poor. Minutes of Evidence vol. 3*, London, 10,992.

41   *Ibid.*, 10,846, 10,849.

42   Parliamentary Papers (1895), *Royal Commission on the Aged Poor. Report*, London.

43   *Industry*, 5, pp.71–2.

44   *Ibid.*, p.73. Compare with Wells, David A. (1887), 'The Great Depression of Trade. A Study of its Economic Causes, Part 1', in *The Contemporary Review*, 52, August.

45   *Industry*, 5, p.74.

46   *Ibid.*, p.75. Compare with Hobson, J.A. (1894), *The Evolution of Modern Capitalism. A Study of Machine Production*, Walter Scott, p.237: 'The loss of employment may be only "temporary", but as the life of the working man is also temporary, such loss may as a disturbing factor in the working life have a considerable importance.'

47   *Industry*, 5, p.83.

48   *Ibid.*, pp.308–9.

49   Booth, *The Aged Poor*, p.v.

50   *Industry,* 5, p.309.

51   Booth, Charles (1902), *Life and Labour of the People in London, Final Volume,* Macmillan, p.93.

52   *Industry*, 5, p.310.

53   Booth, *Life and Labour*, Final Volume, pp.43–4. See also Simey and Simey, *Charles Booth*, p.64.

Part II Methods of social inquiry

4 Comparisons and contrasts: Henry Mayhew and Charles Booth as social investigators

David Englander

I

Henry Mayhew baffled his contemporaries as still he baffles us. A literary hack and humorist, and a master of scissors-and-paste journalism, he was also the author of an acclaimed sociological inquiry that is vivid and compelling and a major contribution to empirical studies of poverty. Biographical details are few and contradictory. One contemporary had him dying in relative obscurity; another dwelt upon his well-attended funeral and continuing popularity. Athol Mayhew began work on a study to set the record straight. But the son, like the father, was better at projecting studies than finishing them, and the 'connected account' of Henry Mayhew's 'literary labours' remained unwritten.[1] It is the metaphor of the social explorer in a distant land which seemed to summarize Mayhew's identity and achievement. 'He was', said one obituarist, 'the originator of that school of journalistic philanthropists of which Mr Besant and Mr Sims, Mr Clark Russell and Mr James Greenwood, are now the popular representatives'.[2] In his prime he was more than that. G.J. Harney, editor of the Chartist journal, the *Red Republican*, readily commended Mayhew's 'excellent letters' on 'Labour and the Poor'.[3] Jevons considered him essential reading. Slop workers, thrust from under the shadows, cast him as their liberator. More effusive still was the Reverend Robert Montgomery who declared that *London Labour and the London Poor* had opened his eyes and his heart to the suffering in their midst.[4] Beatrice Webb, by contrast, dismissed his work as 'good material spoilt by bad dressing'.[5] 'It is really a mass of incidents of low life, told with dramatic intensity and simplicity by the actors themselves', wrote a like-minded critic, 'but it fails to gather up its facts into any connected statement, or to point the way towards any solution of one of the greatest problems of modern civilization'.[6] Modern assessments are equally varied. One school criticizes his allegedly maverick methods, the unrepresentative character of his material and the unreliability of his conclusions.[7] Another insists that his work has been ignored, his achievement undervalued and his stature diminished. An army of redressers has re-discovered, revised and reprinted, in whole or in part, the missing items which, it is claimed, restore his reputation as one of the most creative and significant of social investigators.[8]

The difficulty with all such assessments is that they are based upon a highly selective reading of Mayhew's writings. Sceptics, reliant in the main upon the published text of *London Labour and the London Poor*, have no problem in exposing its undeniable deficiencies. No less partial are their critics who, though seeking to extend the canon by inclusion of the letters serialized in the *Morning Chronicle*, are still prone to abstract from the millions of words that he published only a fraction of his output. The tendency, common in all forms of Mayhew criticism, to detach the author from the totality of his writings, does, however, create problems. The Harrison-Himmelfarb view emphasizes the faults at the expense of the virtues. The alternative view, though, is equally misleading. The Mayhew, re-discovered and re-claimed for posterity, is the Mayhew of 1849–50, the irreverent, social investigator, whose curiosity, sympathy, insight and imagination carried him almost beyond the boundaries of political economy. The Mayhew presented by E.P. Thompson and Eileen Yeo has sloughed off the ideas and attitudes of his bourgeois origins and harnessed the commercial considerations of the jobbing journalist to a higher social purpose. The Mayhew thus created was uniquely close to working people and their immediate concerns, trusted for his commitment and counsel, and at least deserving of consideration for a place in the pantheon of the proletariat. The question, then, naturally arises: why did he proceed no further?

It has been suggested that Mayhew simply was not bright enough to convert his empirical observations into meaningful social theory. Eileen Yeo tells us that he lacked the colossal brain of a Marx necessary for such a purpose and so never realized his true potential. We are thus left with a 'Mayhew moment' or a turning point that failed to turn.[9] E.P. Thompson, her collaborator, though keen to rehabilitate the author of *London Labour and the London Poor* as a systematic sociologist, was uncomfortably conscious of additional defects in Mayhew's make-up. For Thompson, indeed, the problem was one of personality rather than of intellect and of the co-existence of a set of approved enlightened activities alongside certain socially regressive attitudes and opinions. The latter, however, were not addressed. The likelihood of having exaggerated the triumph over social origins and the consequent recognition that the distance between Mr Mayhew and Mr Podsnapp was not so great after all, was simply too difficult to contemplate. Mayhew's chauvinism, pomposity and prudishness were noted as regrettable lapses without further comment.[10] The censorious exposure of cunning beggars and critique of indiscriminate alms-giving, which made *London Labour and the London Poor* recommended reading by the Charity Organization Society, or the numerous passages of commonplace middle-class moralizing which punctuate Mayhew's sociological writings, are either passed over in silence or dismissed as 'uncharacteristic'.[11]

Neither account is satisfactory. The suggestion that Mayhew's sociological writings were the product of some personal identity crisis that required him to step out with the middle class seems likely to remain an interesting but undocumentable speculation. His sociological and non-sociological writings, taken in tandem, supply the basis for a rather different interpretation, which enables us to locate him within the mainstream rather than on the margins of middle-class social reform movements. Mayhew, it will be argued, is better understood not as some deracinated type but as a figure firmly rooted within his class and its outlook. The unknown Mayhew is not the Mayhew of the *Morning Chronicle*; nor the foreigner-hating, flag-waving, anti-semitic, puffed-up Englishman whose bourgeois prejudices persisted in spite of his experiences as a social investigator. Mayhew was both. There was no dual personality; they are two sides of the same coin. Once this is appreciated, the similarities between Mayhew and Booth will be seen to have been more marked than is sometimes suggested.

Henry Mayhew was born on 25 November 1812, the son of Joshua Mayhew and his wife Mary Ann Fenn. His father, a successful London solicitor, was a stern, autocratic paterfamilias; his mother remains a shadowy figure. Seven of the seventeen Mayhew children were boys. All joined their father's practice and all, with one exception, abandoned the law for journalism. From the little we know of them the brothers Mayhew appear to have been spirited sorts who disregarded their father's wishes – but not his allowances – to pursue literary and theatrical interests turning out popular farces, almanacks, comic novels, travel accounts – anything for which there was a ready market – and contributing to regular newspapers and journals while participating in the founding and editing of miscellaneous money-making ventures. Most were failures. None of Mayhew brothers had any business sense, two were bankrupts and all seem to have experienced a good deal of financial insecurity. In the case of the eldest, it led to tragedy. Thomas Mayhew, editor of the radical *Poor Man's Guardian*, who died by his own hand in 1834, was also unusual in his complete identification with the popular radical movement. The descent of his siblings was less steep.

Headstrong Henry, having dropped out of respectable society, fell into a middle-class bohemia where he came into contact with Thackeray, Dickens and Douglas Jerrold, whose daughter, Jane, he married in 1844. It was a comfortable, convivial and creative environment peopled by dramatists, journalists, and witty, talented types meeting in pubs and clubs, scribbling satires and dreaming up all sorts of theatrical and literary projects. Some faces were familiar. The illustrated comic weekly, *Figaro in London*, which Mayhew edited between 1835 and 1839, was owned by his Westminster contemporary and one-time partner Gilbert Beckett. *Punch*, the climax of such ventures, was founded in 1841, and although Mayhew was ousted from the editorial chair in 1842, he continued his association with the journal until 1845. Twelve months later, Mayhew, like Beckett before him, was bankrupted. The next three years witnessed a desperate casting around for cash. There followed several pot boilers, written in collaboration with his brother Augustus, before fortune again smiled in October 1849 with the invitation from the editors of the *Morning Chronicle* to act as the Metropolitan Correspondent for its national investigation of 'Labour and the Poor'.

With this appointment began the three serial inquiries, conducted during the next five years, which together constitute the Mayhew survey, as it will be described below. In 1849–50 Mayhew produced some eighty-two letters for the *Morning Chronicle*, about a million words in all, devoted primarily to the condition of the London manufacturing trades. In the next two years he published the equally weighty *London Labour and the London Poor*, an investigation in sixty-three weekly parts of the metropolitan street trades. Included on the wrappers was a correspondence column, which foreshadowed the attempted critique of political economy that was developed in *Low Wages*, a separate part-work, also published in 1851, which folded after four issues. The same fate befell the *Great World of London*, a projected panorama, which appeared in monthly instalments between March and November 1856. Its most substantial legacy, the partially finished survey of the prison population, was later completed with outside assistance and published in book form in 1862.[12] All three inquiries were closely connected. About a third of the material published in the *Morning Chronicle* was incorporated in *London Labour and the London Poor*, which also supplied the key reference for the sequel, *The Criminal Prisons of London*.[13]

Mayhew's brief was to provide a reliable account of the earnings of labouring London. The survey population for this purpose included:

... all those persons whose incomings are insufficient for the satisfaction of their wants – a want being, according to my idea, contra-distinguished from a mere desire by a positive physical pain, instead of a mental uneasiness, accompanying it. The large and comparatively unknown body of people included in this definition I shall contemplate in two distinct classes, viz., the honest and dishonest poor; and the first of these I propose subdividing into the striving and the disabled – or in other words, I shall consider the whole of the metropolitan poor under three separate phases, according as they will work, they can't work and they won't work.[14]

The trades were largely self-selecting. The weavers of Spitalfields, dock labourers and the slop-clothing workers, universally acknowledged as paradigmatic low-wage trades, supplied an obvious starting point. Attention then shifted to those artisanal trades where, in consequence of the reorganization of the social relations of production, the degradation of working conditions and deterioration of living standards was most pronounced. Included here were the tailors, hatters, boot and shoemakers, carpenters, joiners and cabinet-makers; excluded were the metal and engineering trades, precision manufactures and printing and paperwork. Unskilled labourers and service workers were under-represented. Domestic service, the largest single source of employment, was omitted.[15]

The want of 'trustworthy information' which supplied the rationale for the inquiry posed formidable problems.[16] The growth of the statistical movement, as Michael Cullen has shown, was an expression of middle-class anxieties provoked by the narrow informational basis of the Condition of England Question. Mayhew, though not part of any of the various social reform networks, was closer to the mainstream than is sometimes suggested. The great parliamentary inquiries of the period did not pass over him as the Angel of Death had passed the Children of Israel. Mayhew, like Engels, was an assiduous reader of official publications. The reports of police authorities, Poor Law commissioners, the Registrar-General, factory inspectors and other regulatory agencies were scrutinized for evidence and argument and their strengths as well as their defects readily exposed. The blue book sociology that framed the values, assumptions and concepts of contemporaries also supplied the point of departure for his particular method of social inquiry. The possibilities of a scientific representation of the social order obtained through details in direct personal testimony seized his imagination. Mayhew's solution was to combine the ethos and interrogative approach of the royal commission with the reporting skills of the journalist. The technique, perfected in *London Labour and the London Poor* enabled him to justify the work as 'the first commission of inquiry into the state of the people undertaken by a private individual, and the first "blue book" ever published in twopenny numbers'.[17]

The sanitary science, which in London as in Paris, thrived on the panic provoked by the conjunction of cholera and crime and the displaced fears of social change expressed by them, provided another point of reference. Mayhew, who had spent time in the French capital, knew of the work of the public hygienists, and wrote as though his readers might be familiar with Thenard's researches or with toxicologists like D'Arcet, whose work was published in the *Annales d'hygiène publique*.[18] Here, too, perhaps, he first encountered the work of Alexander Parent-Duchâtelet, a one-time editor and authority on sewerage and industrial hygiene, who was also the author of *De la prostitution dans la ville de Paris* (1836), which Mayhew cites with approval.[19] Parent-Duchâtelet's extraordinary study of the pathology of Paris reveals an intellectual framework of public inquiry that was well in advance of developments on this side of the Channel. Parent-Duchâtelet was remarkable in his use of social statistics and in the path-breaking application of field observation and personal interview to social research. The point at which Mayhew read the Frenchman remains to be established. What is clear, though, is that he fully shared contemporary concerns in respect of the connection between labouring and dangerous classes. His survey, defined as a fact-gathering exercise on wages and incomes, addressed a particular debate on poverty and criminality and the re-establishment of social order.

The requirements of the work led him into strange company. Labourers were summoned by cab to the newspaper offices; testimonies were taken at public meetings, in the workplace, in private interviews held in trade societies and in small gatherings in low-lodging houses. Mayhew consorted with coalheavers and convicts, spoke with street walkers and slop-workers, fraternized with beggars, visited the poor at home, and even received them in Mrs Mayhew's parlour! The extraordinary rapport that developed between writer and audience found expression in the letter columns of the *Morning Chronicle* and in the pathetic appeals from distressed needlewomen, the wives of impoverished railway guards and like-minded correspondents who cast him as a finder of jobs and distributor of alms.[20] These roles he was not willing to perform. Mayhew's mission, as he himself defined it, was to act as an intermediary between the classes, and to explain to one half how the other half lived. The keeping of low company was a requirement of social science, not evidence of weakened class loyalties. 'To this middle class we ourselves belong,' he wrote, 'and, if we ever wandered out of it, we did so but to regard the other forms of life with the same eyes as a comparative anatomist loves to lay bare the organism and vital machinery of a zoophyte, or an ape, in the hope of linking together the lower and the higher forms of animal existence.'[21]

The powerful and compelling quality of the Mayhew survey, though it drew something from his widening social sympathies and the use of open-ended questions, owed more to the ways in which the interviews were written up. Mayhew insisted that the experiences told to him were taken down on the spot and 'repeated to the public in the selfsame words in which they were told to me'.[22] The language of the poor it may have been; spontaneous it was not. To be sure, the actors were unscripted, but the production was carefully staged. Cues were given and the audience prepared for the lines about to be delivered. Eileen Yeo and Anne Humpherys have also noted the heightened effect created by the elimination of the reporter's questions and the presentation of each interview as if it were an autobiographical statement in the 'voice' of the worker.[23]

Mayhew was assisted by his brother Augustus and two former London City Missionaries who acted as stenographers. He also had two clerks 'continually engaged' 'in collecting information and making general statistics for me'.[24] Interviews generally began with questions about wages and working conditions. No reliable wage series existed when Mayhew began his inquiry. Employers, small and large, who paid the lowest wages, were generally unco-operative. Workers, though helpful, were poor record-keepers, 'and it is only with considerable difficulty and cross-questioning that one is able to obtain from them an account of the expenses necessarily attendant upon their labour, and so, by deducting these from the price paid to them, to arrive at the amount of their clear earnings'.[25] Mayhew, in an attempt to construct the average rate of wages, took extraordinary pains to secure reliable information. Assuming that his informants were 'naturally disposed' to understate their earnings and that his readers expected them to do so, he explained his procedure thus:

> My first inquiries are into a particular branch of the trade under investigation upon which the workman is engaged. I then request to be informed whether the individual has his or her work first or second-handed; that is to say, whether he or she obtains it direct from the employer, or through the intervention of some chamber or piece-master. If the work comes to the operative in question second-handed, I then endeavour to find out the prices paid for the work itself to the first hand, as well as the number of work people that the first hand generally employs. This done, I seek to be

informed whether the work of the individual I am visiting is piece or day work. If day work, I learn the usual hours of labour per day, and the rate of wages per week. If it be piece-work, I request to be made acquainted with the prices paid for each description of work seriatim, the time that each particular article takes to make, and the number of hours that the party usually works per day. By these means I arrive at the gross daily earnings. I then ascertain the cost of trimmings, candles, and such other expenses as are necessary to the completion of each particular article; and, deducting these from the gross gains per day, I find what are the clear daily earnings of the individual in question. I then check this account by obtaining from the workman a statement as to the number of such articles that he can make in a week; and, deducting expenses, I see whether the clear weekly earnings agree with those of the clear daily ones. After this I request to know the amount of the earnings for the last week; then those for the week before; and then those for the week before that. Beyond this point I find that the memory generally fails. Out of the scores of operatives that I have now visited, I have found only one instance in which the workman keeps a regular account of his weekly gains ...

When I have obtained an account of the clear earnings of the workpeople during such times as they are fully employed, I seek to procure from them a statement of what they imagine to be their weekly earnings, taking one week with another, throughout the year. Having got this I then set about to discover how often in the course of the year they are 'standing still', as they term it. I inquire into the number and duration of 'the slacks'. This done, I strive to obtain from the operative an average of the weekly earnings during such times. I then make a calculation of the total of the workpeople's gains when fully employed for so many months, and when partially occupied for the remainder of the year. By this means I am enabled to arrive at an average of their weekly earnings throughout the whole year; and I then compare this with the amount I have previously received from them on the subject ...
I finally check the whole account of their earnings by a statement of their expenditure. I generally see their rent-book, and so learn the sum that they pay for rent; and I likewise get a detail of their mode and cost of living inquired into, especially with regard to the truthfulness, industry and sobriety of the individual.[26]

The personal visits and lengthy interviews with operatives required to elicit incomes data were perhaps the most time-consuming part of the whole inquiry. The bias towards the skilled worker, which has drawn criticism in some quarters, owed as much to his developed record-keeping practices as to any other virtues. The comparative expenditure of time and effort in securing reliable information on earnings made Mayhew appreciative of the intelligent artisan, above all of the 'Society' man, who could more readily supply standard list prices and other essential documents. One such informant who 'placed in my hands a variety of statistical papers connected with the trade' was, he concluded, 'a person of superior understanding'. The difference between those who stored information on paper and those who relied purely upon memory was for Mayhew and his associates a personal as much as a cultural consideration. 'Indeed', he wrote, 'the change from the squalor, foetor and wretchedness of the homes of the poor people that I had lately visited, to the comfort, cleanliness and cheerfulness of the operative tailors, has been as refreshing to my feelings as the general sagacity of the workmen has been instrumental in the lightening of my labours.'[27]

Mayhew, though, was concerned with more than the calculation of wage rates. The survey, undertaken at a key moment in the transformation of the urban economy, recorded the changes in manufacturing activity associated with the expansion of the sweated industries. Captivated by the articulate artisans with whom he consorted, Mayhew developed a quite remarkable understanding of the cultural and material changes that flowed from the increasing degradation of labour. Before Marx there were few who had a better grasp of its defining elements. Mayhew, who spent time in the workshops and petty manufactures, separates work into its constituent parts, and proceeds from an analysis of the labour process to chart the changes in the division of labour in order to show how labour power has become a commodity organized and cheapened to suit the needs of its purchasers. He describes the disruption of the labour market, the expansion of the sweated, slop or dishonourable sector and the varying forms of work process, work organization and wage payment that were applied to increase labour productivity.[28]

Mayhew's comparative method – the cross-checking of statements and juxtaposition of empirically grounded conclusions with received truths – did not necessarily yield reliable results, but it did make the investigator increasingly critical of official sources of information and the explanatory framework into which they were organized. In particular, he became sceptical of the representation of society as a spontaneous and self-adjusting order, and began to doubt whether prevailing economic arrangements were either natural or necessary.[29] The gloomy implications of the Malthusian theory of population and its rationalization of the subsistence theory of wages struck him as both vicious and contentious. He took up arms against the wage-fund theory and ridiculed the view, imputed to J.S. Mill, that 'there is no hope for the working men of this country until they imitate the Catholic priests and register vows in Heaven of perpetual celibacy'.[30]

Mayhew not only documented the downward pressures on the artisan at work but also recorded the sense of loss experienced by the destruction of craftsmanship and the communities it sustained. The silk weavers of Spitalfields, 'formerly, almost the only botanists in the Metropolis', with their once-flourishing entomological, floricultural and mathematical societies, exemplify the severance of science and art, and the despair among craft workers at the loss of skill, independence and control.[31]

Mayhew was just as concerned with the social relations of production, with the values, beliefs and assumptions of his informants, with their traditions and memories, and the connection between their work and their way of life. Taking his cue from the craft trades, he recorded the enormous cultural variations between skilled and unskilled occupations and how these distinctions affected their corporate consciousness and political outlook. He noted, with respect to the waterside trades, how regularity of habits was incompatible with irregularity of income. He notes, too, how different groups of workers respond to technical and economic change and the pressures which transformed coal-whippers into special constables and costermongers into Chartists.

Moving from the streets to the prisons and reformatories, Mayhew explored how the prison operated and how it was organized. *The Criminal Prisons of London*, a text that says as much about civil society as about the penal system, has not received the attention it merits.[32] The prison population, so often viewed as an undifferentiated mass, is here disaggregated and presented as men, women and juveniles whose condition highlights the place of punishment and prison in the social system. New punishment regimes were examined, the goals and methods of the organization of penal life scrutinized and the prison assessed as both school and factory. Direct personal testimony taken from inmates, ticket-of-leave men and young offenders, as always makes compelling reading and reinforces the connection between prisoners and civilians.[33]

II

The disjuncture between the process of production and wealth creation as represented by political economy and the exploitation, revealed by his investigations into the manufacturing trades, raised questions

which Mayhew felt impelled to answer. Having been led to the view
that inadequate remuneration rather than inefficient expenditure was
the principal cause of poverty, he switched attention from observation
to analysis.

Apart from a well-thumbed copy of Mill's *Principles of Political
Economy*, the key texts were those of Smith and Ricardo. Mayhew also
read Charles Babbage's *Economy of Machinery and Manufacturers*
(1832), Adam Ure's *Philosophy of Manufacturers* (1835), Chalmers,
possibly McCulloch and others.[34] Of the unorthodox economists there
was no mention. The writings of the Ricardian socialists, who between
1820 and 1840 advanced the claim of labour to the whole product of
industry, seems to have passed him by. So he began with Mill's
statement that the rate of wages was determined by the law of demand
and supply and sought its refutation and reformulation from the
standpoint of workers as observed in the productive process. His
definition of wages as the ratio of the remuneration of the labourer to
the quantity of the work performed, differed markedly from the
orthodox view (in which wages depended on the proportion between
population and capital). It enabled him to focus attention on employer
strategies for controlling the labour process to show how the supply
and remuneration of labour was affected by organizational systems,
wage systems and the mechanization of production rather than by any
increase in population. His conclusion, baldly summarized, was that
overwork rather than overpopulation was the more influential cause of
the surplus of labour.

Mayhew located the crux of the problem in a growing
disequilibrium between the funds available for the maintenance of
labour and the funds absorbed by capital. His conclusions, though,
were almost as pessimistic as those of the classical economists. He
envisaged a future of increasing competition in which the relentless
downward pressure on wages and employment provoked crises of
over-production and under-consumption, distress and disturbance. No
relief was possible, he argued, until wages were made to better reflect
the value created by the worker. Justice, rather than the market, should
rule, and the workman receive a fairer share of the 'increased value
that ... [he] by the exercise of his skill, gives to the materials on which
he operates'.[35] What was required, then, was a 'new partnership'
between 'the man of money and the man of muscles'.[36] The
reconciliation of the classes through the development of an equitable
wage system, he concluded, would best secure material and moral
progress.[37]

Mayhew's claim to revise economic theory in the light of the
evidence he had collected, to be, in his own words, 'the first who has

sought to evolve the truths of the Labour Question by personal investigation', represents an aspiration rather than an achievement.[38] What had gone wrong? Scholarly approaches here are of two kinds. Some assert that Mayhew's 'unreliability and lack of tenacity' accounts for the poverty of his theory; others direct attention to certain shortcomings in his assumptions and procedures.[39] Mayhew, in the second approach, is presented as the victim of his own sources. His economics, it has been argued, express an artisan trade consciousness which helps to account for the uneasy shifting from fact to value to reach conclusions that do not proceed from theoretical considerations.[40]

Low Wages, Mayhew's attempt to gather his thinking into a general statement, is widely perceived as an exercise that displays his limitations rather than his strengths. 'Mayhew's economic analysis', writes Gareth Stedman Jones, 'consisted largely of antinomies – the disclosure of phenomena not easily accounted for, or indeed, even mentioned in the conventional economics of the period, accompanied by an inability or unwillingness to locate them in an alternative theoretical structure. Such an ambivalence made it unclear even to himself whether he was engaged in a critique of political economy or an extension of it.' But whereas previous commentators have fixed upon Mayhew's alleged fecklessness to account for the abandonment of serious social analysis, Stedman Jones presents him as the victim of economic and political change, beached by the onset of mid Victorian stability, and thus deprived of the radical constituency which might have sustained his project.[41]

Plausible though it is, the interpretation rests on a counterfactual that cannot be tested. The outcome of the Mayhew survey, had it been undertaken at the beginning rather than the close of the 1840s, must remain a matter of conjecture. The extent to which Mayhew had been radicalized by his experience as Metropolitan Commissioner may also be questioned. It will be seen below that, for all his advances in respect of the labour question, he accepted far more of the assumptions of liberalism than he ever criticized. Mayhew's commitment to private property, support of emigration, qualified approval of trade unions, and liking for profit-sharing arrangements, locate him squarely within the ranks of the enlightened middle classes. Even his concern with unequal exchange was connected with a continuing preoccupation with the formation of the dangerous and criminal classes. Thus Chalmers, whose opinions Mill considered erroneous, was mustered by Mayhew in defence of the principle that wages should be sufficient to prevent pauperism. The 'immense mass of surplus labourers, who are continually vagabondizing through the country', he claimed, partly reflected the want of such a wage.[42] Viewed in the round his theoretical interventions seem much more like an attempt to modify or moralize political economy rather than to replace it.

Mayhew's search for an organizing framework for his findings was not exhausted by his encounter with political economy. The need of an alternative anchorage became pressing after the break with the *Morning Chronicle* and the shift towards the street trades and the criminal classes. Those readily available did not at first seem promising. 'The phrenologists alone have looked into the subject, but unfortunately they are theorists with a disposition to warp rather than discover facts', he wrote. Of ethnography he was equally critical. 'Ethnologists', he observed, 'have done little or nothing towards increasing our knowledge of the physical conformation of the predatory and vagabond races of the world.'[43] It was the descriptive force and evolutionist assumptions of ethnography that caught his imagination. Two features were striking: the division of mankind into two anatomically and morally distinct classes, the civilized settlers and the unproductive wanderers, and the parasitism of the latter upon the former. The similarities between the social order as portrayed by contemporary anthropology and that which formed the subject of his investigation seemed to Mayhew to constitute

> ... points of coincidence so striking that, when placed before the mind, makes us marvel that the analogy should have remained thus long unnoticed. The resemblance once discovered, however, becomes of great service in enabling us to use the moral characteristics of the nomad races of other countries, as a means of comprehending the more readily, those of the vagabonds and outcasts of our own.[44]

How well versed Mayhew was in the anthropology and travel literature of his day is uncertain. Mayhew himself, one literary scholar has recently noted, 'is unspecific almost to the point of mystification about his ethnographic references.[45]

London Labour and the London Poor, acknowledges but does not engage with the writings of Pritchard, Lewis and others. There was no good reason why it should. Ethnology, as presented here, was not a set of testable propositions, but a strategy that enabled the author to develop his role as social explorer and interpreter of the poor. Mayhew's borrowings were largely for purposes of illustration; his citations were included as a reassurance for disturbed readers rather than as an invitation to further research.

The nomadic poor are likened to primeval savages, who are ruled by brute passions and animal appetites, and live without structure and restraint. They are dangerous and depraved, restless and indulgent, improvident, licentious and lewd. These people, unknown to the census enumerators, supplied the recruits to the vagabond hordes that were said to be roaming the country. Questions concerning numbers, though, were less urgent than the possibilities of redemption and rehabilitation. Here there were grounds for optimism. On closer inspection, Mayhew found regularities and system in the lives of the poor, and shows them trying to create order and meaning out of the, apparently, meaningless chaos of their everyday existence. The significance of this discovery, however, has been obscured by a Whiggish preoccupation with the origins of modern British sociology and the modern idea of culture. Of such things contemporaries knew little. Mayhew, who well understood the needs of his audience, had shown that, notwithstanding appearance to the contrary, the outcast poor might be susceptible to rational analysis and perhaps also to rational reform.

III

Scientist in spirit, and with a lifelong enthusiasm for chemistry, Mayhew had set out to apply the techniques of natural science to the study of social phenomena. 'I have undertaken the subject with a rigid determination neither to be biased nor prejudiced by my own individual notions', he wrote. 'I know that as in science the love of theorising warps the mind, and causes it to see only those natural phenomena that it wishes to see ...'.[46] His self-image as an inductive reasoner, and self-declared role as a recorder of facts and register of opinions, untrammelled by partisan considerations, represents an intention rather than a description of his practice. His alleged empiricism was in fact filled with unexamined presumptions. Mayhew, though not himself a systematic thinker, was influenced by the associationist psychology of the Utilitarians. Whether acquired by extensive reading and careful introspection, or by simple exposure to blue-book Benthamism, Mayhew assumed that the pursuit of pleasure constituted the basis of human motivation and welcomed the possibilities of enlightened social action that were premised upon it. Chadwick's *Report on the Constabulary* of 1839, that 'valuable Report', was for Mayhew a key text, as much for its reasoning as for its information and specific proposals. Benthamite traces were also evident in his plea for educational reform, *What to Teach and How to Teach It* (1842); subsequently these became more pronounced.[47] His paper on the abolition of capital punishment, read to the Society for Promoting the Amendment of the Law in 1856, was a simple restatement of the utilitarian view that capital punishment was inconsistent with that economy of bodily pain that should form one of the main objects of progressive penal policy.[48]

Empirical investigation, too, was influenced by the moral categories of Benthamite social analysis. Less eligibility supplied a perspective on social research as well as a basis for public policy. Mayhew shared with contemporaries numerous preconceptions about poverty and the poor, and readily classified individuals as respectable and worthy or depraved and vicious. Thus the informants and respondents by whom he set such store were all located within the same evaluative framework. With the workshy, thriftless and criminal elements he had no truck. 'Those who desire to live by the industry of others, form no portion of the honest and independent race of workmen in this country whom Mr Mayhew wishes to befriend', he informed one correspondent. 'The deserving poor are those who cannot live by their labour, whether from under payment, want of employment, or physical or mental incapacity, and these Mr Mayhew wishes, and will most cheerfully do all he can, at any time and in any way, to assist.'[49]

The origins of these distinctions were also accountable in Utilitarian terms. Mayhew's analysis of the formation of labouring and dangerous classes thus combined aspects of sensationalist psychology with an appreciation of the special circumstances of time and place. The genesis of criminality, though rooted in an impatience of steady labour, was primarily a result of the neglect and tyranny of parents and masters, and a consequent failure to engender a love of industry.[50] Men and women, Mayhew believed, were born egoists. 'Theft', he wrote, 'is a natural propensity of the human condition and honesty an artificial and educated sentiment. We do not come into the world with an instinctive sense of the rights of property implanted in our bosom, to teach us to respect the possessions of others, but rather with an innate desire to appropriate whatever we may fancy.'[51] Chadwick's formulation – 'Crime is mostly the result of a desire to obtain property with a less degree of labour than by regular industry' – was also cited with approbation.[52] Prostitution, too, he believed, arose among those 'who are born in labour for their bread, but who find the work inordinately irksome to their natures, and pleasure as inordinately agreeable to them'.[53]

Mayhew's concern with the roots of criminality also led him to an appreciation of Mandeville's sensationalist hedonism. Apart from the irreverent tone and mordant wit, and the telling use of vignettes, anecdotes and sketches – all of them no doubt congenial to the founder editor of *Punch* – it was the satirist-philosopher's assertion that pride was the key to social organization that caught his imagination. Mayhew, though he balked at the egoistic reduction of morality, found the idea of self-love as a socializing agent, capable of converting human animals into human beings, particularly pertinent to his inquiries. What was most suggestive about Mandeville's writing was the unfolding possibilities of moral progress through the balancing of the weaker passions against the stronger. The role of the legislator and moralist to promote such adjustments as were necessary to secure the continuing victory of reason over passion seemed equally apposite.[54] Mayhew, like the political economists who drank at the same trough, readily endorsed Mandeville's view that the desire to be admired, and the disinclination to be despised, constituted an insight of great importance in the shaping of social and market relations. The spirit of emulation, properly mobilized, Mayhew asserted, represented 'one of the great means of moral government in a State'. Its absence among the lowest social classes accounted for prostitution and crime.[55] Mayhew, though, did not believe that such people could not be reached. His proposal for the formation of self-regulating street-trading communities was a measure designed to channel restlessness into respectability.[56]

The idea of man as a creature of desires who seeks to satisfy them as abundantly as he can at the least cost to himself served to distance him from Evangelical educational initiatives and allied strategies for social reform. Apart from a misguided preoccupation with externals, Evangelical social action was, he believed, too narrow in its scope to address the labour question effectively. His attempts to demonstrate this empirically by a case study of the Ragged School Union brought down the wrath of the philanthropic establishment upon his head, and opened the rift with his employers that was to culminate in his departure from the *Morning Chronicle*. Mayhew, though 'pelted with dirt from every evangelical assembly throughout the country', declined to go down gently.[57] Charges against the 'religious gentry' were repeated and embellished in subsequent publications. He scorned educational systems in which children were 'duly taught to spell and to write, and to chatter catechisms and creeds that they cannot understand' and condemned the influence of parson and chaplain as harmful. 'No man', he wrote, 'can have a deeper loathing and contempt for those outward shows of godliness – those continued "lip services" – the everlasting "praying in public places", which the revelation of our every-day's commercial and prison history teaches us to believe, constitute the flagrant "shams" of the age.'[58] In place of chaplain and bible worship he recommended 'really good, sound, wholesome, labour training'.[59]

For Mayhew, it was the formation or non-formation of habits of industry that was central to his understanding of the social question. Mayhew, though he was not attached to any particular group or programme, drew selectively upon the stock of ideas that formed the basis of middle-class radicalism and shared in full its civilizing mission. His belief that criminal behaviour reflected a want of self-control due in large part to an unwholesome environment, underscored the importance not only of the family but also of employment in the key initiatory stages of social development. Apart from the production of necessities, work provided the most direct evidence of the subordination of the passions. For Mayhew, as for his contemporaries, an aptitude for labour was readily perceived as a direct measure of the restraint and discipline upon which social order rested. The tripartite division of the metropolitan poor into those that will work, those that cannot work, and those that will not work, as the organizing principle of the Mayhew survey, expressed middle-class fears of the growth of pauperization and the consequent descent of the labouring classes into the dangerous classes. The utilitarian roots of his thinking were also evident in his conception of work as a necessary form of suffering in which pain might be mitigated and industry encouraged. through education, example and deliberation.[60]

Mayhew's concept of education, though, was wider than that sanctioned by philosophical radicalism. Coleridge's insight into the complexities of the human intellect and feelings impressed him. He, in turn, insisted upon the separation of learning skills and knowledge and was critical of those Evangelical initiatives in which the two were confounded. 'Of course', he wrote in respect of the rehabilitation of young offenders, 'the teaching of reading and writing is a negative good; but it becomes almost an evil when people get to believe that it has any positive or moral religious effect, per se, and so to forgo ... all education of the feelings, and principles, and even the tastes, of those confined within them. The most valuable of all schooling is surely that of the heart, and the next that of the hands, especially for the poorer classes, who are mostly the inmates of our jails.'[61] Cooke Taylor's dictum that 'reading and writing are no more education than a knife and fork is a good dinner' was quoted with approval on several occasions.[62] The cultivation of the feelings and education of the moral sentiments, he argued, supplied the basis for a curriculum that directly addressed the social crisis.

Why is it, then, that Mayhew's ideas have proved difficult to place? Mayhew's want of system and failure to locate his ideas within a coherent programme of social reform, suggest one line of inquiry. It is possible, however, that the difficulty lies in ourselves, in our assumptions about the Victorian middle classes and Mayhew's place within them. To be sure, Mayhew's own humanity did get in the way of the utilitarian precepts he was trying to uphold. But was that so unusual? Is it not likely that his alleged antagonism to a unified bourgeoisie makes him seem rather more marginal than was the case? In truth, we do not know. The teleological bias of histories of social science, and the tendency of recent work to focus upon text rather than context, diverts us from the more fruitful study of how his work was received and understood in his own day rather than how it is 'read' in ours.

IV

The social crisis of the 1880s drove the Booth inquiry just as the fears of cholera, crime and Chartism drove the Mayhew survey. Resurgent fears of mass pauperism, vagabondage, crime and social chaos, preyed upon the middle classes of the 1880s as forty years earlier they had preyed upon their forbears. Inevitably the ground traversed by Mayhew was covered by Booth. Homelessness and destitution, slums and overcrowding, labouring and dangerous classes, the casual and sweated trades proved as salient to the Booth inquiry as they had to its predecessor. Both were concerned to relate poverty to employment. Mayhew began with the worst-paid trades, Booth with the most deprived area. From the East End of London, he set out to discover 'the numerical relations which poverty, misery and depravity bear to regular earnings and comparative comfort, and to describe the general conditions under which each class lives.'[63] Mayhew emphasized the inequitable wage system as the principal source of poverty; Booth drew attention to the imperfections of the labour market. Neither accepted liberal social theory without qualification. The Malthusian assumptions of political economy which so vexed Mayhew were likewise rejected by Booth who also came to share Mayhew's scepticism in respect of free trade. Neither, however, was willing to abandon the moral categories of liberal social action. Booth, like Mayhew, possessed a highly differentiated picture of the working classes and a common classification based upon utilitarian principles. For both the key distinctions were between skilled and unskilled, rough and respectable, deserving and undeserving, between the practitioners of self-help and mutual aid who tried to preserve an independent existence, and the 'residuum' of casual workers, loafers, unemployables and ne'er-do-wells, whose moral and physical degeneration threatened to pull down the self-supporting elements above them. Not surprisingly, both shifted uneasily between environmental and personal influences in the causation of poverty.

Significant differences were as much methodological as conceptual. Both were self-taught statisticians. Mayhew applied his considerable skills to the enumeration of the street trades, the numbers engaged in sweated industries and to the calculation of hourly wages. Mayhew's purposes, though, were more often than not rhetorical and literary, and certainly he never shared Booth's ambitions to build a comprehensive statistical framework into which information might be fed and policy created. Although Mayhew readily grasped the possibilities of a poverty line, he never provided an operational definition for its application. Booth not only supplied a basis for measurement and comparison, but set out to separate those perceived as social problem groups from the self-supporting elements of the population and establish the relative size of each. For this purpose Londoners were divided into eight economic classes. Class A 'included the lowest class of occasional labourers, loafers and semi-criminals'; Class B, 'the very poor' living on casual earnings; while Classes C and D, lived on intermittent and small regular earnings and together made up the 'poor'. Classes E and F, who subsisted above the line of poverty, constituted the pukka working class. The boundaries between classes were fluid and variable and difficult to distinguish, not least because Booth included non-material influences, like providence, thrift and sobriety, in an attempt to establish 'the prevailing type' in each class. 'By the word "poor",' he explained, 'I mean to describe those who have a sufficiently regular though bare income such as 18–21 shillings per week for a moderate family, and by "very poor" those who from any cause fall below this standard. The poor are those whose means may be sufficient but are barely sufficient for decent independent life; the very poor those whose means are insufficient for this according to the usual standard of life in this country. My "poor" may be described as living under a struggle to obtain the necessaries of life and make both ends meet, while the very poor live in a state of chronic want.'[64]

The classification of the population according to the degree of want or comfort in which they were found was not, however, based upon household income, which was not available, but on information acquired by the School Board Visitors in the normal course of their duties. No house-to-house survey was undertaken. In Booth's own words, the classification 'was based on opinion only – that is, on the impression made on the minds of the School Board Visitors and others by what they had seen or heard as to the position in the scale of comfort of the people amongst whom they lived and worked.'[65] The opinions of the School Board Visitors were cross-checked against those of philanthropists, social workers, policemen and others. The scope for error was considerable. Booth's poverty line, it is often noted, was drawn arbitrarily in relation to ill-defined and uncertain income groups and applied inconsistently.

We can, if we wish, make sense of his taxonomy by viewing it as an expression of middle-class moralizing, as do Brown and others, or by following Himmelfarb and seeing it as a creative and worthy form of discrimination – a new typology of poverty, as she calls it – separating labour from the poor and responsive to the special requirements of each.[66] Neither argument seems persuasive. The one does not press the evidence far enough. The other presses it beyond what it will bear. A better approach has been suggested by Peter Hennock who directs attention towards the mode of employment in organizing Booth's conceptual scheme. Booth, he observes, 'very quickly identified his classes with the forms of labour and retained this identification throughout the work, with the result that what might have been regarded as classification according to degrees of poverty came also to be thought of as classification according to different kinds of work'.[67] Posing the problem in these terms enabled Booth to advance the case for limited action to resist the downward pressure exerted by outcast poor upon those who might otherwise be incorporated in the working class proper. The removal from the labour market of the helpess, incompetent and unfit elements concentrated in Class B would, he argued, push Classes C and D upwards above the line of poverty into self-supporting habits. The labour-market orientation of Booth's thought also accounts for the unrepresentative nature of the survey population and the omission of the aged.

Booth, though he too presented himself as a simple empiricist, differed from Mayhew in the greater importance he attached to remedial action. 'In beginning my inquiry,' he wrote, 'I had no preconceived ideas, no theory to work up to, no pet scheme into agreement with which the facts collected were to be twisted or to which they would have to be squared. At the same time the consideration and the hope of remedies have never been out of my mind.'[68] Mayhew possessed neither the urgency nor a comparable sense of personal responsibility. Whereas Mayhew's survey began as a commission initiated by the proprietors of the *Morning Chronicle*, Booth's inquiry sprang from a larger vision of social and moral progress. Positivism provided one perspective on the social problem, but it was the onset of the social crisis that roused the imagination and gave a new focus to his thinking. Booth's leading ideas took shape in the early 1880s. In these years, as Hennock notes, Booth abandoned the idea that attributed poverty to excessive population growth and began to consider the potentially liberating role of organization in the solution of the social problem. Socialist attempts to mobilize London labour and the London poor in the name of a unitary working class underscored the need for a counter strategy that would separate and re-arrange the submerged and labouring classes so as to identify the basis for selective social action. The reconceptualization of the social problem in this way enabled him to advance a programme that, at one fell swoop, promised not only to 'secure the final divorce of labour from poverty', but also to preserve property, promote independence and deprive socialism of a constituency.

Mayhew lends support to 'history from below'; Himmelfarb's Booth serves no such purpose. Booth, we learn, 'never seriously considered using the people as a primary source'.[69] Historians who have worked through the contents of Booth's notebooks will find her statement puzzling. Booth's confidence in the validity of his analysis gained strength from a relativistic concept of poverty that was grounded in the testimonies of working people as well as in the statements of teachers, administrators and clergy. A glance at his interview techniques and procedures will serve to establish the importance of first-hand evidence in the development of his ideas.

The Poverty Series addressed the social situation of the metropolitan poor. The Industry Series, though concerned to develop measures of convergent validity, differed in emphasis. 'The first inquiry', Booth explained, 'had been an attempt to describe the inhabitants of London, especially the poorer part of them, and their social conditions, as they lived street by street, family by family, in their homes.' The aim of the Industry Series, by contrast, was 'to review the people as they work, trade by trade, in their factories, warehouses or shops, or pursue their avocations in the street or on the railways, in the markets or on the quays; to consider their relations to those whom they serve, whether employer or customer, and the remuneration they receive; and finally, to examine the bearing which the money earned has on the life they lead'.[70] The primary focus, then, was upon production and distribution – upon London as an industrial, commercial and trading centre; upon the multiplicity of its trades; the characteristics of its workers; the structure and organization of the labour market; the work process and the social relations arising therefrom. From the classification and enumeration of its industries and workforce Booth moved to a description and analysis of London's working life. The salient features included the localization of trades and the systems of production under which they operated; the supply of labour, its training, conditions and rewards; the sphere of trade unions; and the prospects for peace and progress arising from the relationship of employer and employed.

The work-centred approach of the Industry Series made the research interview central to the survey strategy. The absence of a cadre of officials who occupied a position in relation to the workforce, comparable with that of the School Board Visitors to the general population, was an important constraint which precluded a simple replication of the data-collection methods of the previous series.

Information was obtained by interview and personal observation. Employers and trade union officials were circularized and follow-up visits arranged with those willing to give further assistance. Investigators received precise and detailed guidance as to the information required. The questionnaire, prepared by Booth himself, was partly descriptive and partly evaluative. Instructions were given to report on the extent of organization in particular trades and assess the influence exercised by trade unions. Investigators were asked to find out what class of person became a trade unionist, who resisted membership and why; to identify those branches of a trade and those localities in which trade unionism was strongest; and to describe employer response in terms of attitude and company policy. The social value of trade unions was equally significant. Information was collected on the social relations of workers, their sectional rivalries and divisions so as to estimate the degree to which unions 'cause friendship and increase good feeling amongst those who join'. Booth, like Mayhew before him, requested accounts of working life 'with full details where likely to be of general interest bearing in mind that to me and to most of those who will read my book [will] have no ideas or the very vaguest ideas about the actual daily life of working men [sic]'.[71]

The Industry Series, it should now be clear, was something more than a simple survey of industrial relations. In consequence, information was acquired on the character of workplace organization, the place of custom and ritual in relation to the working community, and the influence of certain trade-specific practices upon the control of production. Booth was equally concerned with the ways in which work and work-culture informed everyday life. Investigators were thus directed to probe some possible connections between work, home and family. In the course of the interview questions were raised about residence, meals, dress, family income and expenditure. Respondents were also invited to comment on housing and rents and given the opportunity to supply aspects of industrial biography.

Booth and his associates had interviewed hundreds of people. Informants were recommended by employers and foremen; a fair number came through the informal network of contacts which had been built up in the course of the earlier inquiry. Within the survey population, women, children, the unskilled, the unorganized and white-collar workers were under-represented. The bulk of those interviewed were working men. Some were self-employed; but most were wage earners. No attempt was made to obtain the age of respondents. Booth, like Mayhew, had a preference for experienced individuals who could supply a certain perspective on trade developments, such as George Oliver and William Jeffrey, who led the Bermondsey leather workers in the strike of 1865, and spoke authoritatively about the labour process and the pattern of industrial relations that arose from it.[72]

From the outset investigators were required to check the accuracy of the information received. The verification process applied to people as well as to statements. Informants and respondents were frequently appraised, as much for their moral worth as their substantive knowledge. Political opinions were noted, though more as a source of bias than as the basis for further exploration. Trade questions were the dominant interest of the survey population. Although the majority of those interviewed were probably members of trade unions, Booth discovered varying levels of commitment, some hostility and a good deal of indifference.

The Industry Survey encompassed the whole spectrum of production: from large establishments, like breweries and locomotive engineering works, to back-street braziers, self-employed printers and knife-grinders leading a hole-in-the-corner existence in sheds, outhouses and lean-tos. In each case the work process was carefully monitored. The stages of production were noted and the organization of work reported. Simple line drawings sketched into the notebooks served as an *aide-mémoire* and visual record of labouring London.

Interviews were arranged for the convenience of the respondent. Some were held in office hours, a few in private homes, and a fair number were conducted in licensed premises. Some took two hours; others longer. Notes were sometimes made, but not always. John Edey, Secretary of the Patent Leather Dressers' Society, for example, 'gave information with great hesitation' and only on condition 'that nothing should be put down on paper while he was there'.[73] The transcripts are not, then, verbatim reports of proceedings. They are reconstructions written up from notes or from memory.

There was some variation in interviewer technique. Most interviews were face-to-face encounters conducted in private. Some, however, developed into a dialogue between interviewer, respondent and the respondent's friends or associates. Duckworth, set to interview a hoop-maker, was unexpectedly referred from the office to the workshop. 'The following', he wrote, 'is therefore an interview with the foreman and the six men working there who joined freely in the discussion.'[74] In other cases a public meeting was required to complete the questionnaire. Where a trade union officer did not feel able to provide information, or where he was unable to approve the written-up report, the matter might be referred to the membership.

The state of the trade and the age of respondents were not the only influence upon the supply of information. The effects of class and gender were equally significant. The Industry Series, unlike its predecessor, reserved no space for a special consideration of 'women's work'.[75] Women workers in the trade-by-trade survey were presented in descriptive rather than analytical terms; and there were too few of them. Booth's female respondents also occupied a lower position in the social hierachy than the male interviewees; being drawn largely from the unorganized and depressed sectors of the labour force. Once their confidence had been gained these poor women found their voice. Their statements, as recorded in the notebooks, present a powerful portrait of life at the margins.

Timing was important. The seasonality of production, for example, seems to have discouraged would-be respondents in certain consumer industries. The status of the survey, and above all the confusion of Charles with William Booth, made some informants unduly circumspect. Mr Palmer, a Bermondsey leather manufacturer, might, for example, have been more forthcoming had he appreciated the distinction. 'He was', Duckworth recorded, 'most unwilling to give me any information, and as he said goodbye asked me how long I had been working with the "General" – he seemed much relieved when he found I was no connection.'[76] The use of the data and the effect of publication were important considerations; for then, as now, the expectation of reward, and the extent of which the research interview might contribute towards it, was a key influence upon respondent participation.[77]

Employer response was influenced by similar considerations. Even when informants were readily forthcoming the difficulties were considerable. Duckworth, given access to the wage books of one cooperage company, came unstuck on complex payments systems in which time rates and piece rates were combined.[78] The point was also frequently made that analysis based on total wage costs might obscure significant differences in the position of different individuals within the same factory or work group.[79] The suggestion that the wages data for the Industry Series was obtained from employers without close inquiry is wrong. Booth had no illusions about the reliability of London employers or the unrepresentative character of those who were willing to answer his queries. The evidence of the notebooks shows that questions were asked, statements scrutinized, comparisons made, and all reasonable attempts undertaken to verify the information provided.[80]

It was not only in respect of the collection of evidence that Booth was careful. Questions of interpretation were handled with equal diligence. Drafts on particular industries or sections were not only subjected to meticulous collective examination but were often sent for external assessment. Booth himself was permitted no exemption.[81] The Booth Inquiry sought to combat prejudice, not least its own.

The prominence of work in the Booth survey reflected more than an interest in the production of goods and services. Equally significant was the effect of work on the worker and on his or her place in society. Cultural considerations were in fact as important to Booth as they were to Mayhew. The notebooks are a mine of information on the expectations and aspirations of individual workers, and on the interaction of work with the bonds created by kinship, gender, religion, ethnicity, recreation and locality. Neighbourhood and community – patterns of sociability, of language, dress and politics – often reflected the needs and norms of the trade. The social life of the workplace, too, was logged; the notebooks indeed recreate the sights, sounds, and almost the smell, of Londoners at work. The milieu of the workplace, with its shop clubs and slate clubs and informal support systems, was also noted.[82] Meal-times, and tea-breaks too, offered opportunities for socializing on and off the premises. Arrangements varied both within and between industries. In some trades workers brought their own food and sent out for supplements; in others facilities were provided either by the employer or by the workers themselves.

In productive relations, as in all aspects of London life, it was the infinite diversity that Booth found intriguing. The enormous variation in trade union strength was particularly striking. In some industries unions failed to develop any foothold; in others the boss did as he was told. One of the largest employers of skilled labour in the book trade, for example, considered himself in thrall to the gilders' union. 'The men come in when they like', he told Booth's assistant; he claimed that he 'cannot say anything to them as they can go and get work elsewhere'.[83] His experience was not unique. Small and exclusive craft societies, like the Spanish and Morocco Leather Dressers, guarded the mysteries of the trade to the bafflement of observers and employers alike. 'It's a marvel the leather trade', wrote Duckworth, 'it's that peculiar … The masters don't know how things are got up, and the men won't tell them.'[84]

Employers, though wary of trade union power, were not uniformly hostile. The most common contemporary objection to trade unionism was that it stifled initiative, restrained output and made industry and employment vulnerable to foreign competition. Management practices, in reality, were more varied than employer attitudes. Apart from the process of economic development and the level of technology, much depended upon the size of firm and its labour and product markets. The contest between capital and labour was conducted principally in workshops and petty manufactures. The small master, the typical London employer, operated a simple management structure. In consumer goods industries, like footwear, furniture and clothing, where once-skilled crafts had broken down into a set of semi-skilled processes, workers were subject to close personal supervision. In family firms these supervisory roles were often shared among the proprietor's relatives. In workshops other than sweat-shops effective management was generally vested in the foreman.

The division of labour as described in the Booth notebooks was not a static one. Chief among the changes recorded was the decline of the London artisan. Competitive pressures, provincial and foreign, which had earlier led to the relocation of some crafts and the destruction or degradation of others, continued to erode the capital's manufacturing base. High overheads and falling prices intensified the search for cheaper methods of production. Cost-cutting measures within the existing division of labour included the manipulation of manning ratios and wage payment systems, speed-up, overtime and casual labour. New technologies in some cases sharpened the contest for control.

Shopfloor responses were carefully documented. Some trades surrendered unconditionally. Clerkenwell watch makers, in the face of American competition, vacated the mass market or shifted to repair work. Sail makers succumbed without a fight. Book binders, though more resilient, were still downhearted. The eight-hours movement, contrary to expectations, gave them little relief from employer pressure. 'The eight hours has brought with it more oversight and time is more closely kept', said the secretary of the Vellum-Binders Society. 'The employers have gained by the change.'[85] Compositors were more combative. The issues raised by the introduction of the Linotype machine and the strategies pursued over its manning and regulation fill many pages in the Booth notebooks.[86]

The unskilled were no less prominent. The industrial survey, conducted during the economic downswing, when the shock waves created by the dock strike had subsided, supplies a unique portrait of the New Unionism in the depression of 1892–95. The Industry Series was itself a response to the New Unionism. Booth was prompted to extend his inquiry in order to take account of the renewed signs of hope embodied in that extraordinary creative upsurge in the sweated trades and on the waterfront at the close of the eighties. His intention, from the outset, was that the inquiry would be union-led and worker-centred.[87] The unexpected capacity for organized and disciplined action displayed by hitherto unorganizable elements gave evidence of a peaceful outcome to the Labour Question. Booth wanted to know more about them and the possibilities which their action had created. That the downward extension of trade unionism was a progressive force he had no doubt. Booth, indeed, viewed organization as an antidote to that 'helplessness' which he identified as a defining characteristic of 'sweating'. The diffusion of trade unionism, he told the Royal Commission on Labour, was among the most powerful of the convergent influences by which the social problem would be solved.[88]

Booth's thinking in this, as in other respects, was not static. As class fears subsided, his horizons widened. The contrived classification of the East London survey, having identified a basis for policy in the connection between the system of employment and poverty, figured less prominently as the perceived need for action diminished in intensity. The focus of the inquiry shifted thereafter towards an exploration of the inner life of the working class. Booth, though conscious of his position as a man of the middle classes, came to the recognition that, as Gareth Stedman Jones puts it, 'the working class was not simply without culture or morality, but in fact possessed a culture of its own'.[89] The mapping of that culture and the preservation of the charts remains one of his greatest achievements.

Conclusion

'None of the writers ... including Mr Booth himself, seems to be aware of the value of detail in describing a place or scene. For lack of it they hardly ever succeed in calling up a definite picture before the mind, and that is rather a pity.'[90] To a Victorian audience accustomed to the sensational low-life studies of Manby Smith, Sims or Sala, Booth's matter-of-fact prose may well have seemed remote, impersonal and drab. The *Saturday Review*'s criticisms of the Life and Labour inquiry have nevertheless retained their currency. Modern scholars in search of an authentic working class find it equally deficient. Mayhew's work, we are told, is more lively and more 'scientific'.[91] There is indeed undeniably a disjuncture between the buttoned-up Booth of the printed survey – very grave and very eminent – and the more approachable Booth of the unpublished notebooks. Booth's rejections of the structures and strategies employed in *London Labour and the London Poor* served to differentiate his survey from that of Mayhew, and to impress the reader with its scientific detachment, system and rigour.[92] The curiosity and commitment, enthusiasm and energy, sympathy and humanity, so evident in the notebooks and manuscripts, were all concealed within a set of literary devices that distanced the author and acted as a barrier against reader involvement with the subject of the text.

Booth, like Mayhew, applied a camera technique to the presentation of his findings. The effect, though, was not entirely to his liking. Whereas Mayhew sought to convey his impressions through a narrowing focus, Booth could manage no more than a static image that faded quickly. In the industrial sphere, he confessed, developments had been so rapid 'as to have, perhaps, rather blurred the picture of some of the trades we have studied; disturbing the "instantaneous" character of the "photograph" which we have tried to produce...'.[93] Booth produced a set of snaps which conveyed size, scale and variety but not individuality. Direct quotation and the reproduction of idiomatic expression or the use of dialect – strategems which might so easily have relieved the oppressive weight of detail and humanized his findings – were applied sparingly. It was as though Mayhew operated a zoom facility and Booth a box camera.

Impressions deceive. The Booth of the notebooks, the unknown Booth, presents a less aloof form of inquiry. Unconstrained by the reporting conventions of Victorian social science, the notebooks show us a privileged collective trying to overcome the burdens of birth, rank and property. Not that their prejudices were conquered; rather they were contained so as to enable them to record faithfully the work situation of labouring London, its rewards and satisfactions, and its hopes and fears. The notebooks, in fact, are far more engaging than the published text. Generalization rendered in a passive voice gives way to contemporary profiles in specific settings, generally reported in the first person, which are full of interesting detail and display a sensitivity to the language and sentiments of working people. Booth's associates, though neither shy nor retiring, were by no means predictable in their interventions. We find them evaluating both the data and substance of the survey and also responding to individuals in ways that reinforce our involvement with them. For all the attempts to attain uniformity and comparability, the notebooks remain highly personal documents. Variations in handwriting and syntax, and other idiosyncracies, all serve to enliven the text and assist identification with interviewers and respondents. The notebooks are also a forceful reminder that, notwithstanding assertions to the contrary, Booth did not rely on a door-to-door poverty census, but acquired information in a manner not dissimilar from Mayhew. As Anne Humpherys so rightly observes, 'Booth's ... notebooks have much of Mayhew's quality of vividness, immediacy, and preciseness'.[94]

There are other similarities. Booth, though more careful in writing up his findings, shared with his predecessor a common commitment to empirical inquiry based upon observation and classification. The flaws, too, bear ready comparison. Neither discovered an effective format for their enquiries. Mayhew's belief in the possibilities of a scientifically sound representation of the social order based upon the largest possible number of direct personal testimonies made his project unmanageable and defeated him in much the same way as it defeated Booth. The interviews and investigations that filled the latter's notebooks were too rich and too many to capture in cold print. Slippage was unavoidable and the prose uncontrollable. Time and again the project ran away from him, as earlier it had run away from Mayhew. *Life and Labour of the People in London* expanded through three editions with differing methods, changing objects and much rearrangement of contents and chapters in what was, ultimately, a futile attempt to devise a satisfactory means of reporting its results.

Questions of identity and status were inseparable from survey investigation as practised by the Mayhew and Booth inquiries. Both were conscious of the social distance that separated the well-fed classes from the labouring poor, and both devised stratagems for its reduction. The hindrance to personal understanding that prompted Booth to take lodgings in the East End and Beatrice Potter to take work as a trouser hand, made even greater demands on Mayhew who, with minimal preparation, found himself required to make sense of a world from which reason, it was supposed, had fled. His struggle for self-control and mastery of class prejudice constitutes one of the heroic themes of his survey. Mayhew, though, was not uniquely close to working people. The interview-based form of inquiry required an unusual curiosity and sensitivity which is also found in Booth and his associates. The achievements of working-class culture and its possibilities for further progress impressed Booth as earlier it had impressed Mayhew. Both found much that was admirable in the institutions and values of skilled workers and both were repelled by the social wreckage below them.

Mayhew's position as an expert on social questions, however, was much less secure than that of Booth or his acolytes. Although Booth harboured doubts about his status among professional statisticians, his expertise was widely acknowledged. His methods and procedures were challenged, but not his integrity. The want of specialization and an alleged want of character denied Mayhew a similar standing.

Mayhew drew no distinction between his serious investigative journalism and other writings. The serialized version of *London Labour and the London Poor* thus carried advertisements for the part issues of a novel, co-authored with William Cruikshank, on the Great Exhibition, and also informed readers of *Mr Mayhew's Spelling Book for the Working Classes*, 'explaining the sound meaning and derivation of the Greek, Latin and Saxon words of the English language' issued in eighteen one-penny parts.[95] Mayhew, as a littérateur and journalist, was, in fact, as well known for his non-sociological writings as for his survey research, and was particularly well regarded as a young people's author. 'No writer could have treated the story more successfully than he has done,' ran the review of his *Young Humphrey Davy* in 1855. In respect of this literary genre, declared another, Mayhew was the equal of Miss Edgeworth.[96] His travel writings were scarcely less popular, *The Upper Rhine and Its Picturesque Scenery*, being listed 'among the best gifts of the season'.[97] His works of social inquiry, by contrast, were compromised by his earlier associations and practices. Mayhew found it difficult to live down his reputation as a writer of comic stories and farces, who resorted to scissors-and-paste methods and took as much care with the truth as he did with other people's copy.[98]

Booth will also stand comparison with Mayhew in terms of ideas. In some respect they were remarkably similar. Both were sceptics in regard to political economy. Both felt that it was in need of revision and each hoped to supply some of the necessary empirical data for that purpose. Both became protectionists. Neither was a socialist. Each was convinced that theoretical and social requirements could be satisfied without the wholesale transformation of property relations. In both cases the rejection of political economy was partial. The utilitarian cast of their social analysis, above all its underlying hedonism, gave their social policies a repressive aspect that was separated more by degree than kind. Mayhew's opinions on the poorest elements were not significantly different from Booth's. Their terms varied but not the substance. Booth's distinction between the self-supporting or 'true' working class and the outcast poor would not have seemed odd to the author of *London Labour and the London Poor*, who never used the term 'residuum' in his writings but applied an equally vivid degenerationalist vocabulary to the depiction of its condition. Mayhew also accepted the case for special action outside the Poor Law and found nothing objectionable in the suggestion that 'habitual vagrants' should be placed under police supervision.[99] For habitual criminals he was even more severe. 'Transportation I think very valuable to old and confirmed offenders, people who are called vagabonds, and who have certain primitive notions of society upon them,' he remarked; and added, 'I think it is for the good of society to get rid of such people, and send them into a primitive country, where vagabond habits are consistent as it were with liberty.'[100]

Booth was equally tough on the poor. But, as José Harris suggests elsewhere in this volume, his support for labour colonies for the segregation of the inefficient elements, was more a *cri de coeur* than a programme for action. Booth's emphasis upon the structure and workings of the labour market does, however, indicate a strategic dimension to his thinking which is distinctive. The repudiation of Malthusian economics pointed him towards the possibilities of state intervention to relieve exceptional pressure in the metropolis. Booth's proposals for the decasualization of dock labour and support for non-contributory old age pensions together represented a coherent plan for the rationalization of the labour market and removal of the residual elements from it. Mayhew, though he too had broken with general theories of over-population, found it difficult to think of social advance in other terms.[101] His analysis of the operation and overstocking of the London labour market, for all its remarkable insights and understanding, yielded no specific proposals for reform and reorganization. Mayhew fixed upon the formation of the outcast poor, Booth upon its reduction.

Mayhew's best work was completed before political and economic changes and the erosion in orthodox economics had begun to influence social theory. Booth's work, by contrast, is best viewed as part of the reconstruction process that followed the displacement of classical economics. Positivism, along with Liberalism and Idealism, brought a new optimism to the possibilities of working-class advance. An industrial system of unlimited potential, and a working population capable of being made rational moral beings, presented possibilities for progress which had earlier seemed unimaginable. The dock strike, demonstrating the existence of a reserve power of corporate action among the unorganized, served, if anything, to confirm this prognosis. Booth's expectations were unfounded. Trade unions were not engines of moral growth. His faith in the possibility of improvement, though, remained undimmed. In this, too, he and Mayhew were more alike than is sometimes imagined. Social inquiry and social action were in both cases bent towards the creation of self-disciplined citizens from unrestrained low-lives.

Notes

1   'The Late Mr Henry Mayhew', *Illustrated London News* (6 August 1887), p.158 Cf. 'Mr Henry Mayhew', *The Athenaeum*, (6 August 1887), pp.181–2. Athol Mayhew's promised 'Life and Times' became *A Jorum of 'Punch'* (1895), an unsatisfactory volume that centred on Mayhew's early career.

2   *The Athenaeum* (6 August 1887), pp.181–2. The connection is not fanciful: see Yeo, Eileen (1973), 'Mayhew as Social Investigator', in Thompson, E.P. and Yeo, Eileen (eds), *The Unknown Mayhew*, Penguin, pp.100–01. Some continuities are also identified in Keating, P.J. (1971), *The Working Classes in Victorian Fiction*, London: Routledge and Kegan Paul.

3   *Red Republican*, No.21, (9 November 1850), p.168.

4   Hutchin, T.W. (1960), *A Review of Economic Doctrines, 1870–1920*, Oxford University Press, p.33; Razell, Peter (ed.) (1980), *The Morning Chronicle Survey of Labour and the Poor*, 6 vols, Firle: Caliban (hereafter MCS), 1, p.113. See, too, comments of 'A Working Tailor' in *Red Republican,* No.23 (23 November 1850, p.178; Answers to Correspondents No.11, 22 February 1851) (printed on wrapper of *London Labour and the London Poor*, BL pressmark), 8276c.55.

5   BLPES, Passfield Papers, Beatrice Webb's (Manuscript) Diary, August 1887.

6   Anon (1890), 'Life and Labour in East London', *London Quarterly Review*, 24, p.316.

7   Glass, Ruth (1955), 'Urban Sociology in Great Britain', *Current Sociology*, 4, p.43; Dyos, H.J. (1967), 'The Slums of Victorian London', *Victorian Studies*, 11, p.13; Harrison, B. (1987), 'London's Lower Depths', *New Society*, November, p.638; Smith, F.B. (1979), 'Mayhew's Convict', *Victorian Studies*, 22, pp.431–48; Himmelfarb, Gertrude (1984), *The Idea of Poverty: England in the Early Industrial Age*, London: Faber, pp.212–370.

8   See Humpherys, Anne (ed.) (1971), *Voices of the Poor: Selections from Mayhew's Morning Chronicle Letters*, London: Frank Cass; Thompson, E.P. and Yeo, Eileen (eds) (1973), *The Unknown Mayhew*, Harmondsworth: Penguin; Neuberg, Victor (ed.) (1985), *Selections from London Labour and the London Poor*, Harmondsworth: Penguin, pp.12–23; Razzell, Peter (ed.) (1980), *The*

Morning Chronicle Survey of Labour and the Poor, 6 vols (Firle: Caliban).

9   Yeo, 'Mayhew as a Social Investigator', p.84; Yeo, Eileen Janes (1991), 'The social survey in social perspective, 1830–1930', in Bulmer, M. et al. (eds), *The Social Survey in Historical Perspective, 1880–1940*, Cambridge, p.53.

10   Thompson, E.P. (1973), 'Mayhew and the *Morning Chronicle*', in *The Unknown Mayhew*, pp.9–55.

11   On the popularity of *London Labour and the London Poor* with middle-class philanthropy, see Jones, Gareth Stedman (1971), *Outcast London, A Study in the Relationship between Classes in Victorian Society*, Oxford University Press, p.10; on the non-engagement with the insensitive Mayhew, see Yeo, 'The social survey in social perspective, 1830–1930', p.54.

12   Mayhew, Henry and Binny, John (1862), *The Criminal Prisons of London*, Griffin Bohn and Co.

13   Williams, Karel (1981), *From Pauperism to Poverty*, London, Routledge and Kegan Paul, p.238.

14   *MCS* I, p.40.

15   Williams, Karel, *From Pauperism to Poverty*, p.247; Humpherys, Anne (1977), *Travels into the Poor Man's Country*, Athens: The University of Georgia Press, p.49.

16   *Morning Chronicle*, 18 October 1849.

17   Mayhew, Henry (1861), *London Labour and the London Poor*, 4 vols, Griffin, Bohn and Co. (hereafter *LL&LP*), 1, p.15.

18   See *MCS*, I, pp.34, 36.

19   See Mayhew and Binny, *Criminal Prisons of London*, pp.454–5.

20   Answers to Correspondents, Nos.6 and 9; Thompson, 'Mayhew and the *Morning Chronicle*', pp.46–7.

21   Mayhew, Henry (1864), *German Life and Manners*, 2 vols, London, 1, p.118.

22   *MCS*, 1, p.111.

23   Yeo, 'Mayhew as Social Investigator', p.71; Humpherys, *Travels into the Poor Man's Country*, p.40.

24   Evidence of Henry Mayhew, *Second Report of Select Committee of the House of Commons on Transportation* 1856 (296), XVII. qq.3504, 3742,

25   *MCS* 1, p.170.

26   *MCS*, 1, pp.170, 199–202.

27   *MCS*, 2, pp.89, 93.

28   See Raphael Samuel (1973), 'Mayhew and Labour Historians', *Bulletin of the Society for the Study of Labour History*, No.26, pp.47–52.

29   Answers to Correspondents, No.50, 22 November 1851.

30   Answers to Correspondents, No.14, 15 March 1851.

31   *MCS*, 1, pp.51–63.

32   Mayhew's criminological writings have not received systematic treatment from historians of crime or from students of social theory; the former are either uncritically enthusiastic or cautious and dismissive; the latter unware of the possibilities for further inquiry.

33   *LL&LP*, 3, pp.430–9.

34   J.B. Say, for example, is sometimes cited for his social observation rather than his economic theory. There are also references to Wakefield's work on co-operation, though it is not clear whether he read them in the original or at secondhand in J.S. Mill's, *Principles of Political Economy* (1909), Longman, pp.116–17.

35   Answers to Correspondents, No.22, 27 September 1851.

36   Answers to Correspondents, No.10, 15 February 1851.

37   Mayhew, Henry (1851), *Low Wages*, pp.36–51.

38   Answers, No.16, 29 March 1851.

39   The psychologistic approach is well illustrated by Kershen, Anne J. (1993), 'Henry Mayhew and Charles Booth: Men of their Times?' in Alderman, G. and Holmes, C. (eds), *Outsiders and Outcasts: Essays in Honour of William J. Fishman*, London: Duckworth, p.100; the methodologically-centred approach is exemplified in the work of Karel Williams, *From Pauperism to Poverty*, pp.237–77.

40   Williams, *From Pauperism to Poverty*, pp.257–8. It should be noted, though, that Mayhew did sometimes attempt to locate the theory of overwork outside the skilled trades: see, for example, *LL&LP*, 2, pp.216–60, 297–338.

41   Jones, Gareth Stedman (1984), 'The Labours of Henry Mayhew, "Metropolitan Correspondent"', *London Journal*, 10 (1), 1984, pp.80–5.

42   *LL&LP*, 2, p.236. On Mill's view of Chalmers, see Mill, John Stuart (1909), *Principles of Political Economy*, Ashley, W.J. (ed.), p.75.

43   Answers to Correspondents No.11, 22 February 1851.

44   *LL&LP,* 1, p.2.

45   Herbert, Christopher (1991), *Culture and Anomie: Ethnographic Imagination in the Nineteenth Century*, Chicago and London: University of Chicago Press, p.208.

46   *MCS*, 1, p.52.

47   Reference to Chadwick's report, include, *LL&LP,* 369, 376–7; on the primacy of the pleasure principle in education, see Mayhew, Henry (1842), *What to Teach and How to Teach It*, London, p.18.

48   See Society for Promoting the Amendment of the Law (1856), *Three Papers on Capital Punishment*, London, pp.32–61. On his familiarity with associationist psychology, see Mayhew, Henry (1847), 'What is the Cause of Surprise? and What Connection has it with Suggestion?', *Douglas Jerrold's Shilling Magazine*, 6, pp.561–4.

49   No.9, Answers to Correspondents.

50   *MCS* 3, pp.43–4.

51   Mayhew, *Criminal Prisons of London*, p.408.

52   *MCS* 4, p.135; repeated in *MCS*, 3, p.35.

53   Mayhew, *Criminal Prisons of London*, p.454.

54   On Mandeville's social thought see the excellent assessment by Goldsmith, M.M. (1985), *Private Vices, Public Benefits*, Cambridge: Cambridge University Press.

55   Mayhew, *Criminal Prisons of London*, pp.455–6.

56   *LL&LP*, 3, pp.432–3.

57   On Mayhew and Evangelical effort, see Thompson, E.P.(1967), 'The Political Education of Henry Mayhew', *Victorian Studies*, 11, pp.23–30. Quotation from Mayhew, *Criminal Prisons of London*, p.390.

58   Mayhew, *Criminal Prisons of London,* p.421.

59   Mayhew, *Criminal Prisons of London*, pp.421–2.

60   *MCS* 3, pp.42–3.

61   Mayhew, *Criminal Prisons of London*, p.431.

62   *MCS*, 4, p.135; Mayhew, *Criminal Prisons of London.*

63   *Poverty*, 1, p.6.

64   *Poverty*, 1, p.33.

65   *Industry*, 1, p.11. The contribution of the School Board Visitors is further considered below.

66   Brown, John (1968), 'Charles Booth and Labour Colonies, 1889–1905', *Economic History Review,* pp.349–60; Himmelfarb, Gertrude (1991), *Poverty and Compassion. The Moral Imagination of the Late Victorians*, New York: Alfred A. Knopf, p.122.

67   Hennock, E.P. (1976), 'Poverty and Social Theory in England: The Experience of the Eighteen–Eighties', *Social History*, 1, pp.75–6.

68   *Poverty,* 1, p.165.

69   Himmelfarb, *Poverty and Compassion*, p.98.

70   Booth, Charles (1897), *Life and Labour of the People in London*, 9 vols, Macmillan, 9, p.159.

71   Booth Collection, A23, fos 49–50, memorandum for Mr Maddison 1892/3. Mayhew had earlier requested trade societies to submit 'a brief account of the experiences, privations and struggles of those working men whose lives have been unusually chequered and the publication of which is likely to prove interesting or useful to their fellow workers or the public generally' (Answers to Correspondents, No.6).

72   B95, fos 8–11, 190–22.

73   B96, fo.66.

74   B84, fo.1.

75   Parliamentary Papers (1892), *Royal Commission on Labour: Minutes of Evidence*, Group 'C', [c.6708–vi], (35) q.8,932.

76   B96, fo.5.

77   Kahn, Robert L. and Cannel, Charles F. (1968–79), 'Interviewing: Social Research', in Sills, David L. (ed.), *International Encyclopaedia of Social Sciences*, 18 vols, Macmillan, 8, 149. See, too, Hyman, Herbert H. (1954), *Interviewing in Social Research*, University of Chicago Press, 1954. Quotation from Booth Collection, B95, fo.47.

78   B84, fos 44–6.

79   B93, fos 39–40; Booth Collection, A20 [section 48]. Replies to Questionnaires, fos 3, 7; [section 41], fo.74.

80   See Booth's evidence, Parliamentary Papers (1895), *Royal Commission on Labour*, Group C [c–6708–vi] (35), qq.8,921, 8,936–8,940. Cf. Thompson and Yeo, *Unknown Mayhew*, p.105.

81   A23, fo. 41, Harry Gosling, Secretary of Amalgamated Society of Waterman and Lightermen, to Jesse Argyle, 11 November 1895; A39, [section 7], fos 11–14, Ernest Aves to Charles Booth, 25 April 1902.

82   B96, fos 12, 19, 27, 42.

83   B101, fos 90–1.

84   B95, fo.45.

85   B101, fo.27.

86   For an attempt to set some of the general issues within a comparative context, see Harrison, Royden and Zeitlin, Jonathan (eds) (1985), *Divisions of Labour, Skilled Workers and Technological Change in Nineteenth-Century England*, Harvester.

87   Parliamentary Papers (1892), *Royal Commission of Labour*, Group C, [c–6708–vi] (35), q.8,932.

88   Parliamentary Papers (1893–4), *Royal Commission on Labour*, Group C, [c–7063–i] (39), qq.5,409,5,418, 5,462–5,464, 5,608–5,611, 5,686–5,688.

89   Jones, Gareth Stedman (1983), 'Working-Class Culture and Working-Class Politics in London, 1870–1900: Notes on the Remaking of a Working Class' in Jones, Gareth Stedman (ed.), *Languages of Class: Studies in English Working Class History 1832–1982*, Cambridge University Press, p.183.

90   'Life and Labour in London', *Saturday Review*, (6 October 1894), pp.386–7.

91   Humpherys, *Travels into the Poor Man's Country*, pp.135–44. The 'scientific' status of Mayhew's work has, however, been vigorously contested: see Himmelfarb, *The Idea of Poverty*, pp.312–62.

92   See, for example, A5B, fo.79, press-cutting from *Pall Mall Gazette*, 31 July 1891.

93   *Industry*, 5, p.78. See, too, Llewellyn Smith, H. (1929), 'The New Survey of London Life and Labour', *Journal of Royal Statistical Society*, 92, p.531.

94   Humpherys, *Travels into the Poor Man's Country*, p.221.

95   Answers to Correspondents, No.9.

96   See review of Henry Mayhew, 'The Wonders of Science or Young Humphrey Davy' in *The Athenaeum* (15 December 1855), p.1464; also review of 'The Boyhood of Martin Luther' in *The Athenaeum* (30 May 1863), p.714.

97   *The Athenaeum* (19 December, 1857), pp.1581–2.

98   See unsigned review of *London Labour and the London Poor* in *The Athenaeum* (15 November 1851), pp.1199–201.

99   *LL&LP*, 3, pp.373–4.

100   *Select Committee on Transportation,* q.3516.

101   In his conflict with the Ragged School Union in 1850 Mayhew had argued in favour of a state-assisted scheme of educational and industrial training 'connected with a plan of systematic emigration which would secure honest employment in other lands for those who cannot find it here', *MCS* 4, p.78.

5 Interviews and investigations: Charles Booth and the making of the Religious Influences survey

Rosemary O'Day

Between 1889 and 1903 Charles Booth published the seventeen substantial volumes which together form his study of *Life and Labour of the People in London.* The work which went into this publication began in 1886 with the district inquiry into the extent and nature of poverty. It is this first series on poverty which has in the main commanded the attention of scholars, who have on the one hand sought to evaluate Booth's methodology and on the other used his 'evidence' to support their own arguments about the problem of poverty in late Victorian London.[1] Important though this work is, it is unfortunate that the remainder of Booth's published work has been comparatively neglected. There were no fewer than seven volumes in the Third Series covering Religious Influences. The purpose of this series was very different from that of the earlier Poverty Series and its methodology was differently conceived and practised. Religion, like poverty, was a central concern of Victorian social observers and investigators: if it were for this reason alone, the nature of Booth's religious survey deserves attention. But more than that, this series also represents Booth at the height of his powers; if we wish to study Booth's developed methodology then it is with this last work that the scholar must be concerned. He advanced no further.

It is vital to establish both Booth's purpose in making the study of religious influences and the methods which he employed. Here the historian has a rare advantage. Not only do the seven published volumes exist, but so do many of the notes and papers and much of the correspondence that was collected during the years 1897–1902 and from which Booth wrote his account. These papers enable the historian to gain a unique insight into the making of the survey and to check at first hand Booth's methods for accuracy, reliability and representativeness.[2]

Extensive work on the manuscript collection and on the printed volumes suggests that this exercise, difficult though it is, is essential. It also indicates that scholars would be unwise to use the printed texts as opposed to the manuscript collection. Here is a case where 'the historian must go back to the sources'. Previous assessments of the

Religious Influences Series restricted themselves to a study of the printed volumes.[3] As we examine both the results of the survey, as reported in the notes of the interviews, and the printed account of 'Religious Influences', we can see how Booth, and to some extent his associates, planned the survey and how when they wrote about it they came up against its limitations and tried to resolve the consequent problems. The printed volumes hide 'a multitude of sins'; they also hide a multitude of virtues. At first reading, the Religious Influences Series seems to provide an admirably straightforward, authoritative and lucid account of religious influences in the metropolis. Compared with the notes of the survey, it appears both so much more than that and so much less.[4]

Booth, his associates and his family, were not forthcoming regarding the planning of the Religious Influences Series.[5] Scholars previously have been forced to rely upon Booth's brief description of the survey and its rationale in the printed text. When Booth wrote his Religious Influences Series (which was first published in 1902/3) he felt able to impose a grand plan upon his work on the *Life and Labour of the People in London*. According to this account he had sought to 'enumerate the mass of the people of London in classes according to degrees of poverty or comfort and to indicate the conditions of life in each class'.[6] He had mapped out the streets and plotted the distribution of the various classes. This, together with information concerning the education of the people, formed the First Series on Poverty. Eventually he had used the 1891 Census and reclassified the people according to the occupation of the head of the family 'from top to bottom, testing poverty by the degree of crowding in their dwellings and wealth by the number of servants employed'. In the Second Series on Industry he included with this industrial tabulation an account of the conditions of labour in each group of trades.[7] Booth recognized that he had then achieved his original goal but he was not satisfied to leave matters there, 'for just as life day by day is conditioned by the character of the home, the opportunities of education or recreation and the chances of employment, so there are other social influences which form part of the very structure of life, and some account of them is necessary to complete the picture of things as they are. Among these influences Religion claims the chief part'.[8] The seven-volume Religious Influences Series, as he describes it, represents the fruits of his investigation into the influence of 'organized religious effort in all its forms' and, to a lesser extent, the influence of 'other organized social and philanthropic influences', of the work of local government and the police.

In the printed text, it is clear what Booth was and was not attempting to do by the time that he *published* the Religious Influences Series. He was not pretending to present a detailed account of institutionalized religion in the capital. He was not pretending to discuss matters of religious truth. He was striving rather to describe the *influence* of organized religion upon the people of London. He thought that he was describing 'things as they are'. He dissociated himself from any attempt to explain the nature of this influence, to compare the present situation with the past, or to predict the way in which matters were moving. 'My concern in the matter of religion is solely with the extent to which people accept the doctrines, conform to the discipline and share in the work of the religious bodies, and with the effect produced, or apparently produced, on their lives.'[9] The books speak of the participation of the people in organized religion, not specifically of the work of the ministry.

So, four or five years after the work of the survey was undertaken, Booth described in print the research methods employed to elicit such information. 'We have endeavoured to see, and with comparatively few exceptions have seen, all the responsible heads of Churches of whatever denomination. The account of their work, its successes and failures, forming the basis and material of this work, is contained in written reports of nearly 1,800 personal interviews, of which 1,450 were with the direct representatives of religious work and nearly 350 with other authorities.'[10] By any measure, this was an amazing accomplishment. The reports of the interviews are a veritable gold-mine for the historian: it is the precise nature of the nuggets yielded by this mine which is in dispute.

This was, however, an after-the-event account of his motivation in organizing the survey. And it has many defects as a description. Booth faithfully if briefly described the methodology which was employed in the fieldwork. Yet, in the printed text, he gives no detailed description of the interviews or of the types of questions posed by his interviewers. Moreover, he does not necessarily tell us what questions were in his mind when he initiated the survey – only what questions seemed important to him by 1901–02. We are left with a number of unanswered queries. What form did the interviews take? Did Booth initially have in mind a more elaborate schema for his research which would enable him to discover answers to the questions he posed in the printed volumes, or did he truly believe that the research methodology he employed would suffice? Did he indeed set out in 1897 with the questions in mind which he posed in the printed books?

This article represents an attempt to ascertain what Booth originally set out to discover about religion in the metropolis when he initiated the survey in 1897. It consists of a detailed analysis of the surviving reports of his fieldwork. This represents a necessary step towards a comparison of Booth's research and writing on the subject of religion in London.[11]

1   Fieldwork

Fortunately, we are able to reconstruct the fieldwork methodology in some detail. Booth did not conduct all the interviews personally although he was himself involved. He had a team of select men, who without exception had worked for him before on the earlier surveys and who appear to have been both remarkably skilled in encouraging interviewees to talk freely and profitably and notably perceptive in their assessments of human nature. They were Ernest Aves, George Arkell, George Duckworth, Jesse Argyll and Arthur Baxter.[12]

Booth describes how the 'team' surveyed one area of London at a time: 'We have moved our camp from centre to centre all over London, remaining for weeks or even months in each spot in order to see as well as hear all we could.' London was for this purpose divided into districts dictated by its urban development and not by religious concerns at all. The first camp was set up in London north of the Thames in 1897–98. Beginning with the far eastern corner of the Isle of Dogs the team moved 'along the metropolitan border by way of Poplar, Bromley, Bow and Hackney to Islington, St Pancras, Maida Vale and Hampstead'. This constituted recently built London. Next the camp moved to the 'inner ring' between London north of the Thames and the City boundary. 'Here' said Booth 'old purposes and needs have given way to new, and destruction and rebuilding go on apace.'[13]

There followed the West Central district and then the 'West End of wealth with its rapidly filling hinterland of Hammersmith and Fulham'. The team moved on to the south of the Thames to 'trace the extension of London southward over outward and outermost rings of population, stretching from Roehampton on the extreme West to Eltham on the extreme East'.[14]

Booth approached the appropriate religious authorities to gain their support for the venture. This was duly given. A surviving open letter from Mandell Creighton, Bishop of London (1843–1901) shows that he requested all the clergy in his diocese 'to assist him willingly and to the utmost of their power'.[15] The Bishop of Rochester also instructed his clergy to co-operate.[16] Herbert, Cardinal Vaughan was apparently even more forthcoming: on 2 May 1897 he wrote to Booth recommending that 'At Spitalfields, St Anne's Underwood St, Father

Walters would give much information concerning the district.' After giving other names he provided Booth with certain statistics regarding the work of the Catholics in the metropolis.[17]

Then letters were sent to every minister and missionary working in London, inviting them to co-operate with Charles Booth's inquiry by granting an interview. It was with relative ease that the clergy of the Church of England were identified (using official listings).[18] It was presumably rather more of a task to identify other places of worship and their ministers. It is one of the great strengths of Booth's survey that it allows us to identify and locate geographically all the places of worship in London at the turn of the century and to list ministers working in them.[19]

2   Interviews

One of the most innovative features of Booth's developing survey methodology was his appreciation of the importance of a structured interviewing technique and his refinement of the method over the years 1886–1903.[20] His faith in his method of collecting information probably arose from his long-standing involvement with Royal Commissions of Inquiry, which relied extensively upon interviewing 'experts' to ascertain 'facts'. To appreciate fully the use of interviews in his work on religious influences, it is necessary to explore a little his earlier forays into interviewing. 'The root idea with which I began the work was that every fact I needed was known to someone, and that the information had simply to be collected and put together.'[21]

As a result, he organized in-depth, lengthy interviews of sixty-six School Board Visitors working in the East End of London to obtain information regarding the conditions of life pertaining to those families with school-age children with which the visitors were constantly in contact. When the scope of the survey was extended to include all of London, the interviewing technique was retained but modified in length for practical reasons. Our knowledge of this early technique is mainly derived from the interview notes.[22] One or other of Booth's secretaries visited a School Board Visitor and noted down particulars of the condition of life of the children on the street by dividing them according to class. Beatrice Webb commented: 'On the few occasions when I attended these interviews it was enlightening to watch how Charles Booth, or other of his secretaries, would extract from the School attendance officer, bit by bit, the extensive and intimate information with regard to each family, the memory of these willing witnesses amplifying and illustrating the precisely recorded facts in their notebooks.'[23] The information thus obtained was recorded in what was intended to be a systematic and comparable manner (although uniformity and comparability were not achieved). While it was acknowledged that the interviewees possessed individual bias, it was believed that this bias could be ironed out by the interviewing of such a large cohort and by techniques of accounting. Following the recording of the numerical data, the interviewer noted down the 'general character of the street', based upon the opinion of the School Board Visitor and the interviewers' assessment of its reliability. Thorough interviewing provided the basis for the Second Series on Industry. The surviving notebooks suggest a structured approach to these interviews.

The idea behind the earlier surveys was by interviewing a few hundred people to obtain accurate information regarding millions. This did not mean that he worked with a random sample of the 'people'. He stayed with structured interviewing of persons in authority. Moreover, if Booth was attempting from the start to establish the influence of religion upon the people, he rejected even the census method. Why did he interview ministers? Encounters with ministers of religion yielded much information about 'their work, its successes and failures', but interviews with the people themselves would have yielded much more about the impact of organized religion upon the lives of Londoners. Booth relied heavily on the former, not at all upon the latter. Unfortunately Booth does not discuss his reasoning. We are left wondering whether he was simply unaware that there was a methodological mismatch between the evidence he sought and the source he used, or whether when he set out in 1897 he was contemplating writing a detailed and critical survey of the work of the ministry in the metropolis. There appears to be some indirect evidence that the latter was the case: for some reason Booth changed his mind about what he was trying to write.[24]

When Booth came to work on the religious life of London he had had a good deal of experience of field survey work – over ten years to be exact – and had clearly learned a lot from this work. His initial cartographical plotting of poverty had been based on statistical and other materials provided to his interviewers by School Board Visitors supplemented by reference to the Census and other authorities. During work on the poverty survey Booth's assistants were constantly developing their methodology: the early street notebooks bear little resemblance in their layout and arrangement of contents to the later street notebooks. It was, of course, essential that Booth and his assistants should modify their methods of data collection when they discovered the deficiencies of their existing system, but there were clear problems when it came to compiling the descriptive account of poverty because the data were not collected in a uniform fashion. In the end Booth hid the problem from the public eye by printing only sample streets in the volumes and, otherwise, using only aggregate figures. When it came to his work on religion, Booth made every effort from the start to produce a uniform approach and uniform data.

Much attention was accorded the form of the interviews which were to provide the basis of the survey. With the original letter of invitation was sent a printed schedule of questions: this was to act as a checklist of the issues to be covered by the interview. Although interviewees were not requested to complete the form, many in fact did so and some survive in the notebooks, replete with information.[25] This printed pro forma or schedule for the interviews was produced at headquarters at 8 Adelphi Terrace, The Strand, before any interviewing began. The schedule was in several parts. Which sections were used would depend upon the interviewee and the interviewer. A minister would be sent Schedule A if he belonged to the Church of England; Schedule B if he were a Nonconformist or Catholic. Initially these schedules were broadly similar but by 1900 there were considerable differences. Moreover, if the interviewer felt that the minister had particular knowledge of, for example, local government, he might return on another occasion with a separate schedule to provide the structure for an additional interview.[26]

As can be seen from the questions on the schedule presented to the ministers, Booth was asking for information of a statistical nature: how many clubs are there? how many people attend them? how many people attend morning and evening service? how many people attend weekday services? how many celebrations of the communion are there? what are the average figures of communicants? how many paid workers are there in the parish? how many people are visited? how many children attend Sunday school? what proportion of the parish are touched by the work of the church or chapel?

The questions relate to the formal activities of the church and the extent to which the population at large participates in them or is impinged upon by them. There are no questions relating to the effectiveness of these activities in terms of the spiritual life of the participants. What is asked for is an indication of formal participation in the life of the church. There are no attempts to acquire information about the spiritual life of those people who do not attend church or chapel or participate in the church's social round.

Scholars have accepted Booth's printed statement that religious influences were not susceptible to statistical analysis.[27] He might have concluded this in 1902 but the records of the fieldwork suggest that, if he believed this in 1897, he organized his research in a very strange way. Whatever else, there can be little doubt that when Booth designed the survey he intended the information collected by his associates and himself to be comparable. The questions which were posed and the replies collected cried out for quantitative expression.

There is other internal evidence of the care with which the interviewing programme was designed. Whatever the defects of the interviewing technique, Booth tried to impose uniformity of approach upon interviews undertaken by different members of the team. Neither does the form of the interviews suggest an unsophisticated approach – he was not simply casting his net and trawling for any fish in the vicinity. To state that Booth's Religious Influences Survey was fundamentally flawed and ill-conceived displays an ignorance of the working papers of the survey.[28]

Some individuals were clearly irritated by the increasing number of requests for similar information from many sources. The Reverend S.F. Bridge, Vicar of St Paul's, Herne Hill, wrote back in unpromising terms, 'Dear Sir, As you have the consent of the Bishop of Rochester and Southwark I suppose I must consent to see your representative ... but I am weary and sick of the incessant "numbering of the people" for one cause or another'.[29]

In the great majority of cases an interview was granted, however. Such an interview normally lasted up to two and a half hours (sometimes much longer) and involved intensive questioning and frantic note taking. When the fieldwork had just begun, one of the associates commented on the inordinate length of time 'which it is necessary to give an interview if each of the questions is to be adequately dealt with'. After two hours interviewing the Reverend A. Chandler of All Saints, Poplar, only the end of the church questions had been reached and the general questions had to be crammed into half an hour. 'Unless some means is taken to shorten the matter to be dealt with I foresee difficulty in getting clergymen to give us the necessary time, and I shudder to think what will happen with men who are inclined to be "gassy".'[30]

The extent of co-operation at the interviews varied, as the above interviewer recognized. George Arkell observed: 'Though perfectly polite Mr Ramsey [of the Emmanuel Congregational Church, Barry Rd, Dulwich] was less cordial than is usual with our interviewees. He came in with that air of having little leisure which is always ominous, and it was difficult to get much from him.' When asked for a copy of the year book he replied, 'I think not, it is strictly for private circulation among members'.[31] Help sometimes came from unexpected quarters. When Aves finally interviewed Bridge he found to his surprise that 'the whole of Mr Bridge's growl had found expression in his postcard. Face to face he was very friendly, and genuinely interested moreover in the Inquiry'.[32] But even where the interviewer does not comment in his report upon the co-operativeness or otherwise of the interviewee, the interviews themselves yielded information of variable detail and quality. In some cases this may have been because the person interviewed was unforthcoming or ill informed. Baxter commented that Mr Bedford of All Hallows, East India Docks, 'has been but a very short time in the parish – since November 1896 – and ... therefore did not ask for information on many of the general questions'.[33] When Duckworth interviewed T.D. Bell, Secretary of Camberwell Green Congregational Church, he did so because 'we were passed on to him by the present pastor of the Church (Mr Stephens) on the ground that he as an old church member would know more about the work than Mr S. who had only come 7 months ago'.[34] When Mr Nelson was interviewed, he gave 'the impression of not knowing his district very thoroughly', whereas Vere Barley, Curate to the Revd J. Parry of Bromley, although only there for eighteen months, 'during that time ... has evidently got a thorough grasp of his district'.[35] Perse Hewlett of St Luke's, Millwall, filled in the form and sent it back, 'but I fear is not anxious to meet us'.[36] In general, the interviews conducted with Anglican ministers seem to have been most detailed and extensive. Occasionally someone warranted two visits: Mr Neil of St Matthias, Poplar, was interviewed twice.[37] Because the Anglican clergy might be expected to have information on all parts of parish life and not simply the congregation, they were relied upon for more basic and general information than were, for example, the Methodists, who gave information predominantly about their own congregational experience. This is only true in general – there are instances of lengthy and detailed interviews with members of the leading denominations and with schoolmasters, missionaries and so on. Some variations doubtless occurred because the interviewer was more interested in what one individual had to offer than another. When an interviewee proved particularly useful the interviewing team were keen to exploit the opportunities. For example, W.G. Martley of Poplar Charity Organization Society was interviewed by Ernest Aves on two days using schedules D and E.[38]

* * *

What types of information did the interviews yield? What kind of data did the associates consider it important to record? Clearly it is impossible to give more than a flavour of the results of the 1,800 interviews. Nevertheless, it is important to appreciate both the enormous richness of the archive produced and the categories of evidence which the team thought it important to collect. These might provide indicators of the type of study which Booth initially hoped to produce. There are problems in analysing the interviews. What we have in each case is a *report* of the interview and not the interview itself. The interviewer appears to have taken verbatim notes of the interview and these were then worked up into a carefully tooled report shortly thereafter. Sometimes written notes presented by the interviewee were included: the Reverend A.W. Bedford, Vicar of All Hallows, East India Docks, 'had prepared written notes which I have incorporated in the following report' wrote Baxter.[39] The notes were written up under headings – largely but not exclusively provided by the printed schedules. The schedules formed a skeleton for the interview but we shall never know how closely the interviewer stuck to their letter when questioning the subject. In other words, there are few direct clues to interviewing 'technique' in the reports. We shall never know 'how' the interviewers framed or phrased their questions, or whether they recognized that such factors might influence the replies they received. We do not know the extent to which they were aware of, and reflected upon, the influence which they might be exercising upon the interviewees. The 'chemistry' between interviewer and interviewed might be obvious to us as we read the reports, but how aware were Booth and his associates of its power?

Faced with an absence of direct evidence we are forced back upon the indirect. Although the interview reports do vary enormously in length, detail and coverage, they follow a sufficiently similar layout to make internal analysis of one interview worthwhile. For this purpose I have selected an interview with the Revd H.Q. Mason, Vicar of St Stephen's, North Bow, on 12 and 13 May 1897, using schedule A.[40] The structure of the report, while not necessarily of the interview, broadly speaking follows that of the schedule, although additional material is included. The report begins with a record of the name and status of the subject and the date and location of the interview. There follows a brief description of the interviewee, including his age, the length of his service in this place, and his previous experience. This is followed by a mediated response to the first question on the schedule: 'What is the general character of the population?'. 'Movement of the better class away, mainly out further East, and the advent of a lower class a very noticeable feature', represents a summary of the subject's reply. The interviewer similarly reported Mason's comments on the portion of the population touched by the church's ministrations, illustrating with statistics that 'the constant change [is] a serious difficulty in carrying out the work of the parish. You can't make it permanent or go "deep"'. Mason's information concerning the persons employed by the church and their respective duties (in response to question 3) is duly recorded along with a response to question 8 concerning the work of visiting. Information elicited by questions 4, 5 and 6 is noted. Then the interviewer appears to have departed radically from the schedule. He apparently asked Mr Mason what was the 'Fundamental aim' of his ministry: 'Mr Mason said that it was by the medium of personal contact to exercise an influence "for good". The Church and the home are the two great centres of work. He upheld the "pastoral" idea. Regards himself as a kind of "spiritual official". He is put there by the law of the land and "offers" what he can from the point of view of the national church.' '"I try and do two things: to teach men to fear God and honour the King. If I succeed in that, I don't think that I can go far wrong."' (There is evidence from other interviews in the book that this question was at least occasionally posed. 'I tried to get from Mr Noyes what his aim is but without any great success; the fact is that he has no particular aim' was the astringent comment about the pastorate of Revd J.P. Noyes of All Hallows, Bromley).[41] Later another leading question was put to Mason. 'Asked about the present high-church tendencies said that he anticipated a reaction. Extreme people on both sides are doing a great deal of harm, the ultra Protestant no less than the ultra-Anglican. As regards the latter thinks that in the long-run "people won't stand tom-foolery".' Bow itself is old-fashioned. Its traditions have been evangelical for 150 years. The patrons are evangelical. But still a great change has come over the services.' (Other interviews suggest that a range of supplementary questions might be posed: for example, Adamson of Old Ford Church appears to have been asked what were the 'special difficulties presented by his parish' and to have used the opportunity to compare his situation with Mr Sweetnam's, in Victoria Park.)[42] The report of the Mason interview then returns to the skeletal outline of the schedule, with replies to questions 7, 8, 9 and 10 and the general questions and headings. These are quite informative and include Mason's opinions on a number of issues, including the collapse of nonconformity and its loss of ministers, marital habits and the conduct of local clergy in competing for marriage fees. It would be instructive to compare the use of the schedule by different interviewers.

There is internal evidence that Booth instructed his associates to acquaint him with the people they were interviewing through the medium of their interview reports. Most reports commence with a thumbnail sketch of the minister. These are often very skilfully drawn and reveal much about both the interviewee and the interviewer. Duckworth described the Pastor of Kenyon Baptist Church, Clapham: 'Mr Douglas is an old man, tall, stoops rather, white silky hair and beard, old fashioned, a scholar and an unmethodical dreamer between 60 and 70 years of age: with a very pleasant voice.'[43] The deacon of Denmark Place Baptist Chapel provided a stark contrast. Forty to forty-five years old, of middle height, he possessed a 'clean shaven chin, dark fringe of whiskers joined to one another by his moustache', was 'a clerk in an office in the Smithfield meat market' and had 'no ideas but plenty of facts'.[44] Duckworth's personal prejudices sometimes emerged very clearly. Dracup, the Superintendent of the Hope Mission, Camberwell, had, Duckworth thought, 'the agreeable manners of a shop assistant'.[45] 'Mr Champion is a young man of the most pronouncedly "goody goody" type who was obviously predestined by his temperament and a wretched constitution for some minor part in the religious world', he wrote of the minister of the Primitive Methodist chapel on the Crystal Palace Road. He was, thought Duckworth, more suited to a small mission for 'he has only been in the ministry for 18 months: already he has broken down and ... looked wretchedly ill'. 'Poor gentle Mr C himself would be as likely to "touch" the average public house loafer (with which his area was filled) as to move a sea anemone from its rock by the power of his preaching.'[46] Linnecar, pastor of the Mansion House Mission on Camberwell Road, 'drops his h's freely, and talks with a distinct American twang when excited. Calls himself the sailor preacher and dresses in blue serge with a double breasted coat ... He certainly does "make a Jorkins of the Almighty" but his genuineness prevents him from even seeming to be profane ... Here is a man of the people, paid by the people, who reaches of the people. Is it only by such as him that they can be reached?'[47]

Why was this information thought worthy of record? We are faced here with much more than a group of late Victorians with an urge to demonstrate their powers of literary description. Such thumbnail portraits were intended to facilitate recall of the interview at a later date. They would familiarize Booth with the character and background of interviewees he had not met as a means to assess the nature, bias and reliability of the evidence supplied. They would provide Booth with the kind of personal detail he might require when later writing up the material.

There is even more to these sketches than this. The shape of the reports suggests that Booth and his associates were anxious to record their considered assessments of the nature of the individual ministries in which these men were engaged. The face and person of the man was regarded as a real guide to character and worth. In the absence of a sketch pad or a camera, these descriptions were the associates' method of conjuring up the physiognomy of the men concerned. We note that George Nelson of St Michael's, South Bromley, was an Irishman 'with a slight brogue' and that 'his face is of a type more common in the RC than in the English church'; that A. Wentworth Bennett, Curate in Charge of St Gabriel's, Poplar, was 'mean and undistinguished in appearance with an excellent face for a low comedian ... (unremarkable but) quite a good fellow: a fair average specimen of the average man'.[48] The Revd E.C. Mackenzie was 'probably not a brilliant scholar or a deep theologian, but full of energy and enthusiasm, and just the sort to be popular with working people, and especially perhaps with the boys. His manner is as frank and open as his face'.[49] Baxter confirmed the opinion of the one 'black sheep among the clergy of the district' of the Isle of Dogs, the Revd C.S. Coldwell, by commenting that he was 'a tallish man with an amiable, rather weak face'.[50] Sometimes the interviewer was aware that the face and manner of a cleric were deceptive, as with the Revd W. Adamson of Old Ford Parish Church: 'As you talk to him you are in doubt as to whether he is a saint or a fraud and you incline to the former. But the latter would seem to be nearer the outside judgement. It is in any case difficult to imagine that this low-toned gentle faced divine is the quarrelsome he seems to be.'[51]

The physical portraits of the interviewees merge imperceptibly with on the spot assessments of the character and efficacy of their ministries. Ernest Aves summed up the Revd S.F. Bridge, Vicar of St Paul's, Herne Hill, as a 'sturdy, capable, strong-willed old gentleman of sixty or so', adding, 'There is something of the magnate about him, nothing new fangled. "On whose authority is relief given", I asked. "On mine" was the reply. "I am Pope in that, although not in a great many other things." But, parochially, he probably rules throughout, a solid man with solid services suited to a solid congregation'.[52] The interviewer of J.P. Noyes of All Hallows, Bromley, saw him as 'youngish':[53]

> ... languid in manner and lethargic in temperament, a gentleman and quite a pleasant fellow but devoid of energy, enthusiasm or spontaneity. He is a type of man who has entered the church mainly from a feeling of unfitness for anything else. His position is probably due to interest rather than to merit. He is a man of some private means, with friends outside who also help him with funds.

The associates, who certainly took seriously their mission to collect comparable quantitative information regarding the activities of the various churches and missions, took no less seriously a responsibility to record their own impressions of the approaches and attitudes of London ministers to their life's work. For example, when Aves interviewed Father Benedict Snow, priest of the Lordship Lane Roman Catholic Church in 1900, he was as interested in Snow's response to anti-Papist feeling as in the number of attendants at mass. Snow, who was 'full of friendliness, lunch and wind', 'belched good humour', and accepted that his church could expect only to cater for an established Catholic population: '"There are three high Anglican churches in the neighbourhood, and to come to us would be like going to a little Dissenting Chapel. Besides we are upstairs. Looks like a trap, a Papist trap" he added with a smile, and is clearly no proselytizer.'[54] The assessment of the Revd J. Parry of Bromley was acerbic: 'It was not his object to absorb the nonconformists but if they went to the wall!! Mr Parry is doubtless strictly Darwinian as regards the conflicts of the churches.'[55]

Detailed and often highly critical assessments of the ministries of the men involved are coupled with perceptive comments concerning the difficulties of reaching the people. Ernest Aves' meeting with the uncommunicative wife of Mr G.W. Beale of the East Dulwich Church, Arnott Road, forced him to conclude that she is 'uninteresting and uneducated. She is the President of the 'Ladies' Christian Association of the chapel and we can probably measure something of its vitality by hers' – a sad state of affairs when her husband 'is engaged in some business of his own during the day and is away regularly from 10 to 7'.[56]

It is tempting but mistaken to regard such material as mere 'colour'. The dominance of the assessment element in the interviews provides convincing evidence that the team were setting out in the first instance to compile extremely detailed dossiers of the work of individual London ministers, which would form the basis of the printed assessment of the efficacy of their work. Such dossiers would contain comparable quantitative material on the activities of the church, chapel or mission concerned, but they would also contain information concerning the peculiarities of the parish or congregation, and the problems thereby presented to the ministers, and concerning the approach and efficacy of the ministers in tackling such problems. The interviews and the reports based upon them thus involved a considerable critical input from the investigators themselves.[57]

The interviewee was encouraged to talk. The associates were of approximately the same class as the ministers with whom they conversed; they found relations generally easy and friendly and managed to convince each interviewee of the importance of the evidence he was giving. His opinions, his approach, and his attitude to his work, were as important to the interviewer as were statistics of church attendance. In the notes, the comments of the interviewee were taken down verbatim and some were repeated in the reports. Clearly the interviewer was selective: there is no transcript of the entire interview; he simply picked out what bits of the conversation seemed most interesting either to himself or to the survey or to the interviewee. For example, when the Revd W.A. Carroll of St Frideswide's was interviewed, the report noted that 100 people attended the Wednesday sermon, including the cleric's verbatim comment: 'they do crave so for sermons even if they are utter rot'.[58] Later in the same report we read that Carroll 'tried at first to cooperate with Labour Party: was a pupil of Scott Holland and came here from a West End parish "a tearing socialist", but has completely gone round; with few exceptions the labour men are "more selfish than the most old-fashioned Tory". (Scott Holland is a theorist only: "he does not know the working man a bit")': '"he regrets"' that the clergy '"should have to do so much which is really Laymens work, and which is done badly by the clergy, just because they are parsons and have not time to do it properly"'.[59] The interviewer was picking out from the body of the interview what he considered to be *significant*. This involved a decision-making process and the use of criteria to which we are not made privy. This raises the whole issue of bias and of the nature of the interaction between interviewer and interviewed. Booth nowhere discusses this element in his investigative technique. What we have in the reports are (a) comparable quantitative information provided by the ministers in response to the heads on the schedule; (b) the minister's opinions; (c) the associates' impressions and assessments of the minister and his work in the metropolis.

The information contained in the reports is rich and varied in character. In their pages the researcher can find evidence of the religious, social and charitable efforts of almost every place of worship in London. There are copies of parish magazines, year books and service arrangements. There are detailed accounts of some missions, clubs and congregations. There are verbatim comments from clergymen of all denominations displaying their attitudes and their awareness of the problems of their work. Scholars are able to use these riches for a multitude of purposes, but we must hold on to the idea that the interview reports represent carefully tooled analyses of the efficacy of the ministries involved. Consciously or unconsciously, they do not provide objective data; neither do they supply simple evidence of the attitudes of the men involved.

When Charles Booth reached the stage in his researches of beginning to write up the results for publication he asked his 'secretaries' to produce reports that summarized their findings for each district. These summaries still exist for some areas and they demonstrate what it was that the secretaries thought that Booth was after – critical accounts of the organized Christian ministry in the metropolis, expressed in general terms but with detailed and specific supporting evidence.[60] Duckworth commented on the potential effectiveness of the ministry of St Mark's, Whitechapel, in damning words: 'In view of the staffing of the church, the idea that it can have any important local influence becomes either pathetic or absurd. Both the vicar and the senior curate ought to be superannuated, and the other curate is a converted Jew, whose work seems ineffective except with a poor class that can be bribed. And effectiveness of that kind ought to be described as failure.'[61] Neither were the secretaries afraid to name names:[62]

> In the whole of Whitechapel there is no parson of mark. Nonconformity's weak everywhere, and among the clergy, while there are capable and vigorous men like Davies and Rust; good men like Draper and Allen, there is also the badly placed man, in Bayne (except that he is fairly tolerant of, and quite friendly to, Toynbee Hall); the genial absentee failure, in Bourchier, and the man who ought to be superannuated in Davenport. Take them all in all and I think one has to admit that the Establishment is but indifferently well served in Whitechapel.

Duckworth went to pains to expose in detail the misuse of the Children's Holiday Fund at St Paul's Church, Whitechapel.[63]

The interviews that Booth's team conducted were complex. They attempted a compromise between precision and richness. The schedule or questionnaire was constructed to provide readily comparable factual and statistical data about religious activity; the easy-going purposive conversation with the representatives of the churches on their home ground was designed to elicit their attitudes and to permit the observant associates to make assessments of their pastoral performance. So while it may in a sense be true that Booth's was the first attitudinal survey, the interviews yield much more diverse categories of data than such a description would suggest – statistics; assessments of the ministries of all the individuals concerned; the opinions of the individuals concerned; the 'expert' opinion of the clergy and ministers; the prejudices and preconceptions of Booth and the associates themselves. While we shall always be unsure of the extent of direction and intervention by the team, we can be certain that a form was imposed upon the interviews which shaped the findings.

From the full range of research papers – interview notebooks, secretaries' reports, Booth's digests and lists – we are able to discover what types of information Booth was seeking to elicit from the systematic interviewing technique he adopted. It remains for the scholar to compare the nature of this information with Booth's use of it in the printed volumes. We search there in vain for statistical data presented in comparable form for the various places of organized worship. Equally we search for and do not find a critical assessment of the organized Christian ministry in the metropolis, which employs detailed, specific information and names names.

APPENDIX*

A   The Church of England

Life and Labour of the People in London, Influences. (Mr Charles Booth's Inquiry)

1.   What is the general character of the population?

2.   What portion do the ministrations of the church touch?

3.   What persons are employed (stating duties and whether paid or not)

4.   What buildings are used? (including missions rooms, schools and clubs)

5.   What services or other religious meetings are held and by whom and how many attended?

6.   What social agencies are connected with the Church – institutes, societies, clubs, entertainments, meetings, etc.

7.   What Educational Work is done?

8.   To what extent are the people visited? (by Clergy or District Visitors)

9.   What arrangements are there for nursing the sick?

10.   To what extent is charitable relief given or administered by the Church?

General questions

Under what other religious, charitable or philanthropic influences do the people come?

What co-operation is there between the Church and other bodies?

Remarks with reference to the district are wanted on –

Local Government (including Poor Law Administration)

Police

Drink

Prostitution

Crime

Marriage

Thrift

Health

Housing and Social Condition generally

[signature]

[Where possible, a comparison should be made between Past and Present].

It is not intended that this Form should be filled up, but it may be found useful for making notes to an interview.

* This Schedule is taken from Booth Collection, B222, p.81.

Notes

1   See, for example, Jones, Gareth Stedman (1971), *Outcast London*, Oxford: Oxford University Press.

2   BLPES, Booth Collection, Series A and B; two of the projects of the Charles Booth Research Centre for the Study of Social Investigation at the Open University.

3   Simey, T.S. and Simey, M.B. (1960), *Charles Booth, Social Scientist,* Oxford: Oxford University Press. The Simeys took an unduly pessimistic view of the potential of the manuscript materials, p.71.

4   Such a comparison constitutes one of the major projects being undertaken by the Charles Booth Centre at the Open University.

5   Booth, Mary (1918), *Charles Booth: A Memoir,* London: Macmillan; reissued with a foreword by Ritchie, Margaret (1968), Farnborough. Booth, Charles (1902), *Life and Labour of the People in London,* Third Series, *Religious Influences,* London: Macmillan, Volume 1, p.3. The reader will find a detailed discussion of the planning and meaning of the Religious Influences Series in O'Day, Rosemary and Englander, David (1993), *Mr Charles Booth's Inquiry: Life and Labour of the People in London Reconsidered*, Hambledon, pp.161–98.

6   *Religious Influences*, 1, p.3.

7   *Religious Influences,* 1, pp.3–4.

8   *Religious Influences*, 1, p.4.

9   *Religious Influences*, 1, p.5.

10   *Religious Influences*, 1, p.7.

11   This major project forms part of the work of the Charles Booth Centre at the Open University.

12   *Religious Influences,* 1, Title page. Although Booth acknowledged their assistance in the survey, he reserved entirely to himself the task of writing the series. Work is in progress comparing the printed text with the digest produced by Booth's assistants.

13   *Religious Influences*, 1, pp.5–6.

14   *Religious Influences*, 1, p.6.

15   Booth Collection, A31, fos 1–2. References to Series A and Series B items in Booth Collection are henceforward referred to only by the prefix B and the item number, with page numbers where appropriate.

16   B305, p.29.

17   A31, fos 3–4.

18   e.g. B158.

19   e.g. *Religious Influences*, 1, pp.70–2 + map, supplemented by Booth's own lists in Series A.

20   The history of interviewing remains to be written. This article represents a contribution to such a history. There is an interesting discussion in Madge, John (1967), *The Tools of Social Science,* London: Longman, pp.154–253.

21   *Religious Influences,* Final Volume, p.32.

22   Series B, Notebooks 1–80; see also BLPES, Passfield Papers, Diary of Beatrice Webb for recurrent entries.

23   Webb, Beatrice (1971), *My Apprenticeship,* Harmondsworth: Penguin Books, p.239.

24   See pp.148–50. This, I think, explains why Booth's methodology seems 'extraordinarily ill-conceived for its purpose' to the casual reader.

25   A54, for example, contains numbers of schedules sent to South London nonconformist ministers and duly completed and sent in by them to Booth's secretaries.

26   The wording of the schedule, as taken from B222, is reprinted in the appendix.

27   Simey and Simey, *Charles Booth,* p.222.

28   McKibbin, R.I. (1978), 'Social Class and Social Observation in Edwardian England' in *Transactions of the Royal Historical Society,* 5th Series, Vol.28, p.176. 'The Religious Influences' section of Booth's *Life and Labour* is extraordinarily ill-conceived for its purpose, and its information is redundant to most questions the historian might wish to ask.'

29   B305, p.29.

30   B169, pp.1–4.

31   B306, p.7.

32   B305, p.29.

33   B169, p.168.

34   B304, p.53.

35   B175, pp.l81; 227.

36   B170, p.27.

37   B169; B170 see also, for example, interview with H.Q. Mason, Vicar of St Stephens, North Bow, 12–13 May 1897, in B175, pp.19–48.

38   B173, pp.15–47.

39   B169, p.168.

40   B175, pp.19–48.

41   B175, p.15; see also B175, p.95.

42   B175, p.159.

43   B304, p.1.

44   B304, p.83.

45   B306, p.99.

46   B307, pp.117–124.

47   B306, pp.11, 39.

48   B175, pp 117–18, 169.

49   B169, p.135.

50   B169, p.185.

51   B175, p.167.

52   B306, pp.29–31.

53   B175, pp.1–2.

54   B306, p.151.

55   B175, p.63.

56   B306, p.159.

57   On these problems and approaches, see O'Day, Rosemary (1988), 'The Men from the Ministry' in Parsons, G. (ed.), *Religion in Victorian Britain*, Manchester: Manchester University Press, 2, pp.259–79.

58   B175, p.l03.

59   B175, pp.113, 115.

60   Series A.

61   A39 (34).

62   A39 (8), p.39.

63   A39 (8), pp.37–8.

6 Women and social investigation: Clara Collet and Beatrice Potter[1]

Rosemary O'Day

At least five women investigators assisted Charles Booth in his monumental endeavour: Beatrice Potter, Alice Green, Clara Collet, Mary Tabor and Margaret Tillard.[2] In the late nineteenth century the new woman – educated, socially aware, and forceful – sought a channel for her energies. For some at least social investigation and social observation provided that channel.[3] The documentation exists to allow us to examine just what social inquiry offered two of Booth's female associates, Beatrice Potter and Clara Collet, and what they in their turn offered social inquiry. If Beatrice and Clara were not as unalike as chalk and cheese, then they were as dissimilar as gorgonzola and cheddar.

In *My Apprenticeship*, Beatrice Potter made much of her apprenticeship as an investigator under Charles Booth.[4] While historians and social scientists have noted this fact with interest, none has been concerned with the precise nature of the work she did for Booth and the manner in which she did it. The intention here is to reconstruct in so far as the record allows her work on the Booth inquiry between 1886 and 1888. Such an archaeology of her investigations makes clearer the nature of her relationship with Booth in the late 1880s and allows us considerable insight into the way in which the Poverty Series was researched. Hitherto the perspective on such matters has been largely that of *My Apprenticeship*, published some forty years after the event.[5] The account of her early experience in *My Apprenticeship* has not been rejected here, of course, but the early discovery by the present writer that there were differences between Potter's reconstruction of her work in that book and the contemporary record, has led to much greater reliance on the diary and upon the surviving records of the research itself. Similarly, the realization that there are important omissions and errors of transcription in the typescript diary has meant a return to the holograph diary on many occasions. This new study contributes considerably to our understanding of her experience, the influences upon her and her competence as a researcher in 1889, when she began work on her study of the Co-operative Movement in the company of Benjamin Jones. It allows us to focus more precisely upon that stage in her life where she rejected Charity Organization Society-style philanthropy in favour of social investigation. It is also a vital preliminary step towards an assessment of her findings and their place in Booth's survey.

The sources available for such a study are many and various. Beatrice Potter's manuscript diaries, Beatrice Potter's manuscript notebook of her investigations into the wholesale clothing trade, notes and reports in the Charles Booth Collection (Group A) and Beatrice Potter's autobiography (*My Apprenticeship*) have provided most of the material. One of these sources presents particular problems for the historian. The diary exists in four different forms: a holograph diary, two typescripts and a printed but edited version. Norman and Jeanne Mackenzie concluded that 'the typed versions differ from the original and from each other only in minor respects' which are 'simply errors'.[6] Most of the differences are probably of this minor variety but, from the point of view of this study, some of them are very important. Presumably because they were illegible or regarded as insignificant, most of the notes of Beatrice's researches are omitted from the typescript version and from the Mackenzies' edition. (The manuscript is often appallingly difficult to read.) Important material relating to the Jewish community in particular is omitted. It is, therefore, vital to refer to the holograph version of the diary. In the ensuing text, dates of manuscript diary entries are inserted in brackets after citations. Occasionally, where the date of the diary entry is unclear, a footnote gives the holograph volume reference with folio numbers to facilitate reference. Some of the material is also quoted in *My Apprenticeship*, but because Beatrice frequently altered what she had originally written, if only slightly, it is still preferable to refer to the manuscript diary. This diary evidence must be read in conjunction with that in Beatrice's work diary of her researches into the Wholesale Clothing Trade.[7] Because Beatrice never revised her contributions to the inquiry, citations from the printed articles on docks, tailoring and Jews are from the final (and only full) edition of *Life and Labour of the People in London*.[8]

Clara Collet too, though in a less public and less publicized arena, acknowledged her profound debt to Charles Booth. Hers is not a name that you will often find in the indices of books on nineteenth- and twentieth-century women. When she is noticed it is more often either as the close friend of the novelist George Gissing, or as a commentator on women's work in the early twentieth century than as a woman herself. Yet she is interesting in and for herself. She was, supposedly, the first woman to have gained an MA in Political Economy. She became one of Charles Booth's associates. She went on from there to the Labour Department of the Board of Trade, where she became a senior investigator, with an assistant of her own. She was for a time President of the Association of Assistant Mistresses and a Governor of Bedford College. Achievements aside, she was a fascinating person who expressed something of herself and the problems she faced in her personal as well as her professional life. While it is interesting for the historian to chart events and developments it is even more intriguing to see how particular individuals lived this experience.We are enabled, in a rather episodic manner, to discern how Clara discovered her own identity.[9]

Through this study of Clara and Beatrice we may profitably reflect on the dilemma before the historian as we seek to reconstruct the past from autobiographical and diary materials as well as from more traditional sources. This dilemma is not only, or primarily, whether the materials are available to reconstruct the past experience itself or merely the account of that experience as mediated by individuals. It involves considering the impositions which we as students of the past make upon the discourse of past people. And it involves determining how we employ a variety of different kinds of source (for example, in the case of Clara Collet, her own remembered personal history and her conscious and semi-conscious working out of her personal concerns in different types of writing, alongside empirically derived data, both by herself of working and studying women, and of the world in which she lived by the present historian). It involves examining the way in which we today impose a pattern upon what we have discovered. It involves matching (or mismatching) the Clara who reveals herself with the Miss Collet whom her contemporaries knew and the Clara Collet who emerges from a historian's acquaintance with the records of the Booth Inquiry and with the other people involved in it.

The Collet archive, while small enough, contains a wide variety of types of documentation – diaries, articles, a novel, statistical reports on women's work, and correspondence. In part, at least, this is the Clara who wants to be seen. Miss Collet flits across the consciousness of her contemporaries occasionally and briefly – as a part-time lecturer at Toynbee Hall, as the organizer of a meeting here and a meeting there, as Booth's capable researcher into women's work, as a woman friend, as a bossy relative, as a scholar mourned by colleagues. This is the mature Miss Collet, the outside Miss Collet. From the huge, amorphous archive of Booth's inquiry no one reflects or comments upon Clara Collet, but she emerges as one, if an important one, among many associates – a capable and acute investigator outshone if certainly not outclassed by Beatrice Potter.

This is the retrieved and retrospectively assessed Clara Collet – the important or unimportant Clara Collet.

The facts of Beatrice Potter's life have been rehearsed many times, not least by herself, and the reader is referred for them to her autobiographical account and to the many biographies which have appeared.[10] She came from an affluent and large family of ten daughters. The materially comfortable life she led derived from her family's business interests but contrasted sharply with her emotional deprivation as a child. She was largely self-educated and had had some experience of the world through travel and the conversation of family and friends who were steeped in politics and social activism. In the 1880s, however, family circumstances forced her into a more narrowly domestic life and affairs of the heart also brought her face to face with the whole issue of the proper place of a woman in society.

Clara Elizabeth Collet was born in 1860, the second daughter and fourth of the six children of Collet Dobson Collet and his wife Jane. In the eighteenth century the family had been very prosperous but had lost a good deal of money in India and elsewhere. When Clara's grandfather died young in 1829 he left six children in somewhat impoverished circumstances. Four of the children emigrated to New Zealand but Collet and Sophia stayed in England. Collet became editor of the *Diplomatic Review*, a small radical journal. Her mother ran a small laundry in North London. Although they kept at least one servant (a mark of membership of the middle classes) and sent their five children to good day schools, all the children were expected to work for their living and Clara at least seems to have helped in business, perhaps taking and delivering orders for her father's publications.

We first meet Clara on her sixteenth birthday, 10 September 1876. Her passion for reading was served by the presents she received from her family. 'Louise offers to give me *Wives and Daughters* but I have read it and shall ask for a book by Holme Lee. Wilfred is going to give me one of Black's or Heary's.' A year later Clara was to write, 'the most difficult thing in a diary is to write totally for yourself, try as hard as one will there is always *arrière-pensée* about what people would think if they read it. It has been so with me as almost my only idea is whether people will admire me, the consequences have not been beneficial to the truth of the record', and in truth the early part of her diary has a certain self-consciousness and artificiality. She records her industry, her wide reading, her pronounced opinions. 'Read Byron's Life.' 'He was bad but he is the only person that I ever loved (whom I am not personally acquainted with). I hate his prisse [prissy] prig of a wife with all my heart and all my soul.' 'I swear by all I ever swore that I will never of my own free will read a page of that detestable hound Leigh Hunt.' 'I must study up *Richard II* by myself. It is my duty and I will.' 'Read *For Ever and Ever* by Florence Marryat. Very bad indeed ... I was quite rejoiced when they all came to grief they were such idiotic people. I won't waste my wallible [valuable] time over her again.' 'Actually did a little of *RII*. Read Hollinsheds account. Either those people hasperated their haitches where they ought not to be or they did not where they ought. Henry IV must have had horrible taste to dress in green and black.' 'Read some of J.S. Mill; he is dull and no mistake.'

But through the pages of the diary we catch a glimpse of the day-to-day doings of a schoolgirl at the North London Collegiate School, then situated in Camden Road. And she is *by no means* dull. Travelling to school on the train daily, pursuing a wide curriculum, doing three hours' homework a night (to take more than that time signifies a 'duffer'), going on occasional educational visits – a trip to South Kensington Museum with Miss Buss was 'dreadfully instructive. Very few things that I cared about except the machine for measuring the intensity of thought', spending her evenings reading or, in the absence of a book, retiring early to bed, entertaining friends to tea, taking singing lessons and attending musical evenings and reading parties.

Her family, and therefore Clara herself, moved in that shadowy Grub Street world of which we as historians know far too little. She toyed with becoming a writer herself and at one point wrote a ghost story which she was advised to submit to a magazine for publication. What became of it we don't know. She displayed considerable interest in the literary and dramatic activities of her relatives and friends. Her Aunt Sophy had once stayed for a weekend with Louisa M. Alcott and family, and also knew Emerson. Collet Dobson Collet, in addition to editing the *Diplomatic Review*, had once sung in the chorus at Covent Garden. Her father was a friend of Karl Marx and had published some of his articles in the *Free Press*. Clara was very close to his daughter Tussy (Eleanor) (who was, incidentally, also an acquaintance of Bernard Shaw at this time and a friend of Beatrice Potter somewhat later). Through Tussy, Clara also knew Clementina Black.[11] Clara idolized Tussy, five years her senior; she who was what Clara wanted most to be and was not – 'beautiful' in the eyes of most beholders. Lissagaray, to whom Tussy was secretly engaged, was 'not half good enough for her', and Clara privately wished he would commit 'forgery and suicide'. In 1877 the Marx family, the Collets and the Maitlands (Dolly and Clara and nameless male relatives), Edward Rose, the playwright, and Ernest Radford, formalized their earlier reading parties as the Dogberry Club. The Marxes were the moving spirits and most meetings took place at their home, 41 Maitland Park Road. Adults joined in too. Clara's father seems to have participated although there is no mention of Karl treading the boards. Instead, according to another member, Marian Skinner, he sat at the end of the long double drawing-room enjoying the proceedings. 'As an audience he was delightful, never criticising, always entering into the spirit of any fun that was going on, laughing when anything struck him as particularly comic, until the tears ran down his cheeks – the oldest in years, but in spirit as young as any of us. And his friend, the faithful Frederic Engels, was equally spontaneous.'[12] Clara recorded in her diary performances of *The Merchant of Venice, As You Like It* and *Twelfth Night*. 'Richard III read at the Marxes. Da good as Richard. Tussy perfect as Lady Anne. Ludovic Lorimer deservedly clapped as Edward IV.' By this time dramatics and playgoing were an established part of Clara's leisure. All the proceeds of the subscriptions for the Dogberry Club were devoted to purchasing tickets for Irvings' first nights. Over Christmas and the New Year 1877/1878 she and various members of her family and acquaintance saw numerous plays in the West End and Clara wrote critical review notices of all.

Already in her late teens, Clara was honing her not inconsiderable critical skills. Molière, Byron, Gaskell, Jules Verne, Mortimer Collins, *Paradise Lost*, Mrs Henry Wood and Goethe – all were read and commented upon. She, like so many of her contemporaries, made a point of producing swift pen portaits of any that she met, summing up in just a few well-chosen words both the physical attributes and character of the individual. 'Tussy was Rosalind to Mr Hill's Orlando. They both read very well. Mr Hill awfully tall and thin as a lamp post horribly small feet but he is clever and very nice for all that I think ... Mr Smith is a young man with more muscle than brain as he says himself. He looks very stupid but rather a good young man. Most good young men are stupid.' Already too she was particularly prone to comment upon the lives and experiences of women. On 8 October 1876 she heard a sermon on Anne Askew, the sixteenth-century Protestant martyr. When asked whether she believed that the wafer when blessed became the body of Christ, she answered, 'I believe that God made man but I cannot believe that man can make God.' 'Not bad for a woman', she added.[13] Thus early she was turning over in her mind ideas that emerged in her book on working middle-class women in 1902 – that women might be intellectually inferior to men, or at least, might mature intellectually somewhat later than men.[14] Her suspicion of the durability of male–female relationships showed itself in early September 1876 when she was on the way to school. 'Man in the train today who begged leave to open the carriage window in order to wave goodbye to his wife who was not up when he went away and who lives in a house facing the line.' 'People should always be attentive to their wives and not trample upon their tenderest feelings', he said when someone praised him for this consideration. 'I thought I should have laughed out right', wrote Clara. 'Wonder how attentive he will be two years hence.'[15] She prided herself upon her ability to detect character from appearance. When she visited a friend's house for tea she called for their family albums and proceeded to tell the character of everyone. Proudly she recorded, 'They said I told everyone correctly except one.' And, aside, 'personally I think I was correct'.[16]

In these early and detailed diary entries one detects no teenage moods, no conflict between the girl and her parents or her siblings. The only omission seems to be references to her mother. Was she still alive? Or was it simply that Clara had more contact with her father, with whom she shared interests? Her life seems crowned by success as she passes the London examinations in June 1878, the first to be open to both men and women.[17] Yet later Clara looked back and wondered, 'I wonder if I should have been better or worse if I had been happy and understood when I was a child. Probably not better.'[18]

Our knowledge of the second episode in Clara's life is again largely derived from her diary. The original of the diary exists alongside several undated typed versions. Of these more later. Aged nineteen, Clara became an assistant mistress at the newly founded Wyggeston Girls' School, Leicester, on Miss Buss's recommendation, at an initial salary of £80 – a prospect that in August 1879 she viewed with some trepidation. Leicester would be a far cry from London. 'I am not sure whether I shall like it, but I do know I shall like it better than being at home. The Marxes and Miss Oswald (her poetry teacher) are the only people I care for here.' She took with her a long list of addresses of people with whom to correspond but frankly admitted that she would probably write to hardly any on the list.

At this time Clara reflected on her diary writing. She was still writing for an audience but, this time, it was an unseen and unknown audience – an audience in her future, if and when she made her name and became 'interesting'. 'If I write about my own thoughts there will be one thing gained. I shall still be writing for people who may one day read my diary but it will be for people I do not know and who will only see it if my name becomes known; I could never bear people I know to read sentiment written by me.' There *is* much more emphasis upon Clara's feelings in this episode of her life and her diary.

Strange Leicester might have been, but Clara found it delightful. The working life and the social life which she describes is certainly very different from that she had experienced in London. Skating, swimming, tennis and dancing now form part of her staple diet. 'I was never so happy in any life before' she comments in April 1880, and contemplated that the ability to experience pain depended upon sensitization to pleasure. At first she worked hard and steadily towards her Intermediate Arts examination at London (then known as the first BA) which she took and passed in July 1879, and the final BA (known as the second BA) in October 1880. She was tutored by masters at the Boys' Grammar School in Greek and applied mathematics, but had to 'manage Latin and English subjects by myself'. Clearly she took her work with the schoolgirls in her charge seriously. Her subjects were mathematics and Latin and she noted down assiduously the academic problems and performance of her pupils. She began a debating society at the school: the first topic for debate was 'the occupation of girls on leaving school'. It went on to consider subjects such as capital punishment (11 to 7 against) and cremation (15 to 1 in favour).[19] And in April 1882, 'After tea we had games: amongst other things everyone wrote down a subject for a debate; they were mixed up, one paper given to each person who had to make a speech on the subject given him. Annie Cottrel started on women's rights (my subject) ... I had to discuss Love.' Outside school she was drawn into the world of the chapel and the Temperance Hall. Her family was Unitarian, although Clara seems to have attended other places of worship and to have associated a good deal with secularists. Even this early she was expressing religious views not unsimilar in kind to those of Charles Booth. 'I do believe that there is a divinity that shapes our ends rough hew them as we will.'[20] There was a serious side to her spiritual life. For instance, she records many sermons she heard and especially notes the solemn sermon preached on Darwin's passing in April 1882, when the funeral march was played.[21] There was a philanthropic aspect too. 'There was a mother's meeting and I waited at tea and had none myself.' But there was also a lively and increasingly absorbing social side which derived from this and into which she entered once she had passed her external BA at Bedford College, London. 'I had a good fit and went' to the socials held by Miss Gittins for the Sunday School Scholars 'in order to do good'; on the whole, she reflected, 'I think I have enjoyed them most'. At the first chapel social 'Miss Gittins read a paper on Lady Jane Grey, she did it splendidly and with such pathos that it was difficult to establish mirth afterwards'. On one occasion the topic at the social was anecdotes about dogs. A 'Jabberwocky' one Saturday night included poetry readings, music, epitaphs and essays on such subjects as the 'management of men at home' and the 'best ways to feel bored'. At several points she reports having enjoyed dancing at these socials with a variety of young men.

So interesting was her social life that she resolved to postpone studying for her MA indefinitely. In February 1882 she wrote, 'Last Valentine's Day someone sent me one Cupid breaking his bow at the sight of a lady graduate. "Love gives place to learning". I showed it to Mr Hopps who said the sender did not know me ...' and indeed Clara made learning give way at least to dalliance at this time. Her interest was roused by the three Ginson sons in particular – Sidney, Alfred and Ernest – athough other youths were marked out as attractive. All three were Unitarians like Clara and she met them through chapel activities. Sidney was involved in secularism and Clara found him and his conversation enthralling. Initially she had high hopes that Sidney would become her fiancé and he encouraged her with his attentions, but in March 'S.G. gave me his confession which I read on the way home by the light of the lamps. Our evening walks are over now *ainsi sort il*, and by November Sidney was courting Clara's friend, Polly Blackwell. 'Alfred does not make love to me a bit' she complained. She was less than enthusiastic about the youngest brother's attentions: 'Ernest Ginson has summoned up courage to put his arms around my waist and I nerved myself up to corresponding deeds of heroism.' And she made do with poor Alfred while clearly hoping that Sidney would see the error of his ways. As late as April 1883 she wrote of a trip out with the Social Evenings Group 'S.G. devoted himself to anyone but me.' It was not until Sidney announced his engagement to Miss Loribond in May 1884 that she finally gave up hope.

It is in the context of her social life and her romantic dreams that we should view Clara's despondency during the March 1883 to spring 1885 period, although the difficulties she experienced with her colleagues at the schools were also a contributing factor. She tells us rather less about these problems but they certainly complicated the decisions she made about where she should go next. The first outburst in the diary comes in March 1883. 'I have been indulging in a fit of hysterical crying tonight. I feel so perfectly wretched and miserable and hopeless and worthless.' She was busy working for an examination (perhaps to enter Girton College) but found studying impossible because of her unsettled state. 'The worry of school and the feeling of incompetence make me feel miserable.' 'I do wish I could go to Girton or University College or give up teaching or emigrate.'[22] Her inclination towards teaching was by no means strengthened when she gave a disastrous demonstration lesson at the North London Collegiate School before Miss Buss as part of her teacher's qualification.[23] Then her unsatisfactory relationship with Alfred Ginson gave her cause to reflect upon her situation more deeply in November 1883. 'I begin to feel more and more certain that so long as I live I shall never have any intimate friends and I know that I undoubtedly possess to a remarkable degree the faculty of offending nearly every one.' She was led to comment upon the relationship between her intellectual life and her personal life in a forthright manner. 'This is partly why I have decided to take to study as hard as I can, first, in order to ensure my always being able to hold a good position as a teacher', because she must always be independent in the absence of a supporting partner, 'and secondly to have something to fall back upon when life seems rather dismal.' This said, her future in teaching was uncertain. Work did not necessarily offer a path to happiness any more than did personal relationships either with men or female colleagues. She saw in herself a deep change. 'I think I am leaving off being a girl; the future does not look very bright and that is a pretty sure sign ... that I am losing the power of building castles in the air which has been my chief delight until now I think.' What should she do? Her future course is far from clear: 'How I shall turn out I don't know.'[24] Marriage with one she did not love was not a prospect she could embrace. She would control where she gave her friendship, whether to men or women. Life-long partnership to satisfy another's desires was not on her agenda. 'It is much better to live an old maid and get a little honey from the short real friendships I can have with men for whom I care myself than to be bound for life to a man just because he thinks he cares for me.'[25] Perhaps this was why she turned down the repeated proposals of marriage from one E.W. in the spring and summer of 1884. But the thought of a future bereft of personal relationships troubled her. She did not deceive herself that other activities would compensate or that she would feel whole. And in great measure she saw her inability to have such relationships as her own responsibility. 'With me it is sure to be accompanied later on by a feeling of depression at the thought of how wanting my life will be in the fulness of living owing to my own inability to care much for anyone but myself.'[26] She envied George Eliot her relationship with George Lewes.

The edited versions of this diary offer yet another Clara to the reader. Clara never wrote an autobiography as such. Yet the personal archive which she left her family and which is now housed in the Modern Records Centre at Warwick University shows her self-conscious attempts to 'remember' her experience and to organize it on paper in a way that would be meaningful both to her and to other women. Her diaries, even her novel and her statistical study of social novels all stand somewhere between 'text' and 'experience'. That she saw her diaries, in particular, as recounting a story that would be of general interest is indicated by her edition of part of them as 'The Diary of a Young Assistant Mistress, 1878–1885'. This typescript incorporated some additional material which Clara felt was important to her personal history and which she thought had unaccountably been omitted from the diaries. We might usefully draw a parallel between Beatrice Potter and Clara Collet here. Both women worked for Booth's Inquiry at the beginning of their 'working' lives and both wrestled, although in rather different ways, with questions relating to their identity as women as well as scholars. Beatrice Potter also had her holograph diaries typed up (this time by a secretary) and she modified the entries, usually by omitting material from the typescript. Then in 1930 Beatrice published an autobiographical work, *My Apprenticeship*, which selected and presented the material from the diaries. In the case of Potter, the historian's work in uncovering the experience of her early years is complicated by the fact that the modern editors of her diaries worked from the typescript and themselves omitted large chunks of material from them as a consequence.[27] What led Clara to make an edited typescript of this part of her diary? Perhaps she did it in direct response to the spate of such publications which appeared in the late 1920s by the likes of Beatrice Webb and Margaret Wynne Nevinson.

Clara, then, reworked her diary and her personal history. Obligingly she drew attention to some of her later additions to the text. The details of her appointment at Wyggeston are spelt out for the first time. The appointment gave her a salary of £80 plus the facilities to prepare for her intermediate and final arts examinations at the University of London. As already noted, she received some tuition at the Boys' Grammar School. She added the information that later, following her three week summer school at Newnham College in the midsummer of 1884, which she found 'all delightful', and her reflections upon her unsatisfactory personal and professional life, she decided to enter for an MA at the University of London. 'My diary makes no reference to my decision to go into residence in College Hall, London, in October 1885 to study at University College and take my MA degree in Moral and Political Philosophy (which included Psychology and Economics) nor does it mention that I told Miss ... I was giving up my post in July 1885; nor that notwithstanding this she raised my salary from £150 to £160.'[28] She entered College Hall, Gordon Square on 28 October 1885. This was her first residential experience of higher education and it was one she embraced with enthusiasm. Thus began a life of studying in the Round Room at the

British Museum each day; of reading Jevons' *Currency amd Finance* and Walker's *Political Economy* (a reminder here of the importance laid upon becoming acquainted with the ideas of the political economists); of rekindling her friendship with Tussy (now living with Ernest Aveling who had once taught Clara statistics); of dinners in college and conversations about philanthropic and investigative work in the East End of London and Soho.

Infuriatingly, Clara Collet's diary (and her typescript) give out for a period of some four years in 1886! She began work for Charles Booth in late 1888 (at the point when Beatrice Potter had declined to inquire into women's work and Mrs Alice Green had also backed out of the assignment) and she stayed in his employ at least until late 1890. But how she came to know Booth is a matter for speculation. Their paths may have crossed through the Leicestershire/Unitarian connection; through common connection with Beatrice Potter via Tussy Marx; through Clara's casual position as a lecturer at Toynbee Hall (and participation in the Toynbee Hall conference on women's work in November 1887) and her nodding acquaintance with Henry Higgs, the Le Playist scholar; or through the involvement of some of her friends at College House in philanthropic and settlement work in the East End and Soho.[29] In addition to producing studies of women's work and women's education for Booth, Clara worked for Graham Balfour's Battersea Inquiry in 1889–90 and for Booth's work on Poor Law Unions in 1890.[30] Her work on women and education was given a by-line by Booth but her work for Balfour and on the Poor Law Unions was unattributed and has come to light only through careful analysis of the Booth and Balfour notebooks and Clara's diary. Several of the Battersea notebooks were written in her hand and, characteristically, contained special comment upon women's lives. 'Have done the Ashby-de-la-Zouche workhouse, am just setting to work on elementary scholars in higher schools', she noted in November 1890.[31]

The picture of her that emerges from the records of the Booth Inquiry is very different from the picture she presents of herself as an investigator in the 1890 section of the diary. Interestingly it was Booth, not Clara, who was quizzed by A.J. Mundella before the Royal Commission on Labour in 1892 – this was not because she was a woman, but because as far as the outside world was concerned Booth authored the *Life and Labour*. But Booth gave generous recognition that the investigative work and the writing had been Collet's. Perhaps as a direct result of his recommendation, Clara was employed as one of the four Assistant Commissioners enquiring into women's home work for the Royal Commission on Labour in 1894. But the Clara of the diary is not the assured authority on women's work. She is an educated woman living a precarious middle-class existence through part-time teaching and research work. She sees the years since she left Wyggeston as years of 'real failure'. 'I have burnt my ships; I do not regret it, but I doubt whether I should have done it if I had known what it would be.'[32] 'This investigating work has many drawbacks and just now I feel thoroughly unnerved by the expectation of pinpricks. I would give it up and will give it up whenever I see a chance of earning a certain £60 even by lectures on economics.' 'Not', she continued, 'that I do not like the work when it is done or that I do not find a kind of enjoyment in the risk often involved in facing unknown people, but although I enjoy the personal contact with so many people I should never see otherwise, the work leaves no roots behind.'[33] Even her enthusiastic friend Clementina Black was depressed occasionally by the futility of her investigative work, and Clara was easily thrust into a slough of despond: 'What is the use of anything one does; why not let things slide altogether. Does anything matter? *Ecclesiastes* is my favourite book in the Bible.'[34] In part her despair had economic roots: 'gave five lectures on rent at Toynbee in Mr Higgs' absence … And what I am going to live on next year I don't in the least know'. This disparity between the confident, well-organized, working Clara and the depressive, despairing Clara should make us concerned about the status of our knowledge of the next phase in her working life, which at present is derived almost entirely from a variety of minutes, obituaries, and professional writings. A thorough examination of her correspondence with Gissing and Gabrielle Fleury and later parts of the diary may correct this imbalance.

Just a brief reference now to Clara's later career as a civil servant and professional investigator. In 1903 Booth recommended and secured for her a position as Labour Correspondent in the Board of Trade. Her recent publication of *Educated Working Women: Essays on the Position of Women Workers in the Middle Classes* (1902) in addition to her published work for Booth's inquiry made her amply qualified to do the work required. Like it or not, Clara was destined for the next twenty-seven years to investigate the working lives of women, and to be seen by the outside world for much longer than that as *the* early twentieth-century authority in this field. Today it is Clara's statistics which are trotted out by scholars to set the scene for discussions of women's lives between 1889 and 1930. Within this world she carved herself a professional niche. In 1917 she became Senior Investigator in the Labour Department and remained thus until her retirement in 1920. She was independent financially. By all accounts she would have liked to have been independent in other ways.

In 1910 she threatened resignation because her position prevented her speaking her own mind.

Clara did not fall into the trap into which many social historians are accused of falling – of treating 'women' as a general category and the experiences of individual women as 'a gender constituency which speaks for all women'. Her work as a social investigator, first for Charles Booth, and then for Hubert Llewellyn Smith as an investigator in the Labour Department of the Board of Trade, led her to acquire an enormous fund of 'facts' about working women in all walks of life and to reflect fruitfully upon their diversity of experience.[35]

The emphasis here has been upon the Clara of the two diaries and the Clara we learn about from her professional work as an investigator, first for Booth and then for the civil service. But there are, as intimated, other Claras. One of these was the Clara who filled her leisure time with 'business'. The Clara who was a founding member and President of the Association of Assistant Schoolmistresses; the Clara who was first an elected fellow of the Royal Statistical Society and then a member of its council; the Clara who was a council member of the Royal Economic Society and who organized an evening discussing the Webbs' *Industrial Democracy* to make the members read it; the Clara who sat on Trade Boards until she was in her seventy-fifth year. It was Clara Collet who in 1890 founded the Junior Economic Club at University College. 'All she did was done with zest', said one of her contemporaries. The friendships that she had formed with professional colleagues over the years – for example, Llewellyn Smith – provided her with some social and intellectual life outside her work.

Clara's one surviving attempt at a novel is intriguing. Brief and not very inspiring as literature, it focuses on the experiences of a small group of professional women – doctors and writers – and their attitudes to marriage and love both in the abstract and when face to face with them. Clara uses these women as mouthpieces for a variety of opinions, some of which closely echo those voiced by Beatrice Potter in her diaries and letters.

> 'It makes one quite hopeless for one's kind. Who will believe us when a girl like that goes straight over to the enemy at the first encounter?'
>
> 'Kate Gavin' replied Florence Douglas, 'she is engaged to be married.'
>
> 'She is not the first lady doctor who has done that you know,' said Miss Jenner reflectively, 'I shall never do it myself, and I am quite willing to admit that no one ever asked me to. And I must say it would be inconvenient to have a man in the house who was

perpetually wanting me or the servants to attend him. It would have to be the servants because really when I come back from my rounds I want a good rest. I just lie in the sofa and shut my eyes and forbid anyone to speak to me for a good hour ...'

Maggie, a young teacher, is made to say:

'It is what I have not had and never shall have that makes me sick of everything. Why did we never learn at Newnham that we should be women some day, not merely sponges to absorb knowledge and give it out again? Why were we such fools as to imagine that the study of science could ever satisfy us? How many men are satisfied with merely intellectual life. Why do we learn what makes life living so much later than other girls?'[36]

This is interesting enough, but it is what Clara has to say about the attitude of one of her chief characters who is prepared to marry without love just for security which reminds us of her own concerns when she was courted first by Alfred and then by E.W. Maggie 'loved the adoration that was offered her, which aroused in her a warm feeling towards the adorer which by many women is mistaken for love of the man himself instead'. She 'pictured a restful home of which she herself was the centre and the sun' yet she did not love Frank Rust. Marian, on the other hand, thinks this is gross selfishness and says 'It would be a dreadful thing to marry a man just to round my experience and to help myself realize myself *à la* T.H. Green. Dreadful for him as well as for myself'. Surely there is material here to flesh out an educated woman's quandary when faced with the desire to 'have it all' and to set against George Gissing's treatment of the *Odd Woman,* Clara Collet's perspective.

And her resolution of the plot when Marian, the plain heroine, is made beautiful both by the love of another and her own love for that other, seems to be an expression of Clara's obsession with physical appearance. One of her other short literary pieces is entitled 'The Beautiful Hester Mulso' or 'The Cultivation of the Mind' and it again, though this time through a treatment of one of Samuel Richardson's friends, makes the point that beauty is often 'apparent' rather than 'real'. Hester Mulso was made to make herself appear beautiful by cultivating her mind and her conversation. Tussy, it is sometimes suggested, was a rather plain woman who made herself appear beautiful because of her vivacity. Perhaps Clara hoped to work the same magic? The contemporaries who remembered her 'brilliant mind', 'her charming personality', and her 'keen sense of humour', seem to have fallen under her spell.[37] But it had no effect upon her young great-niece who recalled her 'immense double chin and chilly ways'.[38]

Beatrice Potter was intimately involved in the beginnings of Booth's proposed survey of *Life and Labour of the People in London*.[39] Heeding the advice of friends such as Herbert Spencer and Arabella Fisher that she should 'take up some line of inquiry', she had expressed a desire from the start to be an active participant in the quest for knowledge.[40] In later years she was to describe her involvement in philanthropic rent-collecting as a 'narcotic' which she much needed after her disappointing 'affair' with Joseph Chamberlain.[41] There seems every reason to suppose that sublimation also played its part in her ventures into social observation and social diagnosis. In 1882 her mother died and Beatrice assumed her place in the family home. Worries about her ailing father (who suffered a stroke in 1885) and her younger and difficult sister, Rosie, were added to her personal problems.[42] To suggest that sublimation was all that it was would be incorrect. She, like Clara Collet, was suspicious of sublimation. Beatrice longed to be both educated and useful.

The years 1884–86 marked a watershed in Beatrice's life. In 1883 she had joined the Charity Organization Society and begun work among the Soho destitute. Her consciousness that such people were not representative of the working classes made her glad of the opportunity to visit her mother's working-class relatives in Bacup. This became the occasion for her first exercise in careful direct observation. In January 1884 she determined to 'gain more knowledge of legal and commercial matters' and the theory of government in order to profit from this exercise. It also led her to her work as philanthropic rent collector and visitor of Katharine Buildings in East Smithfield. Her diary shows a Beatrice fully aware of the responsibilities of the work as rent collector/visitor on the Octavian model, exhausted and often depressed by the perceived impossibility of the task (15 March 1885). It was in this context that she determined to 'undertake less of the management, and use the work [as rent collector] more as an opportunity for observation'. During the late summer and autumn of 1885 she made detailed plans for a social naturalist's notebook of the inhabitants of Katharine Buildings (22 August, 23 October, 8 November 1885).[43] The case-study approach of her ledger owed much to the influence of the Charity Organization Society. But her debt to Spencer was greater: two years earlier she had confided to her diary that 'it would be amusing to make studies of human beings with the same care I bestowed on imitating bits of rock, stick and root'.[44] Her hope at that stage was to write up the material as 'stories of East End lives later on'. Perhaps her failure to complete this work owed something to the diversion provided by Booth's investigative work and by Sidney Webb's conviction that documentary research was superior to direct observation – the replacement of the influence exerted upon her by Herbert Spencer and Charles Booth by that of Sidney Webb.[45] Nevertheless the work marked her withdrawal from the world of the philanthropic worker into that of the social investigator. She saw it as such a step. Her research for Booth was a confirmation and further development of the move.

Unlike Clara Collet, Beatrice was involved in the initial discussions which shaped Booth's Inquiry. Her relationship to Booth (cousin by marriage and personal friend), combined with her active involvement in and discontent with philanthropic work in London's East End, rendered such involvement perfectly natural. In early March 1886 Booth had called the first meeting of the so-called Board of Statistical Inquiry, and Beatrice, along with three or four others, attended the second meeting in April 1886. After describing the mammoth undertaking of painting 'a fair picture of the whole of London society', she commented in her diary, 'If I were more advanced in knowledge of previous conditions it is just the sort of work I should like to undertake'.[46] No doubt Beatrice exaggerated her own role in shaping Booth's inquiry, but she was undoubtedly a formative influence and might have been even more so had she not been in the country looking after her father for much of 1886. She discussed Booth's planned inquiry with Samuel Barnett and probably relayed to Booth Barnett's profound scepticism about the project.[47] She met C.S. Loch at Booth's office on 4 May. Loch expressed enthusiasm for 'accurate knowledge of the conditions of the poor'. 'Evidently, from his account, there are many who would like to devote themselves to investigation.'[48] It was at this time that Beatrice contemplated writing an article in the autumn of the year 'to explain what I mean by social diagnosis ... If it were well written it would help Charles Booth's organization'.[49] And in the event it was in large part in conversations with her and letters exchanged with her that Booth refined his approach to the project and its organization. This is not to say that Potter produced the ideas – she did not – but she did make Booth think and she drew his attention, according to Mary Booth, to one of the most important sources of evidence for his first foray into personal investigation – the School Board Visitors.[50] It was in a letter to Beatrice that Joseph Chamberlain put his finger on one of the main problems which would exercise Booth and his co-workers. 'My department knows all about Paupers and Pauperism but has no official cognizance of distress above the pauper line', he wrote.[51] 'Yet this is surely the serious part of the problem. I am trying to collect facts from different sources but it is difficult to make them complete.' It seems highly probable that Beatrice Potter communicated these ideas to Booth when they met that spring. In June 1886 Beatrice was away from London and the inquiry. She was so worried that the project would fold or, what was worse, that she would be excluded from it that she wrote to her cousin, Mary Booth. Mary comforted her: 'He says that though little is done everytime – the thing is alive and that he thinks the men he has got hold of by no means lose their interest in the idea', while 'I think you a little under rate what you do at present towards helping him and the others'. Charles wanted to dine with her the following Wednesday but doubted 'much whether even during the time when your main work will have to be private study of your own [i.e. because she is caring for her father] – you will ever be as much shut out of the labatory [sic] and even the wards as you think you shall be'.[52] For most of June, July and August both Booth and Potter, for different reasons, took a holiday from the inquiry but, in the meantime, Booth was eager to support her work in a practical way. It seems that he probably regarded Beatrice as his 'deputy' with regard to the 'long course of reading' necessary for his work but which he 'could not myself undertake ... to save my life'.[53] His secretary, Jesse Argyle, was left temporarily without work while the inquiry was in abeyance: 'It has occurred to me that he might perhaps be of some use to you in looking up this or that – you being rather far from the British Museum. Can you make any use of him?' One way that had suggested itself to Booth was in help with the interesting essay on social diagnosis: 'Could Argyle help to work up your sketch of the legislation of the last fifty years or did you get enough done yourself ... to prove that "we are not governed by general principles" beyond controversy?'[54] Probably he knew that his wife's cousin was looking for research assistance.[55] Beatrice leapt at the offer and four days later Booth wrote back to her, 'Argyle ... took very kindly to the proposal of doing some work for you. I will write to him and set him agoing in the right direction'.[56]

In these letters to Potter, as part of a written conversation about social investigation, Charles Booth set down some of his own ideas.[57] Potter's correspondence with Maurice Paul also shows that throughout 1886 she was part of an ongoing and detailed conversation about the nature of the inquiry and its proposed methodologies.[58]

Initially Booth had intended her to undertake the interviews of female School Board Visitors.[59] There is no way of knowing whether she did so. There is some suggestion in the correspondence that Ella Pycroft had been asked to participate in the interviewing and she was perhaps intended to fulfil this role. Certainly in *My Apprenticeship*

Beatrice writes: 'On the few occasions I attended these interviews it was enlightening to watch how Charles Booth or one or other of his secretaries...',[60] making it reasonably certain that interviewing School Board Visitors was not part of her work routine.[61]

Her real work for Booth was heralded in December 1886.[62] From its beginning this was a contribution to Booth's survey of trades associated with poverty.[63] Because of family responsibilities investigation became perforce a holiday employment. In late February 1887 Beatrice began the work which she had promised but she did not give 'The Docks' her exclusive attention during the months that followed: she continued beavering away on her articles while simultaneously collecting some material for her 'sweating' industry work.[64] She started with interviews with the Superintendents of the West India and East India Docks, establishing the *modus operandi* of the docks and ascertaining what other types of material she required. She spent time becoming acquainted with the contract system that had been in use for two years at the Millwall Docks. She accompanied Charles Booth to the West India Docks to pursue some lines of inquiry there and to interview Stephen Sim the Secretary to the Amalgamated Stevedores' society. She contrasted the operation of the Millwall Dock with the West India and East India Docks. She recorded in her diary both her pleasure in the work and her dissatisfaction with the level of her knowledge of the subject.[65]

She determined to follow up several lines of inquiry as a result of this reflection: the different classes of worker in the docks; the consequences of the opening of the Suez Canal upon dock business; the work of the Tilbury, Albert and Victoria Docks. Both Booth's opinion and that of the police were to be canvassed. She staged further interviews with, for example, a Master Stevedore; with Mr Thomas, the School Board Visitor of the Millwall area; with Kerrigan the School Board Visitor for Limehouse (Stepney); with Mrs Gibbs, the wife of a worker at the Cutler Street warehouse; with Mr Gibbs, a worker at the wool warehouse; with Mr Bright, the manager of the south side at Millwall Docks; with Mr Coleman, a dock missionary; with Mr Maulty, a chauvinist contractor; and with Mr Wright, manager of the Fresh Wharf. Her brother-in-law, Daniel Meinertzhagen, obtained letters of introduction for her to the wharves. At a dinner at around about the same time she had useful conversations with Mr Cox, Superintendent of the London and St Catherine's Docks, and Mr Beck, the Superintendent of the West India. Although she exaggerated somewhat when she wrote 'Morning after morning I am up early, watching the struggle for work at the dock gates; and observing the leisurely unloading of sailing vessels compared to the swift discharge of steamers', she actively observed the docks.[66] Some of the reports of her work on the docks are wonderfully evocative. Witness her interview with Kerrigan, the School Board Visitor, or her visit to the docks.[67]

She also visited Peabody's dwellings and asked questions there about tenants who worked at the docks; toured a wool warehouse (Goudge-Cousin); spent an evening at a club in St George's Yard, talking to 'Preferables' at the London and St Catherine Docks. One of these was Robinson, a socialist dock labourer. She consulted Charles Booth's notebook on the doss houses which served the docks and noted down interesting information. Unfortunately for us the diary entries relating to the period from 1 June to 11 August 1887 were torn out of the holograph diary.

In many respects a poor note taker, she occasionally comments that she has to interview someone afresh because her original notes were too sketchy or non-existent.[68] She had a flair for capturing the scene there and then, recording the vitality of the speech and observing keenly the life of the people whether or not it had much relevance to the subject at hand. Thus the trip to Victoria Park with Kerrigan told her little about the docks but a good deal about the dockers and their community. More is the pity that this facility did not transfer itself to her articles for the Booth survey! For, despite the richness of the interview material, Beatrice Potter drew directly on little of it for her chapter on *The Docks*. It is perhaps understandable that she eschewed the style of Mayhew; after all she, like Booth, wished to avoid sensationalism. It is rather less obvious why, when she had such a flair for conveying the actual in all its immediacy, she rejected the real examples she had of what happened at the dock entrance in favour of rather strained and architected literary description.[69] On the rare occasions when she did refer to the views of real individuals she, oddly enough, elected to alter what they had said.[70] It is to be noted that she does not attribute the origins of the comment, although she had it carefully noted down in her diary and in fact knew the family well. Sometimes, as with Dartford, she shows a distressing tendency to take over part of the interviewee's comment and present it as her own verdict.[71] Documented examples were felt unimportant to make her case. It was sufficient to say, for example, 'From my own observation as a rent collector, and from other evidence, we know that the professional dock labourer (as distinguished from ...) earns from 12s to 15s a week, supposing his earnings were to be spread evenly throughout the year'[72] without giving examples from her carefully kept Book of the Inhabitants of Katharine's Buildings[73] or saying just what that other evidence was.

And when she reported the activities of the dock police and the irritation it caused in the workers, she understandably neglected to report directly the views of Robinson, the socialist dock worker, who was the first to acquaint her with the views of the men themselves: 'Says he makes a point of secreting tobacco on his person to defy the rule.'[74] She had no statistical support whatsoever for her comment that women's work sapped the men's appetite and energy for work; its support was a comment from Cox of Millwall that 'Sometimes have to sack men for not coming in time. Men depend on the wives' labour and only want to earn pocket money.'[75]

The chapter's useful description of the typical work of the docks was heavily derived from her detailed interviews with the superintendents, chairmen, general managers and occasionally foremen and gangers of the various docks.[76] Similarly the statistics of employers of the different docks came from this source and from, for example, the Secretary of the Stevedore's Union.[77]

In the event her chapter on the docks was a somewhat colourless and countless contribution. It combines the worst of two possibilities. It contained few statistics and the results of poorly documented personal observation. There is little exciting description, and facts and opinions are rarely attributed. It contrasts most unfavourably with David Schloss's chapter on bootmaking, for example.

The article offers few 'facts' and offers assertion in place of proof. Clearly by the time it was published Beatrice Potter did have a good knowledge of dock practices, derived from her interviews, her notes on the tenants of Katharine's Buildings, her personal observation and her reading, but the work itself was unsatisfactory. In reality she knew more about 'attitudes' among managers and men to dock work than she knew about the work itself. She saw what the managers wished her to see; she heard what managers and men wished to tell her. Yet, in the event, she chose to treat what she was shown and told as 'fact' and she presented it to her readers with great authority.

In early August 1887 she 'settled with Charlie on the autumn's work. The Sweating system is to be the subject of my next paper'. 'I have it in my mind to make it more of a picture than my article on "Dock Life".'[78] Her interest in this subject had been fed by her meeting in the spring with Mr Hoffman, a Methodist preacher and a foreman in a shoe factory who had 'made the sweating system a special subject of study'.[79]

By late August she had read Mayhew's *London Labour and London Poor* of 1851, which she described as 'good material spoilt by bad dressing – it is a mine of information – both of personal observation and of statistical enquiry – but there is no opening to it, nor any destination reached. It is overloaded with descriptive detail'. She read it mainly for its entrée to the sweating system, but her comments are revelatory of her approach to the work of investigation and writing itself. Immediately she mapped out an article on the sweating system which seemed to point her in the direction of a study of the boot and shoe industry. In October, even just as she was embarking on the Tailoring Trade Inquiry, she interviewed an Irish worker in the Boot and Shoe Trade.[80]

Work began in earnest in October 1887. Significantly, this time it began with close co-operation with Booth's office and specifically with George Arkell. During 1887 she met with Booth, sometimes twice or thrice in a week.[81] Booth's personal interest in the tailoring trade was important for the immediate direction of Beatrice's inquiry into sweating.[82] Ernest Aves's services were enlisted to interview practitioners in the Boot and Shoe trades.[83] It was not long, however, before Booth called to a halt the plan of including coverage of this industry in a general article on sweating by Beatrice.

Booth then was directing the campaign but under him Arkell and Argyle executed his general plans with flair and precision and exercised remarkable initiative. Arkell conducted interviews himself and wrote detailed reports of his findings on the trade, which were presumably invaluable to Beatrice and the others who worked on the tailoring trade for the first and second series.[84] It was he who compiled the statistical tables and by a careful process of analysis drew Booth's and the others' attention to lacunae and problematical areas.[85] In February 1888 he walked Beatrice through the East End.[86] Sometimes he challenged her ideas – a brave man![87] Arkell lent organization to Beatrice's endeavour and Beatrice owed him a considerable debt.[88]

From 20 October 1887 she kept separate her interview notes for Booth's inquiry.[89] A glance at this book demonstrates that she had determined not to repeat the mistakes of her Dock Inquiry. There was a deliberate attempt to interview a large number of both men and women and to ensure a fair spread across the trade. In her diary for 13 November 1887 she commented: 'Wrote out my notes and shall tomorrow decide on my plan of campaign with Charles for the coming month in London.'[90] On 14 November 1887 she wrote some brief notes to herself (presumably with Booth) which show that she was aware of the need to do this: 'Will get at middlemen through Cohen R Street, Darvin, Spiezel'; 'Jewish workers through A Whathorn Clerg. from St Jermyn in the East and Madden.' 'Employers from Arkell's Book.'[91] The notes show that she deliberately interviewed women workers and that she used George Arkell's interviews of women workers in trouser, vests and juvenile shirt sections of the trade also.[92] She planned and carried out interviews of her own of shopowners, middlemen and workers;[93] used interview material already collected by Booth's team (at least fifty interviews are extant); interviewed officials who might be able to give her privileged information; made it her business to find out through questioning and personal experience the processes of the trade; and searched such records as were available.

Barnett's introductions were of great importance to her: Darvin, the School Board Visitor; Mr Lakeman, senior factory inspector for the East End in Home Office employment; a sanitary inspector; Mr Nash, a post office official, Mr [John] Burnett, who worked for the Board of Trade, David Schloss, Ernest Aves.[94] She also built up contacts with leading members of trades associations.[95] She interviewed the Singer's Sewing Machine Collectors.[96] She cultivated and exploited this network of contacts mercilessly, but they did not always supply her with the information she coveted and expected.[97] As a woman investigator, of course, she was particularly dependent upon the company of others. Often the companion would be a contact such as Nash or Levy.[98] Sometimes she would entertain two informants together,[99] or she would meet a new informant at the house of another.[100] On occasion Charles Booth himself was an active participant in her interviews. This is something that Potter underplays both in her diaries and in *My Apprenticeship* but it is certainly worthy of note. All the more so because according to her Booth's presence was not necessarily advantageous.[101]

The book contains no questionnaire but one is often able to deduce from the notes the line of questioning.[102] There might be questions on issues which had recently been brought to her attention in some way. Thus: 'I asked him why he did not work direct for shipper – He answered "I haven't got the head for business – I've often had the chance, but have got sufficient to do, to do my own part of the business"',[103] and 'Cross-examined him about foreman, whether they took bribes for employment or to conceal bad work – said the manager of the firm for whom he worked had dismissed 3 foreman for taking money to conceal bad work, and had now to look over the work himself ...'.[104] There were further questions about employers and workforce, condition of trade compared with that of twenty years previously; the Jewish sweaters; dishonest practices among the workforce; irregularity of work; demands of the market.[105]

Beatrice shared with Booth a conviction that accurate observation was aided by sharing the experiences of the people.[106] Her diaries and her notebooks permit us to see her attempts in this direction.

The Levy family provided another useful contact: Mrs Levy, a tailoress and inhabitant of Katharine Buildings, introduced Beatrice to her mother, Mrs Moses of Oxford Street, Stepney 'with a view to learning to be a plain hand'. After a false start on 19/20 October because there was no work, Mrs Moses 'a fat cheerful jewess' with 'low forehead, big jaw and greedy, good-natured eyes' and her German Jewish husband 'a rough, uncouth fellow' who 'looked as if he had worked off the outer skin of mind and manners, constant sweating reducing his patience with life to its lowest ebb', welcomed her on Monday 24 October into their workshop for four days. She commented at the end of her stint as a plain trouser hand that when they parted it was as the best of friends although their 'work must have been bad for my sewing was too good for the trade'.[107] In the following April Beatrice obtained employment as a trouser hand at a Jewish sweaters shop on Mile End Road. She lasted two days.[108] The reports of the Potter interviews are reminiscent of many of those later written up for the Religious Influences survey.[109] Perhaps Booth influenced Beatrice's reporting technique – we know that she on occasion interviewed with Booth. On 26 November she went with Booth to interview members of the Jewish branch of Amalgamated Tailors.[110] We also know that from the very early days Booth was convinced of the desirability of making interviews conform to a pattern to ensure the ready transferability of interviewers.[111]

The indications are that Charles Booth and Beatrice together considerably modified her original plan for this paper. Around this time she jotted down the 'Heads of Paper on East End Tailors'[112] which indicated the plan of the essay as it stood at the time. A reading of the printed essay will demonstrate that the plan was not adhered to. For example, the plan in February was to begin by criticizing the whole concept of a 'sweating system' as too comprehensive and vague; the published version began with a seven-page discussion of the relationship between 'the new province of production' and 'the old-established native industry'.[113] Booth himself undertook the discussion of sweating as a phenomenon. The planned section on the Jewish community,[114] which did find a place in the version of this essay she published in the *Nineteenth Century*, was omitted from Booth's survey because she wrote a separate essay on the Jews. Arkell seems to have worked out a more precise categorization of the tailoring trade which appeared in the printed book.[115]

Her work was performed with the peculiar intensity characteristic of her. In part this was because of the pressure of time – it was an investigation which had to be fitted in to the finite time of her holiday – and partly because of the background of personal misery.

The chapter on the 'Tailoring Trade of the East End' is also a disappointment. She did not play to her strengths. In the event she shied away from a discussion of the concept of 'sweating'. There is little drawing upon the wonderful interview material she and Arkell collected; the 'picturesque' sections are grafted on to a colourless general argument. She signally failed to use observed detail to lend proportion to the scene she painted. The statistical infrastructure is more adequate than that of the 'Docks' chapter, but she does not appear comfortable with it and it was indeed provided by others.

Initially Beatrice proposed that her paper on 'sweating' would include a 'General picture of Jewish life in the East End'. She noted that the coat trade was 'in the hands of the Jews' and intended to compare the lives and prosperity of the Jews with the plight of the Christian population. 'They form a community', she observed. Also important were the *chevras* (foreign Jews congregated in synagogue-based confraternities), public opinion, the Jewish Board of Guardians and parental government. Her comment on the plan was telling: 'This must be the striking and graphic part of my article.'[116]

An examination of the archive indicates that her researches were directed by this general plan of campaign: an attempt to understand the Jewish community from within, both through interviews and 'total immersion', followed by a flurry of activity reading *The Jewish Chronicle* and the Minutes of the Jewish Board of Guardians and interviewing Jews and others who might help her to make sense of her earlier work. Much material was collected between October 1887 and April 1888. Her visit to the Levys (who lived in Katharine Buildings) produced a detailed report ranging from their family life to their employment and life-style.[117] The Levy description is keenly drawn and bears the marks of a report written in retrospect (for example, uncertainty of how many children they had). In writing this account Beatrice Potter perhaps consulted the 'Inhabitants of Katharine's Buildings Book' kept by her for the years 1885–86 and had prior knowledge of the family, but the report is full of personal observation and judgement: 'Their home is dirty and untidy and all the money is spent – but Mrs Levy says she must have plenty of food for her work is heavy. Levy is intelligent and glad to read books or newspapers. He has many friends of a respectable character and willingly talks on religion and social questions.'[118]

She worked out from this connection with the Levy family in several directions: to the homes and workshops of Jewish sweaters; to a chevra; to personal experience as a trouser hand; to what she described as 'the Jewish passion for gambling'. The notes she made are extremely valuable for the insights they offer into the life of the

Jewish community in London's East End. In the early encounters with Jewish tailors and their families Beatrice showed herself acutely conscious of their housing standards and eating habits. Mr Aarons, for example, lived in 'well-furnished comfortable rooms'; the Levys had a dirty and incapable Irish woman to look after the children while she worked, had a dirty and untidy home but ate well and had a caring if indulgent home life; the Cohens dwelt in a 'damp and comfortless' house and had a parlour which was 'untidy and without ornament or even sufficient furniture'.[119] The description from the MS Diary in October 1887 of her training as a trouser hand with the Moses of Oxford Street, Stepney, emphasized detail about their housing.[120] Later she was to observe of Samuel Montague MP and his wife: 'They live in a luxurious but gloomy Kensington Palace Gardens mansion and are blessed with ten children – the ugliest and most depressed looking family I have ever set eyes upon.'[121] Her keen eye for detail was apparent.

A note of her timetable for the last week of November and the first fortnight of December 1888 bears witness to a flurry of activity on the essay.[122] This involved not only individual work but consultations with other members of the Booth team with expertise in this area: Fox, who worked on the tobacco trade and the boot and shoe trade, known as Jewish trades; Llewellyn Smith, who was currently working on immigration into the metropolis for the Booth survey; Ernest Aves, a Toynbee man, with an intimate knowledge of the East End and of the furniture trade and the boot and shoe trades; and Clara Collet, of course, who was to write the chapter on women's work for the survey.[123]

The timing seems important. The published text owes so much to the material which Potter collected in the last six weeks of her inquiry into the Jewish community – the only time when she was exclusively concerned with Jews themselves rather than their occupations. Perhaps the description of the Jewish immigrants' arrival owes what immediacy it has to the fact that it had been experienced but a month or so previously – it was reporting rather than research. On 8 January she was 'Hard at work at the paper on the J[ewish]C[ommunity] and more than half through with it'. And on 23 January she confidently confided to her diary: 'my paper not quite finished but in a hopeful condition. Think it will more than satisfy C. Booth and will prove one of the "attractions" of the book'.[124] On 11 February her triumphant entry reads: 'Finished and sent it off to be copied: it has taken me longer than the other two: I trust it is better(?).'

Thus ended an era for Beatrice Potter. Her close association with the Booths was at an end. Already in November she had been aware that 'C. Booth has no more work for me to do' and was looking towards working on her original idea, 'the actual nature of Economic Science'.[125] A study of Co-operation 'under Benjamin Jones' was projected in December.[126] Her amicable relations with the Booths, husband and wife, were ended. She had broken with her dear friend and second cousin Maggie Harkness over a silly argument. Now she looked briefly to the Creightons and to Professor Alfred Marshall for intellectual direction and stimulation, although Toynbee Hall still had its attractions. It is an appropriate moment to leave her.

There are superficial similarities between Beatrice's investigative work for Booth and that of Clara Collet. Both contributed essays to the Poverty Series which were based upon the use of extensive interviewing. It remains to be seen whether the similarities end there. A chapter on women's work had long been on Booth's agenda. In 1887 Alice Green, widow of J.R. Green, was undertaking the work but not progressing well.[127] At Christmas that year Margaret Harkness grumbled to Beatrice that she had not been employed to do the work. In early November 1888 Mrs Green had certainly given up the task, and Booth asked Beatrice if she would undertake the investigation and complete the essay by the following March.[128] As Beatrice was just getting into her stride again with the study of the Jewish Community (which was not completed until February 1889) it is perhaps unsurprising that she did not take up Booth's challenge. Clara's name is actively associated with women's work later in the same month and it seems reasonable to assume that she joined Booth's team during November 1888. She did not devote herself exclusively to this essay, however, but divided her time between Balfour's Battersea inquiry and work on girls' education and the Poor Law Unions. In March 1889 Beatrice was still being pressured to make a study of female labour. 'There is one thing that you and only you can do – an inquiry into that unknown field of female labour' urged the economist Alfred Marshall. She, as is by now well known, reacted unfavourably to the suggestion, arguing the right and the ability of female investigators to explore 'male' subjects.[129] Whether or not Booth was left dangling for so long, Clara had undertaken 'leg work' on the subject well before spring 1889 and was soon to resume responsibility for the chapter. Unlike Beatrice Potter, Clara Collet's sympathies were with feminism.

In his deposition to the Royal Commission, Booth said that he had taken the sheets of the 1881 Census as a general basis for the study of women's work and that lists of factories and workshops known to employ women had been provided by the Factory Department of the Home Office and the Factory Inspectors. Lakeman, the factory inspector, had been helpful, as had various missionary bodies who had provided introductions to working girls, 'so that we might become acquainted with them'. To this end 'Miss Collet took up her residence in the East End and lived there for three months' during which time 'she was continually engaged in trying to come into contact with the girls, and those who were working amongst them'. Like Beatrice, Clara attempted 'total immersion'. Where factory girls were concerned she would 'invite them to come to her house'. 'She found it very difficult to get information that was satisfactory' but, he thought, she did eventually succeed. Clergy introduced her to home workers, the most elusive of all. 'She made full notes as she went along. At first, I was sharing the task (something Booth did with all his associates), as long as it was confined to interviews with factory inspectors, and so on; and afterwards Miss Collet went on alone, and wrote down almost everything that happened in full, and those notes I read as they were written. She then wrote her own chapter – it is entirely her writing. I simply revised what she had written to see that it contained everything that seemed to be trustworthy.'[130] We, of course, might add that, like Beatrice, Collet was deeply indebted to (and acknowledged her debt) the work of George Arkell.

None of Collet's interviews for the chapter seem to survive, although much material collected by Arkell does, and it is therefore impossible to compare her interviewing technique or her use of her own material with that of Potter. An examination of the chapter suggests that Collet was not only thorough in her investigation but creative. Look at her genealogy of shirts. She was not only knowledgeable but highly critical of her sources. For this look at her treatment of the machinists employed in the East End branch of a city firm.[131] She used mature comparative techniques to make points.[132] Her treatment of home work as a general issue is excellent – she delved into it to discover its economic roots and the problems peculiar to married women who must work to make a living.[133] Look then at her study of factory work, and the interesting suggestions she had to make about the explanations of high infant mortality among the children of women factory workers;[134] and her unabashed challenge to the employers to decide whether half a loaf was better than none when times were slack.[135]

Even this is sufficient to convince that *at this time* her skill as an investigator and as an analyst was of a different variety from that of Beatrice Potter. Small wonder that Clara Collet was snapped up by the Board of Trade as a Senior Investigator in the Labour Department on

Booth's recommendation in 1903.[136] Her reports for the civil service, and her independent publications, indicate that, while she built upon both these skills and her knowledge base, her work for Booth was of a formative nature.

In later years Beatrice Potter rendered a triumphal account of her time with Charles Booth's Inquiry as her 'apprenticeship', the years in which she received training in her chosen craft. Close examination of the existing archive, which has involved piecing together tiny fragments of information and sorting out the sometimes distorted account of her activities during the years 1886–89, indicates that Beatrice Potter certainly threw herself into the work with great intensity for limited periods (perhaps a total of eight months were spent on investigation for five essays during the three and a quarter years covered here), familiarized herself with both printed primary sources and sources of information available to the personal investigator, and had the opportunity to observe and draw upon the expertise practised by Booth and many of his earlier associates (often drawn from Toynbee Hall). There can be no doubt that she was very intelligent, very eclectic and very willing to be 'an apprentice' despite her decidedly un-humble personality. Nevertheless she was untutored and she remained untutored. Unlike Clara Collet, she was uncomfortable with the sorts of material Booth, Arkell and Smith made available to her. She remained unable to organize her interviews to produce a systematic run of material, despite the excellent example provided her. She did not know what precisely she should do with the wonderful interview material she collected. Where statistics were used, they were provided by others and analysed by others. She displayed at best hesitancy in manipulating them. Fundamentally she was dissatisfied with her efforts. It was essentially an apprenticeship which had left her, talented as she undoubtedly was, relatively unskilled at the craft she had chosen. Even in her last and best essay for Booth, 'The Jewish Community', we have to laud her enterprise in seeking to open up the unopened to an English public and the richness of her sources (evidence of which survives) rather than her success in describing the community and detailing the dovetailing of secular and religious life within it. Nonetheless this was a much happier exercise in description than either 'The Docks' or 'The Tailoring Trade'. Ultimately she rejected most of Booth's approach to investigation, choosing rather to follow a path mapped out by Sidney and herself.

Notes

1   I wish to thank the Women in the Humanities Group at the Open University for their generosity. Parts of this chapter – that concerning Clara Collet – was first aired at one of the group's seminars and the subsequent discussion was most helpful.

2   Octavia Hill contributed a short essay to the Poverty Series but she can scarcely be described as one of Booth's investigators.

3   For some interesting comments on the ways in which women capitalized on the opportunities social research offered them, see Bulmer, Martin, et al. (1991), 'The Social Survey in Historical Perspective' in Bulmer, Martin, et al. (eds), *The Social Survey in Historical Perspective,* Cambridge University Press, pp.35–7 and Kish Sklar, Kathryn (1991), 'Hull-House Maps and Papers: social science as women's work in the 1890s' in the same book, pp.111–39, which treats the American experience and which suggests English parallels. Jane Lewis has accorded stimulating consideration to the work of several important English women investigators. See Lewis, Jane (1991), 'The Case of Beatrice Webb and Helen Bosanquet' in Bulmer, *The Social Survey,* Cambridge, pp.148–69; Lewis, Jane (1991), *Women and Social Action in Victorian England,* Edward Elgar, and 'Social Facts, Social Theory and Social Change: The Ideas of Booth in Relation to those of Beatrice Webb, Octavia Hill and Helen Bosanquet' above, pp.49–66.

4   Webb, Beatrice (1926), *My Apprenticeship,* Harmondsworth, Penguin edition, 1971.

5   Epstein-Nord, Deborah (1985), *The Apprenticeship of Beatrice Webb,* Macmillan. Epstein-Nord has confused Potter's 1926 account of her work for Booth with her actual work in 1886–88. It is not insignificant that Epstein-Nord calls her Webb throughout. Yet many of the views which Webb held in 1926 were not Potter's in the 1880s. See Webb, *My Apprenticeship.*

6   Mackenzie, Norman and Mackenzie, Jeanne (eds) (1982), *The Diary of Beatrice Webb,* Vol.1, 1873–1892, *Glitter Around and Darkness Within,* Virago, p.20.

7   BLPES, Passfield, 7, i.8.

8   Booth, Charles (1902–3), *Life and Labour of the People in London,* 17 volumes, Macmillan.

9   For a different view of Clara Collet see Miller, Jane (1990), *Seductions,* Virago.

10   Recent biographical accounts occur in Lewis, *Women and Social Action*, and Epstein-Nord, *The Apprenticeship.*

11   Kapp, Yvonne (1972), *Eleanor Marx, Volume I, Family Life, 1855–1883*, Lawrence and Wishart, pp.219, 226.

12   *The Nineteenth Century and After*, 91, no.539, January 1922.

13   Diary, p.13.

14   Collet, Clara E. (1902), *Educated Working Women. Essays on the Position of Women Workers in the Middle Classes*, P.S. King & Son, p.24.

15   Diary, p.6.

16   Diary, p.11.

17   Vicinus, Martha (1985), *Independent Women: Work and Community for Single Women, 1850–1920*, Virago, p.125.

18   Manuscript Diary, MRD, Warwick, MS29/8/1/53, p.97 (hereafter referred to as Clara Collet's Diary).

19   Diary, March 1882, p.49.

20   Diary, p.51.

21   Diary, p.56.

22   Diary, March 1883, p.70.

23   Diary, 15 March 1883, p.70.

24   Diary, pp.88–90.

25   Diary, p.81.

26   Diary, p.97.

27   See O'Day, Rosemary (1993), 'Before the Webbs: Beatrice Potter's Early Investigations for Charles Booth's Inquiry', *History*, 78, pp.219.

28   Clara Collet's typed diary, MRO, Warwick, MSS 29/8/2/76.

29   Clara later became great friends with Higgs. See *Economic Journal* (1940), which printed items in Collet's diary about Higgs and Higgs's letters to Foxwell in 1890, which were in the possession of Miss Collet.

30   BLPES, Booth Collection, B58, B60, B64.

31   Clara Collet's Manuscript Diary, 18 May 1890, p.106.

32   Clara Collet's Diary, May 1890, p.105.

33   Clara Collet's Diary, 18 May 1890, p.106.

34   Clara Collet's Diary, May 1900?, p.107.

35   Smith, Hubert Llewellyn (1931), *New Survey of London Life and Labour*, P.S. King.

36   Warwick, MRO, MSS 29/3/13/4/1 'Undercurrents', p.1, 6.

37   'Two Obituaries of Clara Elizabeth Collet, 1860–1948' (1948), *Journal of the Royal Statistical Society*, Series A, 111, pp.252–4.

38   Miller, *Seductions*, p.70.

39   See O'Day, Rosemary and Englander, David (1993), *Mr Charles Booth's Inquiry, Life and Labour of the People in London Reconsidered*, Hambledon, for more on this.

40   'I wish you would take up some line of inquiry' wrote Herbert Spencer to B. Potter, 8 October 1883 – cited in *My Apprenticeship*, p.152; see also Booth Collection, Fisher to Potter, 24 January 1886, Passfield II i (II) 6, Item 133; Mary Booth to Potter 6 June 1886, Passfield II i (II) 6, Item 23.

41   Webb, *My Apprenticeship*, p.282.

42   See Lewis, *Women and Social Action*, pp.85–96, for an interesting discussion of Beatrice Potter's concerns about social work and the personal identity of women.

43   BLPES, Coll.Misc.43; Epstein-Nord, *The Apprenticeship*, pp.144–7; See O'Day, forthcoming, *Potter, Pycroft and Paul: The Sweet Trinity and Katharine Buildings, 1885–1890*.

44   Passfield, Beatrice Potter's MS Diary, 2 January 1883.

45   Coll. Misc.43 and Passfield make it clear that Beatrice Potter continued to work at Katharine Buildings intermittently throughout the period 1885–89.

46   Passfield, MS Diary, 17 April 1886.

47   Passfield, MS Diary, 18 April 1886.

48   Passfield, MS Diary, 4 May 1886.

49   Passfield, MS Diary, 4 May 1886; see also Webb, *My Apprenticeship*, p.292.

50   The precise circumstances in which this information was communicated are discussed in O'Day and Englander, *Mr Charles Booth's Inquiry*, pp.33–4.

51   Passfield, II i (II), 4, Joseph Chamberlain to Beatrice Potter, 28 February 1886.

52   Passfield, II i (II), 6, Mary Booth to Beatrice Potter, 6 June 1886.

53   Passfield, II i (II), 8, Charles Booth to Beatrice Potter, 27 July 1886.

54   Passfield, II i (II), 8, Charles Booth to Beatrice Potter, 27 July 1886.

55   Passfield, II i (II), 6, Arabella Fisher to Beatrice Potter, 24 January 1886.

56   Passfield, II i (II), 8, Charles Booth to Beatrice Potter, 31 July 1886.

57   For a detailed treatment of these ideas see O'Day and Englander, *Mr Charles Booth's Inquiry*, pp.35–7; for a different perspective upon the relationship between Potter and Booth, see Lewis, above, pp.49–66.

58   See, for example, Passfield, II i (II), 8, Maurice Paul to Beatrice Potter, 3 September 1886.

59   Passfield, II i (II) 8, Item 176, Charles Booth to Beatrice Potter, 5 September 1886.

60   Webb, *My Apprenticeship*, p.239; for the full quotation see my previous chapter, endnote 23.

61   She did interview one or more School Board Visitors in the course of her later work on the docks, for example, but this should not be confused with her earlier involvement in the project in the autumn of 1886.

62   5 December 1886;Webb, *My Apprenticeship*, p.300.

63   Although she first published the work as 'The Dock Life of East London', *Nineteenth Century,* September/October 1887; Webb, *My Apprenticeship*, p.314.

64   The extent to which her work on Katharine Buildings sparked her interest in the docks is a matter of speculation. Certainly she used little of the material assembled during this work in the essay itself. See Coll. Misc. 43; Epstein-Nord, *The Apprenticeship*, pp.144–7.

65   Passfield, MS Diary, 30 March 1887; edited version in Webb, *My Apprenticeship*, p.300; Passfield, MS Diary, May 1887; this also is differently described in Webb, *My Apprenticeship*, p.301.

66   6 May 1887 Diary; Webb, *My Apprenticeship*, p.302.

67   Webb, *My Apprenticeship*, p.302 is a reworking of entry for 11 May 1887 in MS Diary.

68   See, for example, Passfield 8.62r.

69   See *Poverty*, 4, pp.30–1 and compare with, for example, the MS Diary entry for May 1887.

70   Passfield, MS Diary, May 1887 and Webb, *My Apprenticeship*, p.302; *Poverty*, 4, pp.24–5. For greater detail on this point see O'Day, 'Before the Webbs', pp.223–6.

71   See O'Day and Englander, *Mr Charles Booth's Inquiry,* for evidence that Beatrice Potter was not alone in this unfortunate habit. Booth himself was an arch offender.

72   *Poverty*, 4, p.27.

73   Coll. Misc 43, 1885–90.

74   Webb, *My Apprenticeship*, p.302.

75   30 March 1887 Diary.

76   See interviews at West India, East India, London and St Katherine's and Millwall – entries under 25 February 1887 and 30 March 1887 in Diary.

77   For further detail see O'Day, 'Before the Webbs', p.225.

78   *c.*8 August 1887, Diary.

79   24 March 1887, Diary.

80   5 October 1887, Diary.

81   See Norman-Butler, B. (1972), *Victorian Aspirations: The Life and Labour of Charles and Mary Booth*, Allen and Unwin, p.91, based on Mary Booth's *Diary*.

82   Booth Coll. A19 fo.1.

83   He was employed from 14 October 1887.

84   A19 Tailoring, fos 178 ff.

85   Compare *Poverty*, 2, pp.67–8 with BLPES, A19 fos 26–7.

86   Passfield 8.63.

87   Passfield 8.55.

88   For detail see O'Day and Englander, *Mr Charles Booth's Inquiry*, pp.57–82.

89   MS Diary, 20 October 1887; Passfield 7.1.8.

90   13 November 1887, Diary.

91   Passfield 8.21.

92   Passfield 8.40; 8.69.

93   Seventy-one are listed in the index to the volume.

94   Passfield 8.22.

95   Passfield 8:53–54; 8.47–8 Macdonald also wrote for Booth's inquiry, *Poverty*, 4, pp.142–8; 8.43.

96   See her reference to interviewing these men, *Poverty*, 4, pp.45–6 – see 8.

97   Passfield 8.27; 8.48; 8.48–49; 8.2; 8.18; 8.19; 8.19.

98   See below, Passfield 8.6.

99   Passfield 8.57: Hall and Macdonald.

100   See Passfield 8.59: she met N. Joseph, Jewish architect, at the house of the Chief Rabbi.

101   Passfield 8.49; see also 8.53–54; we should not accept Potter's assessment unquestioningly, however.

102   Passfield 8.2.

103   Passfield 8.3.

104   Passfield 8.3.

105   Passfield 8.3–8.4.

106   Other members of the Booth team may have employed this technique. David Schloss certainly did so. See O'Day and Englander, *Mr Charles Booth's Inquiry*, pp.93–6.

107   October 19, 20, 24, 1887 Diary; Passfield, 8.11–16.

108   The notes of her 'working life' are included in Passfield, MS Diary for 11–25 April 1888. These were already retrospective and 'literary' but when compared with the published version reveal small but interesting discrepancies; 'Pages from a work-girl's Diary', *Nineteenth Century*, September 1888; republished as 'The Diary of an Investigator', in Webb, Sidney and Webb, Beatrice (1902), *Problems of Modern Industry,* Longman, originally published 1898; see Epstein-Nord, *The Apprenticeship*, pp.174–7 for a consideration of this episode.

109   O'Day, 'Interviews and Investigations', pp.371–ff.

110   Passfield 8.53.

111   Booth to Beatrice Potter, 5 September 1886. Passfield, II i (II) 8, Item 176.

112   Passfield 8.60.

113   *Poverty*, 4, p.45.

114   Passfield 8.60.

115   Booth Collection, A19, fos 2–6.

116   Passfield 8.61–8.62.

117   Passfield 8.6.

118   Passfield, 8: 6ff; Ledger of inhabitants of Katharine Buildings, Coll. Misc. 43; see Epstein-Nord, *The Apprenticeship,* pp.144–7 for a brief treatment of this ledger.

119   Passfield, 8.5–8.8.

120   MS Diary, October 1887; Webb, *My Apprenticeship*, pp.316–7.

121   December 1887, MS Diary.

122   For a detailed account of the work which Beatrice Potter did at this stage, see O'Day, 'Before the Webbs', pp.236–40.

123   MS Diary vol.12 p.170; not in the typescript as far as I can ascertain.

124   8 January 1889, 23 January 1889, Diary.

125   28 November 1888, Diary.

126   December 1888, Diary.

127   Passfield, II i (II), 6, Mary Booth to Beatrice Potter, 1887.

128   Passfield, MS Diary, 3 November 1888.

129   See Lewis, *Women and Social Action*, pp.96–9, for a good discussion of this position.

130   Parliamentary Papers (1892), *Royal Commission on Labour Minutes of Evidence*, Group C [C.6708–VI] PP.1892 (35), qq 8,909–61; O'Day and Englander, *Mr Charles Booth's Inquiry*, pp.86–7.

131   *Poverty*, 4, p.261

132   *Poverty*, 4, pp.299–311.

133   *Poverty*, 4, pp.299, 301 *et passim*.

134   *Poverty*, pp.325–6.

135   *Poverty*, 4, pp.314–15.

136   ULL, Booth Correspondence, MS 797 I/4803.

7 Paradigms of poverty: a rehabilitation of B.S. Rowntree[1]

J.H. Veit-Wilson

Benjamin Seebohm Rowntree (1871–1954) was a pioneer of social research into poverty. His first social survey of York in 1899[2] not only counted the poor but described their conditions of life. It showed that at least one-third of the poor had too little money to buy enough even for physical existence, let alone for social participation. In the years since his death, many of the reports of his early work and findings have concentrated on Rowntree's development of the instrument by which he showed this (the primary poverty measure). By doing this, some authors have misrepresented Rowntree's work in two important respects. Firstly, they have suggested that the primary poverty measure was Rowntree's sole conception of what poverty was. They wrongly suggest that he held only an absolute, minimum subsistence view of poverty, and they unjustly criticize him for doing so. Secondly, they overlook his actual relativistic definition of poverty which he used in 1899 and in his second survey of poverty in York in 1936.[3] The critical authors also misquote the statistics which these surveys produced, often mentioning only the very poorest and not all those whom Rowntree identified as being poor, or saying that all the poor had incomes below the primary poverty line. Not all authors seem to have misunderstood and misrepresented Rowntree in this way, but some of the best known and most widely published have done so and perpetuated the errors.

There are two reasons why this misrepresentation matters. Firstly, the truth should be told, and error which has been widely spread should be corrected, particularly when personal reputations are at stake. Secondly, British state income maintenance programmes have been justified for the past forty years in terms of Rowntree's early work on minimum subsistence. Such methods have often been promoted on the assumption that Rowntree's work provided a neutral scientific basis for minimum subsistence and showed relative approaches to be no more than matters of individual opinion. On the other hand, academic careers have been devoted to attacking this assumption and Rowntree's work, and to promoting a relativistic paradigm for poverty studies. But a reconsideration of Rowntree's early work shows both the assumption and the attack to be misguided.

Rowntree's paradigm of poverty was relativist and not absolutist. His development of the primary poverty measure in 1899 was explicitly a heuristic device and not a policy prescription, and his views on policy to combat deprivation were far more progressive and redistributive than his critics seem to realize. In short, a reconsideration would restore Rowntree's reputation as the pioneer of policy-orientated poverty research which later workers have not overturned but only advanced.

These are bold assertions, and this paper aims to substantiate them. The first section briefly sets out some examples of the erroneous assertions which are conventionally presented about Rowntree. The second section – which reviews what Rowntree actually wrote about his early measures of poverty and his reasons for using them – leads on to the final section, which considers the implications of this review for the arguments about poverty. Rowntree's minimum subsistence definition of poverty was itself relativistic, as he himself asserted,[4] and the paradigmatic shift which has unconsciously taken place is from relativistic definitions based on standards produced by experts such as Rowntree,[5] to relativistic definitions based on standards derived from the population itself through social surveys such as those carried out by Peter Townsend and his colleagues.[6] Awareness of this distinction shifts the focus in theoretical discussions from the sterilities of argument between experts to the realities of democratic politics, and the new paradigm thus has profound and far-reaching consequences for social policy.

Conventional misreporting of Rowntree's early work

The mistaken assertions which have been made about the methods and findings of Rowntree's early surveys in York[7] range from minor points of methodological detail to major errors about the concepts of poverty with which he was working. One may classify the mistakes roughly into those concerning his survey method, errors in the statistics quoted, confusions between Rowntree's concepts of 'poverty' and 'primary poverty', and confusions between Rowntree's definitions of 'secondary poverty' and his comments on some of its apparent causes. Some of the mistakes are so elementary and obvious that one is forced to assume that the authors had not checked Rowntree's published work (they rarely give references) but had perhaps copied the error inadvertently from some previous mistaken author whom they had trusted. To substantiate this criticism, some examples of these common errors follow.

Many authors seem unclear about Rowntree's research methods. Some say that he or his investigators visited every household in York in 1899,[8] whereas Rowntree pointed out that only working-class households (those not keeping servants) were studied.[9] As a result, some authors give the wrong percentage for the poor,[10] where the reported figure was 43.4 per cent.[11] Some authors give lower percentages for the poor in 1936 than Rowntree does,[12] and some compare statistics of one of Rowntree's three kinds of poverty in 1899 with a dissimilar one in 1936, and draw erroneous conclusions.[13]

Sometimes two or more of these types of error are compounded in one reference, as in the following example:

> A physiological definition of poverty is one which permits relatively easy translation into cash terms. This makes it possible to carry out the measurement of poverty on a large scale. A poverty line is drawn, being the minimal amount of money needed to keep a person out of poverty, and the numbers of people who fall below this line can then be counted. This technique of measuring poverty was first used effectively in Britain around the turn of the century in the pioneering surveys conducted by Booth and Rowntree. At that time the information they collected indicated that, by their rather stringent standards, over one quarter of the population was living in poverty.[14]

In fact neither Booth nor Rowntree used anything like the technique described here, and by confusing the measurement of primary poverty with the identification of the poor, this author makes it seem that all the poor were living below the primary poverty income level, whereas only one-third of them were in fact doing so.[15] It is a succinct complex of inaccuracy.

It is a common error among authors to assume that in 1899 Rowntree used an income measure to identify and count the poor. Such authors suggest that they are unclear about Rowntree's important distinction between the identifying criteria of poverty and the heuristic device of the primary poverty measure. This confusion is found in the well-known works of such authors as Berthoud and Brown,[16] Coates and Silburn,[17] Evans,[18] Field,[19] George,[20] Holman,[21] Jackson,[22] Rein,[23] and Townsend,[24] to name but a few. Many authors also have difficulty in reporting Rowntree's own views about secondary poverty. Their common errors are confusions between the definition of secondary poverty (which describes *who* those poor are) and its causes (which explain *why* they are poor), and the unfounded notion that Rowntree believed that all secondary poverty was caused by improvidence. Among the authors whose work suggests confusion about secondary poverty are Berthoud and Brown,[25] Hagenbuch,[26] Holman,[27] Kincaid,[28] Meade,[29] Rein,[30] Rodgers,[31] Rose[32] and Townsend.[33]

Rowntree must himself bear some of the responsibility for the mistakes. He was sometimes obscure, confused, inconsistent and mistaken. The introduction to his first survey report[34] gives a summary of his method of distinguishing poverty which is quite misleading when one compares it with the detail in later chapters of the book. It seems that some later authors may have based their criticisms simply on their reading of the introduction; its ambiguities about the concepts of 'merely physical efficiency' and secondary poverty may well have seemed good reason for their comments. Sometimes Rowntree changes the meaning of words and ideas from one part of a book to another; for example, 'the minimum standard' means a particular income level on page 34 of the 1941 report, a different real level of living on page 126, and is called 'poverty' on page 460. Quite apart from questionable research assumptions and methods, there are arithmetical errors: not merely what may be misprints (such as the discrepancy between the numbers of working-class people in institutions given on pages 12 and 32 of the 1941 volume) but downright howlers such as adding together disparate percentages to produce a chimerical total.[35] However, we must remember that Rowntree, unlike the authors referred to, was not an academic scholar, but was a socially concerned businessman who could afford to test his ideas.

Thus, in substantiating a serious charge of error, I do not want to suggest there has been deliberate impropriety. Many of the references given are passages in which the authors' attempts at brevity may have compressed disparate elements or only partially reflected Rowntree's ideas, together producing false impressions. But some of them occur in lengthy attacks on Rowntree's minimum subsistence measures in 1899 or 1936 in the erroneous belief that they were Rowntree's sole or even preferred significant concept of poverty, or his ideal prescription for income maintenance. As this seems to have become conventional or at least unexamined wisdom about him, I hope the authors mentioned will excuse my having used their works as merely a few among many examples, particularly because other previous writers have not all misquoted Rowntree. For example, as long ago as 1959, in a paper read to the British Association on 'Seebohm Rowntree's contribution to the study of poverty', Drinkwater quoted Rowntree to refute Townsend's criticisms[36] and added: 'One does not need to disagree with the sentiments which underlie these criticisms to feel that, whatever application they may have to others, they do considerably less than justice to Rowntree himself.'[37]

Similarly, Aronson's critique of the arguments between proponents of minimum subsistence and relativistic approaches to the operational definition of poverty lines in the USA politely criticizes some misrepresentations of Rowntree's concept of secondary poverty, and concludes: 'a historically informed reading of Rowntree suggests that his use of subsistence-based criteria was a rhetorical device that reflected a political strategy'.[38] Her paper is not designed to give the evidence for this assertion and, because Rowntree continues to be widely misrepresented, it is timely to counteract what seems almost a derogatory mythology about him by a review of the facts. The next section returns, therefore, to Rowntree's original works and quotes him to show what he set out to do in defining and measuring poverty, how he did it and why. This review of his early published work is confined to those parts of it that concern the first of his two aims 'to ascertain not only the proportion of the population living in poverty, but the nature of that poverty'.[39] The review is thus not concerned, except where relevant, with the second aim, the report on the social conditions of the working class as a whole, which takes up seven of the ten chapters in Rowntree's first book.[40] Nor is the paper intended to be an encyclopaedic review of the validity of different concepts or explanations of poverty, except as appropriate to illuminating the discussion of the content and current status of Rowntree's early work and indicating the significance of the real change of paradigm which Townsend's research methods facilitate.

Rowntree's own accounts of his methods and their rationale

The 1899 survey

Seebohm Rowntree's first survey of York was carried out in 1899 and the report was first published in 1901. In its introduction, Rowntree set out the aims mentioned above. It was in pursuit of the aim of ascertaining 'the nature of that poverty', Rowntree writes here, that he decided to divide the families in poverty into two groups:

> (a) Families whose total earnings are insufficient to obtain the minimum necessaries for the maintenance of merely physical efficiency. Poverty falling under this head I have described as 'primary' poverty.

> (b) Families whose total earnings would be sufficient for the maintenance of merely physical efficiency were it not that some portion of it is absorbed by other expenditure, either useful or wasteful. Poverty falling under this head is described as 'secondary' poverty.[41]

To find the division between the two kinds of poverty, Rowntree had to discover 'the minimum sum necessary to maintain families of various sizes in a state of physical efficiency'.[42] From this it might seem as if Rowntree was equating poverty with an inability to attain merely physical efficiency, and that it was therefore identifiable by income level, in which case families in secondary poverty were not 'genuinely' poor. But only later in the book did Rowntree show that these were not his beliefs or practices: too late for some readers, who seem to believe that Rowntree was critical of anyone not managing to live a decent life on the primary poverty line. To try to dispel this confusion, we must look first at Rowntree's research method.

The bulk of the survey was carried out by an investigator visiting households, and information was also given by voluntary workers, clergymen and others.[43] The 11,560 households visited were those of almost all the wage-earners in York. Households employing servants were excluded (as were their servants' households on the same premises); to be working class was taken as synonymous with earning wages and not keeping servants.[44] The number of people about whom information was obtained was 46,754 'or almost exactly two-thirds of the entire population'.[45] The 1901 Census had not been published, and Rowntree calculated the number in the servant-keeping class by deducting the wage-earning population, an estimate for the number of domestic servants, and the inhabitants of public institutions, from the total population of the city. He included 'a few families who ... do not keep servants, but who live in the same style as many of those who do'.[46]

Although Rowntree was able to find out the exact wages of some of the workers (he employed some of them in the Cocoa Works), he estimated the earnings of many of them: 'In the case of skilled workers, the earnings were assumed to be the average wage which obtains in the district for the particular trade.'[47] Any precise statements about numbers, percentages and income levels ought therefore to be carefully qualified; it is doubtful if Rowntree's frequent use of two decimal places in percentages can be justified by the reliability and precision of his crude data.

In a pamphlet defending his survey method against criticism, Rowntree described the way in which he established how many people were living in poverty as follows:

> In order to arrive at the total number of those who are living in poverty, my investigator in the course of his house-to-house visitation noted down as being in poverty those families who were living in obvious want and squalor. From this total number I subtracted those who were living in 'primary' poverty; the remainder represented those who were living in 'secondary' poverty. Now, in order to ascertain the number who were living in 'primary' poverty, reference to the definition of the term will show

that it was necessary first to ascertain what were the minimum sums upon which families of different sizes could be maintained in a state of physical efficiency. Having settled these sums, it was only necessary to compare the income of each family with the standard in order to see whether that family was above or below the 'primary' poverty line. It is clear, therefore, that the fixing of my 'primary' poverty line depends absolutely upon a money basis, while the fixing of my 'secondary' poverty line depends upon observations regarding the conditions under which the families were living.[48]

The distinction between primary and secondary poverty was not designed to identify the poor but was intended to illuminate 'the nature of that poverty' – 'that poverty' being conceptually distinct from either primary or secondary poverty, and consisting of the characteristics of families identified by the investigators as being poor. It is essential to note that the precise criteria used by Rowntree's investigators to determine which members of York's working class were or were not poor *did not include income*. As Rowntree noted above, the precise criteria used by his investigators to identify poverty were not financial; they were *behavioural* and *visible*. In the body of the 1901 volume, Rowntree elaborated the method summarized above, to give greater depth to the meaning of 'obvious want and squalor':

> Direct information was often obtained from neighbours, or from a member of the household concerned, to the effect that the father or mother was a heavy drinker; in other cases the pinched faces of the ragged children told their own tale of poverty and privation. Judging in this way, partly by appearance, and partly from information given, I have been able to arrive at a fair estimate of the total persons living in poverty in York.[49]

Rowntree stated clearly that these identifications of who was poor did not thereby define any particular income level as the poverty line. A family might maintain the outward appearance of not being poor while having an income less than that of families which did not maintain this appearance:

> The investigator, judging by appearances, would place such families above the poverty line, whilst he would no doubt place below it some families living in the slums who should not have been so counted.[50]

Furthermore, comparisons between the table classifying the population of York by income level,[51] and the bar chart showing the number and proportion of the population in and out of each kind of poverty,[52] show that Rowntree was quite clear that classification by the visible signs of poverty did not correspond with particular income categories.

That it was appearance and behaviour, *not income*, which were foremost in Rowntree's mind in identifying the poor and thus implying the criteria comprising the definition of poverty is unambiguously clear throughout this section. Continuing the passage quoted above[53] Rowntree writes: 'From this total number I subtracted the number of those ascertained to be living in "primary" poverty; the difference represents those living in "secondary" poverty',[54] and to make sure it was clear he repeats it later.[55] Lest anyone suspect that this interpretation is a mere matter of emphasis, Rowntree returns to it yet again in his concluding chapter:

> The number of those in 'secondary' poverty was arrived at by ascertaining the *total* (italics in original) number living in poverty, and subtracting those living in 'primary' poverty. The investigators, in the course of their house-to-house visitation, noted those families who were obviously living in a state of poverty, i.e. in obvious want and squalor ... sometimes the external evidence of poverty in the home was so clear as to make verbal evidence superfluous.[56]

We can summarize Rowntree's method of identifying the poor diagrammatically thus:

Rowntree's concepts of poverty, 1899

THE WHOLE POPULATION
   consisting of
THE NON-POOR
   distinguished *by life-style* from
THE POOR (ΣP)
   who consist of those people
IN SECONDARY POVERTY (P2)
   who are distinguished *by income level* from those
   people
IN PRIMARY POVERTY (P1)

His procedure can be shown as: ΣP minus P1 leaves P2. As demonstrated, his procedure was *not* P1 plus P2 totals ΣP, as it is often misquoted.[57]

The difference between primary and secondary poverty was by no means inconsiderable in quantitative terms. Of the whole domestic population of York, 27.84 per cent were living in poverty[58] but only

9.91 per cent were living in 'primary' poverty.[59] Thus a large majority of all the poor people in York were living in 'secondary' poverty, 17.93 per cent of the whole population.[60] From many other commentators' later accounts of Rowntree's findings, some of which were referred to above, one might assume that primary poverty was the principal (or only) form of poverty, while secondary poverty was a mere wasteful fringe on the massive volume of primary poverty. In fact, most of the York poor were in secondary and not primary poverty – but they were all in poverty, by Rowntree's definition. Table 7.1 summarizes the essential statistics.

It should now be clear that Rowntree and his investigators were working with a relative definition of poverty which compared the living conditions of the people they surveyed with the living conditions which were conventionally recognized and approved. Apart from differences in measuring 'convention', they used a definition essentially comparable with Townsend's celebrated definition of relative poverty in the first paragraph of chapter one of *Poverty in the United Kingdom*:

> Individuals, families and groups in the population can be said to be in poverty when they lack the resources to obtain the type of diet, participate in the activities and have the living conditions and amenities which are customary, or are at least widely encouraged or approved in the societies to which they belong. Their resources are so seriously below those commanded by the average individual or family that they are, in effect, excluded from ordinary living patterns, customs and activities.[61]

Charles Booth used a similar relative definition of poverty in his surveys in London to that used by Rowntree:

> I made an estimate of the total proportion of people visibly living in poverty, and from amongst these separated the cases in which the poverty seemed to be extreme and amounted to destitution, but I did not enter into the questions of economical or wasteful expenditure. You too have enumerated the cases of visible poverty; but you enumerate separately those whose income is such that they cannot by any means afford the expenditure which your argument sets forth as an absolutely necessary minimum.[62]

'As a result', writes Rowntree,[63] 'I feel no hesitation in regarding my estimation of the total poverty in York as comparable with Mr Booth's estimate of the total poverty in London, and in this Mr Booth agrees.'

Table 7.1 Population statistics and percentages in poverty, York 1899

Rowntree's method of calculating numbers in each category	Numbers in total population	% of total population	% of domestic population	% of wage-earning class*
1. Whole population (estimated)	75,812	100.0	–	–
2. *less* inmates of institutions	2,932	3.9	–	–
3. *leaves* domestic population (line 1 minus line 2)	72,880	–	(100.0)	–
4. *less* domestic servants (estimated)	4,296	5.7	–	–
5. *less* members of wage-earning households	46,754	(61.7)	(64.2)	100.0
6. *leaves* members of servant-keeping class (line 3 minus lines 4 and 5)	21,830	28.8	–	–
7. PEOPLE VISIBLY IN POVERTY (ΣP)	20,302	(26.8)	27.84	43.4
8. *less* people in primary poverty (P1)	7,230	(9.5)	9.91	15.46
9. *leaves* people in secondary poverty (P2)	13,072	(17.2)	17.93	(28.0)

Source: Numbers and percentages given by Rowntree (1901, pp.1, 28, 31, 111, 117) with the author's calculations given in brackets. Rowntree describes the statistics of the poor as percentages of the whole population (1901, pp.111, 117), but the calculations show that they are in fact percentages of the domestic population only.
* Rowntree's wage-earning class base excludes the inmates of institutions and domestic servants, almost all of whom were, however, members of the working class (1901, p.26).

The problematic issue for Rowntree and his contemporaries was not the identification of poverty as life-style but the question of cause. Hence most of Rowntree's efforts did not go into defining poverty (ΣP), but into the line separating those whose income was too low however they spent their money. The differences between Booth's and Rowntree's surveys in this respect were not conceptual but methodological. Rowntree explained: 'As soon as I came to deal with the question, "What proportion of the population of York is living in poverty?"' (i.e. ΣP) 'I saw that in a town so comparatively small as York, it would be possible to distinguish between the two kinds of poverty' (i.e. P1 and P2).[64] Booth could not do this because, as he wrote to Rowntree in 1901, 'The methods adopted by you are more complete than those I found available for the large area of London.'[65] In a glowing contemporary review of Rowntree's book, Nash wrote:

> The subject of poverty ... never comes up for discussion without bringing forth a disagreement as to what are the immediate causes of poverty ... Mr Rowntree's book will do much to clear up this question, which is a very important one ... Mr Rowntree's conclusions, too, are confirmed in a remarkable way by their coincidence with Mr Charles Booth's estimate of London poverty.[66]

Like Rowntree, Booth was conscious that his definition was conventional and relative. In their biography of *Charles Booth, Social Scientist*, T. and M. Simey wrote:

> In sum, Booth's poverty line must be regarded as being so drawn as to coincide with popular opinion, and all depended, in the last analysis, on the judgement of his interviewers. The key phrase is in the Second Paper; those families are 'very poor' whose means are insufficient '*according to the usual standards of life in this country*' (authors' italics); it was not his fault if his endeavour to translate this into shillings and pence for illustrative purposes was regarded by others as the main factor in his evaluation ... Many misunderstandings, and many false comparisons have arisen, however, from Booth's use of estimates of family income.[67]

Not only Booth's 'very poor' but also his 'poor' were defined in terms of conventional standards: their means were insufficient 'for decent independent life'.[68] As Marshall puts it:

> Though Booth may be said to have invented this concept (i.e. 'the line of poverty') he used it rather carelessly and inconsistently. This was, perhaps, because poverty for him, as for his predeces-

sors, was not a matter of income only, but of the conditions obtaining in the home and of the nature and regularity of employment. He was interested in the qualitative differences between the classes.[69]

This clearly conscious distinction between poverty (which is a relative condition defined by visible life-style) and the primary poverty income level runs through Rowntree's first book, from the introduction onwards. The very ordering of the chapters indicates it. Chapter Three on 'The Standard of Life' shows that poverty is not treated as life on a given income level, but in terms of the style or state of life which is experienced at an imprecise or varying cash income level. Only in the next chapter does Rowntree elaborate the distinction and consider the basis of the primary poverty line. Even here the distinction is unequivocal. The chapter concludes with a reiteration of the emphasis on the poor as visually identifiable, not on the primary poverty line. Its penultimate paragraph gives Rowntree's own priorities: 'That nearly 30 per cent of the population are found to be living in poverty is a fact of the gravest significance.'[70] Yet it was his attempts at late Victorian scientific precision which have been seized upon by later commentators (and misrepresented) as Rowntree's sole significant measure of poverty. Their later misapprehensions may have been encouraged by the emphasis which Rowntree's own contemporaries gave to his development of a cash primary poverty line as a precise survey tool[71] and as a focus for argument. In responding to these two forces, Rowntree's own interest in all the poor may arguably have later shifted towards an interest in an income level on which the poorest could live.

Nevertheless, it is very important that readers comprehend just how clearly Rowntree realized that even the primary poverty line was relative and not in any sense 'scientifically absolute'. Rowntree's critics seem to overlook his remark: 'It is thus seen that the point at which "primary" passes into "secondary" poverty is largely a matter of opinion, depending on the standard of well-being which is considered necessary.'[72] To show this, he gave calculations for the proportions of the poor in each category if he had taken weekly family incomes two shillings (10p) and six shillings (30p) higher for the primary poverty line: at the lower level, for example, nearly half of the poor would have been in primary poverty instead of one-third; at the higher level the proportion would have been over three-quarters of all the poor.[73]

One of the most prolific of his statistical contemporaries, A.L. Bowley, carried out a number of studies in British towns using a form of the primary poverty line as the measuring instrument. But Bowley did not suffer from misconceptions about the status of that instrument any more than Rowntree did. Bowley wrote: 'Though this calculation appears to have a scientific basis, and so far as knowledge of nutriment goes is accurate, it is in fact conventional rather than absolute.'[74] Bowley seems quite aware that the primary poverty line was not an income on which anyone could live: 'We are far from arguing that larger incomes are not to be desired ... We are only concerned here to establish a standard below which a family is *prima facie* in want'[75] – *prima facie* meaning that there was no need at that low income level to argue about *other causes* of poverty.

So far I have only discussed Rowntree's method of counting the poor in 1901. I turn now to the reasons he gave for adopting this method. The problem of poverty at the end of the nineteenth century was not how to define it (since there seems to have been general agreement that poverty was a visible condition, 'obvious want and squalor', in which some people lived), but to find out what the scale and causes were. The obvious effects of poverty were poor health and physique among the working class (as Rowntree also showed)[76] which – to the middle classes who were asking the question – reduced their value as workers and soldiers. A conventional explanation of poverty, held by many among the middle classes and exemplified by the work of the Charity Organization Society, was that people who looked and acted poor did so because they wasted their money, not because they had too little of it. To test this assumption one does not have to believe in the validity of a minimum subsistence approach oneself: it is enough if the proponents of the individualistic assumption are prepared to believe in it, as they generally were because it had the stamp of approval of nutritional science on it. As a research chemist by training and practice, Rowntree wanted to use these respected and persuasive methods and language to find out which explanation was the more plausible. To do this he had to see if there was any level of income at which the individualistic hypothesis would no longer hold true; that is, could there be an income level at which people could not maintain a non-poor life-style however hard they tried? Assuming for the sake of the experiment alone that all forms of social expenditure are disputable, but that scientifically proven minimum subsistence expenditures are irreducible, Rowntree was able to show that one-third of the poor had incomes too low even to keep physically fit, and that nearly three-quarters of these inadequate family incomes came from full-time regular earnings.[77]

In spite of this, Rowntree was criticized by those (like the Charity Organization Society) who rejected the implications of his findings, that state action was required to raise incomes. One such critic was Mrs Bosanquet: the only frankly hostile one, according to

Rowntree.[78] Both Rowntree and Mrs Bosanquet agreed that poverty *might* be caused by individual improvidence; the question at issue was whether some of it was caused by too little income. Mrs Bosanquet considered that the standard of living on which the primary poverty line was based was extravagant, and that the nutritional standards were too generous. Rowntree answered her:

> Had Mrs Bosanquet devoted some years of her life to the study of chemistry, as it has been my lot to do, she would have observed that, in every instance where ... the analyses may be inaccurate, the possibility of error ... may be *overstated*, but ... the inaccuracies are never on the side of *understatement.*[79]

His pamphlet replying to Mrs Bosanquet goes into detail on his survey and nutritional methods, and he concludes that:

> Her criticism suggests a lack of acquaintance with the science of dietetics, and of the relative status now accorded to those who have written upon it. She surely cannot imagine that I made so important a decision as to that of the standard to be adopted without the most careful enquiry;[80] ... probably sufficient has been said to show that my facts are capable of surviving criticism, and may, therefore, to quote her own words 'take their place in the body of approved knowledge by which men are willing to guide their actions'.[81]

As I have shown, primary poverty was defined in money terms, and so its causes were expressed as reasons for low incomes. But secondary poverty was the residual category: in it were all those who were poor but whose incomes were more than the primary poverty level. What were the causes? Unfortunately, Rowntree confused the answer. In the 1901 Introduction he wrote about 'other expenditure, either useful or wasteful', and glosses this comment: 'It need hardly be said that an expenditure may be in the truest sense "useful" which is not necessary for the maintenance of *merely physical efficiency*'.[82] These comments are both essentially correct in terms of his definition of what secondary poverty *is*. But in considering *why* some people 'act poor', he returned to contemporary middle-class convention, and answered in terms of individual improvident behaviour.[83] Few of the readers who criticize him for this seem to have turned over the page to see that Rowntree then locates these individual behaviours firmly in social context:

> Though we speak of the above causes as those mainly accounting for most of the 'secondary' poverty, it must not be forgotten that

they are themselves often the outcome of the adverse conditions under which too many of the working class live.[84]

He then expands this structural explanation to include:

> ... questions dealing with land tenure, with the relative duties and powers of the State and of the individual, and with legislation affecting the aggregation or the distribution of wealth.[85]

The common criticisms of Rowntree are that he prescribed the primary poverty income level as enough to live on and, following from this, that in concentrating on human physical efficiency alone he disregarded all human social and psychological needs. Both of these criticisms can be shown to be unfounded if one examines what Rowntree actually wrote.

> As do so many of today's campaigners, Rowntree felt the need to counter any charge that his findings might exaggerate the extent of poverty: hence his constant emphasis on a minimum subsistence approach.[86]

Field is wrong to refer to 'the extent of poverty', since that was not in dispute; what Rowntree himself was perfectly clear about was that he was using these natural science methods not to define or measure poverty (ΣP) but to distinguish primary from secondary poverty. 'The work done towards determining the relative proportions of the two classes has been valued by many experts as marking an advance in social information and in statistical exactness'.[87] In this way, he contributed to the later misunderstandings about his views and methods. Remembering that he was concerned with the causes of poverty (ΣP), we can better understand the emphasis he gave to the use of a measure which distinguished causes in currently conventional terms at a minimal level:

> My primary poverty line represented the minimum sum on which physical efficiency could be maintained. It was a standard of bare *subsistence* rather than *living* (italics in original). The dietary I selected was more economical and less attractive than was given to paupers in work houses. I purposely selected such a dietary so that no one could possibly accuse me of placing my subsistence level too high.[88]

This extract shows Rowntree choosing his method of comparison to persuade his audience, not because he believed anyone could live a social life on the primary poverty line, but because they believed it to be possible. To accept an opponent's premises for the sake of argument as a basis for one's criticism is a normal debating practice, but it has been turned against Rowntree.

Rowntree repeatedly returned to this point. His view that his minimum subsistence primary poverty line was not a realistic prescription for even a minimum income to live on, but was no more than a heuristic device, is evident throughout his writings. It is implicit in his famous and much-quoted description of what minimum subsistence would mean in real life.[89] He wrote in his study of *How the Labourer Lives*: 'We ... state our own strong conviction that such a minimum' (i.e. one equivalent to the primary poverty line) 'does not by any means constitute a reasonable living wage', and further on: 'we have assumed a poverty line so low as to be open to the criticism of serious inadequacy'.[90] In 1937 he was still making the same point in his revised edition of *The Human Needs of Labour*: 'No! my standard cannot be successfully attacked because it is too liberal. Rather it is open to the criticism as being too low, and yet millions of our fellow citizens belong to families whose breadwinners earn less than my minimum figure.'[91]

'I chose this criterion', Rowntree wrote in 1952 about 'merely physical efficiency', 'because I didn't want people to say that Rowntree's "crying for the moon".'[92] But why should they have done so? The comment makes sense only if one remembers that Rowntree was using his methods to show that even opponents of social reform could not resist the conclusions about the causes of poverty. As he wrote in 1941 about his *Human Needs of Labour* poverty standard used in 1936:

> I purposely adopted a standard which the most hard-boiled critic could not say was extravagant. Had I given any justification for such a criticism, those who wanted to excuse the present state of things would have fastened on any items which might be regarded as extravagant and thus sought to neutralise the effect of my book.[93]

It was a matter of political judgement, and was, in Briggs's own view, correct:

> As in 1901, however, the austerity of Rowntree's standards was more telling, at least to better-off people, than a more generous analysis, tinged with what in the conditions of the 1930s might still have been dismissed as 'sentimentality'.[94]

As we have seen, Rowntree defended his standards against critics of their generosity and justified them in terms of their political realism, but not as an income level on which real people should have to live. Similarly, when the common confusion between primary poverty and Rowntree's actual views about poverty is dispelled, it is clear that he was probably a good deal more aware of the social and psychological dimensions of poverty than his critics seem to realize. Writing about expenditure on 'non-essentials' in 1941,[95] he refers to the resources needed for the satisfaction of postponable psychological human needs as opposed to immediate non-postponable physiological human needs; he treated the satisfaction of the latter needs to a level of merely physical efficiency as 'essential'. But this does not mean that Rowntree thought that psychological needs should not be met before physiological ones, as he is commonly misinterpreted as suggesting; it means only that he was aware that both sets of needs could not be met simultaneously from an inadequate income. In answering the question: 'why do poor people spend their inadequate incomes on social recreational activities instead of food?', he wrote:

> The explanation is that working people are just as human as those with more money. They cannot live just on a 'fodder basis'. They crave for relaxation and recreation just as the rest of us do. But ... they can only get these things by going short of something which is essential to physical fitness, and so they go short, and the national standard of health is correspondingly lowered.[96]

In other words, he is once again addressing a debate, in this case about the national standard of health, and he is demonstrating not that health could be maintained on so low an income by ordinary humans, but that it could be maintained only by an inhuman disregard of the satisfaction of conventional psychological needs.

People such as Mrs Bosanquet may have felt justified in criticizing the primary poverty line as generous because they may have been using a narrower version of the life-style criterion of poverty than Rowntree worked with. When Rowntree defended himself against them, he pointed also to the wider aspects of deprivation, collectively suffered and visible but not always manifest in any one poor individual (and, as the following extract shows, he was well aware of the sexual division of diswelfare in poor families). Briggs, who as Rowntree's biographer was very conscious of his genuine concern that poor people should be provided with the resources and opportunities needed for complete and fulfilled lives in their own contemporary society, repeatedly shows Rowntree trying to get people to understand what poverty really meant:

> Rowntree warned his readers not to pit their uninformed feelings about poverty against his facts. If they saw people who by his

standards were in primary poverty appearing to live well (in terms of smoking, drinking, dress or recreation), let them not confuse 'things that are seen' with consequences of poverty which are not seen: 'We *see* that many a labourer, who has a wife and three or four children, is healthy and a good worker, although he only earns a pound a week. What we do *not see* is that in order to give him enough food, mother and children habitually go short, for the mother knows that all depends upon the wages of her husband ... These unseen consequences of poverty have, however, to be reckoned with – the high death rate among the poor, the terribly high infant mortality, the stunted stature and the dulled intelligence.'[97]

Writing in 1923 about the inadequacy of benefits for the unemployed, Rowntree again shows what he really felt about the primary poverty line:

> Do we want the workers always to spend only what is needed for purely physical efficiency? Are amusement and all luxuries to be taboo? Surely not! Those who, often thoughtlessly, speak of the inordinate thriftlessness of the working class, would not like to see their own households condemned to such an iron regime as the thrift they recommend would involve.[98]

Briggs bluntly states that Rowntree 'condemned people who had misinterpreted his own writings about minimum subsistence'.[99] Although Rowntree was addressing mainly critics of his profligacy, his words are as relevant to those who, after his death, criticize what they believe was his parsimony.

The 1936 survey
In his second survey of social conditions in York, Rowntree used a new tool in his attempt to show scientifically that some poverty was caused by incomes too low even for good managers to live on decently. The second survey was started in 1935 and work continued for some years; the results were published in 1941, but it is generally referred to as 'the 1936 survey'.[100] The new tool was based on the estimates which Rowntree had made for minimum wage purposes. During the First World War, Lloyd George had commissioned Rowntree to oversee the welfare of the workers employed by government in the munitions industry. In trying to improve their conditions and pay, and having argued that the primary poverty line was a criticism of, and not a prescription for, minimum wage levels, Rowntree worked on what he thought could represent a defensible minimum wage for a family:

'defensible' meaning that Rowntree's use of the heuristic device of the minimum subsistence approach would show the need to *raise* wages. The calculations were published as *The Human Needs of Labour* in 1918 and extensively revised and republished in 1937. He used them as the basis for his cash poverty line in the 1936 survey. Both versions were based on surveys of the actual budgets of working-class households, augmented by a 'minimum but conventional' diet, somewhat more generous than that of the primary poverty line in 1899. In particular, the sums included allowances for rents to pay for decent housing, thus at a much higher standard than most working-class people occupied, and they allowed for a limited range of conventional social expenditures of the sort which had been explicitly excluded from the primary poverty line in 1899. The total represented a recommendation for a minimum living wage large enough to cover Rowntree's estimate of the basic needs of a family with three dependent children: the family would thus live at a higher level while there were fewer children, and Rowntree called for children's allowances if there were more. Ignoring housing costs, this sum (43s 6d, £2.18) was nearly half as much again in real terms as the primary poverty line for the same household (30s 7d, £1.53).[101]

Rowntree's survey method in 1936 was not the same as in 1899. The basis of the survey was in principle a census of all households whose chief wage-earner was earning not more than £250 a year. Rowntree's method of finding these households was, however, simply to interview all households 'in all the streets where such people are likely to be living'.[102] He admitted this would omit manual workers earning more than £250 per annum, and households earning less who did not live in the streets covered by the survey. He also pointed out that some low-paid middle-class households were included. We must therefore note that the survey was based neither on class, occupation or income level, but on households living in what were assumed to be 'low-income household' addresses – and these are what Rowntree refers to for simplicity as the working classes.[103]

The house-to-house visitations covered 16,362 families, including 55,206 people, comprising about 57 per cent of the city's total population. Income data were *not* obtained during these visits; as in 1899, Rowntree obtained them from employers for about 60 per cent of the households. For the remaining 40 per cent of households, Rowntree estimated their incomes from 'information gathered regarding the normal earnings of people engaged in the occupations concerned'.[104] Again, the amount of well-informed guesswork, which Rowntree openly admits to, probably would not support finely distinguished decimal points of percentages.

As in 1899, Rowntree used various arguable estimates about the size of the total population of York (within changing boundaries) and of the population employed as domestic servants or living in institutions, and he included some inconsistencies and misprints.[105] Comparisons with 1899 must therefore be made only with care and qualification. Rowntree himself commented: 'The only figures that are absolutely comparable are those for primary poverty.'[106] Table 7.2 shows the chief categories relevant to this discussion, in 1936 and in 1899.

Rowntree's aims in the 1936 survey were to find out how many people were in poverty and what changes had taken place since 1899. The way in which he defined poverty (ΣP) had not changed in principle, although naturally its relativistic components were not the same. However, he did not feel he could operationalize this definition in the same way as in 1899; he could not identify the poor

> ... by direct observation, partly because the methods of doing this adopted in 1899 appear to me now as being too rough to give reliable results, and also because even had I done so the results would not have rendered possible a comparison with 1899, for ideas of what constitutes 'obvious want and squalor' have changed profoundly since then. There is no doubt that in 1899 investigators would not have regarded as 'obvious want and squalor' conditions which would have been so regarded in 1936, and on the other hand a large proportion of the families living below the 1936 poverty line would not in 1899 have been regarded as 'showing signs of poverty'.[107]

Therefore, instead of using the 1899 method, Rowntree used his estimates of actual wage rates to estimate how many people lived below the minimum wage level (31 per cent), and augmented the result of this *cash* measure by more than a quarter (7–10 per cent) to reach his 'guestimate' of those people who lived in poverty defined as *life-style* even though their incomes were higher than the cash measure. Rowntree summarized the position thus:

> We shall not, I imagine, be very far wrong if we assume that *about* 40 per cent of the working class population of York are living below the minimum standard, 31 per cent through lack of means, and 9 per cent because of expenditure on non-essentials.[108]

This point seems to have been overlooked by later commentators.

Rowntree's 1941 report shows that his concept of an adequate level of living included many factors other than income: the conditions of housing, health, education and a variety of recreational and leisure

Table 7.2 Population statistics and percentages in poverty, York, 1936, and comparisons with 1899

Rowntree's categories of the population	1936			1899		
	Number	% whole population	% low income residents	Number	% domestic population	% wage-earning class
1. Whole population (estimated)	96,980	100.0	–	75,812	–	–
2. People living in lower income streets in 1936	55,206	56.9	100.0	–	–	–
3. People in working-class households in 1899	–	–	–	46,754	(64.2)	100.0
4. People living below 'minimum standard' (ΣP)	–	(about 23.0)	'about 40' 38–41	20,302	27.84	43.4
5. People living below 'Human Needs of Labour' level	17,185	17.8	31.1	–	–	–
6. People living in 'primary poverty' (P1)	3,767	3.9	6.8	7,230	9.91	15.46

Sources: Numbers and percentages given by Rowntree (1941, pp.11, 13, 28, 34, 96, 108, 108, 126 and sources for 1899 as in Table 7.1) with the author's calculations given in brackets.
Rowntree's note: 'The only figures that are absolutely comparable are those for primary poverty' (1941, p.461).

activities and facilities. Although this level of living was composed of social and not physical factors, and was relative and not absolute, Rowntree gave openings to his critics by measuring aspects of it in cash terms and calling it a 'minimum'. Thus many of them[109] quote only the statistics of the poor who also have low incomes instead of giving correctly the statistics of *all* the poor. If we take the correct estimate, we find that the proportion of the population which was poor in York in 1936, about 23 per cent, is surprisingly the same percentage as Townsend found was poor in the United Kingdom in 1969 using his deprivation standard.[110]

Rowntree was very concerned that historical comparisons should be facilitated for their social value: 'it is *most* important to be able to measure accurately the success which has attended the efforts made by the community since 1899 to improve the condition of those living in abject poverty'.[111] To do this precisely he needed an unvarying measure of poverty apart from the relativistic and thus changing measures by which he defined poverty (ΣP). For the purpose, therefore, he took the 1899 primary poverty line and adjusted it for 1936 prices. The resulting comparison is shown in Table 7.2: a fall from roughly one in ten of the population of York to around one in twenty-five. It is in the course of this discussion of comparisons that Rowntree made a serious statistical error. In quoting the 1899 figures, he added together the 15.46 per cent of the *working-class* population in primary poverty[112] and the 17.93 per cent of the *whole* (domestic) population in secondary poverty,[113] and then wrote:

> The fact that in 1899 only 33.39 per cent of the working class was regarded as living in poverty, either primary or secondary, whereas in 1936 31.1 per cent are living below the minimum through lack of income, and a further unknown proportion, possibly 7 or 10 per cent, are living in 'secondary' poverty, have no relation to each other.[114]

The correct figure should of course have been 43.4 per cent,[115] and Rowntree seems to mean that we cannot compare it with the estimate of about 40 per cent in poverty in 1936 because the standards were not constant. But if we focus on the changing standards according to which people were defined as poor, then such a comparison becomes as valid as is the one based on unvarying standards. Between 1899 and 1936 in York, unvarying poverty (P1) diminished significantly but relative poverty (ΣP) remained relatively constant. Rowntree showed that he was using both of these standards of comparison in the subsequent passage where he expresses the conviction that there has been immense (possibly 30 per cent) improvement in the economic condition of the workers but

> ... the satisfaction which we may rightly feel at this great improvement must be qualified by a serious sense of concern that so large a proportion of the workers are living below a poverty line which few, if any, will regard as having been fixed at too high a level.[116]

Rowntree's own writings quoted here demonstrate irrefutably what he really said. In view of their antiquity and accessibility, it is puzzling to find recent commentators still writing passages such as these:

> In 1934–35 Rowntree repeated his study of York using a slightly more generous poverty line than in 1902 ... He found 18 per cent of the York population to be in poverty, half of these in 'primary' poverty.[117]

> It was found that the extent of poverty, measured in this dynamic sense, far from falling had actually risen from 10 to 18 per cent between 1899 and 1936. This meant that there had been a considerable increase in the proportion of the population unable to attain currently minimally acceptable standards despite an overall improvement in social conditions.[118]

Perhaps later editions of these and other popular books could correct such errors and help to restore Rowntree's reputation for intellectual integrity and social responsibility.

The theoretical status of Rowntree's concept of poverty

This final section considers the theoretical status of Rowntree's early work on poverty in relation to the claims of the relativists such as Townsend, and the implications of a changed perspective on the relation between theories of poverty and political action. As Mencher writes:

> ... the trite observation should be made that differences in the definition of concepts in studies of income are not abstract issues, but can only be resolved in view of their practical consequences in clarifying the problem of poverty.[119]

Townsend's massive work on *Poverty in the United Kingdom* not only presents the findings of the most searching survey of the levels of living of the British population a decade earlier, but a large part of the book is also devoted to detailed discussions of differing concepts and measures of poverty and deprivation and their implicit or explicit relationships to policy prescriptions. On the second page of his first chapter, Townsend opens a discussion of 'Previous Definitions of Poverty'.[120] He acknowledges that his new relativistic approach 'is new only in the sense that the implications and applications do not appear to have been spelled out systematically and in detail', and quotes Adam Smith's famous definition of 'necessaries' which include 'whatever the custom of the country renders it indecent for creditable people, even of the lowest order, to be without'. But Townsend refers to Rowntree's work in such a way as to exclude Rowntree from consciousness of this relativism:

> Previous operational definitions of poverty have not been expressed in thorough-going relativist terms, nor founded comprehensively on the key concepts of resources and styles of living. The concern has been with narrower concepts of income and the maintenance of physical efficiency. Among the early studies of poverty, the work of Seebohm Rowntree is most important

– and then follows a description solely of *primary* poverty, concluding: 'A family was therefore regarded in poverty if its income minus rent fell short of the poverty line' (i.e. the primary poverty line).[121] No mention here of secondary poverty or of any other kind.

Of course the critical point is what Townsend means by the word 'operational'. Was Rowntree's survey operational? Townsend says Booth's survey was 'on a larger scale but employed a cruder measure of poverty' than Rowntree's.[122] He thus seems to compare Booth's 'cruder' poverty line with Rowntree's *primary* poverty line. But, as we have seen, this is not to compare like with like, as both Booth and Rowntree realized.[123] Both of their surveys operated a similar definition of poverty, but it was a visual one which measured the quantity and quality of housing and its contents (including inhabitants) against prevailing conventional assumptions about what non-poverty was.

Townsend's own method (1979) of operationalizing relative poverty standards may be stated briefly as follows. First, exploratory studies are carried out[124] to generate indicators of deprivation – items of goods, services and experiences which people consider necessities, the lack of which constitutes deprivation. These provisional indicators are then tested in national surveys to see how far they are valid as deprivation indicators across the whole population, and at what income levels people lack necessities they want because they have too little money and not because they choose to do without them. In this approach, both the list of necessities and the income level at which they are achieved are derived from the population itself through surveys, and not from expert prescription or calculation.

But at the time of Booth's and Rowntree's first surveys, the concept of conventional life-style and the visual identification of the poor were not in themselves problematic. I have outlined Rowntree's reasons for concentrating his attempts at precision in 1899 on primary poverty rather than poverty as a whole. Thus, to count the poor, Booth and Rowntree were entirely dependent on an operational definition based on 'styles of living', and to show 'the nature of that poverty' Rowntree was crucially concerned with conventional resources, as can be read in Chapter 3, 'The Standard of Life', in his first book (1901) and extensively later.[125]

Townsend is perfectly right that even the primary poverty line is narrowly relativistic in conception,[126] but he nowhere seems to admit that Rowntree's definition of poverty (ΣP) was as relativistic, though not as precisely delineated or empirically derived, as his own. It seems that he too may have misunderstood Rowntree's definitions of poverty, and this impression is strengthened by his consistent misquotation of Rowntree. As long ago as 1962 Townsend wrote in his seminal essay on 'The Meaning of Poverty': 'In 1901 Seebohm Rowntree stated that families living in poverty were those "whose total earnings are insufficient to obtain the minimum necessaries for the maintenance of merely physical efficiency"',[127] and in the latest work he writes: 'Poverty as mismanagement (or Rowntree's "secondary" poverty)'.[128]

Asa Briggs suggested that many influential people at the end of the nineteenth century (let alone many social scientists and politicians since) approvingly or disapprovingly believed that Rowntree had overturned the widely held view of poverty as a life-style caused by misuse of sufficient resources, and had substituted a new perspective of poverty as too little money for minimum subsistence, and a new and scientifically reliable method for discovering what resources were necessary for subsistence.[129] As explained and acted upon, this might be said to be paradigmatic: the theory that human needs can be met at an income level corresponding to this minimum level of living; the creation of a new scientific instrument to determine this minimum level and its price; a set of rules concerning the question of the goods and services to be put in the minimum 'shopping basket' and priced; and a body of practitioners applying the theory and methods to conduct surveys and devise minimum income maintenance programmes for the state.

Townsend's entire academic career has been marked by his desire to overturn this paradigm of minimum subsistence poverty which he implies Rowntree established, and to substitute an explicitly relativistic one, where the theory is that human needs can only be conceived and expressed in terms relative to the social norms peculiar to social context, time and place; measured by standards of relative deprivation; with rules to determine the resources to be considered. The approach in itself has precedents, since the concept of potential relative deprivation has long been accepted in Britain as the basis of, for example, the design of earnings-related pensions and insurance schemes, but it has not previously been systematized and applied, as Townsend has now done, to examine the issue of poverty.

Contrary to the paradigmatic view ascribed to him, in 1899 Rowntree seems to have held a simple and unarticulated version of the relative deprivation view, although it can be argued that in later life Rowntree was seduced by the support his work received into accepting the viability of the minimum approach. But his own words show that he had not started from those premises: he had no intention of changing the definition of poverty as a deprived life-style, but only of discovering its extent and nature, and of convincing his readers that the reasons for a part of it were not within the control of the poor themselves. Those who read Rowntree's works may at times be surprised that he could arrange his ideas in such unsystematic or taken-for-granted ways, and one may note that his references to the concepts and measures of forms of poverty changed in his books as he grew older. Briggs calls Rowntree's sociology 'unacademic and unsystematic',[130] but Drinkwater considers that in the application of scientific method it is Rowntree's critics and not Rowntree himself who are to blame for the confusion.[131]

Townsend's criticisms are validly addressed to Beveridge and others who maintain the defensibility of a minimum subsistence measure of cash need to be embodied in the state's social policies, but one may ask if they rightly apply to the early Rowntree. As shown above, he started from the premise that poverty was to be expressed in terms of conventions about life-style, as does Townsend. Rowntree's concern about poverty – as Townsend's – did not exist in a moral vacuum but arose from a dissatisfaction with the condition of the poor and the intolerable disparity in control over resources which caused those conditions. When Rowntree wanted to convince his readers of the quality of poverty, he showed them – in a scientific language they respected – that some of the poor had too little money to satisfy their physiological needs, let alone the conventions of life-style. Instead of using a different word for the income measure he devised to emphasize this point, he unwisely also called it poverty, though with the qualifying adjective 'primary'. Townsend distinguishes between deprivation (equivalent to Rowntree's ΣP) and a notion of poverty the role of which is to convince Townsend's readers that the quality of deprivation is caused by lack of money (as opposed, that is, to the idea that the deprivations are caused by other lacks or are voluntary choices of behaviour).

The problem here is not merely semantic. McLachlan has argued at length that it is pointless to disagree about differing stipulative definitions of poverty: 'poverty' is what people use it to mean, and to be considered in the context of action.[132] I have suggested elsewhere that discussion would be helped by using an agreed terminology in which deprivation is the condition of unmet need, which is caused by lack of control over resources of all kinds (tangible, intangible, interpersonal, intrapersonal) over time; and where the term poverty is used in its conventional sense as the condition of lacking *money* resources. In this usage, deprivation may be caused by other factors besides poverty, and money can only meet those needs which can be satisfied in markets.[133] Titmuss was among the first to demonstrate the importance of channels other than markets through which resources flow to meet the needs of individuals.[134] Rowntree considered the question of how far there were other sources of real income available to households, such as the products of allotments, or presents, beyond the cash earnings of the family, and wrote: 'I have come to the conclusion that the extent to which incomes are augmented by such irregular means is very small, and would not materially affect the figures we have been considering.'[135] The occupational, fiscal and social welfare channels which Titmuss identified were, in 1899, either undeveloped or unavailable to the poor. The concepts of deprivation and poverty could thus be treated at that time as largely coterminous, and a comparison between Rowntree's and Townsend's use of the terms is feasible. In these terms, Rowntree's concept of poverty (ΣP) could be described as deprivation identified by observers, while Townsend's method is based on social actors' perceptions of deprivation.

The belief that popular perceptions of deprivation are a valid basis for defining necessities has a long and respectable provenance. Aronson quotes no less than Alfred Marshall's *Principles of Economics* (1890) to show that his views of economic efficiency embraced the idea that class-bound cultural habit created conventional necessities, to be given no less weight than, say, the hypotheses of nutritional science in deciding what necessities were.[136] Aronson's study of the setting of poverty lines in USA in the period 1885–1920 shows how proponents of equality promoted the use of workers' own consumption preferences in defining necessities, while those who supported national efficiency preferred to prescribe how workers should spend their money. She suggests that the idiom of natural science as a means of expressing subsistence minima achieved greater public attention in situations in which there was a low level of agreement on the principles of distributional justice to be applied to anti-poverty policies, and that Rowntree used it only as a rhetorical device to persuade people.[137]

Rowntree's critics often overlook that he used 'natural science' methods to establish solely the nutritional component of the necessities included in primary poverty: the components of clothing, lighting, fuel and rent were in fact based – as many critics suggest they should be – on empirical budget studies of working-class households in York. Not many people know that Rowntree actually discussed with his respondents what *they* considered to be the minimum conventional necessities and their cost, and he then used these responses for his primary poverty minima.[138] Nor was this an isolated instance of attempts to operationalize convention in poverty lines. In Harris's biography of William Beveridge, she described how he was advised that Assistance Board experience showed that 'any practical definition of "subsistence" was largely dependent not merely on what was necessary but also on what was customary'.[139] Beveridge rejected this advice, just as he rejected Rowntree's view that minimum income levels should not be based on a primary poverty approach: Beveridge's recommended income scales were substantially lower than Rowntree's recommendations for minima in *The Human Needs of Labour*.[140] The widespread misrepresentation of Rowntree as the effective originator of the minimum subsistence levels embodied in the income scales of the Beveridge Report *National Assistance and Supplementary Benefit* is particularly ironic in the light of the calculations by Atkinson and his colleagues which show that the poverty line used by Rowntree in his 1950 survey of York was higher than the prevailing National Assistance scale rates by a factor of between 30 and 40 per cent.[141] When one examines the relationship between Townsend's empirically derived 1969 Deprivation Standard and the contemporary supplementary benefit scale rates, one finds that (even allowing for all the methodological reservations which both Atkinson *et al.* and Townsend express) Rowntree's poverty incomes for households of varying compositions are relatively higher than Townsend's (see Table 7.3).

Table 7.3 Rowntree's 1950 poverty line and Townsend's 1969 deprivation standard compared with National Assistance or supplementary benefit scales

Type of household	1950: Rowntree's poverty line as % of NA scale rates	1969: Townsend's deprivation standard as % of SB scale rates
Man under 60	138	131
Woman under 60	119	132
Man and woman both under 60	131	116
Man and woman plus 1 child	134	116–119
Man and woman plus 2 children	136	119–125
Man and woman plus 3 children	136	124–131

Sources: for 1950: Atkinson *et al.* (1981, p.67); for 1969: Townsend (1979, p.269).

Conclusion

To sum up, the evidence from Rowntree's life's work does not suggest that he promoted an absolutist or minimum subsistence conception of poverty, and it does suggest that his measure of overall poverty was relativist and quite comparable with that promoted on empirical grounds by Townsend.

What distinguishes the work of Rowntree and Townsend is not the clash of absolutist versus relativistic paradigms; it is the shift from relativist standards for defining deprivation as *prescribed by observers* to relativist standards *derived from surveys*. The effect is shattering. Decades of futile argument between middle-class experts, administrators and politicians about what goods and services should or should not be included in the list of necessities for the poor are swept away, and the value of sociological expertise is revealed as the power to enable whole populations to speak for themselves systematically and incontrovertibly about what deprivation means.

In Rowntree's class society at the end of the nineteenth century, convention expected clear cultural stratification and the issue of middle-class identification of the key criteria of deprivation was scarcely seen as problematic. What *was* problematic for the power classes was the question of whether to give the poor money and, if so, how much. In Townsend's latter part of the twentieth century the idiom of rigid cultural stratification is widely unacceptable, and the politically contested issue has become more sharply whether the state's social security levels are sufficient to combat deprivation.

This process of change, via Beveridge's adoption of sub-Rowntree poverty lines, has produced a further confusion in Britain. We have to be clear that the scientific establishment of a poverty line is a separate and technical activity which must be firmly distinguished from the quite different activity of taking political decisions as to how much money any government chooses to pay the poor. The public discussion of this issue has been bedevilled for decades in Britain by the inability to distinguish these two activities, and in 1985 Britain still has no official poverty line other than that implied by social security scales. I have discussed elsewhere how this relationship might be clarified and adjusted: that is, how governments may both apply the Townsend paradigm to establishing valid poverty lines, and also consider those factors (such as the intensity of deprivation or other characteristics of deprived categories) they should take into account in setting income maintenance levels for a social security programme.[142] The distinction has been blurred or even obscured by those governments and others who have thought to benefit by deciding first how much money to spend on all the poor and then defining poverty as the income levels which that sum provides.

Like Townsend, Rowntree was not only an investigator but was also politically active and advised the major progressive political party of his day on social policy issues. But, as we have seen, the mixture of roles and goals led to confusion and misunderstanding. Similarly, T.H. Marshall, reviewing Townsend's survey, draws attention to the problems Townsend encounters in 'trying to straddle two horses, one a sociological horse concerned with the scientific analysis of social structure, the other a social policy horse, concerned to expose an evil and to seek a remedy'.[143] Facts do not speak for themselves: the exposure of inequalities, deprivations and poverty is not thereby a motive force for political action or a prescription for the form it should take. The uses made of Rowntree's primary poverty measure should act as a warning to us all to preserve clarity about the pursuit of each set of distinct goals: elucidation, persuasion or policy-making.

Notes

1   I want to acknowledge gratefully the constructive criticism and suggestions which several previous versions of this paper have received since it was first given at the British Sociological Association's annual conference in 1981. I owe a great personal debt to Peter Townsend and my criticism of some of his views must not be taken as detracting from my respect and gratitude to him. The paper has also benefited from the advice of A.B. Atkinson, J. Higgins, K. Judge, H.V. McLachlan, R.A. Sinfield, A.J.C. Wilson, H.C. Wilson, the participants in seminars at the BSA conference and at Newcastle-upon-Tyne Polytechnic, and the anonymous referees of this journal.

2   Rowntree, B.S. (1901), *Poverty: A Study of Town Life*, London, Macmillan.

3   Rowntree, B.S. (1941), *Poverty and Progress*, London, Longmans Green.

4   Rowntree, *Town Life*.

5   Rowntree, *Town Life*; Rowntree, B.S. (1937), *The Human Needs of Labour,* London, Longmans Green.

6   Townsend, P. (1979), *Poverty in the United Kingdom*, Harmondsworth, Penguin.

7   1899 and 1936.

8   Thane, P. (1982), *The Foundations of the Welfare State*, London, Longman, p.6.

9   1901, p.14.

10   For example, '28 per cent of his survey', Evans, E.J. (ed.) (1978), *Social Policy 1830–1914*, London, Routledge and Kegan Paul, p.12.

11   Rowntree, *Town Life*, p.117.

12   For example, Townsend, *Poverty*, p.160; Thane, *Welfare State*, p.168; see Rowntree, *Poverty and Progress*, pp.108, 126.

13   For example, Brown, M. and Madge, N. (1982), *Despite the Welfare State*, London, Heinemann, p.53.

14   Brown, M. (1982), *Introduction to Social Administration in Britain*, London, Hutchinson, p.23.

15   Rowntree, *Town Life*, pp.111, 117.

16   Berthoud, R. and Brown, J. (1981), *Poverty and the Development of Anti-Poverty: Policy in the United Kingdom*, London, Heinemann, p.15.

17   Coates, K. and Silburn, R. (1970), *Poverty: The Forgotten Englishmen*, Harmondsworth, Penguin, p.22.

18   Evans, *Social Policy*, pp.12–13.

19   Field, F. (1982), *Poverty and Politics*, London, Heinemann, p.116.

20   George, V. (1973), *Social Security and Society*, London, Routledge and Kegan Paul, p.42.

21   Holman, R. (1978), *Poverty*, Oxford, Martin Robertson, p.5.

22   Jackson, D. (1972), *Poverty*, London, Macmillan, p.23.

23   Rein, M. (1970), 'Problems in the definition and measurement of poverty', in Townsend, P. (ed.) *The Concept of Poverty*, London, Heinemann, p.50.

24   Townsend, P. (1954), 'Measuring poverty', *British Journal of Sociology*, p.131; Townsend, P. (1962), 'The meaning of poverty', *British Journal of Sociology*, pp.211, 215; Townsend, P., *Poverty*, p.33.

25   Berthoud and Brown, *Policy*, p.8.

26   Hagenbuch, W. (1958), *Social Economics*, Cambridge, Cambridge University Press, p.167.

27   Holman, *Poverty*, pp.4–5.

28   Kincaid, J.C. (1973), *Poverty and Equality in Britain*, Harmondsworth, Penguin, p.53.

29   Meade, J.E. (1972), 'Poverty in the welfare state', *Oxford Economic Papers*, 24 (3), p.289.

30   Rein, M. (1970), 'Problems in the definition and measurement of poverty', in Townsend, *Concept*, p.49.

31   Rodgers, B. (1969), *The Battle Against Poverty, Volume 1*, London, Routledge and Kegan Paul, p.52.

32   Rose, M.E. (1972), *The Relief of Poverty 1834–1914*, London, Macmillan, p.29.

33   Townsend, *Poverty*, p.239.

34   Rowntree, *Town Life*.

35   Rowntree, *Poverty and Progress*, p.461: quoted without reference or apparent awareness of the statistical error by Walker, C.L. and Church, M. (1978), 'Poverty by administration: a review of supplementary benefits, nutrition and scale rates', *Journal of Human Nutrition*, 32 (5–18), p.8.

36   Townsend, 'Measuring poverty'.

37 , Drinkwater, R.W. (1960), 'Seebohm Rowntree's contribution to the study of poverty', *Advancement of Science*, 16, p.193.

38   Aronson, N. (1984), 'The Making of the US Bureau of Labor Statistics Family Budget Series: Relativism and the Rhetoric of Subsistence', Paper presented to the American Sociological Association Meetings, San Antonio, p.26.

39   Rowntree, *Town Life*, pp.7–8.

40   Less than half of the working class was poor, and only one-seventh of the working class had incomes below the primary poverty line – Rowntree, *Town Life*, p.117 and see Field, *Poverty and Politics*, p.119.

41   Rowntree, *Town Life*, p.8.

42   *Ibid.*

43   *Ibid.*, p.14.

44   *Ibid.*, p.14.

45   *Ibid.*, p.26 and elsewhere – but note the error on p.85 where the number given is 47,754.

46   *Ibid.*, p.28.

47   *Ibid.*, p.26.

48   Rowntree, B.S. (1903), *The 'Poverty Line': A Reply*, London, Henry Good, pp.19–20.

49   Rowntree, *Town Life*, pp.115–16.

50   *Ibid.*, p.117.

51   *Ibid.*, p.31.

52   *Ibid.*, p.117.

53   *Ibid.*, pp.115–16.

54   *Ibid.*, p.116.

55   *Ibid.*, p.140.

56   *Ibid.*, pp.297–8.

57   For example, by Jackson, *Poverty*, p.23.

58   Rowntree, *Town Life*, p.117.

59   *Ibid.*, p.111.

60   *Ibid.*, p.117.

61   Townsend, *Poverty*, p.31.

62   Letter from Booth to Rowntree, quoted by Rowntree (1901), p.300.

63   Rowntree, *Town Life*, p.299.

64   Rowntree, *Poverty Line*, p.19.

65   Quoted in Rowntree, *Town Life*, p.300.

66   Nash, R. (1902), *How the Poor Live*, Manchester, Women's Co-operative Guild, p.3.

67   Simey, T. and Simey, M. (1960), *Charles Booth, Social Scientist*, Oxford, Oxford University Press, p.279.

68   Booth, C. (1892), *Life and Labour of the People of London, Volume 1*, London, Macmillan, p.33.

69   Marshall, T.H. (1981), *The Right to Welfare and Other Essays*, London, Heinemann, p.37.

70   Rowntree, *Town Life*, p.118.

71   Bowley, A. L. and Burnett-Hurst, A.R. (1915), *Livelihood and Poverty: A Study in the Economic and Social Conditions of Working-Class Households in Northampton, Warrington, Stanley, Reading (and Bolton)*, London, King.

72   Rowntree, *Town Life*, p.141.

73   *Ibid.*, p.112.

74   Bowley, A.L. and Hogg, M.H. (1925), *Has Poverty Diminished?*, London, King, p.13.

75   Rowntree, *Town Life*, p.14.

76   *Ibid.*, Chapter 8.

77   *Ibid.*, Chapter 5.

78   Rowntree, *Poverty Line*, p.3.

79   *Ibid.*, p.21, original emphasis.

80   *Ibid.*, p.22.

81   *Ibid.*, p.25.

82   Rowntree, *Town Life*, p.87n.

83   *Ibid.*, pp.142–3.

84   *Ibid.*, p.144.

85   *Ibid.*, p.145.

86   Field, *Poverty and Politics*, p.116.

87   Rowntree, *Poverty Line*, p.19.

88   Rowntree, *Poverty and Progress*, p.102.

89   Rowntree, *Town Life*, pp.133–4.

90   Rowntree, B.S. and Kendall, M. (1913), *How the Labourer Lives*, London, Thomas Nelson and Sons, pp.30–1.

91   Rowntree, B.S. (1937), *The Human Needs of Labour*, London, Longmans Green, p.125.

92   Letter from Rowntree to Caradog Jones, 18 January 1952, Rowntree Archive, York, item SR/p.21.

93   Briggs, A. (1961), *Social Thought and Social Action: A Study of the Work of Seebohm Rowntree*, London, Longman, p.296.

94   Briggs, *Social Thought*, p.297.

95   Rowntree, *Poverty and Progress*, p.126.

96   Rowntree, *Human Needs*, pp.126–7.

97   Briggs, *Social Thought*, pp.36–7, quoting Rowntree, *Town Life*, p.135n.

98   From an unpublished paper on unemployment insurance, quoted in Briggs, *Social Thought*, p.204.

99   *Ibid.*, p.204.

100   Rowntree, *Poverty and Progress*, p.7.

101   *Ibid.*, pp.102, 104.

102   *Ibid.*, p.11.

103   *Ibid.*, p.11.

104   *Ibid.*, p.25.

105   *Ibid.*, pp.12, 32.

106   *Ibid.*, p.461.

107   *Ibid.*

108   Rowntree, *Poverty and Progress*, p.126.

109   Townsend, *Poverty*, p.160.

110   *Ibid.*, p.302.

111   Rowntree, *Poverty and Progress*, p.101.

112   *Ibid.*, p.461.

113   *Ibid.*, p.460.

114   *Ibid.*, p.461.

115   Rowntree, *Town Life*, p.117.

116   Rowntree, *Poverty and Progress*, p.462.

117   Thane, *Welfare State*, p.168.

118   Brown and Madge, *Welfare State*, p.53.

119   Mencher, S. (1967), 'The problem of measuring poverty', *British Journal of Sociology*, 18 (1), p.2.

120   Townsend, *Poverty*, p.32.

121   *Ibid.*, p.33.

122   *Ibid.*

123   Rowntree, *Town Life*, p.300.

124   Such as those of Land, Marsden, Sinfield and Veit-Wilson: for details see Townsend (ed.), *Concept of Poverty*, and Townsend, *Poverty*.

125   Rowntree, *Human Needs*, and *Poverty and Progress*.

126   Townsend, *Poverty*, pp.38–9.

127   Townsend, P., 'The meaning of poverty', *British Journal of Sociology*, 18(3), p.215.

128   Townsend, *Poverty*, p.239.

129 Briggs, *Social Thought*.

130 *Ibid.*, p.3.

131 Drinkwater, *Study of Poverty*, p.192.

132 McLachlan, H.V. (1983), 'Townsend and the concept of "Poverty"', *Social Policy and Administration*, 17 (2), pp.97–105.

133 Veit-Wilson, J.H. (1981), 'Measuring poverty', *New Society*, 58, No.986, p.76.

134 Titmuss, R.M. (1958), 'The social division of welfare', in *Essays on the Welfare State*, London, Allen and Unwin.

135 Rowntree, *Town Life*, p.112.

136 Aronson, N. (1984), 'The making of the US Bureau of Labor Statistics Family Budget Series: relativism and the rhetoric of subsistence', Paper presented to the American Sociological Association Meetings, San Antonio.

137 *Ibid.*, p.26.

138 Rowntree, *Town Life*, p.108.

139 Harris, J. (1977), *William Beveridge: A Biography*, Oxford, Clarendon Press, p.397.

140 See, for example, Veit-Wilson, J.H. (1984), 'Seebohm Rowntree', in Barker, P. (ed.), *Founders of the Welfare State*, London, Heinemann, p.82.

141 Atkinson, A.B., Corlyon, J., Maynard, A.K., Sutherland, H. and Trinder, C.G. (1981), 'Poverty in York: a true analysis of Rowntree's 1950 survey', *Bulletin of Economic Research*, 33, p.67.

142 Veit-Wilson, J.H. (1985), 'Consensual Approaches to Poverty Lines and Social Security', *Journal of Social Policy*, 16 (2), pp.269–301.

143 Marshall, T.H. (1981), 'Poverty or Deprivation?', *Journal of Social Policy*, 10 (1), p.82.

Part III Retrieved Riches: using the Booth archive

8 Charles Booth and the social geography of education in late nineteenth-century London

William Marsden

The reverential review of the first series of Booth's *Life and Labour* surveys in the *Pall Mall Gazette* in 1891, ranking its author as a 'social Copernicus', drew special attention to the important educational component in Booth's surveys, in contrast to the later neglect of this aspect. Like others, the reviewer identified education as the most likely cure for the social diseases of urban life:

> We rise from them feeling that here, more probably than anywhere else – in this splendid educational and disciplinary work that is being done for London by the Board and voluntary schools – lies the solution of our hardest problems.[1]

The *School Board Chronicle* had already acknowledged the 'value to educationists' of Booth's earlier paper to the London Statistical Society on 'The Condition and Occupation of the People of East London and Hackney', and used it as an argument for regarding the provision of schooling also as a means of redress in the case of gross disparities in social opportunity:

> We must get rid of the false idea that education is the privilege of the few to be used chiefly for their mere personal advantage. In a civilised country everyone must be able to render service in some form or other which the community requires, or become a burden upon it. There is no alternative: we must either bear the cost of extending fitting education for all or pay an accumulated penalty hereafter, and though short-sighted views of personal self-interest may induce some to evade the duty, the true instinct of national interest and indeed of self-preservation calls aloud for its full performance.
>
> If the paramount need of modifying our school system and organising all those resources which in the broader sense of the word are educational, be once recognised, we may hope to do much to reduce the amount of human suffering.[2]

While Booth offered some reassurance on the extent of this suffering,[3] he too subscribed to the widely held pathological interpretations of life in the metropolitan slums and to this unrealistic elevation of education to a leading position on the list of possible rescue agencies. Booth and his team relied heavily on the education service in their own work, double-checking their relatively objective survey results, based on School Board Visitors' Reports, against subjective estimates they elicited from teachers in their school visits. The former indicated 8.4 per cent of the population existed in dire poverty and 22.3 per cent in poverty or precarious comfort. The schoolteachers' estimates suggested 11.8 per cent in the former and 33.2 per cent in the latter categories.[4]

These close contacts with School Board Visitors and teachers are one of the major benefits the Booth surveys provide for the social historian of education. The very timing of the surveys is of help for, by the late 1880s, the London School Boards had come of age, having grappled effectively with the problem of providing accommodation of a standard well in advance of its time for hundreds of thousands of children, having attacked vigorously, some claimed over-vigorously, the problems of attendance, and having initiated sophisticated bureaucratic structures and wide-ranging curricular extensions that demoralized the voluntary providers, many still functioning on early nineteenth-century definitions of what constituted an appropriate 'education of the poor'.

Booth and his team were able to use the carefully delineated London School Board districts and blocks as a basis for the survey of poverty and comfort in the metropolitan region. The maps were collected in an appendix to Volume 2 of the first survey. For the more detailed ecological surveys at individual street level, the result was the extraordinary and now justly celebrated series of colour-coded maps,[5] of compulsive interest and unique value to the urban historian of education. Booth claimed validity for his surveys in part on the basis of the thorough details obtained from the School Board Visitors:

> The School Board visitors perform amongst them a house-to-house visitation; every house in every street is in their books, and details are given of every family with children of school age. They begin their scheduling two or three years before the children attain school age, and a record remains in their books of children who have left school. The occupation of the head of the family is noted down. Most of the visitors have been working in the same district for several years ...
>
> They are in daily contact with the people, and have a very considerable knowledge of the parents of the school children, especially the poorest amongst them, and of the conditions under which they live. No one can go, as I have done, over the

descriptions of the inhabitants of street after street in this huge district and doubt the genuine character of the information and its truth.[6]

The reliance on these reports and on official School Board boundaries clearly enhances the potential of the surveys for educational research. The first series, *Labour and Life of the People*, thus provides critical data at two scales: those of the metropolitan region, and of the individual community or even street, the latter immensely important particularly where the admissions registers of individual schools can be found and catchment areas mapped. In no other town or city is so revealing a resource-base available.

The second series of *Life and Labour of the People in London*, the so-called 'Industry Series', is useful in a different way, in that one of the 'trades' was that of schoolteacher. From this information, the pattern of residential preference of teachers is revealed, an issue which Booth and his team took up in their final series. In some ways this third series, 'Religious Influences', is the most valuable of all, in that it extends the territorial coverage of the first series, identifies ecological change as it took place in some districts during the 1890s, and is also assertive, characteristically from the high moral ground, on a number of values issues, *inter alia* making judgements about the relative successes of church and school in influencing the morals and manners of a volatile urban population.

In sum, for the social historian of education the Booth surveys provide an unparalleled source for the investigation of disparities in urban educational provision, including:

(a)   *territorial variations* in access to schooling at the metropolitan scale, which were

(b)   closely associated with a growing residential segregation in society in turn generating a *hierarchical gradation of schooling*, as evident in the elementary phase as the secondary;

(c)   at the micro-level, studies of *individual schools and their social catchments*, particularly in the poorer areas which so preoccupied Booth and his team;

(d)   examination of the mismatch between the location of schools in which they taught and the residential preferences of teachers;

(e)   explorations of the attitudes of teachers to their work, again especially among poorer children, and their views on the intellectual, social and moral impact of the work of the London School Board.

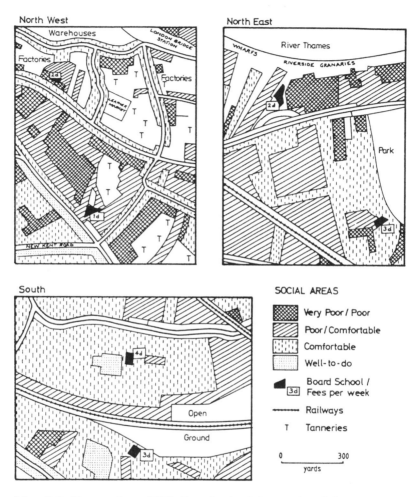

Map 8.1 Bermondsey, 1875: Board school fees and social area
differentiation (after Booth)

Territorial variations at the metropolitan scale

The first *Labour and Life* survey was complemented by an investigation of social indicators contained in the 1891 census. A close correlation was revealed between the house-to-house visitation, the basis of Booth's poverty comfort spectrum, and the evidence of overcrowding drawn from the census material. Thus the 30.7 per cent in poverty and 69.3 per cent in comfort in London was paralleled in the 31.5 per cent crowded and 68.5 per cent not crowded ratio he worked out from the census.[7] Together these delineated enormous territorial variations in poverty and comfort over the metropolitan area. On the basis of his surveys and the census figures, Booth found, with one exception, the same areas in the top twelve of both poverty and overcrowding.[8] Thus St George's-in-the East headed both the table of poverty (48.9 per cent) and of crowding (57 per cent). St George's indeed topped six out of seven of Booth's indices of poverty, while in 'Hampstead, happy Hampstead, there is neither poverty nor crowding, or at least much less than anywhere else in London'. As Booth observed, in these two districts 'we have our alpha and omega'.[9]

Fifty of London's School Board blocks had ratios of over 55 per cent poverty. Parts of Bermondsey, Southwark, Bethnal Green and South Lambeth rose to over 75 per cent. In general the East End, dockland areas to the south of the Thames, and the northern fringes of the West End and the City, had poverty levels of over 60 per cent, about twice the average of London as a whole. Within these areas, there were individual black spots. Bethnal Green had the largest percentage of the 'residuum', 17.2 per cent, while St George's-in-the-East with 48.8 per cent had the largest percentage of the poor.[10] At the other extreme, about three-quarters of the population of the School Board divisions of Marylebone, Chelsea and Westminster were living in comfort. But even in relatively prosperous areas there would be individual communities in poverty. Thus, while Greenwich division as a whole had a poverty ratio of only 28 per cent, this masked a range from 18 per cent to nearly 37 per cent. Marylebone's average of 26 per cent covered a range of from 13.5 per cent to 30.4 per cent. Even more strikingly, the deviation in Finsbury's 33.5 per cent average in poverty was from 18.8 to 48.9 per cent.[11]

It is significant that it was in the areas of great poverty that, on the one hand, the voluntary providers prior to the 1870 Act had left the most yawning gaps in accommodation and, on the other, that the London School Board achieved its greatest quantitative success in having plugged most of the gaps by the time of Booth's survey. In 1871, for example, the London School Board's own survey revealed huge deficits in accommodation in all its eleven districts, the smallest deficits being in the City and Westminster. These two areas had a small surplus of school places for girls, but everywhere else was in deficit. There were small surpluses in accommodation for boys in four of the most well-to-do districts, the City and Westminster again, and Chelsea and Marylebone.[12] The 'filling in the gaps' principle laid upon the School Boards by the 1870 Education Act can therefore be redefined in considerable part in terms of the resolution of spatial inequalities.

The hierarchical grading of elementary schools in London

Booth's general map of London poverty/comfort was divided into 134 areas with about 30,000 people in each, and was compiled from information collected in 1889–90. The details could be combined at the School Board division level, or fined down to individual School Board blocks.[13] Stemming from the categorization of groups along the poverty–comfort spectrum, and from the territorial diversity, Booth proceeded to classify the elementary schools of London on a social grading basis. In so doing he drew attention to a, by then, well-established process of hierarchical adjustment to the perceived social/educational needs of children from the lower middle classes downwards, based on an officially approved graduated fees structure, with school payments ranging from 1d. to 9d. per week.[14]

Booth's classification of schools relied heavily on information derived from teachers who, on the basis of the appearance of the children, regularity of attendance, attitudes towards fee-paying, and so on, could form 'a fair idea of the character of the home', and in so doing opened up a rich 'mine of knowledge'.[15] What emerged was a graded classification of elementary schools according to the percentage of children they contained in each of Booth's social classes. This was followed by a more systematic investigation of selected schools. The classification of schools of the elementary sector into six classes, then three linked grades, is shown in Table 8.1 (overleaf). Illuminating differences were found between the voluntary schools of the religious bodies and the Board schools.[16]

The Board sector was in an intermediate position in terms of social intake. The Catholic schools accommodated the largest proportion of poor children, with nearly 25 per cent in the two poorest categories and about 70 per cent in all in poverty. By contrast, nearly 75 per cent of the children attending Anglican and Nonconformist voluntary schools came from comfortable backgrounds. The Board Schools took approximately 60 per cent of children from poor and 40

Table 8.1 Six classes and three grades of elementary schools

Class	Characteristics	Grades of elementary schools
I	Accommodating the 'poor' and 'very poor' with a sprinkling of the lowest semi-criminal class	Lower
II	Accommodating the 'poor' with but a slight mixture of 'very poor'	
III	Accommodating the 'poor' and comfortably off together	Middle
IV	Accommodating the comfortably off with but few 'poor'	
V	Accommodating the comfortably off and some fairly well-to-do	Upper
VI	Accommodating those who are fairly well-to-do only	

per cent from comfortable backgrounds.[17] In terms of fees, Booth found that about 5000 Protestant and 5500 Catholic children were being schooled free, and 6700 and 2800 were paying 1d. per week, out of totals of 175,000 and 32,500 respectively. At the other end of the scale, over 40,000 Anglican children were being charged 6d. and above, as against less than 500 Catholic.[18]

A striking instance of territorial variation at the detailed community scale resulting from the differentiated fees mechanism can be found in Bermondsey. The case was interesting also in that it made explicit the fact that the Education Department gave the London School Board tacit approval to gear the fee to what the local market would bear. Thus in the poverty-ridden and malodorous tanneries district in north-west Bermondsey (Map 8.1), there was a 'penny board school'; the riverside and other industrialized zones generally had board schools with 2d. fees; less crowded areas of east and south-east Bermondsey 3d. and more. The one 4d. school in the area in 1875 was Monmow Road, from an early stage the most prestigious Board school in Bermondsey, and located in the most extensive well-to-do area according to Booth's classification (Map 8.1). On at least two occasions the school fees were raised in reflection of this fact. When the London School Board resolved to raise the fees from 4d. to 6d. in 1880, radical local groups protested. Divisional members of the Board supported their case, but the Education Department insisted that its aim was to secure that fees be fixed 'so as to suit the particular class of children for which a particular school may have been erected', relying on local knowledge to judge the suitable level of fee.[19]

Individual schools and catchment areas

Having graded the schools into 'classes', Booth and his team probed more deeply, paying particular attention to the poorest schools. His assistant, Mary Tabor, provided background on the three broader grades: Upper, Middle and Lower (Table 8.1).

The upper grade schools excited warm approval. 'A more inspiriting and satisfactory sight can hardly be desired':

> The great bulk of the children are wholesome, bright-looking, well-fed, well-clad, eager for notice, 'smart', and full of life. 'Smartness' is much cultivated in schools of this class, and the superiority in nervous power is often very noticeable as compared with those of the lower grades. The work done, though often mechanical, too clerkly, and narrowed under past regulations by the defects of a rigid and imperfect Code, is still in quality, scope, and teaching power, distinctly in advance of what even middle-class parents, a few years ago, could secure for their children in the ordinary private school.[20]

The middle grade school was marked by between 26 per cent and 37 per cent of children in groups E and F, only a sprinkling in A, about 10 per cent in B, and the great majority in C and D. A key factor in the quality of this grade of school was seen to be the success of the headteacher. Under good leadership, a middle-grade school would show 'as many open intelligent faces among the boys, as much refinement and decision among the girls, as one of quite the upper grade that has been managed by a mere mechanical driver for "results"'.

Such headteachers won the confidence of parents, and more children stayed on into Standards V and VI. Mary Tabor viewed with favour also the introduction of penny banks, libraries, Swedish drill, Bands of Hope, and cricket and football clubs into such schools, with the penny bank in particular seen as the 'best corrective' to spending money at the sweet shop, 'the child's public house', regarded as 'an excellent training in those habits of heedless self-indulgence which are the root of half the misery of the slums'.[21]

The lower grade, Class I schools provoked much more detailed attention. These included the 'schools of special difficulty' set up by the London School Board in 1884. There were twenty-two such schools at the time of Booth's survey, taking about 21,000 children. In them, headteachers were paid £20 and assistants £10 per year extra. Criteria for designating 'special difficulty' were 1d. fees; few children in attendance over school exemption age; a transitory school population; and parents and children of such a character as to impose special difficulties on the teachers.[22] The type locale was

> ... usually on the skirts, or standing in the midst of a crowded, low, insanitary neighbourhood. The main streets, narrow at best, branch off into others narrower still; and these again into a labyrinth of blind alleys, courts and lanes; all dirty, foul-smelling, and littered with garbage and refuse of every kind. The houses are old, damp and dilapidated ... Not that the children are much at home. Their waking hours are divided between school and the streets. Bedtime is when the public-houses close. The hours before that are the liveliest of all the twenty-four, and they swarm about undisturbed till then. They have no regular meal times ...[23]

Tabor found the atmosphere and character of children in the infant departments of such areas less disturbing than that in the junior departments. She saw the slum mother as liable to expend extra toil on the little ones, leaving the older siblings to fend more for themselves. She instanced a Standard I boys' class of 'dull and backward children', a 'sorry group' of fifteen to twenty:

> One or two are tidy-looking boys; one has a clean washed face, and a white collar on. The rest are ragged, ill-kept and squalid in appearance. Some are filthily dirty, others sickly looking, with sore eyes and unwholesome aspect. One or two seem hopelessly dull, almost vacant. Another, a scare-crow little fellow, alert and sharp, with a pair of black eyes twinkling restlessly around as if he were meditating escape, had made his own living, we are told, in the streets before the officer ran him in.[24]

But even among this group, 'fully half the homes are decent in their way', and it was from such that pupils were more prone to move into the higher standards. Thus after Standards III and IV, a marked improvement in atmosphere was apparent, those staying on to V and VI coming from more respectable homes. But such children generally formed no more than 6 per cent and in some schools only 2 to 3 per cent of the total on roll. In the very worst schools, there was no leaven at all:

> The slum look is everywhere. It penetrates like a slimy fog into the
> school itself. 'Slum-born' seems written on the faces of the
> children, hardly one of whom impresses us as well up to the
> average ... We see numbers of half-imbecile children throughout
> the school; big boys in low standards who cannot learn, try as they
> may; children of drinking parents chiefly ...[25]

As already noted (reference 9), for Booth, St George's-in-the-
East and Hampstead represented the omega and the alpha in his social
spectrum, and these offer useful detailed studies of particular schools
and their catchments. In an earlier survey, Booth had judged St
George's-in-the-East to be 'more entirely poverty-stricken' than either
of its poor neighbours, Whitechapel and Stepney.[26] He found it a
peculiarly depressing place:

> ... a walk down to St George's is always ... into comparative
> colourlessness. There is a feeling of going away from the heart of
> things. It is off the main beat and monotony reigns ... the
> temptation to drink to excess there comes with especial strength.[27]

In an earlier appraisal he had been even more gloomy:

> Of all the districts of that 'inner ring' which surrounds the City, St
> George's-in-the-East is the most desolate. The other districts each
> have some charm or other – a brightness not extinguished by, and
> even appertaining to, poverty and toil, to vice, and even to crime
> ... a rush of human life as fascinating to watch as the current of a
> river to which life is so often likened. But there is nothing of this
> in St George's, which appears to stagnate with a squalor peculiar
> to itself.[28]

Of all the districts of London, St George's was worst in terms of
poverty, domestic crowding, death rate per thousand, and on a
combined position of all the variables of social difficulty considered by
Booth, based on information in the 1891 census.[29] One concern
peculiar to Whitechapel and adjacent parts of St George's was the
influx of European Jews at this time, which Booth saw as an important
cause of overcrowding:

> The German Jew is coming into St George's in large and
> increasing numbers. They can live under conditions and so close
> together as to put to shame the ordinary overcrowding of the
> English casual labourer ... There were at one time only Irish
> colonies in St George's but these are slowly giving way before the
> German Jew who occupies their quarters and supplants them in
> other ways.[30]

The influence of this almost unique example, aside from the Irish, of significant foreign immigration, was seen by Booth's secretaries as mixed, in that although the Jews contributed to appalling overcrowding, they presented a 'favourable contrast to the promiscuity of many of the English poor', and could be seen 'as cleaners or scavengers of districts of Irish poor'. But in better districts they were said to hasten decline.[31]

They had a major impact on school provision in Whitechapel and neighbouring parts of St George's:

> I can remember when even at Chicksand Street school [in Whitechapel] less than half the children were Jewish and now there are hardly any Christian children in the place. Bink's Row, Rutland Street, Lower Chapman Street [Map 8.2] and Betts Street schools are all now Jewish or being Judaized.[32]

At the time of the formation of the London School Board, St George's-in-the-East was a classic area of educational under-provision. The situation was gradually improved by the Board's energetic school-building programme, and by the time of Booth's survey St George's had been provided with large Board schools, accommodating over 1000 children in each, such as Berner Street and Lower Chapman Street.

Map 8.2, showing Board schools only, illustrates how thick on the ground schools had to be to service so densely packed an area. By the end of the School Board era, apart from the three Board schools whose catchments are shown on the map, there were also Betts Street, Cable Street, Christian Street, the 'Highway' (a 'school of special difficulties' in St George's Street) and in Wapping, Brewhouse Lane and Globe Street. With the exception of that of Lower Chapman Street, fractured as it was at this time by the presence of London Docks, the catchment areas were very compact. Blakesley Street appears to have catered for the most concentrated area of serious poverty, to the south of Commercial Road, though the 'Highway', for which the appropriate information is not available, would no doubt have been worse. The relatively homogeneous social nature of the area appears to have precluded a clear-cut internal hierarchy of elementary schools based on differentiated fees. In 1877, for example, the two Board schools then in existence in St George's, Berner Street and Lower Chapman Street, had fees of 1d. or 2d. respectively. Of all the Board schools of St George's only Cable Street, small for a Board school with accommodation for 400 only, attained higher grade status.

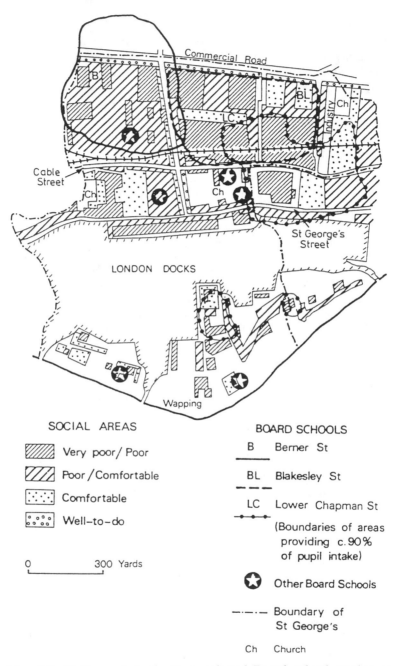

Map 8.2 St George's-in-the-East: selected Board school catchment zones and social area differentiation in the 1890s (after Booth)

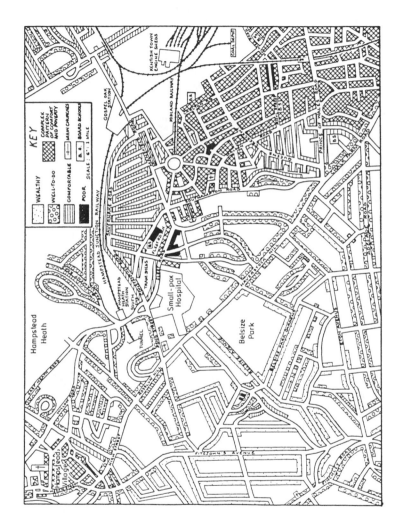

Map 8.3 Hampstead and environs, 1890s: social area differentiation (simplification of Booth's map)

They were conspicuous by their absence in the lists of successful London scholarship schools.

By contrast, notwithstanding pockets of poverty in the old village, most of Hampstead was prosperous. The inhabitants discerned no need whatsoever for Board schools in Hampstead proper, as distinguished from its fringes, and successfully resisted attempts to introduce them until the very last years of the London School Board.

Of particular interest, however, is the transition zone between Hampstead village and Kentish Town (Map 8.3). In this block the London School Board built Fleet Road School in 1879. Fleet Road was appropriate territory for the construction of a Board school. It was at the end of a tram route. (Trams were the low status form of transport at the time and had been excluded from Hampstead itself.) It was the site of a smallpox hospital.[33] Close to the working-class housing of Kentish Town, creeping north-west and threatening the slopes of Hampstead itself, Fleet Road, described by Besant as 'this dreary street',[34] represented very much the 'fag-end' of Hampstead. The intention was that the school should cater for the escalating population of West Kentish Town and Gospel Oak.

This was a socio-economically mixed urban zone, as Booth described:

> Many find employment in the railways and in Brinsmead's and other piano makers ... Wives of working-class work in the laundries round about. Not much distress but majority live from hand to mouth ... some shopkeepers, mixed with labourers, some of the latter in struggling poverty.

In the immediate neighbourhood of Fleet Road, Booth referred to 'modern roads containing decent artisans and their families',[35] an area with nearly three-quarters of the population living 'in comfort'.

In the seven years between the opening of the schooling, and the sittings of the Cross Commission on Elementary Education, the Headmaster, Mr W.B. Adams, had established Fleet Road as one of the most celebrated Board schools in London. In the evidence he gave to the Commission, he insisted that his catchment area was not especially privileged:

> The population is a very mixed one; we have the children of brick-layers and labourers: a considerable sprinkling of the parents of the children are employed on the Midland and North-western Railways. The great industry of the neighbourhood is pianoforte making ... and a great number of the parents of the children are employed there. Then we have a new neighbourhood springing up

of small villas, which are occupied by people engaged in city warehouses, and so on.[36]

It would seem that Mr Adams spotted the potential in this 'new neighbourhood' from an early stage. Just to the north of the school, between Mansfield Road and the railway (Map 8.3), it was immediately obvious as a lower-middle-class area. The esteem of the school was quickly established by expert public relations. The successes of the school in the London School Board scholarship stakes and choral competitions were given maximum publicity through prize days and school concerts, to which influential educational and political figures were invited, and through entries in the local press. Competition for places at the school became intense, as the catchment area was pivoted towards the north, and more and more children were entered from other parts of London, making use of the railways which focused on Gospel Oak for daily transport. Unlike the situation in other areas, where board school headteachers complained of voluntary schools foisting difficult children on them, the opposite seems to have occurred in the case of Fleet Road.

On the fringes of the 'Hampstead of the villas', Fleet Road School provides a vintage case study of the interpenetration of residential and school choice, in the peopling of an area closely associated with the 'great age' of three major social developments: railways, domestic music and popular education. Parents who worked as engine drivers and station-masters, skilled piano craftsmen, and as clerks travelling by the North London line to offices in the City, were at one with the aspirations of a headmaster who made Fleet Road the best-known, if not the best, of the London Board Schools. It was a school at the cutting edge in the rise of the meritocracy.[37]

It would be grossly deterministic to suggest the social catchment necessarily dictated the success of a school in the competitive scholarship stakes, though it was in general accepted that social advantage favoured higher quality provision and scholastic achievement. One of W.B. Adams' guiding principles was to give priority to the attraction of highly trained staff and to this as much as the nature of the pupils he attributed the school's success. The quality and attitude of head and assistant teachers was also an issue of concern to Charles Booth.

The residential preferences of teachers

In the 'Population Classified by Trades' part of his survey, Booth turned to education under the general heading of 'Public Service and Professional Classes', published in volume 8 in the second edition.

The section of 'Literature and Education' was undertaken by Jesse Argyle.[38] On the basis of the 1891 census enumeration, 26,521 people were classified as teachers, of whom 19,794 were women, and 1040, including School Board Visitors, were also identified as being in 'school service'. Map 8.4 shows the distribution of persons engaged in education in the metropolis, and reveals a pattern which far from replicates those of poverty and overcrowding. Thus the Surrey docklands, the East End, and the city centre and its northern fringes were avoided by the teachers. Neither were significant numbers found in the affluent parts of London, such as Chelsea and Westminster, St John's Wood and Hampstead.

The teachers generally resided in quintessentially lower-middle-class areas, such as Hackney and Fulham, Wandsworth and Camberwell. They generally lived in adequate though far from affluent circumstances. Teachers were very much on the fringe of the servant-keeping class. About 30 per cent kept at least one servant.[39] The modal age of the teaching population was thirty, about seven years higher than that for the occupied population of London as a whole.[40]

The mismatch between the catchment areas of the poorer elementary schools and the residential preferences of their staffs was striking. Comparing two of Booth's tables by taking rank orders, the top six areas for the percentage of the population engaged in education were Fulham, Lewisham, Hackney, Greenwich, Wandsworth and Camberwell. These were respectively 17th, 25th, 21st, 7th, 15th and 13th (out of 25 districts) in the rank order of poverty. Similarly, the six districts most unpopular as places of residence for teachers, Shoreditch, Bethnal Green, the City, Holborn, St Saviour's and St Olave's, both in Southwark, were respectively 6th, 2nd, 10th, 1st and 5th in the poverty scale.[41] For the most part, Booth was complimentary about the headteachers and assistants he met. Where interviews were reproduced in the Third Series volumes such staff remained anonymous, but in the original archive the names of those interviewed remain. The head of one school, Mr D., was declared to be:

> ... a man of volcanic energy, pleasant bright face and dancing eyes, full of enthusiasm for his work, and with a tremendous idea of the importance of the schoolmaster's mission. ... The dullest, the idlest and the most apathetic must be stirred to some extent by contrast with a spirit so keen and vivacious.[42]

Mr H.J. Dare, Headmaster of Barrow Hill Road Board School and once an assistant at Fleet Road School, gained equally enthusiastic praise:

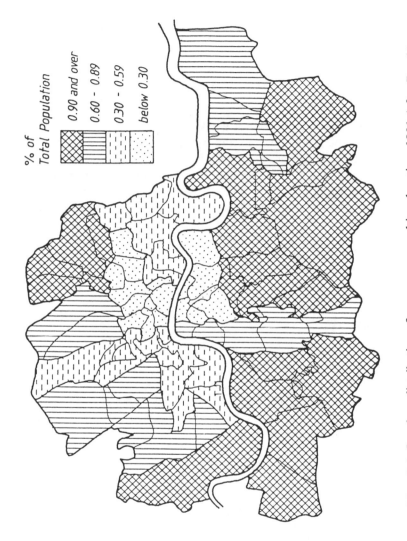

Map 8.4 London: distribution of persons engaged in education, 1891 (after Booth)

% of
Total Population

0.90 and over

0.60 - 0.89

0.30 - 0.59

below 0.30

> He is a man of 40 looking much younger ... He has been at this school for five years. He is exceedingly keen and intelligent ... I enjoyed my interview and walk round with him immensely, coming away with a renewed conviction that as an elevating influence the school swamps the rest.[43]

Similarly Miss Newland, at Belvedere Place Board School, Borough Road:

> ... a model teacher ... Scotch, quiet, forcible, clear-headed and sympathetic ... Methodical in her ways; rigorous in her discipline; firm and kindly ...[44]

At the same time, Booth was quick to pick up evidence of lack of interest of any headteacher in the social mission of the school, especially in the poorer areas. Of such he could be very critical. Thus the headmaster of one Board school in Saffron Hill was described as 'going and coming from the school daily like a City clerk', knowing the locality little, and interested only in the educational side of the school.[45] The headmaster of a Limehouse Board school lived in Forest Gate, beyond the boundary covered by the London School Boards, and surprised Booth by how little he knew of the activities of the boys out of school. He took children only after seeing them, and appeared to attract a larger than expected percentage of children of shopkeepers and mechanics.[46] The head of a Battersea school was similarly said to live some way from the school and see as little as possible of his school district.[47]

One School Board Visitor Booth interviewed had a poor overall view of the social pretensions of schoolteachers: 'The teachers generally are the children of artisans, and rising as they do into a different social stratum they suffer from "swelled heads" and think more of their social position in the suburb in which they live than of the welfare of the children in their school.'[48]

The social impact of education

The teachers also provided Booth with a largely positive assessment of the impact of education, particularly since the establishment of Board schools. A number commented on the benefit which had accrued from the children being second generation schoolgoers.[49] One of the fullest responses came from the headmaster and a member of the staff of Summerford Street school in Bethnal Green. The head found little mental improvement, but an enormous progress in manners and morals. In the early days, the slightest rebuke brought filthy language but, while bad language was still heard in the playground, an oath was rarely evident in school hours. His assistant teacher spoke even more strongly:

> I have emphatically to record that a great and pronounced change has in my time taken place in the whole demeanour of the native born child, and for the better. The old ruffian child is fast disappearing. Where are the rebels and outlaws and young villains of a dozen years ago? The school has not existed for nothing.[50]

Similarly the headmaster of a poor Board school in the inner south of London found the boy of 1890, as compared with that of 1880:

> Much more docile; insubordination, then endemic, now almost unknown ... Cheerful and eager now, then often sullen and morose. Relations with teachers generally friendly, often affectionate – no street-calling of them or stone-throwing as there used to be.[51]

A number of the headteachers displayed a certain hostility to the church and were dismissive of its social influence. Thus at Portman Place Board School the head, Mr T.C. Bray, referred to the clergy of his district as a 'poor lot', negatively regarded by working-class people, and having little success in attracting children to Sunday school. Bray also judged religious teaching in the Board schools to be superior to that in the voluntary sector.[52] Similarly the master and mistress of a Board school in Greenwich found religion to have no present place in the lives of the families of their pupils, and thought schools had greater social influence than any other medium. Religious influences were seen here by Booth to 'fail even to an unusual degree to penetrate' the lives of the people.[53]

Even though a large number of interviewees asserted the value of education in softening the manners of the poor, there remained constant reference to the social problems of schooling in the slum areas, having to grapple with the perceived thriftlessness and drunkenness of parents, and the poor attendance, dullness, and lack of attention of the children.

At the time of the First Series, Booth and his team clearly shared the optimism the London School Board's efforts had created in promoting the schools as a force for social and moral improvement. Their influence was symbolized in the Board school buildings, 'uniformly handsome, commodious, and for the most part substantial and well arranged ... the high-water-mark of the public conscience in this country in its relation to the education of the people'.[54]

Nowhere more than in the East of London does the 'extravagance' of the School Board stand justified. It was necessary to strike the eye and hold the imagination, it was worth much to carry high the flag of education and this is what has been done. Each school stands up from its playground like a Church in God's acre ringing its bell ... The effect of the tall school buildings with their characteristic architecture is heightened by the low-browed houses amongst which they stand. Such situations have been deliberately chosen and the clearance for the school-house has been made very often in the midst of the worst class of poverty.[55]

By the time of the Third Series, 'Religious Influences', Booth was more circumspect in his judgements though still of the opinion that the schools remained the most potent influence on social well-being, especially when compared with the churches and charitable agencies.[56] Yet there had been a 'palpable failure to secure the results anticipated'. Further,

A whole generation has been through the schools, but in scholarship there is not much to show for it. Almost all can, indeed, read, though with some effort; and write, after a fashion; but those who can do either the one or the other with the facility that comes of constant practice are comparatively few.

But the effort had been 'far from wasted' on the moral dimension: 'Obedience to discipline and rules of proper behaviour have been inculcated; habits and order and cleanliness have been acquired; and from these habits self-respect arises.'[57]

As one who believed the ultimate purpose of education was religious, it may be that the survey's findings on this score were depressing to Booth. Was the answer to infiltrate religion through education and hope by this means for a downward social diffusion of respectability and religious-mindedness? Let Booth conclude:

Thus with regard to the working classes we seem to arrive at a deadlock ... It is a serious *impasse*, yet something may be done to avoid it. Individual working-class homes may be brought within the religious circle, and individual young people may be induced to join in the life and work of the Churches.

To this gradual movement, largely dependent as it is upon economic progress, general education and rising standard of life provide the key. Beyond this, is it too much to hope that as a result of education a ferment may be set up in the minds of young people of the working classes, who, thereupon, discussing for themselves and amongst themselves the ways of God with man, a subject which is never stale, shall reach at last the confines of religion?

Such a movement could only be gradual; an influence percolating downward; but would be helped forward by every other improvement that can be made in the conditions of life. It would apply first only to the very cream of the working classes, but might in time reach all those (and they would become an increasing proportion) who earn fair wages for fair work, and have learnt how to manage their own lives.

For the many who are, and perhaps must for long, if not always, remain below the level of independent existence, the work of the churches is, for the most part, based on charitable assistance. The aim as regards the training of the children hardly rises above order, discipline, cleanliness, decency, and general good behaviour. Religion must be reached through these things, not these things through religion. They are the road, though religion may be the goal.[58]

Notes

1   *Pall Mall Gazette*, 31 July 1891, p.2.

2   *School Board Chronicle*, 22 September 1888, pp.291–2.

3   See for example, Hennock, E.P. (1976), 'Poverty and Social Theory in England: the Experience of the Eighteen-eighties', *Social History*, 1, p.75.

4   Booth, C. (ed.) (1891), *Labour and Life of the People: Vol. 2* London, Williams and Norgate, pp.482–3.

5   See Hyde, R. (1975), *Printed Maps of Victorian London, 1851–1900*, Folkstone: Dawson, p.239.

6   Booth, *Labour and Life*, 1, pp.5–6.

7   Booth, C. (1893), 'Life and Labour of the People in London: First Results of an Inquiry based on the 1891 Census', *Journal of the Royal Statistical Society*, 56, pp.557–96.

8   The map 'London Poverty by Districts' can be found in Booth, *Labour and Life*, Appendix to 2.

9   Booth, 'Life and Labour', 1 pp.569–74.

10   Booth, *Labour and Life*, 1, p.36.

11   Booth, *Labour and Life*, 2, Appendix, Classification of the Population of London by Registration Districts and School Board Divisions.

12   For a map showing these disparities see Marsden, W.E. (1977), 'Education and the Social Geography of Nineteenth-Century Towns and Cities', in Reeder, D. (ed.) *Urban Education in the Nineteenth Century*, Taylor and Francis, p.52.

13   Booth, *Labour and Life*, 2, Appendix, Map 1.

14   See Marsden, *Nineteenth-century Towns and Cities*, pp.61–2.

15   Booth, *Labour and Life*, 2, p.477.

16   For a fuller account of these differences, see Marsden, W.E. (1985), 'Residential Segregation and the Hierarchy of Elementary Schooling from Charles Booth's London Surveys', *The London Journal*, 11, pp.131–4.

17   Booth, *Labour and Life*, 2, p.481.

18   *Ibid.*, pp.484–5.

19   Letter from Education Department to London School Board dated 5 July 1881, printed in *School Board Chronicle*, 16 July 1881, p.31.

20   Booth, *Labour and Life*, 2, pp.507–8.

21   *Ibid.*, pp.504–5.

22   See Gautrey, T. (1937), *'Lux Mihi Laus': School Board Memories*, Link House Publications, pp.93–4.

23   Booth, *Labour and Life*, 2, pp.491–2.

24   *Ibid.*, p.497.

25   *Ibid.*, pp.500–2.

26   Booth, C. (1887), *Conditions and Occupations of the People of Tower Hamlets 1886–1887*, Edward Stanford, p.42.

27   BLPES, Booth Collection, Reports by Secretaries, A.39, p.1.

28   Booth, *Labour and Life*, 1, p.66.

29   Booth, 'Life and Labour', pp.569–74.

30   Booth Collection, Notebooks, Group B, 333, p.3.

31   Booth Collection, Reports by Secretaries, A.39, pp.8–9.

32   *Ibid.*, p.6.

33   See Thompson, F.M.L. (1974), *Hampstead: Building a Borough 1650–1964*, Routledge and Kegan Paul; p.294.

34   Besant, W. (Sir) (1911), *London North of the Thames*, A. and C. Black, p.386.

35   Booth, *Labour and Life*, 2, Appendix, pp.15–16.

36   Parliamentary Papers (1887), *Cross Commission*, 2nd Report, p.45.

37   See Marsden, W.E. (1990) *Educating the Respectable: a Study of Fleet Road Board School, 1879–1903*, The Woburn Press.

38   Booth, C. (ed.) (1896*), Life and Labour of the People in London: Population Classified by Trades*, 8, Macmillan, pp.149–89.

39   *Ibid.*, pp.384–7.

40   *Ibid.*, p.160.

41   Based on *Ibid.*, p.385, and Booth, *Labour and Life*, 2, Appendix.

42   Booth, C. (ed.) (1902) *Religious Influences*, 3, p.214.

43   Booth Collection, *Miscellaneous Districts*, Group B, 211, p.83.

44   *Ibid.*, 283, p.215.

45   *Ibid.*, 240, p.39.

46   *Ibid.*, 173, p.139.

47   Booth Collection, *Miscellaneous Districts*, Group A, 51, p.10.

48   *Miscellaneous Districts*, Group B, 233, p.89.

49   Booth Collection, *Parish Notes*, Group A, 40 pp.22–3.

50   *Miscellaneous Districts,* Group B, 225, p.55 and insert at p.67.

51   *Religious Influences*, 4, p.202.

52   *Miscellaneous Districts*, Group B, 225, p.89.

53   *Religious Influences*, 5, p.46 and p.50.

54   *Industry*, p.486.

55   *Poverty*, 1, p.129.

56   *Religious Influences*, 5, p.53.

57   *Religious Influences*, Final Volume, p.202.

58   *Religious Influences*, 7, p.405.

9 Working-class religion in late Victorian London: Booth's 'Religious Influences' revisited

Hugh McLeod

One morning in October 1967 I was sitting in the British Museum Reading Room, lethargically scanning the book on Charles Booth by the Simeys.[1] I suddenly perked up when I came across a reference to the fact that Booth's notebooks were available at the London School of Economics. I had been working on my PhD for a year, but up to that time my attempts to discover new sources had been largely abortive. I immediately went down to Houghton Street, and by 9.20 that evening (the hours of work in the LSE library's special collections room were then very liberal) I was a Booth addict. The Booth Collection is the kind of source that every research student in history dreams of, and the section that most interested me had apparently remained almost untouched since being deposited in the library in the 1920s. This was the material, consisting of some twenty folios and 150 notebooks, which provided the basis for Booth's 'Religious Influences Series'. Characteristically, the first person to discover them seems to have been Raphael Samuel, who was working on the collection in the summer of 1967, though the 'Religious Influences' material was a side-interest for him. Through the rest of that autumn, I was a regular visitor to LSE, and I got to know the distinctive style of the various 'secretaries', who assisted Booth in his work, by interviewing hundreds of clergymen, lay church officials, Board school headmasters and representatives of the Charity Organization Society, and by preparing reports on the general religious characteristics of the various districts. I came to enjoy the opinionated and often malicious reports of the mercurial Arthur Baxter, to groan when faced with another blandly factual contribution from the staid George Arkell, and to cheer when the interesting but often illegible items provided by Ernest Aves came in typed. Charles Booth himself conducted relatively few interviews and his contributions mainly consisted of accounts of his Sunday walks, in which he popped in and out of churches, listening to sermons and observing the congregations, attended Men's Owns and Pleasant Sunday Afternoons, or joined the crowds on Peckham Rye sampling park oratory.

I

I am going to begin by looking at the material on religion in the Booth Collection, and discussing the ways in which it was used both by Charles Booth himself and by recent historians. Then I shall look at what the Collection reveals about the religious outlook of Booth and of his assistants. Finally I shall suggest how the Booth Collection might be combined with other sources to produce a more adequate religious history of working-class London than any that has been written up to now.

There is a strong temptation to use the Booth Collection primarily as a quarry for colourful quotations. And it certainly provides plenty of those. Many of the clergymen interviewed were ready with pungent comments on their parishioners, their colleagues, or life in general. For instance, there was the Camberwell vicar who divided his parishioners into: '(1) The Common or garden materialist (the great majority). On Sunday morning he copulates about ten times with his wife, and reads *The Referee*. (2) The Superstitious who turn to Ritualism, and (3) The Devout, who in nine cases out of ten go to chapel.' Booth's assistants tended to reply with equally pointed comments on the people they interviewed and the services they attended. The above mentioned vicar was described as 'a strange blend of the ascetic saint and the Piccadilly rake', and A. Osborne Jay, the well-known Anglo-Catholic vicar of Holy Trinity, Shoreditch, was 'a stout, plain, coarse-looking fellow with the appearance of a prize-fighter out of training'.[2]

But the Collection can be used in a variety of more systematic ways. Firstly, it is an unrivalled source of information about the clergy of all denominations in the 1890s. The reports tell us what the clergy looked like, how they dressed and spoke, what sort of houses they lived in, what their views were on a variety of theological, liturgical and social issues. The longer interviews include a wealth of anecdotes, reflections, self-criticism and/or trumpet-judgements of their own.

Secondly, Booth's secretaries attempted to collect systematic information on the personnel employed by each parish or congregation, the buildings maintained, the services held at them, and the social, educational and charitable work that was being carried out.

Thirdly, the material in the Collection throws interesting light on the interrelationships between the various participants in the investigation. Clergymen were invited to comment on the work both of their colleagues and of rival denominations. Secular agencies, such as the Charity Organization Society, were given the chance to comment on the churches. Particularly interesting are the views, stated or implied, of Booth's own team.

No one, I think, has yet done full justice to the riches of the material on religion. The first to attempt to do so was, of course, Charles Booth himself. The most memorable sections of Booth's seven volumes of 'Religious Influences' were his vivid evocations of the local atmosphere in the various quarters of London, his attempts to define the collective mentality of particular social classes or religious denominations, and his eye for the revealing small detail. As examples of the latter: in the very poor district of Hackney Wick he noted 'the positive cleavage between Church and club' among the men associated with the Anglican parish, 'the churchgoers refusing to join the club, and the club members declining to go to church'; and in the upper-working-class district of Southwark Park he commented that 'Anyone walking through the district cannot but be conscious of the extent to which public attention is called to the affairs of the Churches. In every street there are bills – sometimes half the houses have them in their windows – bearing announcements of special services, or lectures or 33 entertainments of one kind or another connected with the Churches'.[3] As an example of one of the many eloquent and much-quoted passages in which Booth attempted a collective religious portrait, I shall quote his description of the religious attitudes of working men in Hackney:

> They like their club with its pot of beer, its entertainments, its game of cards or billiards, or the 'pub' and its associates and a bet on tomorrow's race, but they look on these things as inconsistent with a religious profession, and every form of religious association thus becomes (if they think seriously about the matter at all) something from which, in honesty, they must hold themselves aloof. They are unwilling to accept a restraint that would deprive them of these everyday pleasures, and the step to denounce as hypocrites those members of religious bodies who live mundane lives is thus easily made ... Coupled with this there is some class feeling against joining churches which are supposed to side with the rich, so that to go to church may even be regarded as disloyalty to class. Thus there springs up a public opinion amongst themselves which in their workshops may make a favourite, if not a hero of the man who most defies religious restraints; who is even most reckless in his life and conversation.[4]

There are, however, weaknesses in Booth's interpretation of the material that he collected. Perhaps the most significant point is that in attempting to gain an overall view of the religious attitudes of each class and of the character of each denomination he tends to oversimplify, and to miss many of the nuances. In his dealings with individuals, Booth would appear to have been more humane and more broadly sympathetic than most of his assistants; but in describing groups he tended to draw on a remarkable collection of hostile stereotypes. Roman Catholics were drunken and habitual beggars; Jews were grasping and dirty; Wesleyans were pretentious and insincere; and so on.[5] So far as the relationship between religion and class was concerned, he tended to suggest in the summary passages that this was more neatly predictable than his own evidence warranted.[6] As a result, his overriding stress on religious indifference led him to underrate even the organized religion, let alone the more informal religiosity, of the working-class districts. Conversely, in stressing middle-class religious activism, he did not follow up the many hints in the interviews that this was declining, or the evidence that the middle class was more religiously active in some parts of London than others.[7]

Two other blind spots limit the value of Booth's analysis. The first is that he tends to take for granted a male perspective. Except where women are explicitly mentioned, accounts of working-class religious attitudes and practices evidently refer to working-class men.[8] It is not that Booth is unaware of differences between the views of women and men, but merely that he assumes that the views of the men are more important. The second point is that Booth was so hostile to the charitable efforts that absorbed a large part of the churches' resources in the poorest areas, that his account of their work is strongly negative, and shows little empathy either with the church workers or with the very poor themselves. Booth legitimately pointed to the danger that charitable aid by church workers could become a means of 'bribing' the poor to attend their churches, and that the poor might respond by 'hypocritically' feigning piety, in order to maximize their opportunities. But this overriding fear of 'pauperization' led him to play down the urgency of the need that led mothers to go through the humiliation of asking for food and clothing for their children. When he dealt with the destitute, there was even a note of callousness in Booth's judgements. Thus, a Spitalfields church specializing in providing bread and coffee for the homeless was criticized for making 'mere existence, and often harmless existence, more possible'.[9]

There have been three recent studies which made substantial use of the religious material in the Booth Collection, and each, I believe, has added important points to Booth's own interpretation. They were my own book on class and religion in late Victorian London, Jeffrey Cox's book on the churches in Lambeth, and Alan Bartlett's thesis on the churches in Bermondsey.[10]

While I have been accused (on the whole, fairly) of the same stereotyping tendencies as Booth, I think that the most important respect in which I went beyond Booth's interpretation of his own material was in identifying various distinctive subcultures within the London working class. While broadly accepting, and attempting further to develop Booth's account of the predominant working-class attitudes, I attempted to explore the distinctive outlook of a number of somewhat untypical groups, including Roman Catholics (who also received special treatment from Booth), secularists, those whom I called 'ultra-evangelicals', and those who favoured an undogmatic form of Christianity with a strong emphasis on political radicalism. I accepted Booth's view that only the Roman Catholics established much of a following among the poorer working class, but I attached more importance than he did to the religiosity (or, in some cases, the committed irreligion) of a section of the more prosperous workers.[11]

The most thorough analysis yet made of Booth's material on religion (more intensive, though less extensive, than that by Booth himself) is by Jeffrey Cox. Booth also played a more crucial role in Cox's work than in that of Alan Bartlett or myself, as he provided a large part of the evidence on which Cox's most important arguments are based. Cox made a systematic study of Booth's data on the charitable and quasi-charitable activity of the churches, from direct relief, to mothers' meetings, to the provision of cheap recreational facilities, specially highlighting the role of the large corps of church-sponsored district visitors. He concluded that it was this multi-faceted charitable and social activity that did more than anything else to keep the churches in business as a major force in late Victorian England. The poor needed the services that the churches provided, and the élite used their money and influence to support the churches because of the belief that these efforts were essential to the stability of society. Thus Booth and Cox were agreed in emphasizing this aspect of the churches' work. But while Booth repeatedly stated that these efforts were 'a failure' and in some respects positively harmful, Cox regarded them as rather successful at least in the short run: they made a small, but none the less significant contribution to alleviating poverty, and as such they were a genuine expression of Christian concern, and they also gave the churches a position of power and respect in society. In the longer term, admittedly, undue concentration on social work would leave the churches unprepared for the sudden loss of their accustomed role when central and local government took over most of the churches functions in education and charity in the later nineteenth and early twentieth centuries. According to Cox, this is the major reason for the decline of the churches in the twentieth century.[12]

Cox also offered a more positive reinterpretation of two other points made by Booth. Reversing the cliché about the irreligion of working men, Cox suggested that in a culture where so many vital household decisions were made by women, the relative religiosity of working-class women was more significant than the indifference or hostility of their husbands.[13] More generally, Cox argued that what Booth (and many clergymen) called 'indifference' might often be better understood as 'diffusive Christianity' (a phrase borrowed from Bishop Talbot of Rochester). Instead of focusing on the one religious act which the clergy and middle-class observers regarded as most important, but which most working-class people abstained from (regular attendance at Sunday services), Cox looked at those kinds of religious observance which were popular with the working class – for instance, christenings, churchings, harvest festivals and Watch Night services. He also argued that ignorance of, or lack of interest in, many of the doctrines of orthodox Christianity, should not be confused with irreligion or apathy. 'The people of Lambeth thought of themselves as Christians, but insisted upon defining their own religious beliefs rather than taking them from clergymen.'[14]

Many of Cox's arguments were accepted by Alan Bartlett, whose study of Bermondsey made considerable use of the Booth Collection, as well as oral history and Diocesan Visitation Returns. While not going so far as Cox in emphasizing charitable activities over and above all other aspects of the churches' work, Bartlett went even further in correcting Booth's negative evaluation. He stressed how much church-based health-care, youth clubs, savings banks, and so on, met real needs, and how much these efforts were motivated by an admirable humanitarianism.[15] Bartlett is also inclined to take seriously and to look sympathetically at 'diffusive Christianity'.[16] In fact, Bartlett goes further than either Booth or Cox in emotionally identifying with both clergy and people. A good example of the difference in approach can be seen in Cox's and Bartlett's treatment of the mother's meeting. Cox discusses the phenomenon briefly, his main points being that there were a great many of them, and that they attracted 'a deferential class of working-class women'. Bartlett rejects the latter claim, arguing that 'the women had clear expectations of what was needed and what was unnecessary and where the church responded, the result was a popular religious institution'. Noting the friendly, relaxed atmosphere of the mothers' meetings, and the fact that they often met in local mission halls, he describes them as 'informal, neighbourhood "churches"', supplying the 'women's needs for a blend of recreation, relief and religion'.[17] In keeping with this attempt to see things through the eyes of the participants, Bartlett highlighted the local boundaries that mattered so much to contemporaries, but easily disappear from the view of historians. In this he was very much in the tradition of Charles Booth himself, whereas Cox largely sacrificed local colour in his pursuit of a coherent overall vision. Thus Bartlett stressed the crucial role in Bermondsey geography of the east-west thoroughfare, Jamaica Road. Catholic strength lay to the north of this line, whereas Nonconformists were heavily concentrated to the south. Meanwhile, the Anglicans had their own stronghold in the isolated dockside district of Rotherhithe, where an active vicar had planned the early formation of a series of new parishes in the 1830s and 40s.[18]

II

Although users of the Booth Collection (with the partial exception of Cox) have been mainly interested in what it reveals about the religion or irreligion of the working class, the materials contained there have one major deficiency: out of hundreds of people interviewed, no more than a handful were themselves working-class people. The interviews offer opinions and anecdotes galore, but little direct testimony. However, I would suggest that they are at least as interesting for what they reveal about the views of Booth and his collaborators as for what they reveal about the views of working-class Londoners. I want to look next at the views expressed by Booth's team both about specific religious denominations and about the social role of religion more generally.

Booth himself came from one of Liverpool's leading Unitarian families, but seems, after a period as a Comtian Positivist, to have adopted a 'reverent unbelief'.[19] He viewed all of the churches with detachment, but a fair degree of sympathy. At least three of his assistants (Aves, Baxter and Duckworth) came from an Anglican background, though Baxter was evidently an agnostic, as, probably, was Aves. The other two contributors, Arkell and Argyle, tended to keep their opinions to themselves.

Most obviously, the interviews reveal the social distance between upper or upper-middle-class Anglicanism, and lower-middle-class Dissent. Thus, Duckworth, who has been described as 'a man of the world in excelsis' 'and, it has to be admitted, a snob',[20] found something positively comical in his surroundings at the City Temple:

> The way you were shown to your place and the people round reminded me irresistibly of a well-organised drapery establishment: the people looked like decent shop-walkers and decent shop-girls.

He went on to suggest that the minister, Joseph Parker, was no more than an entertainer – 'not a bad one, but not a very good one' – and that all 'mystery', all 'feeling of the "Presence"' was lacking at the City Temple, though he granted that 'it does seem to suit the sort of mind for which it caters'.[21] If Duckworth was inclined to sneer, Baxter seems to have been genuinely fascinated by the exotic figures whom he encountered in his voyage of discovery into the lower-middle-class suburbs:

> I had never before consciously met a Deacon in the flesh, but Mr G. was almost to a button what I had pictured the typical Deacon: medium height, grey hair and full but trimmed beard and whiskers, plain but not unpleasant face; inclined to be stout; dressed in a frock-coat of shiny black broad-cloth, with waistcoat opening rather low and showing two gilt studs; black bootlace tie tied in a bow. He saw me at his home in Church Crescent, Hackney: everything very hideous and very philistinish: large portrait of Spurgeon on the wall.[22]

Thus Baxter began his account of an interview with the senior deacon of a Congregational Church. The interesting point is that he ended by commenting quite warmly on the deacon's 'genuine enthusiasm for philanthropy'. Indeed this was characteristic of the whole encounter, at least so far as Baxter was concerned, since he ended the enquiry by finding himself more in sympathy with the Nonconformists than with the church of his birth. After comparing the Nonconformist ministers of Islington and Hackney very favourably with the Anglican clergy of that area, he asked, 'Am I right in suggesting that as a body they are more intelligent, better educated, and better trained?'[23] There were still aspects of Nonconformity that grated on him: for instance, he disliked extempore prayer because of the hackneyed language that tended to be used, and he clearly regarded the more traditional kinds of evangelicalism as an anachronism.[24] On the other hand, especially among the Congregationalists, there were a lot of ministers who combined an earnest manner with wide intellectual interests, strong social concern and liberal theology in a way that he found congenial. (He was particularly impressed by the number of Congregational ministers who had a set of *Life and Labour* prominently displayed on their shelves – and this was certainly the surest means of obtaining a favourable mention from Baxter and his colleagues.)[25] More generally, Baxter was impressed by the number of striking and original personalities among the ministers he met, and by the fact that fewer Nonconformists than Anglicans seemed to have entered the ministry by default.[26] This favourable judgement applied even to some ministers whose theology Baxter explicitly repudiated.[27] Part of this preference appeared to arise from a feeling that the Nonconformists were more virile – this being a theme that frequently entered into his favourable or unfavourable judgements on clergymen. A typical approving comment was that a Hackney vicar was 'chock full of go and energy, a good practical head, a sympathetic heart, a slap-you-on-the-back sort of man, sure to be immensely popular with men and boys'.[28] An important aspect of his dislike of the Anglican clergy seems to have been a feeling that many of them were effeminate. This charge was especially directed against Anglo-Catholics,[29] and, together with Roman Catholics, they could also be subjected to accusations of 'priestcraft' and of encouraging superstition and/or craven submission to ecclesiastical authority.[30] In dealing with people like Baxter and Aves, the distinctly unclerical style of many Nonconformist ministers was an advantage. While some of Baxter's anti-clericalism probably had its origins in his own personal history, it is interesting to note that his criticisms of the practical effectiveness of a large part of the Anglican clergy were shared by a large proportion of the lay witnesses interviewed by Booth's team. One East End witness wrote to Aves: 'Why can't they give us some decent parsons?'[31] Admittedly, many of the lay witnesses were officials of the Charity Organization Society, whose disagreements with the clergy's approach to poor relief may have coloured their judgement. Whether or not there is any objective basis for these criticisms, they provide interesting evidence of the attitudes of many nominally Anglican upper-middle-class men in the 1890s.

This may throw some light on the late Victorian transition, identified by Cox, from the assumption that the social progress depended on the efforts of the churches to the assumption that the churches were concerned with 'religion' and that the progress of society depended on purely secular agencies.[32] The split ran down the middle of Booth's team, and the division is probably partly a generational one. Booth (born 1840) accepted that 'religious influences' were the best hope for the changes in individual character that were the foundation of social progress.[33] Appropriately, therefore, after losing his Unitarian faith he became a Comtian Positivist. Though he later abandoned this creed, and did not find another that satisfied him, he continued to attach a lot of importance to the favourable influence that religion could exercise on others. Aves (born 1857) and Baxter (born 1860) were more sceptical, and they got plenty of support from the Charity Organization Society officials and Board school headmasters most of whom were eager to minimize the influence of the churches and chapels – often in order to aggrandize their own influence.[34] Baxter, referring to evidence of a decline in 'drunkenness, savagery and rowdyism' in north-east London, attributed the improvement to 'more efficient elementary and secondary education, greater vigour in local government, and increased religious and philanthropic activity' – in that order. Summing up the situation in Shoreditch, he suggested that the best of the clergy could exercise a better social and moral influence as laymen.[35]

Cox has very effectively pinpointed the change in attitude to the solution of social problems that was taking place. But in explaining why it was taking place I think he attaches insufficient importance to changes in religious belief. Clearly several processes were at work here. Firstly, and probably most importantly, intervention by local authorities or by the state, with their vastly greater resources, permitted a far more comprehensive provision of schools, low-rent housing, or whatever else it might be, than was within the means of the churches or any other voluntary body – and as Cox shows, ministers of religion frequently welcomed state intervention for this reason.[36] Secondly, the establishment of each new secular agency had the effect both of showing that the churches were less necessary to the well-being of society than people had thought, and of establishing a further body of specialists with a vested interest in questioning the clergy's claims to universal competence. But two other points also seem relevant. First, there did seem to be a lot of evidence that the churches were failing to make an impact on the majority of the people, and that if any general regeneration of society were to be achieved, new methods would therefore have to be tried. Baxter's confidence in the Board schools was as naively optimistic as his criticisms of the churches were often exaggeratedly severe. But it is easy to see how from the perspective of the 1890s the dual panacea of universal, free, unsectarian education, together with a vigorous reforming local government, seemed to offer the prospects for real improvements in the conditions of life of the working class. My second point, however, is that it was precisely because people like Baxter had already rejected Christianity, and because they believed that many of their contemporaries were doing the same, that they were so sceptical of reforming efforts based on religion. Aves, for instance, defined 'the real needs' of the East End in terms that seemed expressly designed to make most of what the churches were doing irrelevant or misconceived (though he did regard their temperance campaigning as useful).[37] Baxter felt that human beings were basically irreligious, and he also argued that positive rejection of religion was on the increase. He claimed that anti-religious views were more widely held by working men than the clergy recognized, and referred approvingly to declarations that 'We don't want nothing to do with no bloody parsons'. He felt that if middle-class men went to church it was largely under pressure from their wives.[38] (Baxter, whose male chauvinist tendencies seem to have been more pronounced than those of any other member of Booth's team, does not seem to have had much interest in the views of the middle-class women themselves.) With views such as these, it is not surprising that his hopes for social improvement rested on secular agencies.

III

Because the Booth Collection offers so little direct evidence about the views of working-class people, historians have been obliged to seek new sources. One objective has been simply to obtain more precise information about the extent of working-class participation in the churches and chapels. Cox and I used marriage registers in order to investigate the social composition of the various Nonconformist denominations. Bartlett identified the members of a Bermondsey Baptist chapel in the 1871 and 1881 census enumerators' books.[39] All of these sources suggest that most chapels had a substantial working-class membership, though the proportion of working-class people was usually lower than in the population as a whole. The deficiency tended to be greatest in the case of unskilled occupations. Bethnal Green, where about half the men marrying in chapel at the turn of the century were in manual occupations, was fairly typical in this respect: white-collar occupations were over-represented, skilled workers appeared in about the 'expected' proportions, and unskilled occupations were very much under-represented. Bartlett's analysis of Drummond Road Baptist chapel in the 1880s suggested a wider occupational spread, but with a tendency for members to live in the more 'respectable' streets, rather than the poorest parts of Bermondsey. This evidence suggests that the proportion of working-class people attending some kind of church or chapel was greater than Booth and many of his informants tended to assume. This suggestion is strengthened by the evidence of oral history. The huge oral history survey of Edwardian Britain carried out by Paul Thompson and Thea Vigne[40] included about fifty interviews with people brought up in working-class families in London. Of these, 24 per cent reported that their mother had attended church with some degree of frequency during their childhood, and 20 per cent reported that their father had done so. While these figures were considerably lower than those obtaining for the industrial districts of Lancashire, Yorkshire, south Wales or central Scotland, they are considerably higher than the various estimates contained in the Booth Collection,[41] and higher than I myself would have estimated before seeing the evidence of this and other oral history surveys. The oral evidence also lends plenty of support to Cox's claim that the churches were 'an obtrusive part of the social landscape' even in areas where church-going was lowest.[42]

Oral history has come to be recognized as a vital resource for historians of the working class in the late Victorian and Edwardian period. We must be grateful that the pioneering work of such historians as Thompson, Vigne and Raphael Samuel in the 1960s and 1970s, as well as the more recent work of Bartlett, created a bank of valuable oral material before it was too late. However, there are also some documentary sources that give working-class people some chance of speaking for themselves. While oral evidence may over-represent the 'respectable',[43] the poorest and least 'respectable; sections of the working class are heavily represented in the sources, such as court and Poor Law records, used by Ellen Ross in her research on working-class women.[44] While this is not primarily concerned with religion, references to the churches, and especially to their charitable facilities, frequently occur in these sources. The poorer areas of London also provide the characteristic settings for the diaries of City Missionaries, who engaged in door-to-door religious propaganda, sometimes mixed with charitable relief and visiting the sick, and who provided verbatim records of the conversations they had.[45] Cox and I both made considerable use of autobiographies, of which some excellent examples from London in this period exist. However, interviews have the great advantages over against autobiographies that they tend to include less self-justification, less discreet omission, less attempt at literary effect, and that their subjects tend to be less distanced from the milieu they are attempting to recall. A skilful interviewer may also play a crucial role in encouraging reflection on particular episodes – admittedly, the ones that interest the interviewer, which may not be those that interest the interviewee.

By combining the Booth Collection with sources of the kind just mentioned, which reflect more directly the ideas and experience of working-class people themselves, it should be possible to produce a more rounded portrait of London working-class religion than any that has yet been achieved. I want to suggest next how this might be done.

My first point is that we need to be aware of the full range of working-class religious positions, and to avoid the stereotyping of which both Booth and most subsequent historians have been guilty at one time or another. The portrait has to include a significant minority of convinced secularists, as well as a probably larger minority of convinced believers, and many shades of attitude in between. Older accounts, such as those by Eric Hobsbawm and Gareth Stedman Jones, tended to lay too much stress on secularism.[46] More recently, Jeff Cox, with his valuable work on 'diffusive Christianity', more or less ignored secularism and gave rather little attention to the committed church-goers. Bartlett has given the latter more serious attention than any previous writer, but he too has little to say about the secularists. No one has yet entirely succeeded in getting the balance right between these different elements.

Secondly, any balanced picture needs to give due weight to differences between female and male perspectives. Bartlett has gone further than any other historian of London religion in doing this. More still needs to be done to take account of the implications for religious history of Ellen Ross's work on women's networks, household management, and marital conflict. Ross notes that in working-class London, 'women and men lived in quite separate material worlds organised around their responsibilities in a fairly rigid sexual division of labour. Marriage was not viewed as creating a new social unit: the fissure between wife and children on the one hand, and husband on the other was accepted as a normal part of it'.[47] She shows how this rigid separation led to different patterns of sociability, often to different perspectives and priorities, and sometimes to severe antagonisms between husband and wife. So far as the churches were concerned, one reflection of this separation was the fact that many religious meetings were held exclusively for one sex or the other. Those for men tended to be on Sunday afternoon and those for women on Monday afternoon or evening.[48] There were also many church organizations which catered exclusively for young women or young men. In each case the style and content of the meetings reflected the specifically male or female nature of the audience, and part of the attraction lay in the fact that most people found it easier to relax with members of their own sex. There were also differences between the aspects of religion that most interested the two sexes. Religious debate, whether in halls, parks, or informally in a workshop or pub, was a male speciality: as Booth put it, 'The London working man is great in all forms of discussion ... Any subject will do, but religious subjects are the most popular.'[49] On the other hand, women's concern with the care of babies and of the sick, with the bringing up of children, the laying out of the dead, and with ensuring that everyone in the household had enough food, warmth and clothing, led them to give more weight to more practical aspects of religion, including praying for help in time of crisis,[50] ensuring that the appropriate rituals were performed at the times of birth and death,[51] instilling children with ideas of right behaviour,[52] and maintaining the family's reputation in the eyes of neighbours, retailers, and public officials. The household division of responsibilities meant that women were more likely than men to come into direct contact with the churches, especially if they needed charitable help. Of course, this did not necessarily mean that women had a friendlier view of the churches and clergy; but it did mean that their relationship was likely to be different. One question that needs to be considered here is how far differences in religious attitude between women and men led to antagonism between them, or how far these were accepted as simply being an aspect of the sexual division of labour. There is some evidence that in nineteenth-century France, where women were much more strongly Catholic than men, this was a cause of conflict between spouses;[53] in England, where religious differences were in any case less sharp, I have not seen much evidence that this was so.

Two aspects of the religion of this time that particularly need re-evaluation or further exploration, and which relate to the division between male and female spheres, are the charitable activity of the churches and the nature and extent of 'diffusive Christianity'. Church charity has been studied from the perspective of the clergy, from that of the Charity Organization Society, from that of radical critics of the churches' role in social control, but seldom from the point of view of the consumer. Here again, Ellen Ross has introduced a salutary change of focus by trying to start with the working-class mother and her strategies for family survival.[54] In this instance, however, the problems of bias in the sources may be particularly acute, as the child's enthusiastic gratitude for a good meal, which the interview or autobiography tends to record,[55] may drastically simplify the more ambivalent feelings of the mother. As for 'diffusive Christianity', the evidence suggests that this too played a bigger part in the lives of women than of men. Aspects of this form of religion mentioned by Cox include the rites of passage, Sunday schools, the popularity of certain religious festivals, and the prevalence of some kind of fairly vague Christian belief.[56] The fact that the rites of passage largely fell within the mother's sphere has already been mentioned. The same may have been true of the task of ensuring that children went to Sunday school, though the evidence is less clear.[57] Women may even have taken more interest than their husbands in Watch Night services, to judge from Ernest Aves' account of a service in Somers Town on New Year's Eve, 1897 – though one probably cannot draw any conclusions from this one example.[58] As for the nature of popular beliefs: it is clear that irreligious ideas circulated much more readily in the male environment of workshop and pub than in the predominantly female environment of the home.[59]

Thirdly, the church-going minority of the London working class deserves more than the meagre and stereotyped accounts with which most writers have contented themselves. Oral history offers the best prospects of a fuller and more nuanced portrait, and again it is Bartlett, making extensive use of interviews, who has taken us furthest in the right direction. If, as the Thompson/Vigne evidence suggests, they made up more than a fifth of working-class adults in the early twentieth century, they deserve attention on the grounds of numbers alone. Whether they enjoyed an influence comparable to that of some other church-going minorities at that time (for instance, the Durham Methodists)[60] is more questionable. For instance, church-going Londoners were highly fragmented, with Roman Catholics forming a group apart, Anglicans being divided from Nonconformists, and supporters of undenominational missions tending to form a fourth group.[61] Their most conspicuous role was perhaps as exemplars of a style of life – thrifty, self-improving, industrious, above all 'respectable' – which powerfully attracted some of their neighbours and repelled others. The hostile view was given graphic expression in an interview with a man born in 1891 and brought up in Donald Street, Bromley, marked dark blue on Booth's map of London:

'In your street - were there social differences – were some more respectable?'
'Oh yes – you had one or two church-goers – you know. They'd never mix with anybody else. They'd pass the time of day with you but they never mixed in any shape or form.'
'Would their kids mix with you?'
'No – they sent them to play the violin and all that stuff. They wasn't – we was too rough for them.'
'Did they go to the same school?'
'No. They'd private schools somewhere. There's about three of them lived down 'ere.'

He went on to suggest that most of the church-goers had office jobs, that their children were much better dressed than the others around, and that they were 'escorted to school – to church', whereas 'We ran wild'.[62] Other interviews in the same collection by Raphael Samuel suggest that by no means all church-going East Enders had office jobs or sent their children to private school. But the emphasis on respectability, on 'strict' standards, is a frequent theme. Here is how a woman born in 1884 in North Place, Mile End New Town (marked purple and pink on Booth's map), described her strongly Anglican mother, who had been a cook and was married to a brewery horseman. 'She was a very strict woman. Yes. Very strict woman. Never used bad language, nothing like. Or make any rude remarks. Or make any fun of anybody.' On Sunday evening, when the family went to church together, 'you always 'ad gloves on – your shoes cleaned and a hat on your head. Always went respectable.' The children were indeed allowed to play with all the neighbouring children, 'but they were all nice children like ourselves – because they nearly all worked at Truman's Brewery [a bastion of regular employment amid the chronic insecurity of most areas of the East End economy] ... Or they was a policeman.' Though strict, her mother was not aloof: 'But she was very good my mother. If anyone was sick she'd go and 'elp them always always. If anyone was ill or say anyone has passed away and they want to lay someone out run and fetch Mrs Carter.'[63]

The suggestion here is of an enclave of comparative respectability in which the devout enjoyed a sense of community that they did not feel in a 'rougher' area such as Donald Street. No doubt there were a number of such enclaves scattered across the poorer districts of London.[64] For some of those, however, who felt little affinity with their neighbours, their only experience of community was in church or chapel. A classic expression of this viewpoint is the autobiography of George Acorn, a Bethnal Green cabinet-maker, who complained of the 'mechanical lives' of the people among whom he grew up, who 'live, marry, produce children, fight, quarrel, all by rote, and never think'. From an early age, he had 'a leaning towards religion. Places of worship were so clean that I often felt the desire to go into a local church. The brooding feeling of peacefulness seemed to smooth one's turbulent desires.' Eventually a friend persuaded him to start attending a Nonconformist chapel, 'probably the most important step I ever took in my life', where he seems to have valued both the intellectual stimulus and the more refined atmosphere. He was influenced by the secretary of one of the chapel organizations, who 'wore down many of my jagged edges and shaped me into the image of an ordinary middle-class youth'.[65]

Such restless self-improvers as Acorn were often anxious to move from such uncongenial surroundings and to find a home in a 'nicer' neighbourhood, a little further out. Churches and chapels in such areas as Bethnal Green and Bermondsey constantly complained of the loss of members through migration.[66] Important as this image is of churches and chapels as stepping-stones for those en route to the suburbs, it can be misleading if it is presented in a one-sided way that neglects the fact that some churches had become an integral part of the life of ordinary working-class neighbourhoods. This was most obviously true of the Roman Catholic churches in Irish areas of London.[67] But in reading some oral testimonies, it is clear that some (by no means all) Anglican and Nonconformist churches achieved the same acceptance. Arthur Harding, in his account of Bethnal Green in the 1920s and 30s makes a significant distinction between St Paul's, the church where he himself was married, and various other neighbouring churches, such as St Matthew's, the parish church. The rector of St Matthew's is by implication accused of snobbery and various of his church-going neighbours in the impoverished Gibraltar Walk area are presented as standoffish; on the other hand, references to Father Jones of St Paul's are consistently eulogistic, and a Mr and Mrs Johnson 'were ordinary Bethnal Green folk and attended Father Jones's church on Sunday'.[68] Another of Raphael Samuel's interviews may also be relevant here. This was with Bill Brinson, born on the Isle of Dogs in 1894, whose family later moved to Poplar, where he lived all his life, and was for many years Labour Party chairman. In his childhood, Brinson regularly attended All Hallows' Anglican church with his mother, and he continued as a young man to be active in the church, though he later rejected it. Two points seem worth mentioning here. The first is that Brinson's childhood was one of constant struggle, as a result of his father's frequent unemployment and heavy drinking, which forced the family to rely on what his mother could earn by working appalling hours with a sewing machine. Not by any stretch of the imagination could the family be termed superior or upwardly mobile. The second is that Brinson was strongly influenced by a group of radical clergy at All Hallows', and his first involvement in politics was as a result of the 1912 dock strike, when his Bible class ran a soup kitchen for the strikers.[69] This illustrates the fact that the forced attendance by working-class children at church or Sunday school led to some of them forming close personal ties with the clergy, which carried through into adulthood.[70] It also indicates that although committed church-goers were sometimes people on the way out of the local community, religious involvement could also be the first step towards a deeper commitment to working *for* the local community. The most obvious example was participation in the charitable work of the church, which was not the exclusive preserve of visitors from the suburbs, but was also the concern of local working-class and lower-middle-class church-people.[71] In other cases, as with Brinson, religion led the way into political activism. This pattern was probably less typical of London than of some other parts of the country, though it was more common than the heavily secular popular image of London socialism and radicalism might lead one to expect. For instance, a study conducted during the 1929 Parliament of the religious backgrounds of Labour MPs showed a very large number who claimed to have come to their belief in socialism through some form of

Christianity. This was particularly characteristic of MPs from the mining and textile districts, but there were several examples from London too. The best known was George Lansbury. But others included Charles Ammon, a Wesleyan postman from Camberwell; Fred Messer, a Baptist french polisher from Tottenham; and John Scurr, a Catholic docker from the East End.[72]

Finally, I would plead for a more comparative approach to London's religious history. This comparative approach might well begin at home: although material on Judaism was collected by Booth's team it was not used in the final version;[73] the histories of Christianity and Judaism in London have very largely been written in isolation from one another, and in this paper I have continued that tradition. It must be hoped that more historians will attempt a broader religious history that embraces both communities, and strengthens our understanding of both by drawing comparisons between them.[74] London also needs to be compared with, for instance, Liverpool or Manchester, Berlin or New York. Only thus can we determine what was distinctive or interesting about London's religious development, and which trends reflected more general patterns of change. Comparison with New York highlights the formidable influence exercised by Roman Catholicism in the American metropolis, and the fact that none of the churches in London was able to draw active support from such a wide social range, or enjoyed such a strong popular base. The latter was underpinned by a rich culture of folk-belief that had little parallel in the soberly rational world of London Protestantism. On the other hand, comparison with Berlin suggests that in matters of secularity London still had a long way to go. The multiplicity of small places of worship in London reflected a level of popular interest considerably greater than in Berlin, where huge Protestant churches physically dominated many neighbourhoods, but attendances averaged only 0.5 per cent of the adult population in working-class parishes. The free churches did a bit better, but they were considerably weaker than in London. However, by comparison with the militant irreligion of the Social Democratic Party, whose *Kirchenaustrittsbewegung* (movement of mass resignations from the church) was then in full swing, London secularism seemed rather a small-scale affair.[75]

Notes
1   Simey, T.S. and Simey M.B. (1960), *Charles Booth, Social Scientist*, Oxford University Press.

2   BLPES, Booth Collection, B281, pp.99, 111; B228, p.37.

3   Booth, C. (1902-3), *Life and Labour of the People in London*, 17 vols. *Religious Influences*, 1, Macmillan, p.97; 4, p.145.

4   *Ibid.*, 1, pp.89–90.

5   *Ibid.*, 7, p.401; 2, pp.3–4; 7, pp.135–6.

6   *Ibid.*, 1, pp.165–6; 7, pp.394–401.

7   For comments on the decline of middle-class church-going, see Booth Collection, A35, p.67 (Baxter's summary of evidence from north London); B263, pp.3–5; B267, p.131; B287, p.7; B305, p.69 (remarks by clergymen). As regards differences between regions of London, two ministers interviewed in Putney stated that middle-class church-going was lower in south-west than in north London (B297, pp.25–7, 59–61), and this was confirmed by the results of the 1902–3 *Daily News* religious census of London, for which see McLeod, Hugh (1974), *Class and Religion in the late Victorian City*, Croom Helm, p.28.

8   See, for instance the section on 'Church-going and Working Men' in *Religious Influences*, 1, pp.85–90.

9   *Ibid.*, 2, p.16.

10   McLeod, *Class and Religion*; Cox, Jeffrey (1982), *The English Churches in a Secular Society,* Oxford University Press; Bartlett Alan, (1987), 'The Church in Bermondsey 1880–1939', University of Birmingham PhD thesis. This paper was written before the publication of Rosemary O'Day's work on the portrayal of the clergy in the Booth Collection: see her chapter on 'The Men from the Ministry' (1988), in Parsons, Gerald (ed.) *Religion in Victorian Britain*, 4 vols, Manchester University Press, 2, pp.258–79 and 'Interviews and Investigations: Charles Booth and the Making of the *Religious Influences* Series', *History* (1989), 74, pp.361–77. Other recent works on religion in later Victorian London include McIlhiney, D.B. (1977), 'A Gentleman in every Slum: Church of England Missions in East London 1837–1914', unpublished Princeton University PhD thesis, which did not use the Booth Collection; Marchant, C. (1979), 'Interaction of Church and Society in an East London Borough (West Ham)', unpublished University of London PhD thesis, and Morris, J.N. (1986), 'Religion and Urban Change in Victorian England: A Case-Study of the Borough of Croydon, 1840–1914', unpublished University of Oxford DPhil thesis, which concern two of the outer London districts, which Booth's survey excluded.

11   McLeod, *Class and Religion,* pp.60–80.

12   Cox, *English Churches*, pp.48–89, 177–210, 271–4.

13   *Ibid.*, pp.34–5.

14   *Ibid.*, p.92.

15   Bartlett, 'Church in Bermondsey', pp.135–52, 267–70.

16   See for instance his discussion of baptism, *ibid.*, pp.182–8.

17   Cox, *English Churches*, pp.71–2; Bartlett, 'Church in Bermondsey', pp.165–8.

18   'Church in Bermondsey', pp.253–4, 57–8.

19   Simey and Simey, *Charles Booth,* pp.47–8, 60.

20   Woolf, Leonard (1964), *Beginning Again*, Hogarth Press, pp.73, 159.

21   A42.4, pp.14–21.

22   *Ibid.*, B183, p.95.

23   *Ibid.*, report on districts 14 and 16, pp.73–4.

24   B387, p.177, 7–9; A40, report on districts 5–6, pp.55–6.

25   B218, pp.157–9. A good way for a clergyman to damn himself in advance was to begin by asking if Mr Booth was something to do with the Salvation Army: see for instance B314, p.77.

26   Baxter characteristically referred to one vicar as a member of 'the large class who are fit for no career but the Church', B211, p.155.

27   For example, the strongly evangelical Campbell Morgan of Tollington Park Congregational Church, described by Baxter as 'a preacher of extraordinary eloquence', B206, pp.67–9.

28   B196, p.157. A eulogistic account of a Deptford vicar referred to 'the intense virility that is his salient characteristic', B284, p.33.

29   Thus a Hackney vicar was described as a 'pale young curate type … clothed in a cassock, and altogether priestly in appearance', B186, p.83.

30   Noting that the outstanding clergy in Shoreditch and Clerkenwell were extreme High Churchmen, Baxter concluded: 'Hateful as are the methods of Mr Kensit [of the Protestant Truth Society] and his followers, I am not persuaded that the protests which have been raised against the danger of the growth of superstition and sacerdotalism are not justified'. A40.7, p.24.

31   A39, report on Stepney, pp.7–9.

32   Cox, *English Churches*, pp.181–3.

33   Simey and Simey, *Charles Booth*, pp.47–8, 60, 139.

34   See for instance B225, pp.41, 145.

35   A37.11, pp.60–5; A40.7, p.40.

36   Cox, *English Churches*, pp.164–5, 174.

37   A33.12, pp.56–60.

38   A33, report on district 10, p.36; A40.7, p.41; A35, report on districts 14 and 16, p.67.

39   McLeod, *Class and Religion*, pp.309–11; Cox, *English Churches*, 303–4; Bartlett, 'Church in Bermondsey', pp.401–2. See also Field, C.D. (1974), 'Methodism in Metropolitan London 1850–1920', (University of Oxford DPhil thesis), which includes extensive discussion of the social composition of the various branches of Methodism.

40   Essex Oral History Archive, at the Department of Sociology, University of Essex. See also Thompson, Paul (1977), *The Edwardians*, Weidenfeld and Nicholson; McLeod, Hugh (1986), 'New Perspective on Victorian Working-Class Religion: The Oral Evidence', *Oral History Journal*, 14, (1), pp.31–49.

41   The evidence collected by Booth included a number of estimates of working-class church-going rates. Fairly typical was Baxter's estimate of an average of 5 per cent for Hackney, rising to 10 per cent in Dalston and dropping to 2 per cent in Hackney Wick. Booth Collection, A35, report on district 13, p.49.

42   Cox, *English Churches*, p.104.

43   I have discussed this possibility in McLeod, 'New Perspectives', p.31.

44   Ross, Ellen (1982), '"Fierce Questions and Taunts": Married Life in Working-Class London, 1870–1914', *Feminist Studies*, 8, (3) Fall, pp.575–602; (1983) 'Survival Networks: Women's Neighbourhood Sharing in London before World War I', *History Workshop Journal*, (15), pp.4–27; (1986) '"Feeding the Children": Housewives and London Charity, 1870–1918', (unpublished paper, read to Davis Center, Princeton University), and (1990), 'Hungry Children: Housewives and London Charity, 1870–1918' in Mandler Peter (ed.), *The Uses of Charity: The Poor on Relief in the Nineteenth Century_Metropolis* (Philadelphia), pp.161–96.

45   See for instance McLeod, *Class and Religion*, pp.49–54.

46   Hobsbawm, E.J. (1971), *Primitive Rebels*, 2nd edn, Manchester, p.128; Jones, G. Stedman (1971), *Outcast London*, Oxford University Press, pp.337, 339–41. Stan Shipley has also laid a lot of stress on the importance of secularism. See for instance (1971), *Club Life and Socialism in Mid-Victorian London*, Routledge and Kegan Paul, pp.40–1. The best-balanced treatment of London secularism is Thompson, Paul (1967), *Socialists, Liberals and Labour: the Struggle for London 1885–1914*, London, pp.30–3 and *passim*, who notes its significance without making exaggerated claims for its influence, and also gives more serious consideration to the churches than other London histories that highlight the role of secularism.

47   Ross, 'Fierce Taunts', p.578.

48   See for instance Booth's account of 'Men's Own' services in *Religious Influences*, 4, pp.147–9, and his report on attending a packed Monday evening Mother's Meeting at a mission in Islington in Booth Collection, B198, pp.95–9.

49   *Religious Influences*, 1, pp.87–8. As one example of the popularity of religious debates, a 'stand-up fight' at Oxford House in Bethnal Green in 1888 between the then Warden, Hensley Henson, and a well-known secularist on the topic of 'The Historical Origins of Christianity' attracted an audience of 'eight or nine hundred men'. McIlhiney, 'Church of England Missions', p.306.

50   *Religious Influences*, 1, pp.27–8, in summing up 'the response to religion' in Poplar, stated that: 'In family life religion has a certain recognition, as for instance we are told in the habit of private prayer among the women, though how far this is really common I do not know.' The subject is not an easy one to investigate, but autobiographies give some examples: Woodward, Kathleen (1928), *Jipping Street*, p.131 (describing a Bermondsey woman praying with a sick neighbour); Scannell, Dolly (1975), *Mother Knew Best*, p.16 (describing her mother, then living in Beckenham praying for money when the family ran out of food). See also McLeod, 'New Perspectives', pp.37–8.

51   Bartlett notes, 'Church in Bermondsey', p.185, the responsibility of mothers for arranging baptisms (and, of course, churchings).

52   One aspect of this could be teaching the children their prayers. A Kensal Green woman, born in 1905, reproached her laundress mother for never having taught her her prayers, feeling that this showed a lack of affection on her part. Raphael Samuel, interview with Mrs Prentice,

tape 1, p.36. I want to thank Raphael Samuel for letting me see transcripts of this and other taped interviews in his possession.

53 Gibson, Ralph (1989), *A Social History of French Catholicism 1789–1914*, pp.81–2, 187.

54 Ross, 'Hungry Children'.

55 For one example of memories of free breakfasts in mission halls, see Samuel, Raphael (1981), *East End Underworld: Chapters in the Life of Arthur Harding*, pp.24–7.

56 Cox, *English Churches*, p.104.

57 Bartlett, 'Church in Bermondsey', pp.194–5.

58 B386, pp.85–89.

59 *Religious Influences*, 1, pp.27–30; McLeod, *Class and Religion*, p.55.

60 See Moore, Robert (1974), *Pit-men, Politics and Preachers*, Cambridge University Press.

61 Undenominational missions, numerous but mostly small, tend to be ignored. See Bartlett, 'Church in Bermondsey, pp.286–94, for an unusually detailed portrait.

62 Samuel, interview with Mr C. Causon, tape 2, pp.22–4.

63 Samuel, interview with Mrs Stone, pp.11, 32, 35, 37.

64 Another example seems to have been Blackwall Buildings in Whitechapel, where another woman interviewed by Raphael Samuel lived. Her father was on the railways. She mentioned that most of the other tenants had secure jobs, also that they used to 'flock in' to services at a nearby mission. Interview with Ethel Vargo (born 1895), tape 2, p.19.

65 Acorn, George (1911), *One of the Multitude*, pp.51, 65, 151, 173–9.

66 McLeod, *Class and Religion*, p.115; Bartlett, 'Church in Bermondsey', p.284.

67 Bartlett, 'Church in Bermondsey', pp.312–4; see also the chapters by Raphael Samuel, Sheridan Gilley and Gerard Connolly (1985), in Swift, Roger and Gilley, Sheridan (eds), *The Irish in the Victorian City*, Croom Helm.

68 Samuel, *East End Underworld*, pp.241–5, 264. See also Richman, Geoff (1976), *Fly a Flag for Poplar*, p.97: 'in Poplar, the

priest tends to be drawn into the collective feeling rather than remaining remote'.

69   Samuel, interview with Mr Bill Brinson, tape 2, pp.4, 16, 23. See also Richman, *Poplar*, pp.87–90.

70   Another Poplar example is Joseph Williamson, who as a choirboy at St Saviour's fell under the influence of Fr Dawson, and eventually became a well-known East End vicar himself. Williamson, J. (1963), *Father Joe*, p.50.

71   Samuel, interview with Mr C. Causon, tape 1, pp.8–10.

72   Linden, Franz, (1932), *Sozialismus und Religion,* Leipzig; pp.111, 113, 123–5, 127.

73   B197. There is, however, a brief account of the Jewish community by Beatrice Potter in one of his volumes on Poverty: *Poverty*, 3, pp.166–92.

74   The pioneer in this field is Todd Endelman whose comparative study of nineteenth-century Jewish communities has highlighted the influence on their religious development of the forms of Christianity locally prevalent. See, e.g. (1985), 'Communal Solidarity and Family Loyalty among the Jewish Elite of Victorian London', *Victorian Studies*, 28, pp.491–526.

75   The differences between religion in London and New York can be seen at their most extreme in Orsi, R, (1985), *The Madonna of 115th Street*, New Haven. See also McLeod, Hugh (1988), 'The Culture of Popular Catholicism in New York City in the later nineteenth and early twentieth Centuries', in Heerma van Voss, Lex (ed.), *Working Class and Popular Culture*, Amsterdam; pp.71–82 and (1987), 'Catholicism and the New York Irish c.1880–1910', in Obelkevich, Jim, Roper, Lyndal and Samuel, Raphael (eds), *Disciplines of Faith*, Routledge and Kegan Paul. For Berlin, see Wendland, W. (1930), *700 Jahre Kirchengeschichte Berlins*, Berlin and Elm; Kaspar and Loock, Hans-Dietrich (1990), (eds) *Seelsorge und Diakonie in Berlin*, Berlin. See also McLeod, H. (1982), 'Protestantism and the Working Class in Imperial Germany', *European Studies Review,* 12, (3), pp.323–44.

10 Booth's Jews: the presentation of Jews and Judaism in *Life and Labour of the People in London*[1]

David Englander

When in 1886 Charles Booth started his investigation into the condition of the people of London, the effects of Jewish immigration from Eastern Europe had begun to register both in Whitechapel and in Westminster. Pogroms in Russia and the expulsion of the Poles from Prussia led to a rapid increase in the number of Jews in London and concern about the absorptive capacities of the East End where the bulk of them settled.[2] The first of several parliamentary inquiries had already considered the issues raised by 'foreign immigration' while the effect of the newcomers upon wages, sanitary conditions and living standards supplied the subject of everyday exchanges in pubs and parks and of anxious comment in polite periodicals.[3] At the close of the 1890s, when research was concluded for what had grown into the multi-volumed survey of *Life and Labour of the People in London*, the Jewish population of the metropolis stood at an estimated 140,000–150,000 persons. The greater part of it was still concentrated in Stepney but there was also a significant and growing Jewish presence in north and north-east London and in the more select suburbs of the north-west.[4]

In size among ethnic minority populations in London, the Jewish minority was second only to the Irish. The newcomers from Eastern Europe were, however, less widely scattered than the exiles from Erin. The Irish slum communities of mid Victorian London, described by Henry Mayhew and others, were by the time of the Booth survey under severe pressure; several had been destroyed, others destabilized, by the relentless development of the inner ring; and some were now threatened by Jewish immigration.[5] As a result, the Irish in late Victorian London were geographically more dispersed and socially less visible than their compeers from Eastern Europe. Here and there were particular streets and buildings, clusters of courts, and identifiable riverside communities; but neither in scale nor in concentration was there anything comparable with the Jewish ghetto of East London. Jews, moreover, looked different. The immigrant Irish, though known by national stereotype, were not seen as exotics like the Jews from 'the East', the women did not have 'olive complexions' and

there were no 'dark-bearded men in Russian-Polish dress' to evoke a
sense of extravagance and mystery.[6]

Not only did the Irish not look like foreigners; legally they were
not foreigners. Unlike the Jews, the Irish were citizens of the United
Kingdom and not persons of foreign birth. Their condition, if less than
satisfactory, was settled and familiar. The extent of occupational and
social differentiation, or the degree of variation between Irish Catholic
communities, did not register with Booth and his coadjutors, whose
perspective on these and cognate matters tended to be Protestant and
prejudiced. To Booth and his associates, neither the Irish nor their
faith had much to commend them. The Irish were devout but
disorderly, their religion being neither dynamic nor socially uplifting.[7]
Judaism, by contrast, was a religion of improvement: Jews moved
upwards; the Irish moved outwards. The influx of poor Irish had,
moreover, slowed considerably by the close of the Queen's reign. The
fears of labour displacement and social unrest, which their coming
once aroused, had also subsided. A simple comparison of the Booth
and Mayhew surveys indicates the diminished importance of the Irish;
for late Victorian social science the problems posed by the immigrant
Irish were no longer pressing.[8] Not so those of the Jews.

It would have been unthinkable for Booth and his associates to
omit the Jewish community from their survey. The extraordinary
emergence of East London Jewry and its influence upon the earnings
and occupations of the metropolitan poor directly addressed the central
concerns of late Victorian social investigation and rendered its
inclusion automatic. The Jewish presence was monitored and explored
through a number of carefully conducted studies which, for precision
and penetration, were without precedent.[9] The coverage was wide as
well as deep: an extended study of the Jewish community, which
embraced customs, beliefs and institutions, was specially
commissioned; immigration and the immigrant trades were likewise
closely scrutinized. Booth's inquiry, however, went beyond the
measurement of poverty. For all his protestations to the contrary,
Booth found it both necessary and desirable to make use of individual
facts to which no quantitative value could be assigned. Classification
and enumeration, though essential to serious social analysis, supplied
but a partial insight into the condition of the people. Thus, having
tested poverty by various indices – income, crowding, educational
attainment, servant-keeping and so on – Booth felt impelled to extend
his survey to incorporate other non-quantifiable social influences
'which form part of the very structure of life' and without which it was
not possible 'to complete the picture of things as they are'.[10] The
seven densely packed volumes that comprise the Religious Influences

Series embody this extraordinary attempt to probe the spiritual and moral health of the people. In terms of survey research these volumes represent a gigantic trawling operation which netted huge quantities of data, some of it precious, some of it worthless, and some of it on Jews and Judaism.

The information obtained was considerable and is preserved in the reports, notebooks, correspondence and supplementary materials relating to the survey that are currently held at the library of the London School of Economics.[11] Its importance as a resource for the social history of Anglo-Jewry has been acknowledged by different scholars in precept or in practice.[12] These materials can, however, be put to other uses; for not only do they illuminate the condition of the Jewish community in late Victorian London; the ways in which these data were assembled and processed also has implications for the history of survey methods in social investigation. A study of the presentation of Jews and Judaism by Booth and his associates should, therefore, deepen our understanding of Anglo-Jewry and contribute, albeit in a small way, towards a reassessment of the status and significance of *Life and Labour of the People in London*.

Booth's guiding assumption throughout the survey was that systematic bias could, and would, be eliminated by consulting and comparing the widest possible range of sources. 'I have relied first and chiefly on mere average and consensus resulting from the great number and variety of my sources of information', he wrote. 'Statements on which reliance could be placed would tend to enforce themselves, and errors balance each other and drop out of count'.[13] What precisely this meant in operational terms was not properly explained. Booth, having stated his principles, concluded that further discussion of comparative method and procedure was superfluous. In consequence, we do not know how opinions were selected and weighted, or how far the published results accord with the unpublished data. As I hope to show, the discrepancies were both real and significant.

I

Apart from D.F. Schloss, who contributed an essay on the trades of East London, none of those connected with the survey were Jews. Booth was a Positivist of sorts; Llewellyn Smith, who was responsible for the analysis of immigration, came from a Quaker family; Aves, a resident of Toynbee Hall, was religiously minded, as was Arthur Baxter, his colleague; G.H. Duckworth was an Anglican. Their experience of Jewry, native and foreign, was limited. Beatrice Potter, who came from sturdy Nonconformist stock, was remotely connected through her paternal grandmother, a 'tall dark woman of Jewish type' who loved music, read Hebrew and went mad. Beatrice, a striking woman of aristocratic and 'somewhat Jewish appearance', who did not read Hebrew but sometimes doubted her own sanity, was tickled by the association.[14] Her direct contacts with Jews were slightly more extensive than those of her co-workers on the Booth inquiry. As an apprentice social worker, she served her time managing Katharine Buildings, Stepney, a block of model dwellings inhabited by 'the aborigines of the East End'. The impressions thus formed were not always flattering.[15] But whereas Booth regarded foreign Jews as an unpleasant people next to whom no Gentile could live, Beatrice claimed to enjoy their company. Social research was from this point of view a pleasurable experience. 'The society I have been seeing most of is Jewish of all classes', she wrote to a friend during the course of her investigations into the garment trade, 'and on the whole I like and respect them – I almost think I have a *true* feeling for them'.[16]

Whatever their differing experiences and personal antipathies, all members of the Booth inquiry shared the dominant view of Jews as a peculiar people. The existence of a Jewish racial type to which individuals corresponded or from which they deviated was taken for granted. Its physical expression was most frequently encountered in the facial features of contemporaries, in the pigmentation of their skin, and in the presence or absence of a correct bearing. George Arkell, who interviewed Messrs Posner and Gluckstein in connection with the East London fur trade, classified them thus: 'Mr G.', he wrote, 'belonged to the fair type of Jews, his partner however was darker and sharper featured'; M. King, also 'a fair Jew', cut a surprisingly striking figure, 'with a frank bearing, looking more like the typical Anglo-Saxon than a Jew'.[17] Along the Whitechapel Road, wrote Llewellyn Smith, 'the observant wanderer may note the high cheek-bones and thickened lips of the Russian or Polish Jew, [and] the darker complexion and unmistakable nose of his Austrian co-religionist'.[18] Of course, you did not have to be a Jew to look like one. The Revd J. Mahomed, chaplain of the London Hospital, was described by one of Booth's investigators as a tall, handsome, bearded gentleman with a commanding presence and a kindly face who 'looks as if he might have some Jewish blood'; the Church Secretary at Bedford Congregational Church reportedly had 'a Jewish type of face'; while Sidney Webb, according to Beatrice, possessed 'a Jewish nose'.[19]

These outward identifiers, however, expressed but one dimension to the racial peculiarities of the Jews. Equally important was 'the Jewish agility of mind', which was something more than a capacity for smart-alec responses to unexpected questions.[20] Beatrice

Potter, in seeking to account for 'the superior mental equipment of the Jew', pinpointed the effects of environment on belief. Reviled and persecuted, East European Jews found solace and strength in the faith of their fathers. Miss Potter pictured them, within their closed communities, steeped 'in the literature of their race – in the Old Testament, with its magnificent promises of universal dominion; in the Talmud, with its minute instructions as to the means of gaining it'. The intellectual outcome of such absorption – a trained memory, the power of sustained reasoning and the capacity for elaborate calculation, 'admirably adapted to commerce and finance' – made the Jew a truly formidable figure as an industrial competitor.

The self-regarding character of his religion, though, was deemed to be of greater significance. Through its dietary practices, sanitary observances and family-centred values, Judaism served to promote the physical health and mental stamina of its practitioners, but left them devoid of social morality; for 'with the emotions directed into the well-regulated channels of domestic feeling, the mind remains passionless'. This, the most significant absence from his emotional make-up, accounted for the extraordinary market-responsiveness of the East European Jew. 'Anger, pride and self-consciousness with their counterparts of indignation, personal dignity, and sensitiveness, play a small part in the character of the Polish Jew', she observed. 'He suffers oppression and bears ridicule with imperturbable good humour; in the face of insults and abuse he remains silent. For why resent when your object is to overcome? Why bluster and fight when you may manipulate or control in secret?'[21]

Jews, in short, were programmed for profit. 'It is this dominant race impulse that has peopled our Stock Exchange with Israelites; it is this same instinct that has made the Rothschilds the leaders of European finance and the bankers of emperors and kings.'[22] Shaped by the Old Testament and the Talmud into a perfect money-making machine, and indifferent by experience towards those without the faith, the immigrant Jew was untiring, unceasing, and unstoppable in his relentless ascent through the social scale. It was the same innate individualism which also made the immigrant an impossible trade unionist. All Jews, were by nature competitive, she wrote. 'But in the case of the foreign Jews, it is a competition unrestricted by the personal dignity of a standard of life, and unchecked by the social feelings of class loyalty and trade integrity.'[23] To sum up, the *Poilishe Yidl* was Economic Man incarnate. Faith and experience had combined to produce in him those forms of rational calculative conduct which the political economists prescribed for mankind.

Potter was pleased. The chapter on the Jewish community, she wrote, 'will more than satisfy Charles Booth and will prove one of the "attractions" of the book'.[24] On both counts she was right: the Booths pronounced it 'the best thing I have yet accomplished';[25] *The Times* was complimentary.[26] For Booth, indeed, it remained the last word on the subject. With its organizing concepts and underlying assumptions he was in complete accord. Self-employment, for example, was described as 'a natural ambition … that appeals with peculiar force to the Jews'.[27] Upward mobility, if not always attractive – 'It is not a pleasing picture, nor one which we have any wish to see copied too closely by our own industrial classes', said *The Times* of 15 April 1889 – was difficult to condemn. Not so gambling. The Jew as gambler, another racial stereotype, was readily upheld as an indisputable social fact. The Polish Jew, as one of 'a race of brain-workers', was particularly susceptible to gambling, 'that vice of the intellect' which, according to Beatrice Potter, was his sole distraction 'from a life of continual acquisition'.[28] 'The Jews especially, of all classes', Booth concluded, 'are great gamblers.' The autodidact mastering the rules of the game in the solitude of the slums left an indelible impression. 'I have in my mind the picture of a little Jew boy in a very poor street, playing pitch and toss all by himself, studying the laws of chance in this humble fashion', he wrote at the close of the survey.[29]

In varying degrees, and with some exceptions, Booth's co-workers shared these perceptions. Llewellyn Smith, for example, portrayed immigrant Jewry in terms almost identical with those of Beatrice Potter.[30] And though he denied that the immigrant was an innate rate-buster and indifferent trade unionist, David Schloss agreed that their progress out of the lowest forms of industry was remarkable. As with Beatrice Potter, he presented their alleged preoccupation with social advancement as the secular expression of sacred precepts. But, unlike Miss Potter, he emphasized the desire for self-improvement rather than possession by profit as the motive force. The immigrant's incorrigible optimism, he wrote, reflected 'the extraordinary faculty, which the Jewish race possesses, of emerging scatheless and with renewed vigour from the most terrible adversity'.[31] The belief in a specific achievement-oriented Jewish ethos, the product of race and religion, formed part of the intellectual baggage of the period. The resort to cultural rather than structural explanations to account for the upward mobility of the immigrant was, in fact, common to Jew and Gentile alike. The Jew, the secretary of the Jewish Board of Guardians told the House of Lords Committee on the Sweating System, 'has a natural aptitude for pushing to the front'; a view which Jewish trade unionists heartily endorsed.[32]

II

These preconceptions and prejudices, then, supplied the theoretical framework in which the images and impressions of the Jewish immigrant were perceived and structured. These data were, however, obtained by a rational process of statistical inquiry and personal observation. To penetrate the nascent immigrant community Booth relied upon the visitors employed by the London School Board, that volunteer observer corps, whose impressions supplied the empirical basis for much of the Poverty Series. On the strength of their assessments, he told the Royal Statistical Society in 1887 that three-quarters of the Jewish population of Tower Hamlets were in poverty.[33]

The School Board Visitors were on the face of it an inspired choice. For purposes of enrolment and attendance they undertook an annual census of all schoolchildren within their division and in the process acquired an intimate knowledge of working-class life. The School Board Visitors' schedules contained the particulars of all families with children under fourteen years of age, and also included information on wages and rents of certain households. As a group the visitors varied in both perception and penetration. Capacity and experience counted for much. Ex-policemen and soldiers, who made up a fair proportion of their number, doubtless possessed acute powers of observation. None, though, possessed a right of entry. Some crossed the threshold during the course of their duties; others were kept on the doorstep. But in general their assessments were based upon externals; except in cases of non-attendance, remission or non-payment of fees, impressions as to the standards and conditions of householders were formed without access to incomes or expenditure, and, in the case of the shifting population of the common lodging houses, without access to the children. Their opinions and attitudes were on the whole unexceptional; people and places were graded by degree as rough or respectable. These perceptions, moreover, were deeply influenced by their own work situation and the ways in which the poor affected it. Impoverished and migratory parents created additional cases for visitors who already felt themselves overburdened and underpaid. In short, the poor were undeserving because they generated the most work.[34] Booth, who was not himself noticeably sympathetic towards the poor, did not find the absence a shortcoming in others.

'It is not difficult to recognize the Jews', he remarked; 'the School Board Visitors know them well.'[35] The evidence of his notebooks, though, does not support this statement. Significant data on wages and rents, acquired by the School Board Visitors in the course of their duties, were collected but not processed; guesswork rather than social science supplied the measure of poverty. The notebooks record

Booth's attempt to force their impressions into the eight economic classes that he had devised for this purpose. Those relating to the street survey of the Jewish East End, while containing much of substance, display no particular insight or understanding of the people observed. Often the lapidary comments of the School Board Visitors register their own dismay at the appalling conditions in which the immigrants lived. Buckle Street, Whitechapel, packed with Polish Jews – 'they are shot in here' said visitor Golding – was, for example, 'a very poor and crowded place' full of half-clad women standing about on the landings. 'Still', he added, 'it is a better place than Plough Buildings'. The latter was indeed the pits, 'filthy to the last degree', 'a working model of Jerusalem – a fearful place'.[36] The diet of these 'poor class Polish Jews' was equally wretched. 'This class', said Mr Bowsher, 'usually live on specked potatoes, stale bread, wurst (a kind of sausage), bagles (a light kind of bread), wh. [sic] they soak in soup made up of the coarsest parts of animals, stale or decayed fish, i.e., they have very little "legitimate" food.'[37] Others were quite simply perplexed by what they saw. Grace Alley, Whitechapel, said Mr Pointer, was 'a queer place'; and as to Brunswick Buildings, he could manage no more than that the occupants, mainly Jews, were 'decent working people'. 'Visitor knows very little about them', Booth's assistant concluded.[38]

The immigrant East End posed problems of access for which the School Board Visitors were ill prepared. The religious, ethnic, cultural and linguistic differences that separated observer from observed were of a different order from those that separated the professional classes from the proletariat. To penetrate the ghetto required strategy and assistance. Booth appeared to possess both. Himself a pioneer of participant observation, he was ably assisted by the resourceful Miss Potter who, in pursuit of authenticity, secured employment as a trouser hand in a Jewish sweatshop. Beatrice Potter's performance as a Whitechapel workgirl was brave but short-lived. In spite of her claim to extensive work experience (given in evidence to the House of Lords Committee on Sweating), she appears to have worked in only one shop for barely two days.[39]

Potter's fieldwork has been the subject of a careful study by Rosemary O'Day which shows not only the industry and application she brought to the work, but also the considerable range of her informants.[40] Particularly important to the analysis of sweating were the agents of the sewing-machine companies who were to the investigation of the tailoring trade what the School Board Visitors were to the analysis of poverty. Messrs Singer and Bradbury, the two largest suppliers of sewing machines, had raised an army of agents who each week collected the hire purchase payments owed by the master tailors, and spent the remainder of their time combing the area in search of new custom. 'Thus the whole of the East End is mapped out into districts; and the past, present, and possible customers in each street scheduled.' As with the School Board Visitors, these collectors were interviewed separately and their impressions recorded. By such means 'detailed particulars about each individual sweater' were obtained.[41] Others consulted included wholesalers, local labour contractors and assorted workers. Cross-checked against information supplied by the School Board Visitors, factory inspectorate and Home Office, these provided the empirical basis for her subsequent account of the 'Jewish method of production' and the sweating system.[42]

Her account of the immigrant quarter, too, was greatly influenced by an Anglo-Jewish Establishment that shared her prejudices and was both courteous and co-operative. The fledgling investigator was startled and flattered by their attentions. 'The Jews have opened their arms to the dark-eyed Christian who is studying their East End life', she wrote after having dined with the Chief Rabbi. At least two of the guests were poised to open their hearts as well! 'I am a wonderment [sic] in their well-regulated social life, a strange thing curious to behold and pleasant to look upon.'[43] Although she did not in fact like her hosts – the Chief Rabbi was charming but as a Jew manipulative; his wife 'like all Jewesses' possessed 'a sort of "bitterness" of manner and mind'[44] – a certain rapport was evidently established. The Chief Rabbi arranged introductions to various authorities and agencies, religious, educational and philanthropic. The dominant image with which she was presented was that of the 'pauper immigrant' as seen by the Jewish Board of Guardians. The image so formed was confirmed and consolidated by the *Jewish Chronicle*, an indispensable source, which she is known to have read.[45]

For the rest, the Booth inquiry relied principally upon school teachers, social workers, trade union officers, local administrators, police and clergy. Personal interviews were sought with ministers from all denominations who also received a questionnaire indicating the areas on which information was required. Booth's purse and persistence secured an exceptionally high response rate; and it is the written reports of these 1450 structured interviews that forms the basis and material of the Religious Influences Series. Similar interviews with some 350 local officials, charity administrators, educationalists and others, added a substantial input to the stock of information thus accumulated.

III

For the clergy of East London the coming of the Jews was seen as a disaster. Before their arrival the spiritual situation was difficult; afterwards it was impossible. Virtually all the local clergy lamented the immigrant presence. 'The changes', said the Minister of Commercial Road Baptist Church, 'have been as sudden as if the good ship of the church had encountered a cyclone.'[46] The Revd Walter Bourchier, of St Olave's, Hanbury Street, a one-time Fellow of New College, Oxford and former vicar of Steeple-Morden, Cambs., who came to Mile End New Town in 1886, considered his ministry superfluous and himself redundant. A.L. Baxter, who recorded their interview, found the clergyman in sombre mood. 'Mr B's [sic] difficulties', he explained, 'arise from the fact that his is practically a Hebrew parish and he has almost given it up in despair. Of a population of some 6,000 only 600 are Gentiles.'[47] The Revd George Bennett of St John's, Commercial Road, feared for the future of Christianity. The Wesleyan Chapel in Cannon Street Road, he explained, had been turned into a synagogue 'and holds a thousand or more', while at a nearby chapel in Cable Street where once 'you could not get a seat, now you can get a gallery'.[48] Mission work had been disrupted and missionaries relocated; and even in areas not yet affected the Jewish invasion was awaited with apprehension.[49]

Personally as well as professionally the position was hopeless. Bourchier gave Baxter 'a terrible account of the filth and insanitary habits of his Jewish parishioners'. Indeed, so intolerable was the neighbourhood that, for the sake of his wife and children, he had quit the vicarage and taken a house outside the parish.[50] Booth, in his pilot study of Tower Hamlets, classified 75 per cent of Jews as 'quite poor' or 'moderately poor'.[51] In the ten years that followed the conditions in which they lived did not much improve. 'Some of the people even sleep on the landings', said a London City Missionary of one block of dwellings crowded with Polish Jews.[52] 'The Jews', a colleague concluded 'give a lower tone – to the streets they enter.'[53]

The displacement of the church-going population did more than lower the tone of parish life; in some cases it lowered the incomes of the clergy and the subscriptions on which church work largely relied. Where a significant proportion of clerical incomes depended upon fees and pew-rents, and where the living was without an endowment, population movements might have an important influence upon ministerial living standards and professional performance. The material effects of these changes, said the minister of Commercial Road Baptist Church during the course of his interview, 'has been to make them careful in financial matters'.[54] The Revd Dolfan Lewis, minister of Trinity Congregational Church, Hanbury Street, was more to the point. 'We should have been starved out long ago but for the endowment', he told a fellow clergyman.[55]

The difficulty, moreover, was not confined to the East End. By the close of the Queen's reign the rise of Jewish suburbia was well under way.[56] 'There are about 3000 Jews in the parish', said the vicar of St Marks, Dalston. 'Most are Whitechapel folk who have got on and have come to this district to live and enjoy their wealth.'[57] His Nonconformist colleague, the Superintendent of the Hackney Circuit, saw Jewish settlement as an impediment to the forward march of Wesleyan Methodism. 'The newcomers are respectable people and even well-to-do but naturally will not attend the Weslyan Chapel nor have they much respect for the Sunday on which they usually hold garden parties.'[58] From the north-west came a similar story. 'The crucial fact about us', said the vicar of St Marks, Maida Vale, 'is that we are rapidly becoming Hebrew';[59] 'the steady influx of the wealthy jew [sic]', said the pastor of Abbey Road Baptist Church, St John's Wood, was one of 'the chief features of the changes within recent years';[60] and according to the vicar of St Mary's, Kilburn, one in four of his parishioners was Jewish and the proportion was growing.[61]

St Mary's was a pew-rented church, a fact that did not escape the attention of interviewer Ernest Aves.[62] The presence of so many Jews – 2000 in a parish of less than 8000 – gave cause for concern. 'The latter', wrote Aves, 'are a decent set of people, and Mr Stone [the incumbent] maintains very friendly relations with them ...'

> But their rapid increase, in spite of the prevailing friendliness, is by way of being the fly in the ointment ... and Mr Stone did not mention with complete satisfaction the fact that of the six applicants for a house just going to be vacated by a friend of his (rent £125) all had been Jews, and that of eight new houses recently built on open ground behind the Vicarage, seven were already taken by children of the same wonderful race.[63]

The Revd G.A. Herklots of St Saviour's, South Hampstead, a living also dependent upon pew-rents, attributed the diminished vigour of parochial life to the influx of Jews and others of 'low social standing'.[64]

Among the clergy of East London, however, morale had collapsed. The advance of Judaism seemed relentless; the recession of Christianity even more so. 'It needed a good deal of pluck and energy to keep on, owing to the changes in the people', said the Congregationalist minister of Ebenezer Chapel, Watney Street.[65] And so it did. At St Olave's, Hanbury Street, Sunday morning service attracted barely a half-dozen people. As a local missionary remarked: 'You could put the congregation in a 4-wheel [sic] cab.'[66] The bishop of Stepney said that it was a very sad state of things. 'It is, my Lord', the incumbent replied, 'but I can't manufacture Gentiles.'[67] In Spitalfields the future of the church hung in the balance. 'The parish is rapidly becoming Judaised', said the vicar of St Stephen's, 'and if things go on at the present rate in about ten years St Stephens must be turned into a Jewish mission.'[68] 'It is even a question', said his neighbour at St Marks, 'whether his parish, like that of some others in Whitechapel, ought not to be merged again in the parent parish of St Mary and worked from there as mission districts. The very rapid Judaising of the neighbourhood opened up the whole question of the appropriate parochial areas.' His interviewer concurred. 'Apart from the schools', ran the entry in his notebook, 'there is little to be found in St Marks as at present worked to justify its existence.'[69]

The remaining role, that of missionary to the Jews, aroused little enthusiasm among those interviewed. At the commencement of the Queen's reign Jews occupied a special position in Protestant thought as the most powerful witnesses to the fulfilment of prophecy and the truth of revelation.[70] By the close of her reign, the evangelization of the Jews was a marginal concern to all but a handful of committed Christians.[71] The East End clergy, with a few exceptions, declined to redefine their ministry in terms of an out-moded activism. 'This growth of the Jews is the one thing that grieves me', said the Revd Alfred Allen, vicar of St Stephens's, Spitalfields, 'for I don't want to be just a missionary to them.'[72] Allen quit the area shortly afterwards while his Congregationalist colleague prepared to follow suit. The Revd Dolfan Lewis, accepting the inevitability of Jewish settlement, said that, 'as there is no work for them he wishes his deacons to consider [the] advisability of removing the church to the suburbs'.[73] Off the record some clergy thought that, in any case, missionary work among the Jews was misguided, if not mischievous: 'their religion is just as good as ours, and better for them'.[74] The work of conversion, in so far as it was undertaken at all, was consigned to a curate, preferably a 'Jewish curate' [i.e. convert from Judaism], or left to the initiative of the laity.[75] The Jews 'are left entirely alone and their religious scruples completely respected', said the vicar of St Jude's, Whitechapel. 'His mission woman, however, is consumed with a desire to bring the Gospel to her Jewish neighbours, and though quite an uneducated woman, is learning Yiddish for the purpose.'[76]

Spiritual work among the Jews relied largely upon the energy and enthusiasm of a whole retinue of missionaries, scripture-readers, district visitors and Bible-women, the bulk of them trained personnel working directly in connection with local churches and chapels, but also including an assortment of freelance operatives of uncertain status.[77] Among incumbents, the Revd John Draper, the evangelical vicar of St Mary's, Whitechapel, was unusual in the priority he assigned to the saving of the Semites. 'The ever increasing Jewish population causes much spiritual anxiety', said his annual report for 1897, 'and the responsibility has laid heavily upon us of bringing the Gospel to the thousands of unconverted Jews.' To reach 'these ancient people of God', visitation meetings and other forms of provision were arranged. Saturday afternoon services, held in the open air during the summer months, enabled 'respectable Jews ... who would not enter a "Mission Hall"' to attend; special services held in the parish church on the principle Jewish festivals, with the sermon in German and the hymns in Yiddish, were said to be equally inviting.[78] Speaking in tongues was evidently given a whole new meaning by the vicar of St Mary, Spitalfields, who, while awaiting the appointment of a Jewish missionary, proceeded to deliver suitable services 'in Hebrew and jargon'.[79]

The Revd W.H. Davies of Spitalfields Parish Church, who was equally solicitous for the souls of the Jews, made no distinction between his Jewish and Gentile parishioners. 'They alike may participate in the charities and alike are assisted, nursed, or nourished in times of need', he wrote, and, by way of illustration, added, 'There is a Jewish Mothers' Meeting, a Band of Hope for Jewish Children; a Sewing Class, a Sunday School and a Night School'.[80] Davies, moreover, preferred a softly-softly approach to disarm criticism and diminish resistance. 'At the meetings and classes', he explained, 'the New Testament is not used at all: but the Old Testament is carefully taught, especially with reference to the Messiah in the hope that when the attributes to be expected in the Messiah are pointed out the curiosity of the Jews may be awakened and they may be led by enquiry to recognise that Jesus was the Messiah.'[81]

Something more, though, was required to encourage would-be converts to come-out for Christ. The Hebrew Guild of the East London Mission to the Jews, with its satellite societies, refuges and clubs, sought to create a counter community, a haven on the road to Heaven. The need for infrastructural provision of this sort was pressing as those who left the Faith also left the community which sustained it. The baptized Jew immediately became an outcast for whom *kaddish* was said; for to family and friends the convert was as good as dead.[82]

Notwithstanding the expenditure of time and effort, and very considerable sums of money, the outcome was disappointing. In two years the Revd A.W. Schapira, a 'Jewish curate' who worked as an agent of a parochial mission to the Jews of East London, brought but one Jew to the baptismal font.[83] Mr Neugewitz, the London City Missionary, scored better. Even so, his superior performance – four baptisms per year – meant that the millennium would have come and gone and left the Jews of Whitechapel still awaiting salvation.[84] For some the conclusion was clear: conversion was counter-productive. 'I don't mind a Jew', Bourchier told Baxter, 'but I hate a converted Jew: he's usually a mean sneaking brute. However, for heaven's sake don't publish that, that's not my clerical opinion, only my opinion between man and man.'[85] Bourchier's low opinion of the East End conversionist societies, found ready support from other members of the cloth, who were likewise convinced that converts were essentially creatures of Christian charity with an instrumental interest in loaves and fishes and little else.[86] 'All the work among the Jews is thoroughly unsatisfactory', said the Revd H.C. Dimsdale, vicar of Christ Church, Watney Street; 'it is simply bribery.'[87]

Booth, who thought these charges unfounded, agreed that conversion was largely ineffective but that progress in the conversion of the Jews, if it was to be made at all, must be attained through the activities of apostates. 'In the effort to win the Jews', he concluded, 'one of their own race who has become convinced of the doctrine of Salvation through Christ is the best agent.'[88] This, though, was not the view of the incumbent clergy. Bourchier, in his interview with Baxter, took pains to emphasize the adverse effects upon relations between the religions. 'Under the pressure of public opinion', ran the record of their interview:

> Mr B. [sic] has found it necessary at times to make efforts towards the conversion of the Jews, and for some years he had a converted Jew as a curate: this he thinks however is the worst plan possible; for not only are the converted Jews poor creatures but they are looked upon with intense hatred by their race as renegades: the Jews therefore used to spit at the curate in the street and hiss the most horrible blasphemies through the door of the vicarage where he lived. If anything is to be done it must be done through ordinary Christians.[89]

The Revd George Davenport, the aged vicar of St Mark's, Whitechapel, though equally convinced that conversion did more harm than good, was in two minds as to how best to proceed. Duckworth, described the predicament of 'poor old Davenport' thus:

> He knows quite well that he ought to try to convert his neighbours and so he has a Jewish convert curate. But on the other hand he wants to be friends with his neighbours, so he appeared to me to

hold himself somewhat aloof from what his own curate was doing, and to do his best to be liked by everybody while the latter did the necessary minimum of proselytising and making ill feeling ... I feel sure that if it were not for the pressure of an outside opinion he would send his Jewish curate to Jericho and live in quiet (perhaps indolent) peace with all men.[90]

This view, that conversion was not merely ineffective but positively harmful, found unwitting support from the missionaries themselves. Insistent that 'all prejudices are passing away' and that they were no longer 'looked upon as spies and enemies', they were equally certain that fear of rejection, isolation, loss of employment, verbal abuse and even physical violence continued to deter thousands of potential converts.[91] The Revd Michael Rosenthal, a former rabbi who conducted the East London Mission to the Jews, the most successful of such enterprises, told his interviewer that Jews 'regard attempts to convert to Christianity as an insult', that 'many orthodox Jews believe that it is their duty to persecute any member of their own faith who secedes' and that missionaries were despised and molested.[92] 'Mr Rosenthal', the interviewer concluded, 'is himself a very marked man.'

> He has, I gather, never been insulted, but 'hatred shows itself in the gnashing of the teeth; the shaken fist; the fierce look'. He never visits alone; nor even walks unaccompanied. In the Jewish districts he has always a man with him, and in his own neighbourhood either the same attendant or his daughter. He is never alone away from home. In the Mission they have always four (?) policemen at the door during the services.[93]

The Revd John Draper readily conceded that, even when the missionaries were well-received, relations between the faiths remained tense. 'Outwardly at all events the Rabbis are very friendly to Mr D. [sic] and his workers', wrote Booth's investigator, 'but there is no doubt that they resent the attempt to proselytize. Mr D. referred to a Medical Mission for the Jews, where as usual relief is contingent on listening to the Gospel: the Jewish authorities have lately started a free dispensary in opposition.'[94] Rosenthal referred to a Jewish Anti-Conversionist Society which, he claimed, 'works by the methods of evil reports and of slander'.[95]

Conversion was, in short, a dead loss. Booth, though he made no attempt to conceal or minimize its failings, seemed curiously unaware of the ethnic and religious antagonisms excited thereby.[96] The interactive character of host and minority group was a secondary consideration when it was considered at all. For the Booth survey the problematic supplied by 'pauper immigration' meant that with Jews the engagement was indirect; with Judaism it was negligible. 'Questions of poverty, of crowding, of industrial displacement, of insanitary life – insofar as they are connected with Jews, are invariably connected in the public mind with the foreign Jew', wrote G.H. Duckworth.[97] Booth's approach reflected these priorities. Upon the effects of Jewish immigration his eyes were steadfastly fixed.[98]

Duckworth himself thought that the failure of the conversionist societies reflected a want of vigour on the part of the East End clergy and in confidence condemned 'the flabby catholicity and invertebrate theology that leaves the Jews alone'.[99] Booth, who tried to maintain a sympathetic rather than a critical attitude, merely referred in the published text to the 'half-hearted' approach of the local clergy.[100] However, the interview notes indicate that some of the pusillanimous parsons were simply perplexed by the aliens in their midst. 'We don't understand them', said one who had abandoned all idea of conversion.[101]

IV

The clergy were by no means alone in their puzzlement; the police were equally nonplussed by the newcomers. Policemen as professional observers were invited to give their opinions on the social class analysis of London street by street. During the 1890s selected members of the force participated in a large-scale exercise designed to help revise and enlarge the Poverty Map of 1889. For this purpose the metropolis was parcelled out into a number of beats, each of them patrolled cojointly by interviewer and respondent. Not only were policemen required to identify so-called Jewish streets, they also presented much incidental information about the character of the community. 'During these walks', wrote Booth, 'almost every social influence was discussed, and especially those bearing upon vice and crime, drunkenness and disorder.'[102]

The police and public order perspective reflected the origins of the inquiry in the social crisis of the 1880s. Booth, in his preliminary survey of the East End Jewish settlement, had noted and discounted the prospects of political violence from this quarter. 'These foreign Jews', he observed, 'are straight from the pressure of grinding despotism; some may add nihilism and the bitterest kind of socialistic theories to very filthy habits; but the meek and patient endurance with which they live their hard lives, and their ready obedience to the law, do not suggest any immediate fear of violent revolutionary activity on their part.'[103] East Enders themselves sometimes saw the immigrants as dangerous subversives.[104] Police observation, though, tended in general to support Booth's initial assessment. 'Polish Jews and Russians who come here are mostly strong socialists', said one informant. 'Their first inclination on coming over here and finding their liberty is to break out', but, he added, 'they don't do it long.'[105]

The Jewish community was said to produce criminals, but no criminal classes.[106] Petty and irksome, Jewish crime was not considered unmanageable. The lodging houses in Gun Street 'where the Jew thieves congregate' were all known to the police,[107] as were their gaming houses – 'Jews gamble rather than bet'.[108] Even juvenile crime, a serious problem, was perceived as an age-specific rather than a permanent condition, unlike the native variant. As one policeman put it: 'they seldom get an old Jew as a thief – with the Englishman once a thief always a thief'.[109] Jewish criminality, in short, was containable. The more serious threat to public order came from inter-communal conflict; from the *goy* rather than the *gunov*.

Problems of peacekeeping inevitably directed police attention towards the process of ghetto formation. Booth himself likened the coming of the Jews to the slow rising of a flood.[110] Police observation, however, presented the growth of the ghetto not as the natural or irresistible outcome of foreign immigration, but as a negotiated process. The assertion of Jewish territoriality was contested street by street by an indigenous population that was alarmed by the inflationary influx on rented accommodation.[111] Peace reigned only in those streets in which the issue had been decided; where native and immigrant lived side by side, uncertainty persisted with 'friction and quarrels the inevitable result'.[112] In streets colonized by Jewish and Irish immigrants tensions ran high. Thus Duke Street and Black Lion Yard, with their mixed populations, were both considered dangerous, while Spring Gardens, with its mixture of poor Jews and Irish, was said to be 'a rough place for the police'.[113] The trend, though, was towards complete segregation; streets tended 'to become all Jew or remain all English'.[114]

Street supremacy, once established, was not usually subject to further challenge. Only very occasionally were the victors vanquished. Shepherd Street, where 'the Jews have been turned out by a set of rough English and Irish', was one of the few streets to have changed hands twice.[115] In general, the non-Jewish population, indigenous and immigrant, appears to have relied upon intimidation without combination to prevent Jewish settlement. The existence of exclusion zones, which Jews entered at their peril, was acknowledged by the police. The Boundary Street area, following the clearances of the slums around Old Nichol Street (the district fictionalized as the Jago), was one such quarter. 'No Jews have their foot as yet in this district', said Sergeant Trench. 'They would not dare to, they would be so roughly handled.'[116] The area bounded by Balls Pond Road on the north and the Regents Canal on the south was likewise said to be 'singularly free of Jews'. 'The people will not neighbour with the Jews', a local policeman explained.[117]

Police perceptions were conditioned partly by prejudice and partly be professional self-interest. 'On the whole', said Superintendent Mulvaney, head of H (Whitechapel) Division of the Metropolitan Police, the immigrants were 'not rough towards the police'. 'They knife one another but not those in authority.'[118] Sergeant Trench agreed. 'The Jews', he added, 'are not man enough to be rough.'[119] The newcomers, though submissive and respectful, were a nuisance – 'dirty, messy and great cheats', said Inspector Drew of Stepney Green; 'they bring their private quarrels to the police station each charging the other with crimes. It is impossible to believe either'.[120] 'Englishmen', said a colleague, 'were rougher but the Jew more tricky', a statement lent support by Judge Montague Williams whose dictum, 'A Jew never tells the truth except by mistake', was cited by police officers with approbation.[121]

Essentially an artisanal profession, the police force shared the prejudices of the people it policed. To the eye of the respectable Englishman, the newcomers, though not wanting in decency or discipline, appeared to live in dirt and disorder. Streets, strewn with decomposing fish-heads and fruit, or lined with litter and rotting vegetation, were automatically classified as 'Jewish' as though there was some necessary connection between faith and filth.[122] Cleanliness was immaterial. 'Jew children', said Inspector Drew, 'are always messy.'[123] The state of the windows, condition of curtains, fixtures and flowers, also advertised the Jewish presence. Clean curtains, tidy blinds, wax flowers, fruits displayed under a glass case in the front window – these, the signifiers of respectability, were significant absences from Jewish homes.[124]

But if not respectable, Jews were not rough. It was the singularity of Jewish culture and customs that was most striking. The newcomers, though quarrelsome and noisy, were essentially private people not much given to brawling and boozing or the lower forms of street life. Their home-centredness found expression in the attention lavished upon children, in the rarity of wife-beating and in their generally orderly conduct. The 'Jewish type' of child, said Inspector Reid, was fairly dressed, clean, well-fed, and booted.[125] 'Jews rarely get drunk', said Inspector Barker, his colleague from the Bethnal Green Division. 'Jew women as a rule lead happier lives than Gentile women, more respected by the husband and more faithful.'[126] Jews, in short, did not fit easily into the language of class.

The exclusive character of immigrant pastimes accentuated Jewish separatism and left the bobby on the beat more bewildered than ever. 'Jews drink very little in the public houses', so Duckworth was informed; 'the police cannot understand them at all. They shut themselves up in their clubs and there is no getting at them.'[127] Part of the difficulty was linguistic. Members of the 'Met.' were not on the whole Yiddish-speaking while those whom they policed often spoke nothing else.[128] For the puzzled policeman the sense of incomprehension was further deepened by the distinctive garb of the ghetto. The men with their dark beards, fur caps and long boots; the women, bareheaded, bewigged, their coarse woollen shawls draped over their shoulders, made both Inspector Reid and Sergeant Trench feel as though they were present in a foreign town.[129]

Immigrant Jews, it seemed, lived within English society but were not part of it. The fact that they were neither rough nor respectable; that they appeared clean in person but dirty in habits, or that they possessed middle-class virtues but lower-class values, made their location within the class structure exceptionally difficult to determine. The growth of the ghetto and the transitory status of streets affected thereby compounded the problem. Booth's policemen hesitated to assign 'Jewish' streets an appropriate class colour on the 'Poverty Map'.[130] Inspector Drew, Duckworth noted, had 'great difficulty in distinguishing between streets that shd. [sic] be purple and those that should be pink'. Drew's uncertainties reflected a discrepancy in the appearance of the houses and the character of the people. 'As far as outward appearances are concerned', the police officer observed, 'nearly all the streets belonged to the "pink" category.' The interiors, however, raised doubts. 'In the Jewish ho. [sic]', he explained, 'with its greater crowding there is no china pot with an evergreen plant in the front window on a round table which in north London used to be the sure mark of a "pink" character. Again there is greater visible dirt in a fairly well-to-do working-class Jewish house than in an English one.'[131] Drew's confusion was shared by his colleagues. 'Again difficulty of telling by appearance whether some of the small Jew streets should be pink, purple or light blue' Duckworth wrote of another police informant. A further entry in the same notebook records the recurrent problem respecting the colour classification of streets in process of Judaization. 'Seemingly a great mixture of well to do, poor and very poor in adjacent houses or even in the same house, among Jews than among Gentiles.'[132]

The pace of embourgeoisement compounded the difficulty. The uncertain status of immigrant Jewry and its location within the class structure in part reflected the extraordinary rate of social mobility within the Jewish community. The movement from 'greener' to 'gov'nor', and from Whitechapel to Willesden, was, indeed, upheld by Beatrice Potter as proof of the essentially progressive character of the Jewish race. The yeasty properties of the people, signified by their departure for the smart suburbs, was subsequently confirmed by both police and clergy. The upwardly mobile East Enders travelled north by north-west along a well-charted course that took them through Victoria Park, Highbury New Park – '"Highbury Jew Park" Baxter calls it'[133] – Dalston, Stoke Newington and Clapton, terminating, for the most successful, at Hampstead or London West Central. 'It takes three generations to get from Whitechapel to Kensington', said a Congregationalist minister: 'Hackney is the first step.'[134] Of Dalston, a police informant said, 'It is the intermediate stage of their march from Whitechapel to Hampstead'.[135] At Shackewell Lane, Duckworth espied a former tally tailor, now gone up in the world, who seemed to personify the process. 'Round the green was driving a Jew smoking a cigar with his wife by his side, a servant in livery with cockade in his hat behind.' In nearby Sandringham Road with its smart three-and-a-half-storeyed houses, the state of the gardens advertised the Jewish presence: 'in none of them', Duckworth was told, 'were there any signs of care or order or flowers'.[136]

V

Booth, though aware of its condition, did not find the situation of suburban Jewry engaging. A submissive, sober, industrious community which – its unkempt gardens notwithstanding – posed no threat to property, fell outside the parameters of the Labour Question, and so was largely excluded from the portrayal of metropolitan life. Jewish social and economic advancement, in any case, seemed to vindicate his own initial thesis about the improvability of the immigrant and validate that of Miss Potter who, apparently saw no need to revise her account during the fourteen years that lay between the first and final editions of the survey.[137]

The decision to proceed thus supplies a striking confirmation of the extent to which Booth's empirical sociology was prejudiced by its assumptions and methods.[138] Discrepancies between the Booth–Potter analysis of immigrant trades and immigrant workers and the evidence presented by associates were simply ignored. Stephen N. Fox, writing on tobacco workers, for example, rooted his account firmly in the material circumstances of the trade.[139] Ernest Aves, who also presented a structurally determined rather than an ethnically determined analysis of the immigrant in the furniture trade, was severely critical of her conceptual and explanatory framework. The Polish Jew, with his indefinitely elastic standard of comfort, was, according to Aves, bunkum. 'As regards wages', he wrote, 'the average of the better workmen would seem never to reach that of the better class of Gentile labour, but there is no evidence to show that the Jew often works for that low pittance, not even reaching to a bare subsistence rate, so often quoted as though it was his customary wage.' On working hours, too, he was equally dismissive. 'The abnormally long hours per day, and the seven days per week during which Jews and foreigners are frequently stated to work, appear to be exaggerations of prejudice.' The degradation of life and labour, said by Beatrice Potter to be a characteristic of the Jewish immigrant, he expressly repudiated. 'The "foreigner" is indeed a convenient stick with which to strike out the solution of industrial difficulties, but the cudgel that should be more often used is one very difficult to wield, and is for the most part grown in the home woods.'[140]

The value of the survey as it related to metropolitan Jewry was much diminished by Booth's failure to recognize or reconcile these discrepant perceptions. The belief that the social and industrial situation of the immigrant was but an expression of a unique culture and creed, an autonomous and ultimately progressive force, was a distraction and a distortion reflected in a misplaced emphasis upon class dissolution rather than class formation. The 'Jewish worker', as several scholars have recently shown, is a fiction; the want of permanent organization among immigrant workers reflected the structure of the workshop trades and the division of labour within them rather than a deficient sense of social morality. The native working class, though presented by Miss Potter as a paradigm of proletarian solidarity, was, as David Feldman observes, no more than a mirror-image of its immigrant analogue.[141]

The Booth–Potter analysis is equally invalid as an explanation of the social mobility of the Jewish immigrant. 'The major cause ... of the swift social and economic advancement of the Jews', runs the conclusion of a comparative study of the subject, 'has been their reaction to the attitudes and actions of their Gentile neighbours'.[142] Alas, it is precisely in the area of host-minority relations that *Life and Labour of the People in London* is most unsatisfactory. The position of the Jews as a minority-immigrant group, and the possible connection between status and achievement, was obscured by *a priori* assumptions about the profit-maximizing propensities of the Polish Jew, and by prejudice rather than empirical analysis.

Booth's preoccupation with immigration and industrial displacement created additional blindspots and a staggering indifference towards Judaism as a spiritual force both within Whitechapel and in the secondary areas of settlement. Judaism, as presented by Beatrice Potter, was primarily a system for the acquisition and diffusion of transferable skills. Sacred learning adapted to secular purposes transformed the immigrants into a race of brain-workers with which no class of manual labourers could compete. Booth, who discounted Judaism as a 'religious influence in London', felt that additional comment was superfluous.[143] Of, for example, the impact of Anglicanism upon Anglo-Jewry, he appears to have been oblivious.[144] The erroneous assumption that Jewish separatism rendered further investigation unnecessary deprived him of a unique opportunity to set the salient issues of the survey in comparative perspective. That it might have been fruitful to compare native with immigrant Jews, and Jews with Gentiles, in order to explain observed differences in levels of piety and worship, and that such explanations might have said something of significance about the crisis of Christianity on the one hand, and host-minority relations on the other, was beyond him.

These constraints were not entirely ideological; problems of method also created difficulties. The School Board Visitors, though close to the metropolitan poor, possessed an uncertain grasp of the standard of life of the Jewish immigrant. In spite of his reticence respecting the evaluation and selection of evidence, it seems clear that Booth himself must have entertained doubts about their reliability. Significantly, the startling statistic (announced to the public in May 1887) which placed three in four Jews in poverty, was omitted from the first edition of the survey. The quality of the data, however, was not easily improved. Neither police nor clergy were able to penetrate the ghetto, while those who knew most were prone to talk least. The chamber masters and small employers whom Arkell sought to interview 'did not care to say much', were 'very suspicious' and 'very anxious to know why I wanted the information'.[145] Then there was the language difficulty. The capmakers' union in Commercial Road conducted its proceedings in Yiddish; the Hebrew Cabinetmakers' Association was formed to protect those who had no English from exploitation.[146] But with the exception of David Schloss, none of Booth's co-workers spoke Yiddish. Beatrice Potter's dependence upon intermediaries supplied by the Anglo-Jewish Establishment was the outcome. Her distinction between native Jews, 'who have enjoyed the freedom, the culture and the public spirit of English life' and the immigrants in whom was represented 'the concentrated essence of Jewish virtue and Jewish vice', accurately reflected the prejudices of the Chief Rabbi and his circle.[147] It did not, however, reflect the outlook of the immigrant community.

Booth himself was unconcerned by the resultant imbalance. Among the Jewish clergy interviewed for the Religious Influences Series was no representative of the Jewish immigrants. The Chief Rabbi was known to immigrant East Enders as 'the West End *goy*'; while his lieutenant, the Revd J.P. Stern bore the nickname 'the Jewish Bishop of Stepney'.[148] The want of symmetry was, however, avoidable. Duckworth, for example, warned Booth against an uncritical acceptance of the Chief Rabbi's replies. 'The characteristic formalism of the religion of the foreigner, mentioned by Dr Adler, must not', he wrote, 'be regarded as true of the whole class as there is a considerable socialist and free-thinking section – Jews in nothing but birth.'[149] Booth, alas, was not interested in probing the politics of the ghetto. Its interior life formed no part of his picture of the close of the Queen's reign. The plurality of approaches to Anglicization he ignored. The conflict between revolutionary socialist, zionist and orthodox Jews as analysed by David Feldman, or the marvellously evocative studies of W.J. Fishman, find no anticipation in Booth's portrait of metropolitan Jewry.

An unquestioning use of sources is also suggested by Booth's presentation of Jews as a peculiarly family-centred people. Duckworth, who thought that the immigrants 'are often given a clearer moral bill than they deserve', instanced the frequency of wife-desertion in support of his claim.[150] Booth, however, made no mention of conjugal roles within the immigrant community.[151] Why so? The answer is not immediately apparent because, in describing his procedures, Booth rarely takes the reader into his confidence. *Life and Labour of the People in London* provides a partial account of his methods of social enquiry. There is an almost total silence about Booth's own role in the selection and interpretation of evidence. The comparative method, as Booth saw it, was a process of bias-elimination that was unaffected by his own arbitrary interventions. In this he was mistaken. The preceding analysis suggests the need to reconstruct his methodology both as a measure of what he did achieve and as a measure of what he might have achieved.

Finally, how does the presentation of Jews and Judaism relate to Booth's place within the British sociological tradition? The Booth survey, it has often been noted, was geared towards practical rather than theoretical conclusions. 'What is missing,' writes John Madge, 'is any grand theory of poverty and social immersion to set against the theories, for example, of Marx and Engels'; for Heinz Maus this deficiency is sufficient to debar Booth from 'sociology proper'.[152] But, if no great theorist, Booth did possess a social theory: first and foremost he was an empiricist confident that in the science of statistics lay the key to social progress. His and Potter's ideas about Jews and Judaism further combined a number of inherited assumptions common to their class and culture with a large dose of an unreflective Lamarckianism that was to signal a feature of Victorian social science. Looking back over four decades, Llewellyn Smith was thus confident that, as a result of the Booth survey, the Polish Jew had been absolved of responsibility for the existence of the sweating system, even if the immigrant presence made it worse.[153] This is pure moonshine. There is in fact little evidence to suggest that attitudes towards Jews, élite or popular, were positively affected by the Booth findings.

In terms of survey research, too, the outcome must be deemed a disappointment. The inclusion of the Jewish community, as noted earlier, was a historical accident, a result of the coincidence of mass immigration with the genesis of the Booth inquiry rather than any supposed organic relationship with the life of the metropolis. Similarly, its retention among the special studies in *The New Survey of London Life and Labour* forty years later supplied a basis for comparison rather than a pointer towards a sociology of inter-group relations.[154] By then, the concept of the Jewish worker and the intellectual apparatus that accompanied it had disappeared from the language of social investigation. With it, however, had also disappeared all significant interest in the Jewish ethnic minority. Serious survey research had to await the creation of the Research Unit of the Board of Deputies of British Jews in 1965. Metropolitan Jewry deserved better.

Notes

1   Booth, Charles (1902/3), *Life and Labour of the People in London*, 17 volumes (First Series: Poverty in 4 volumes; Second Series: Industry in 5 volumes; Third Series: Religious Influences in 7 volumes; Final Volume: Notes on Social Influences and Conclusions) London: Macmillan.

2   *Poverty*, 3, pp.103–11.

3   See evidence of Revd R.C. Billing, Rector of Christchurch, Spitalfields, Parliamentary Papers (1884–5), *Royal Commission on the Housing of the Working Classes*, PP 30, QQ. 4989, 5054–5056, 5125, 5232–5235, 5300–5305; 'Report of the Lancet Special Sanitary Commission on the Polish Colony of Jew Tailors', *The Lancet*, 3 May 1884, pp.817–18; Fishman, W.J. (1975), *East End Jewish Radicals*

1870–1914, London: Duckworth, p.69; Webb, Beatrice BLPES, Unpublished Diaries, Vol.2, 13 May 1887.

4   Lipman, V.D. (1954), *A Social History of the Jews in England 1850–1950*, London: Watts, pp.97–100, 157–60.

5   On the situation of the Irish, see Lees, Lynn H. (1979), *Exiles of Erin: Irish Migrants in Victorian London*, Manchester: Manchester University Press; Swift, Roger and Gilley, Sheridan (eds) (1985), *The Irish in the Victorian City*, London: Croom Helm, is a general but suggestive survey.

6   *Religious Influences*, 2, p.104.

7   *Religious Influences*, 7, p.401.

8   Significantly, the index in none of the four volumes of the Poverty Series contains an entry for the Irish community.

9   Previous studies include Margoliouth, Revd Moses, (1851), *The History of the Jews of Great Britain*, 3 volumes London: Richard Bentley; Mills, J. Revd (1853), *The British Jews, Their Religious Ceremonies, Social Condition, Domestic Habits, Literature, Political Statistics*, London: Houlston and Wright; Mayhew, Henry (1861), *London Labour and the London Poor*, 4 volumes, London: Griffin, Bohn and Co., 2, pp.124–32; Stallard, J.H. (1867), *London Pauperism amongst Jews and Christians*, London: Saunders, Otley; Davies, C.M. Revd (1876), *Unorthodox London: or Phases of Religious Life in the Metropolis*, London: Tinsley Bros., pp.188–98; and Escott T.H.S. (1890), *England: Its People, Polity and Pursuits*, London: Chapman and Hall, pp.474–8.

10   *Religious Influences*, 1, 4.

11   These are currently being indexed and calendared at the Open University by Rosemary O'Day, David Englander and Judith Ford.

12   Lipman V.D. (1981), 'The Booth and New London surveys as source material for East London Jewry (1880–1930)', in Newman Aubrey (ed.), *The Jewish East End 1840–1939*, London: The Jewish Historical Society of England, pp.41–9; Feldman David, (1994) *Englishmen and the Jews: Social Relations and Political Culture, 1840–1914*, London: Yale University Press.

13   Final Vol., 32.

14   Webb, Beatrice (1971), *My Apprenticeship*, Harmondsworth: Penguin Books, pp.38, 81; Galton, F.W. (1949), 'Investigating with

the Webbs', in Cole, M. (ed.), *The Webbs and their Work*, London: Frederick Muller, p.34.

15   Her diary records an approach by a broker – 'typical Jew' – whose services she accepted. 'Was I done?', she wondered. 'Paid 5s. for three warning visits. If her gets two disreputable women out without further charge, I have made a good bargain' (unpublished diaries, Vol.7, 22 August 1885). This is no isolated example. Her unpublished diaries, according to one authority, reflect 'a near obsession for delineating between Jewish and non-Jewish persons and describing what she considered to be typical Jewish traits': see, Colbenson, Peter D. (1977), 'British Socialism and Anti-Semitism, 1884–1914' (unpublished Ph.D. thesis, Georgia State University), pp.75–80.

16   Beatrice Potter to Mary Playne, 30 April, 1888, in Mackenzie, Norman (ed.) (1978), *The Letters of Sidney and Beatrice Webb*, 3 volumes, Cambridge: Cambridge University Press, 1, p.64; for Booth's repugnance, see *Religious Influences*, 2, p.3.

17   'Fur Trade: Interviews with Mr Posner and Mer Gluckstein, 14 January 1889; and with Maurice King, 16 January 1889', BLPES, Booth Collection, A2, ff. 76, 85.

18   *Poverty*, 3, 100.

19   B221, 161; B216, 63; Mackenzie, Norman and Mackenzie, Jeanne (eds) (1982–6), *The Diary of Beatrice Webb*, 4 volumes, London: Virago, 1, p.324.

20   Cf. B205, 27.

21   *Poverty*, 3, pp.189–90.

22   Potter, Beatrice (1888), 'East London Labour', *The Nineteenth Century*, 24, p.177.

23   *Poverty*, 3, p.191.

24   Mackenzie, *Diary*, 1, p.271.

25   *Ibid.*, pp.278–9.

26   *The Times*, 15 April 1889.

27   *Poverty*, 4, p.335.

28   *Poverty*, 3, pp.188–9.

29   Final Volume, p.57.

30   See Parliamentary Papers (1894), *Board of Trade (Alien Immigration) Reports on the Volume and Effects of Recent*

Immigration from Eastern Europe into the United Kingdom, PP, 68 (1894), pp.40–3.

31   Schloss, David F. (1891), 'The Jew as a Workman', *The Nineteenth Century*, 29, pp.108–09.

32   Parliamentary Papers (1888), *First Report from the Select Committee of the House of Lords on the Sweating System*, PP, 20, Q. 5504; Dyche, John A. (1898), 'The Jewish Workman', *The Contemporary Review*, 73, pp.42–3.

33   Booth, Charles (1887), *Condition and Occupations of the People of the Tower Hamlets, 1886–87*, London: Edward Stanford, p.49.

34   On the situation and outlook of the School Board Visitors, see *Royal Commission on the Housing of the Working Classes*, QQ. 1437–1438, 1481–1483, 1525, 1544, 4346, 4365, 4858, 4913–4919; B10, 47; *Industry*, 4, pp.186–9; Webb, Beatrice, Unpublished Diaries, Vol.11, 10 October 1887; Rubinstein, David (1969), *School Attendance in London 1870–1906, A Social History*, Hull: University of Hull Occasional Papers in Social History; Lewis, Jane (1982), 'Parents, Children, School fees and the London School Board 1870–1890', *History of Education*, 11, pp.291–312. On the potential importance of the data collected by the visitors, see Bales, K. (1986), 'Reclaiming "Antique Data": Charles Booth's Poverty Survey', *Urban History Yearbook*, Leicester, pp.75–80.

35   Booth, 'Condition and Occupations', p.45.

36   B9, fos 21–22, 25.

37   B8, fo.70.

38   B10, fo.15, 33.

39   Mackenzie, *Diary*, 1, pp.241–9; Beatrice's bogus claims were publicly exposed by Lewis Lyons, the Jewish trade unionist, who also criticized her ignorance and class prejudice. Significantly, the account of these experiences which first appeared as 'Pages from a Workgirls' Diary' in *The Nineteenth Century* of September 1888, had become 'The Diary of an Investigator' when republished along with other pieces in Webb, Sidney and Beatrice, (1902), *Problems of Modern Industry*, London: Longman, pp.1–9. Her misleading evidence is in *First Report of Select Committee of the House of Lords on the Sweating System*, QQ. 3410–3412; for Lyons observations thereon, see *Pall Mall Gazette*, 18 May 1888.

40   See O'Day, Rosemary (1993), 'Before the Webbs: Beatrice Potter's Early Investigations for Charles Booth's Inquiry', *History*, 78,

pp.218–42. Cf. Himmelfarb, Gertrude (1991), *Poverty and Compassion: the Moral Imagination of the Late Victorians*, New York: Alfred A Knopf, pp.142–3.

41   Still, there were some places where the collectors refused to go. Booth Street Buildings was one of them. Mr Ruderman, the Singer's agent who guided Booth's assistants around the small workshops of East London for the Industry Series, knew little of the Polish Jews who worked there because he considered the buildings a health hazard too dangerous to enter (B108, p.12).

42   *Poverty*, 4, pp.45–6.

43   Mackenzie, *Diary*, 1, p.250.

44   Unpublished Diaries, Vol.13, 11 February 1889.

45   Mackenzie, *Diary*, 1, attitudes and opinions as presented by the organ of Anglo-Jewry are analysed by Kaplan, Stanley (1955), 'The Anglicization of the East European Jewish Immigrant as Seen by the London *Jewish Chronicle*, 1870–1897', *YIVO Annual for Jewish Social Science*, 10, pp.267–78; and for a general survey of relations between native and immigrant Jews, see Gartner, Lloyd P. (1973), *The Jewish Immigrant in England_1870–1914*, Second Edition, London: Simon Publications; Sharot, Stephen (1973), 'Religious Change in Native Orthodoxy in London 1870–1914: Rabbinate and Clergy', *Jewish Journal of Sociology*, 15, pp.167–87; *Idem*, 'Religious Change in Native Orthodoxy in London 1870–1914: The Synagogue Service', *Jewish Journal of Sociology*, 15, pp.57–77.

46   B224, 51.

47   B221, 51.

48   B222, 00.

49   B226, 5–27; B228, 81; B229, 55.

50   B221, 51–3.

51   Booth, 'Condition and Occupations', p.49.

52   B223, 97.

53   B175, 21–2.

54   B224, 49.

55   B223, 117.

56   Lipman, V.D. (1926–7), 'The Rise of Jewish Suburbia', *Transactions of the Jewish Historical Society of England*, 21, pp.78–103.

57   B199, 7–9.

58   B187, 24.

59   B219, 101.

60   B220, 5.

61   B217, 63–5.

62   The living, a very good one, was in fact exclusively dependent upon fees and pew-rents: see, 'Stone William Henry', *Crockford's Clerical Directory*, (1901), London: Horace Cox, p.1307.

63   B217, 63–5.

64   B217, 39.

65   B224, 35.

66   B223, 89.

67   B221, 53.

68   B221, 223.

69   B222, 79.

70   Vrete, Mayir (1972), 'The Restoration of the Jews in English Protestant Thought 1790–840', *Middle Eastern Studies*, 8, pp.8–50; also see Katz, David (1982), *Philo-Semitism and the Readmission of the Jews to England 1603–1655*, Oxford: Oxford University Press.

71   On Christian attempts to evangelize the Jews, see Endelman, Todd M. (1990), *Radical Assimilation in English Jewish History 1656–1945*, Bloomington: Indiana University Press, pp.144–72.

72   B221, 223.

73   B223, 121.

74   B221, 59.

75   According to a contemporary estimate, there were 126 ordained clergymen in the Anglican Communion who were formerly Jews including three bishops: *Church Congress Report* (1895), London: Bemrose, p.122.

76   B221, 87, 141–3, 189; B222, 83.

77   Some missionary activity was also externally funded from wealthy West End congregations (B 237, 99). On missionary enterprise, proper and improper, see Bateman Charles T., (1904), 'Missionary Efforts in the Metropolis' in Mudie-Smith, Richard (ed.), *The Religious Life of London*, London: Hodder & Stoughton, pp.314–19; *Industry*, 4, 193–201; and for a spectacular example of

fraudulent conversionist activity among the Jews, see B224, 101–09; also in *Religious Influences*, 2, pp.231–2.

78   B221: *Parish of St Mary, Whitechapel, Annual Report & Statement of Accounts* (1897), p.23.

79   B222, 17.

80   B221: *Spitalfields Parish Church, Report & Statement of Accounts* (1897), p.20.

81   B221, 121.

82   B222, 117–25.

83   B221, 141–3.

84   B229, 99–101.

85   B221, 57.

86   B221, 233.

87   B221, 143.

88   *Religious Influences*, 2, p.8.

89   B221, 57.

90   A39, 34–5.

91   B229, 107, 121; B221, 23.

92   B222, 109–11.

93   B222, 115.

94   B221, 41–3.

95   B222, 115.

96   *Religious Influences*, 2, pp.7–9.

97   A39, 7.

98   Booth, reviewing the inquiries begun fifteen years earlier in Whitechapel and St George's-in-the-East, omitted from the printed text all reference to the communal antagonisms highlighted in Duckworth's digest and analysis of the evidence relating to those districts: Compare A39, 41–2 with *Religious Influences*, 2, pp.3–4.

99   A39, 35.

100   *Religious Influences*, 2, 9.

101   B221, 141.

102   Final Volume, 136.

103   Booth, 'Conditions and Occupations', p.48.

104   Parliamentary Papers (1903), *Royal Commission on Alien Immigration*, PP, 9, QQ, 399–402, 2934–43, 2977–82, 5362–5400.

105   B350, 45.

106   Holmes, Colin (1979), *Anti-Semitism in British Society 1876–1939*, London: Edward Arnold, p.43. There is as yet no serious study of Jewish criminality. A good starting point is provided by *East End Underworld: Chapters in the Life of Arthur Harding*, Samuel, Raphael (ed.) (1981), London: Routledge and Kegan Paul.

107   B351, 101.

108   B350, 79.

109   A39, 13; B351, 247; B352, 59–60.

110   *Religious Influences*, 2, p.3.

111   On the housing crisis in the East End and its attendant social tensions, see Gainer, Bernard (1972), *The Alien Invasion, The Origins of the Aliens Act of 1905*, London: Heinemann, pp.37–74; White, Jerry (1981), 'Jewish Landlords, Jewish Tenants: An Aspect of Class Struggle within the Jewish East End, 1881–1914' in Newman, *The Jewish East End*, pp.205–15; Englander, David (1983), *Landlord and Tenant in Urban Britain 1838–1918*, Oxford: Oxford University Press, pp.120–1.

112   B351, 49.

113   B351, 49, 101, 133, 137–9, 147.

114   A39, 4.

115   B351, 117.

116   B351, 199.

117   B347, 121.

118   B350, 45.

119   B351, 151.

120   B350, 65.

121   B350, 231.

122   B351, 35, 49, 67, 69, 77.

123   B350, 35.

124   B350, 197; B351, 151.

125   B351, 69, 81.

126   B352, 63.

127   B351, 87–8.

128   B351, 81.

129   B351, 49, 109.

130   For an explanation of the colour code, see *Poverty*, 2, pp.40–1.

131   B350, 111–13.

132   B351, 115, 155.

133   B348, 167.

134   B187, 37.

135   B347, 97.

136   B347, 85, 89.

137   Her chapter on the Jewish community, reprinted in the second and third editions of the enquiry with minimal changes to the footnotes, was also included in Webb, S and B, *Problems of Modern Industry*, pp.20–45; Booth's view respecting the improvability of the immigrant is in 'Conditions and Occupation', p.48.

138   On the attitudes, beliefs and norms that informed Booth's methods of social inquiry, see Jones, Gareth Stedman (1971), *Outcast London*, Oxford: Oxford University Press; Hennock, E.P. (1976), 'Poverty and Special Theory in England: the experience of the eighteen-eighties', *Social History*, 1, pp.67–91; Himmelfarb, *Poverty and Compassion*; O'Day, Rosemary and Englander, David (1993), *Mr Charles Booth's Inquiry*, Hambledon.

139   *Poverty*, 4, pp.69–137.

140   *Poverty*, 4, pp.211–12.

141   Schmiechen, James A. (1984), *Sweated Industries and Sweated Labour, The London Clothing Trades, 1860–1914*, London: Croom Helm; Feldman, *Englishmen and Jews*, pp.185–209, 234–51.

142   Gottlieb, Paul (1970), 'Social Mobility of the Jewish immigrant. A Study in Social Mobility focused on the Baghdad Jews of the Far East Living in London', unpublished M. Phil. thesis, University of Nottingham, p.173.

143   *Religious Influences*, 7, p.148.

144   For a summary of recent scholarship, see Englander, David (1988), 'Anglicised not Anglican: Jews and Judaism in Victorian Britain' in Parsons, Gerald, *Religion in Victorian Britain*, 2 volumes, Manchester: Manchester University Press, 1, pp.235–73.

145   A2, 87, 89, 96.

146   B81, 41; B110, 83.

147   *Poverty*, 3, p.182.

148   Russell, Charles and Lewis, H.S. (1900), *The Jew In London, A Study of Racial Character and Present-day Conditions*, London: T. Fisher Unwin, p.211; Simmonds, Lionel (1988), 'East London Synagogue Memories', *The Path: The United Synagogue Magazine*, 4, pp.13–14; Finestein, I. (1981), 'Joseph Frederick Stern (1865–1934): Aspects of a Gifted Anomaly', in Newman A., *The Jewish East End*, pp.75–98. Notebook B197 contains interviews with Jewish clergy.

149   A39, 8–9.

150   A39, 8.

151   On wife-desertion, see Englander, David (1992), 'Stille Huppah (Quiet Marriage) Among Jewish Immigrants in Britain', *The Jewish Journal of Sociology*, 34, pp.85–109.

152   Madge, John (1963), *The Origins of Scientific Sociology*, London: Tavistock; Maus, Heinz (1962), *A Short History of Sociology*, London: Routledge and Kegan Paul, p.49.

153   (1930–35) *The New Survey of London Life and Labour*, directed by H. Llewellyn Smith, 9 volumes, London: P. S. King and Son, 6, p.21.

154   Adler, Henrietta, 'Jewish Life and Labour in East London', in *New Survey*, 6, pp.268–98.

West along Royal Mint S! small shops with lodgr
above for carmen, general labours + dockers.
all English. purple not marked in map. South
down Glass House S! all peabody Dwellings. They
are very strict + will not allow any noisy family
to remain, purple. not marked in map, no
Jews here, Dwellings 5 storied with large asphalt
yards. The whole block between Glass House
S! + Cartwright S! is a mass of Dwellings
all purple. built either by the Peabody Trust
or the Metropolitan Industrial Dwellings Co.
[3 rooms from 6/9. 2 rooms from 4/6 + one room
from 3/3]. Reid said that there were a few
thieves in the Dwelling, but no known bad
characters. Many young girls who work in the
City in the single rooms, a respectable class.
All these dwellings are strictly kept.
Between Glass House S! + Dock S! is Shorters Rent.
dark blue on map, poor but no trouble to the police.
rather lt than I blue.

Smith

11.1 George Duckworth's notes of his walks around London indicate
the manner in which the Maps Descriptive of Poverty were
revised and the sources which were used. Duckworth's
information about the model dwellings in Cartwright Street was
derived from the police and was deficient. The colour code of
one street was changed from dark to light blue because it was
not troublesome to the police. (Booth Collection, B351, p.3)

11 Representations of metropolis: descriptions of the social environment in *Life and Labour*

David Reeder

Until recently, Booth scholarship was mainly concerned with his standing as a social investigator. Since the Simeys' early claims for Booth as a pioneer social scientist,[1] a critical literature has downgraded *Life and Labour of the People in London* in relation to later surveys as lacking in objectivity and too discursive. Commentators have been especially critical of the Poverty Survey for its dependence on indirect information and the way that moral attitudes and assumptions were incorporated into the classifications. However this approach to Booth has in turn been criticized for assuming some kind of unilinear evolutionary progress towards a modern positivist ideal of objective social research.[2] It can be argued that such an approach abstracts the Survey from its historical context. From the perspective of an historian, what matters more is the significance of the Survey in the context of its times: how it reflected and shaped contemporary social thinking in the crisis decade of the 1890s and in what ways it extended and improved on a line of nineteenth-century social investigation concerned with gathering moral statistics about the poor, sometimes in house-to-house surveys, and discoursing about their way of life frequently on the basis of first-hand observation.[3]

From the standpoint of this latter tradition, the distinctive features of Booth's Survey were its scale, the complexity of its methodology and its socio-spatial approach to the presentation and description of social data. Notwithstanding the urgency of the task of investigating the extent of poverty, Booth seems to have had a grander plan in mind when he set out to extend the initial survey of poverty in the East End to the rest of the metropolis. Writing about the first meeting of the Board of Statistical Research, Beatrice Webb explained: 'Objects of the Committee: to get a fair picture of the whole of London society, the four millions'[4] Booth's way of getting a fair picture was to represent London society in terms of eight categories of well-being. These categories (set out as letter classes) were used both to organize statistical material and to provide a social classification for all London streets as displayed in colour coding on the *Descriptive Map of*

London Poverty 1889.[5] The poverty map, revised and updated and cut up into smaller pieces, was subsequently used as a guide for the commentary in the volumes on Religious Influences. Each of these volumes contained a social description of the London districts in an introduction and *inter alia* throughout the text. Brief summary details were appended on the character of the London districts, local administration, population, amusements, open spaces and so on.

The novelty of mapping the distribution of poverty in relation to the social character of London as a whole was not lost on contemporaries; and it had as much if not more impact than the Survey itself in the press commentary.[6] Modern commentators have been impressed by it also and the descriptions of the different London districts have been utilized in the work of local historians, as for example in the topographical surveys of the London parishes in the recent volumes of the VCH Middlesex. Sociologists and geographers have also highlighted the way that Booth identified the demographic and ecological forces shaping the social character of the metropolis.[7] But again, some commentators have been less concerned with the contemporary significance of this approach than in making claims about the way that Booth anticipated later ecological analysis or as the founding father of the modern urban survey. However, contemporary representatives of the Chicago school of urban sociology did not regard Booth as anticipating their work. The social map was already a feature of American sociology, and although Booth's contribution was recognized by members of the Chicago School, no debts were expressed. Park made reference to Booth's survey as 'a memorable and permanent contribution to our knowledge of human nature and society', but he also claimed the approach was 'pedantic and largely descriptive'.[8]

The survey as social reportage

What then was the nature of this description? Why was it attempted and how did it function in the Survey? What information was it based on? And how successfully did it represent the social diversity of metropolitan London? This paper attempts an assessment of the descriptive quality of the Survey based on a reading of the published volumes and taking into account the sources that Booth used, with particular attention to the so-called police notes. This way of proceeding is in keeping with the current emphasis in Booth scholarship on studying the methodology and sources of the Survey.[9]

We know very little, however, about Booth's motives in developing a spatial approach to the presentation of social data or why he subsequently elaborated on this in the Religious Influence volumes.

The effort of mapping the data from the Poverty Survey is best understood perhaps as part of Booth's endeavour to reveal things as they were. The map might be thought of as exposing the underlying rationality of metropolitan growth and development. We know that Booth had experienced some sort of personal crisis on his move to London, and there are indications of a sense of confusion over the apparent chaos of metropolitan life. Through the Survey he was able to cast himself in the role of an explorer, a 'social copernicus' in the words of the *Pall Mall Gazette*,[10] in what had become *terra incognita*, finding out how things really were by setting his camp down in various parts of the metropolis. In this context the mapping of London might have had a symbolic importance in the heyday of Imperialism.[11] The effect could be somewhat different, however, from that intended, serving to reinforce rather than to allay the confusion of readers. The social commentator, Charles Masterman, for example, regarded the detail of the Religious Influences volumes along with its maps of 'picturesque bewilderment' as showing a city 'beyond the power of individual synthesis, a chaos resisting all attempts to reduce it to orderly law'.[12] But the whole point of Booth's work in a way was to reveal the regularities in the metropolitan condition, to expose its orderliness, and thus to make London comprehensible once again.

The social description also had a functional importance in the Survey. It was regarded as necessary to understanding the non-quantifiable social influences which Booth felt had to be studied as forming part of the structure of metropolitan life. It was important to describe the kind of social environment within which religious and educational activity was conducted. Yet he goes to greater lengths in the representation of London's social geography than might seem to be required if the aim was simply that of providing an environmental context for probing the religious and moral health of the people. What fascinated Booth as he explained in the first volume dealing with East London, was the way each of the London districts had its own character, its distinct flavour:

> One seems to be conscious of it in the streets. It may be in the faces of the people, or in what they carry – perhaps a reflection is thrown in the way from the prevailing trades – or it may be in the sounds one hears, or in the character of the buildings.[13]

There seems to be a tension in the Survey between the effort to provide a systematic descriptive account and Booth's evident fascination with the individual character of London's central and suburban districts.

Finally, in these preliminary remarks, we should note that, whatever the retrospective criticisms of his methodology, Booth went about the task of operationalizing his ambitions and collecting data in a very different way from any survey that had been held before. The key to Booth's methodology was the elaborate process of systematic social reporting which he initiated. The Survey was based on reports from hundreds of volunteer observers and a series of structured interviews. Among this volunteer corps were School Board Visitors, schoolteachers, policemen, clergymen, social workers, and local administrators, each of them contributing to various parts of the Survey, some of them providing the primary evidence, others being used for supplementary or confirmatory information. Booth's guiding assumption throughout was that systematic bias would be eliminated by utilizing the widest possible range of sources. Thus it was not a weakness but a strength from Booth's point of view to draw on opinions and individual observations, provided these were widely gathered.

As is well known, the social data for the classification of London streets came initially form the School Board Visitors. These Visitors (the School Attendance Officers) had access to data on wages and rents of certain households, and they knew about parental occupations, as part of their work on school enrolment and attendance. But the crucial element in determining the colour classification of the streets was the personal, visual and hearsay knowledge they provided of the habits of life and behaviour of the working-class inhabitants – in contrast to the classification of middle-class London, which was based mainly on rateable value and servant keeping. The initial classification of the streets of working-class London depended very much on the opinions of the School Board Visitors, most of them ex-policemen or army personnel, and from the outset the classification scheme embodied environmental and cultural elements. Booth's continuing preoccupation with gathering information about the habits of life of the people was impelled by a belief in the possibility of validating by this means the authenticity of his categories – the letter classes –as true social classes.

Booth also went to some lengths to revise and update the descriptive map initially in a rather *ad hoc* way by pinning up a copy in Toynbee Hall and asking individuals to make changes as they thought necessary. However, between 1897 and 1902 members of the police force were involved in an altogether more systematic revision which in effect amounted to a survey within a survey. It was organized and mainly conducted by one of Booth's assistants, George Duckworth, who divided the metropolis up into beats and walked most of them himself in the company of a policeman recording observations on the right-hand side of a notebook. The twenty books and 2000 pages of notes covered virtually the whole of London.[14]

On the left-hand side of the notebooks were sketches, hand-drawn maps, and Booth's summary index and occasional comments. The notebooks are extraordinarily detailed on the appearance of houses and streets (and gardens), with information on types of houses, condition, number of storeys, age, rents and inhabitants. The objective was to check the colour codes against a new assessment of the social tone of the streets with a list of changes up and down compiled eventually from the notebooks and incorporated in the map. Duckworth relied heavily on the observations of the police for determining the colour of the lower-class streets even though both he and Booth were of the opinion that the police tended to unduly mark streets down.[15] Duckworth seemed to be aware too of how police judgements might be affected by their relations with a particular district. Nevertheless whether a street was known to the police was decisive for the lowest classification, for as Duckworth frequently observed, black always carries a moral significance.[16] He also interrogated the police on particular aspects of their work, and made notes on such matters as the distribution and character of prostitution in different districts, the incidence of gambling and the fancy, the extent of drinking and police relations with publicans. Some of this material Booth drew on for Volume I of Religious Influences in a section entitled, 'The Police, Drink and Disorder'. But it is necessary to trawl through all the volumes to gauge the extent to which it was utilized as a source of social description, particularly of streets and neighbourhoods, and not only explicitly so in places where Booth refers to 'our survey' or 'our notes' and makes deliberate quotation from Duckworth, but also the unacknowledged references and illustrations. The latter tended to be slipped in between the anecdotes and comments on the lives and attitudes of the poor that came from the interviews with clergymen and others.

Duckworth's notes also offered comments on the middle-class streets, with information obtained from all sorts of local enquiry and personal observation, which included peering into second-floor windows to see if they were being used as bedrooms or living rooms. In one district of Elm Park, Duckworth observed that information had been obtained from the vicar of a local chapel and from the oil man who called on the houses.[17]

What Booth must have found of most value, however, were the pen portraits that Duckworth provided at the end of each beat describing the general character of quite small areas, highlighting the changes that had occurred, saying what was distinctive about the social make-up of the district, and pointing to the micro-economics of local neighbourhoods with references to the role of local high streets and the availability and nature of local employment. Thus the existence of these notebooks accounts for much of the environmental detail in the later volumes of *Life and Labour* and helped to turn these volumes into a large-scale ecological surveillance of the late Victorian metropolis, an elaborate exercise in social topography.

Social patterns: a theory of urban change

In his commentary Booth describes the social character of late Victorian London in two ways: first, in terms of a social patterning, based on displaying the social make-up of different parts of London; secondly, in terms of cultural patterns, based on observations of the attitudes and habits of life of different sections of the working class in different neighbourhoods. These aspects were inter-related since Booth ascribed cultural meaning to particular streets and districts in a way that reflected and bestowed status and stigma.

The selection of detail was not random but informed by a notion or theory of urban change which was related to Booth's general outlook on society. Booth represented London's residential development as being shaped by powerful centrifugal forces, impulses from the centre pushing people into an inner ring, the attractions of the suburbs pulling them from the inner to the outer ring, changing the social map of the city. In the central districts competition for sites, the influence of industry and the consequent raising of rents set the sequence of change in motion, while railway and other transport improvements helped to maintain its suburban momentum. The Survey presents London as a city in motion, albeit mainly it has to be said in terms of a rather banal imagery of human flows. Thus in west London the pace of change is set by 'the tide of fashion and favour which for some time flowed towards Brompton but is now exhausted in the Wild West'.[18] In south London the inner suburbs are represented as a vast 'reservoir' from which 'drifts' and 'flows' of population move from inner to outer London districts: 'Southwark is moving to Walworth, Walworth to North Brixton and Stockwell, whilst the servant keepers of outer South London go to Croydon and other places.' Wandsworth, Clapham and Putney in south-west London are represented as a huge 'pool' into which the 'living stream flows', a region of rapid and recent changes of 'wholesale but for the most part wholesome migrations'.[19] The volumes also contain descriptions of the outer suburbs, although those south of the Thames seemed to defeat him because of the scattered and fragmentary nature of settlement.

London's social map was presented in the Survey volumes as the culmination of tendencies in the development of the metropolis which operated with the force almost of natural laws. One tendency was for people to settle in neighbourhoods similar to themselves in wealth and social standing; another was the tendency for people to move out of a district perceived to be going down socially, leaving room for other people to replace them in an orderly sequence of class residential succession. In the former case Booth notes not only the influence of suburban social pretensions but the importance of local industry in determining the character of the suburbs. The concept of residential succession, however, is seen as the dynamic element in urban change. It was introduced at an early stage in the Survey, with Hackney being instanced as showing the general law of successive migration, while in the Poverty Survey of south London, Booth's assistant commented that 'everyone I have consulted has mentioned this centrifugal tendency of the better off, and almost all have complained that in consequence of it, their district is going down'.[20]

In the Religious Influences volumes, benefiting from Duckworth's commentary on, and revisions to, the social map, the concept of urban change comes into its own, with the law of successive migration affecting districts all down the social scale. Thus in Battersea: 'The red and yellow classes are leaving, and the streets which they occupied are becoming pink and pink barred; whilst the streets which were formerly pink turn to purple and purple to light blue'.[21] The references made to middle-class London are almost entirely in respect of districts showing symptoms of social decline. Thus at the top end of the scale in west London, what Booth bothers to pick out for comment is the existence of shabby gentility in yellow streets and the difference between a red street which might almost be yellow and a yellow street that is suffering decay:

> In the one live prosperous people whose houses are homes. They employ few servants but live in great comfort; in the other pretence in one form or another reigns supreme. People live not only up to but quite without regard to their incomes. Homes are now occupied, now empty; there are guests who pay or the drawing room floor is let or at length the fatal word Apartments appears in the fanlight over the door.[22]

The letting of houses for apartments is everywhere taken to be a symptom of social decline and especially characteristic in Duckworth's notes of the borderland between red and pink barred. Booth accepts the

Duckworth rules as, for example, the rule that if a road is to keep up its status for any length of time it must be formed either of good detached or semi-detached villas with some space about them, or of two-storeyed houses; the former are attractive in themselves while the latter are more within the means of a single family than the three-storey houses which grow rapidly to apartments and then to tenements.[23]

This obsession with social decline was not merely a matter of keeping up middle-class property values, even if Duckworth's notes read like an elaborate estate agents' guide, but had the more serious purpose of illustrating the pressure on housing accommodation in the city and the tendency of decline to slide rapidly into deterioration and decay. A continuing theme in the accounts of the inner suburbs is the pressure on living space, and housing, pushing the belt of overcrowding outwards. This process accelerates dramatically in the poorer suburban districts and especially those having to absorb people displaced by improvements in the centre. This is depicted in terms of Booth's favourite metaphor of the stream of humanity. Thus he writes: 'Whilst the main stream of life and prosperity sets due south, the scum and wreckage carried with it are thrown off upon the western edge.'[24] The wreckage consists of the displaced poor of central London, although he also notes a stream within a stream formed by migratory bands of gypsies. The result is social deterioration. Hence Booth selects from the police notes examples to illustrate this deteriorative tendency. He notes it beginning in the pink of working-class comfort with the subdivision of houses and quotes from the police notes to show how the pressure of industry or commercial development or some new addition to the ground plan, such as the building of a gas works, might trigger it off.[25]

Occasionally, the police notes failed to offer clues as to why a district had gone wrong and Booth had to turn elsewhere. But in general there were ample pointers especially to the relationship between features of the London ground plan and the migratory flows. In describing south London, for example, Booth draws on the notes to explain how wealth is attracted to the higher ground and commons while poverty is associated with the railways and the river. In Putney, where higher ground and river come together, every class is represented from yellow to black. Booth seizes on the evidence in the police notes of the importance of the ground plan making several references to the innumerable dead ends, closed up vistas, and backwaters in the layout of the London streets. He repeatedly draws attention to the significance of physical barriers, noting, for example, how in south London poverty was caught and held in successive railway loops, while in other districts the poor were cut off from the mainstream of urban life in districts lying between canal and railway. Frequently he puts his own gloss on the laconic comments of the police. He notes Sultan Street and adjoining streets, a very poor district in Camberwell, drawing on the details of the police notes – narrow houses, lack of privacy, dirt, neglect, lack of access – but registering his own feelings about this enclosed area, like a fortress entered only on one side. He seems to have been particularly affected by the inwardly looking, hostile world he found on penetrating this block of streets: 'There are places more squalid', he writes, 'in which may be people more debased, but none whereon the word outcast is so deeply branded.'[26]

While Booth's initial concern was with measuring the extent of poverty, the imaginative underpinning of the Survey was the slum, a feature that reflects the importance of the housing question to the social question in the 1880s, but is also a logical development in terms of Booth's analysis and the materials available to him. Given the relatively small proportions of Londoners classified as in the A and B groups he gives disproportionate attention to the poorest and most degraded streets, albeit as I have suggested within the context of an analysis of the housing market for the metropolis as a whole. In his description of these poor districts, Booth identifies from the police notes a string of degraded streets across London sharing common characteristics. All of them are rough – meaning that they were given to public brawling and domestic violence, but they are also low – meaning that they had poor social habits, and vicious – meaning semi-criminal and a base for prostitutes. Roughness is seen as a core feature of the black and blue localities. The archetypal districts were Notting Dale in west London, the Fenian Barracks off Limehouse Cut in east London, and the Dusthole in Woolwich, the centre of the latter being the notorious two or three streets of lodging houses known as Ropeyard Rails. The Dusthole, to take this as an example, had three features according to the police notes: first, a migratory population of dock and waterside workers, costers, hawkers and tramps – a house of call for all the tramps from London to Kent, and with a regular interchange of tenants with Byrum Street in Deptford and Bangor Street, Notting Dale, in west London – the 'casual loafer floats between the two districts south and north of the Thames', observed Duckworth; secondly, it was a district of prostitution ('the younger prostitutes in appearance akin to the sailor's wife of the Ratcliffe Highway, clean white apron and frizzed hair is the mark of the class'); thirdly, roughness, Nelson Street the roughest of them all: 'women with broken noses, swollen faces, draggled skirts, coarse Irish faces, bare arms. No men about, no law runs in these streets, the priest is powerless, the police only come when summoned, missiles showered on them when they interfere.'[27] Districts such as these function as a kind of sump or settlement tank into which the detritus of the metropolis is poured. They also function as a vortex drawing into the deteriorated neighbourhood the incapable and incompetent poor of class B. Such a view was important to Booth's evolutionary and residualist outlook on the poor.

On the other hand Booth goes out of his way to avoid treating all the blue and black districts as homogeneous. Thus he makes a distinction between old established and new poverty, not only as between the poverty districts of the central areas compared with the suburbs, but in the suburbs too between local village poverty and the new importations. Another distinction is between districts exhibiting what he called 'sturdy' and 'wastrel' poverty. The point here is not that he considers it his task to determine the relative influence of character in the causation of poverty. Environment and character he sees as operating together in a changing situation. Even among wastrel districts there are distinctions to be made – the rough districts are not necessarily bad and some districts are simply low. Thus he compares the rude and ragged poverty of Kensal Green in west London with the degraded poverty of Notting Dale. In the former case, he notes, the men are simply dependent on the earnings of their wives as washerwomen – an unusual reference incidentally to the role of women in the domestic economy – and are not bad or vicious. The district is characterized mainly by poor living conditions. However, what distinguishes Notting Dale according to the police notes is the number of cadgers in the district.[28] Similarly Booth compares two districts in Bermondsey: the one a rough district where disorder, brawling and violent outbreaks under the influence of drink are common and a gross virility prevails, and the other, in the neighbourhood of the Bermondsey New Road, neither vicious nor rough to any marked degree. This district Booth points out has not

> The Whitechapel Jew, the Hoxton Burglar, the Nottingdale [sic] Tramp, nor is it like parts of Fulham, a receptacle and dumping ground. It has not even the Spitalfields dosser in full force. It is neither vicious nor criminal in any marked degree; it is simply low; but for debased poverty aggravated by drink this portion of Southwark and Bermondsey falls below any other part of London ... A somewhat closer comparison may lie with the western half of Bethnal Green. The people there may be more brutal, but are certainly less poor; they hold a stronger industrial position.[29]

The permutations are made nevertheless with the standardized labels of the police notes and incorporate the stereotypes that language embodies. Thus the Irish cockney and the costermonger, sometimes, though not always, the same thing, are almost invariably classified as roughs. In Shelton Street, East London, for example, where drunkenness and bad language and violence were common, reaching at times even to murder; or the Nichol which for 'brutality within the circle of family life' nothing in all London quite equalled; or the Clare market, which was full of a poor rough class of labourers, market porters, costermongers, and flower girls.[30] In these districts the women though portrayed as having black eyes are not regarded as victims, but rather as engaged in drinking and violence themselves, loud mouthed and foul mouthed. A typical characterization was the picture of the Fenian Barracks where the general appearance of the street according to the police notes bore out its unrespectable character: 'Drunk women, women without hats or bonnets, truanting children, playing pitch and toss, all the signs of semi vicious poverty.'[31] Again in relation to the Jews, Booth uncritically accepts the judgements of a police force that as an artisanal profession shared the prejudices against newcomers of the people they policed. As David Englander has pointed out in his paper on this subject in this volume, the Jews were a cause of some confusion for the colour coding of the map since they had social characteristics of being neither rough nor respectable. This made their location within the class structure extremely difficult to determine.

Booth was not interested in going behind the conventional categorizations. He was content to notice the incidence of domestic violence but did not ask questions about the reasons for it; he noted the extent of gambling among the poor but mainly as another index of unrespectable and uneconomic behaviour, and he did not identify youthful gambling despite the frequent contemporary references to this as symptomatic of a problem of juvenile delinquency.

Cultural patterns: working-class London

Booth made use of police and clergy anecdotes to construct a picture of a residuum class combining A and B and as having a lifestyle defined by the apparent contrast between their shared culture and that of the respectable. This picture, as developed in the Survey, was concerned essentially with attitudes towards family and home. In poor districts lives were lived out on the streets with little care for standards of home comfort in conditions of overcrowding, or an environment of block dwellings. The ideal environment is that represented by the model suburban estates and districts that were affected by the beneficial influence of estate owners. Examples cited were the districts of pink, pink barred and purple in south London on the Shaftesbury Park estate and that belonging to Lord Battersea, districts forming a social fortress of a very different kind from Sultan Street, where everything is done to maintain order and respectability and the people of upper-grade artisan status and lower-grade middle-class status mixed freely. Similarly in the neighbourhood of Southwark Park in south-east London dwelt a houseproud and comfortable working and lower-middle class whose readiness to share in religious life and respectable amusements is in strong contrast to the indifferent attitudes of the poor districts where Sunday is taken up with hedonistic pastimes, drinking, sport and outings.[32] Thus Booth polarizes differences between the districts occupied by A and B and those occupied by E and F. The differences extended to domestic and sexual relationships. The more respectable were closely integrated into family life, class E representing the wholesomeness of family life and affectionate relationships. In the districts occupied by A and B there was little or no tradition of family life.

Booth thought that attitudes to family life constituted one of the clearest lines of demarcation between upper and lower grades of the working class.[33] While he sometimes admits to family life existing among the poorest, there are clear differences to be seen in the domestic and even the sexual behaviour of the most rough and the most respectable sections of metropolitan working-class society. He suggests, for example, that young men from the rougher sections were highly predatory and exploitative as far as their relations with women were concerned. Casual sexual encounters were common among the rough but the respectable male found definite norms of propriety regulating his behaviour: 'free and honourable terms of companionship under a very definite code of rules, between those who are recognised as "keeping company"'. However, among the rougher class cohabitation was common; girls were frequently pregnant when they got married. Booth's findings also support the idea that males were reluctant to support their families when they did marry. Indeed it is noted that the bonding of males to the family was sufficiently loose for norms to exist that supported extraction from it if things became too much: 'licence is granted by public opinion to the evasion of bonds of marriage of those who have found it a failure'. Attitudes to children and to schooling constituted another point of difference.[34]

Because of the way that Booth conceptualizes the working class into this well-established polarity we are left with a somewhat indistinct impression as to where C and D fit into the picture. Booth seems to be reduced to hinting that they are somehow involved in behaviour and relationships intermediate between the two polar groupings. For example, the majority of the residents of Bethnal Green are represented as neither very rough nor very respectable. They seem to have been bound into patterns of living and spending that had elements from the lifestyle of both. Here roughness seems to be decreasing, there is much life and good humour on the streets, drinking is not so excessive and the pleasures and habits of Bethnal Green people turn largely on the keeping of domestic pets, song birds and whippets. On Sundays, however, 'Beer and the newspapers are in demand and great parties go by breaks into the country for the day.'[35]

There is something of a paradox too in the somewhat lukewarm attitudes of both Booth and Duckworth towards the suburban life. There is not much of a positive kind said about this. Indeed Booth frequently portrays the inner suburbs as having more life and vitality, especially in districts with rumbustious street markets. He goes to some lengths to illustrate in 'side lights' the more colourful aspects of metropolitan life. In contrast the new housing estates are frequently referred to as dull. Thus he explains that in St George's where 'the life that springs from the river and docks has become less active', the district is becoming 'at once more monotonous and more respectable'.[36] Although repelled by aspects of the street life of the poor, he can understand its attractions. As he notes of the district around the Elephant and Castle: 'there is more street life here even than in the East End; more women gossiping at the doors; more children playing in the gutters. In some places there is almost village life. The poorest and lowest cling resolutely to this spot.'[37] There could not be a greater contrast than the style of life to be found in the respectable working-class and lower-middle-class suburbs. Here, for example, is the description of a district in Plumstead in the police notes which Booth copied almost verbatim. This district

> ... is dull and ordinary outwardly but it is remarkable in many ways. The houses are ugly, two storied, yellow brick and for the most part new. The streets are straight and empty except when children tumble out of school and leave a litter of small paper bags which once held pennyworth of sweets or fruit. They are also full of a hurrying straggling crowd of men on their way to and from home during the dinner hour. Otherwise they are empty, the house doors shut, the windows and blinds drawn and everything seems asleep. The women are at home and busy, but they are busy in the yards and small gardens behind and in front. Street life is not amusing. At night the roads are dull and dark. More of the doors are open than in the daytime for many of the men seem to take their evening pipes in front. Villainous strumming on cheap pianos

is also a feature. So is the absence of old people. New houses, newly married couples, young families, wives at home, daughters not yet grown up and expecting marriage and home life not factory work as a career; husbands and sons in full work earning more money than they really know how to spend.

Booth's comment in the left-hand margin was 'Oh Happy Plumstead!'; and his own write-up reflects a degree of ambiguity to what was a portent to the future of residential London.[38]

No other Victorian survey matches the scale or the refinement of *Life and Labour* as an exercise in social topography. The dependence on observations that reflect social assumptions and prejudices common at the time is a source of strength as well as of weakness. Booth's moral categories may seem standardized, but he succeeds in using them to organize descriptive material in a way that represents late Victorian London as a metropolis made up of a myriad of subcultures.

Notes

1   Simey, T.S. and Simey, M.B. (1960), *Charles Booth: Social Scientist*, Oxford University Press.

2   Williams, K. (1981), *From Pauperism to Poverty*, London, Routledge and Kegan Paul, ch.7, pp.309–44.

3   See Hennock, E.P. (1976), 'Poverty and Social Theory in England: the experience of the eighteen-eighties', *Social History*, pp.67–91; Cullen, M.J. (1979), 'Charles Booth's Poverty Survey: some new approaches', in Smout, T.C. (ed.), *The Search for Wealth and Stability: Essays in Economic and Social History*, London, Macmillan, pp.155–74.

4   Webb, B. (1926), *My Apprenticeship,* Penguin, p.220.

5   For details of this map and the background to it, see the introduction by David Reeder and Ralph Hyde to the edition published by the London Topographical Society, Publication No.130 (London, 1984).

6   See the album of press cuttings in class A58, BLPES, Booth Collection.

7   The classic statement is in Pfautz, H.W. (1973), *Charles Booth and the City: physical patterns and social structure*, Chicago University Press. For subsequent refinements see Marsden, W.E. (1986), 'Residential Segregation and the Hierarchy of Public Schooling from Charles Booth's Surveys', *The London Journal*, and

Davies, W.K.D. (1978), 'Charles Booth and the Measurement of Social Character', *Area*, 10.

8   I am grateful to W.E. Marsden for this reference.

9   A fine example of this is the study by O'Day, Rosemary and Englander, David (1993), *Mr Charles Booth's Inquiry: Life and Labour of the People in London Reconsidered*, London and Rio Grande. For a report on other work mainly in connection with the Poverty Survey, see Bales, Kevin (1986), 'Reclaiming antique data: Charles Booth's poverty survey', *Urban History Yearbook*, Leicester, pp.75–80.

10   6 August 1891.

11   I am grateful to Raphael Samuel for this suggestion.

12   Masterman, Charles (1902), 'The Social Abyss', *Contemporary Review*, 81, pp.23–35.

13   *Poverty*, 1, p.6.

14   I made use of the microfilm copies of the notebooks, concentrating on reels 13–19. These form part of the microfilm edition of the Booth Archive which is now completed. Prepared by Kevin Bales it is published by Research Publications International, Reading, in 6 Parts with the title *Life and Labour of the People of London: The Charles Booth Collection, 1885–1905*. The Police notebooks come in Part 1 along with manuscript notes on Industry, Workhouse and Asylum Inmates.

15   For example the Inspector, Clyne, had downgraded all the streets of a district in Woolwich (Reel 17, district 45), but Duckworth thought the streets looked fairly comfortable, the windows and blinds too clean, and the steps too white for there not to be a good deal of pink in them, although he admitted that this might only be a reflection of the extra prosperity of the year.

16   As, for example, in South Lambeth, where Duckworth was again complaining that the streets were not as poor as the map represents (Reel 18).

17   This is in Reel 19, District 48.

18   *Religious Influences*, 3, ch.2, The Inner West, pp.107–8.

19   *Religious Influences*, 5, Part 2, ch.22, p.176, ch.1, p.149. See also the introductory sections to the south London volumes: *Religious Influences*, 4, Inner South London, 5, The South-East and the South-West, and 6, Outer South London.

20   *Poverty,* 1, Part 1, East London and Part 11, South London.

21   *Religious Influences,* 1, p.3. and 5, Part 11, ch.1, Battersea, p.194.

22   3, ch.2, The Inner West, pp.108–09.

23   This is in Reel 19, District 64.

24   *Religious Influences,* 5, Part 2, p.164.

25   See, for example, the account of Brixton in Reel 18, District 48.

26   Camberwell is in Reel 17. For the references in the Survey: *Religious Influences,* 1, p.192, 5, pp.189, 194.

27   The Dusthole is in Reel 19, District 48, especially pp.160–3. Compare the description of the Fenian Barracks especially Gale Street and Farge Street in Reel 13.

28   These references are in *Religious Influences,* 3, Part 2, chapters 3 and 4, The Outer West. The corresponding districts in the Police Notes are in Reel 16.

29   *Religious Influences,* 4, ch.3, p.122. See also pp.101–02.

30   These references are from *Poverty,* 2, pp.47, 67, 178; *Religious Influences,* 1, pp.47–9, 57; 4, pp.14, 17, 101. There are many other references to violence in these localities.

31   Police Notes, Reel 14, District 13.

32   This section is drawn from *Religious Influences,* 6, ch.2, Beyond the Belt of Crowding, sections 1 and 2; 5, South East and South West London, ch.2; 4, ch. 2, Newington, esp. pp.41–50; ch.2, The North East, section 7, Police, Drink and Pleasure Seeking.

33   *Religious Influences,* 1, p.59.

34   *Religious Influences,* 1, Outer East London, section 7, Marriage and Thrift, pp.55–7, 158; Final Vol, p.45.

35   *Religious Influences,* 2, Bethnal Green, esp. p.97.

36   *Religious Influences,* 2, ch.1, section 4, p.64.

37   *Religious Influences,* 4, ch.1, p.10.

38   Police Notes, Reel 19, District 48. Compare *Religious Influences,* 5, Part 1, The South East, section 4, Plumstead.

12   Women in Victorian religion

Rosemary O'Day

No one really knows the story of women in Victorian religion. People know bits of it. They know about a few upper-middle-class philanthropists – about the move towards a women's ministry – about a few working-class bible women – about a few missioners. Few have used the Booth survey materials.[1]

This essay aims to indicate how the Charles Booth Archive Collection might be exploited to tell us more of the story. It also suggests, in a tentative way, some of the substantive points which arise out of the archive.

Booth set out to describe things as they were – the material and spiritual conditions of life of all the people. He was not only concerned with the poor. Neither was he only concerned with men. The entire archive could be exploited by scholars to reveal much about the lives of women in late Victorian times. This essay concentrates on the riches contained in the Religious Influences material. Very little of the information which was collected about women in religion was used in the printed volumes and so it is a service in itself to outline what is there. The limitations of the archive are, of course, very real: attention is drawn to these limitations throughout the essay. The collection of materials associated with the Third Series also contains considerable amounts of material about women in other capacities but this is not referred to except in passing here.

The reports of the interviews, entered into no fewer than 146 notebooks, provide many insights into the role of ordinary women in church life as perceived by the ministers.[2] It is obviously important to note this – the view given of women through the Booth archive is of women through men's eyes. That isn't always the case but it usually is. There will not be many direct comments from women describing their involvement or their lot. So a note of caution is in order. Look out for male attitudes to women – specifically clerical attitudes. These are, however, in themselves very important for women's studies. Part of the purpose of this essay is to delineate the attitudes and approaches of the ministers of the various denominations to women. However, a good deal of the archive is concerned with statistical detail – for example, how many women attended church; how many women acted as unpaid helpers. So there will probably be fairly reliable information of this kind.

Victorian London was a city full of contrasts – wealth and poverty. London's religious life was no less variegated. There were fashionable parishes and unfashionable. There were Anglican churches responsible for population in the tens of thousands and dissenting chapelries answerable to two hundred members. There were churches and chapels worked by enthusiastic and capable ministers and lay workers, and churches and chapels scarcely worked at all – lethargy was their chief characteristic. It is not to be expected that women's involvement in religious life was any more uniform. Women were not any more much of a muchness than were men.

When we look at the place of women in Victorian religion we are faced with a paradox. On the one hand, women were denied the major orders in both the Catholic and the Anglican churches and leading positions in Methodist, Congregationalist and Baptist denominations. On the other hand, women were the mainstay of Victorian religion. The Booth papers allow us to explore this paradox a little. Three linked aspects of women's involvement command attention – congregation, clubs and carers.

First of all, let us start with the place of women in the churches' congregation. Without women, some churches would have had no congregation to speak of and all would have had even sparser congregations than they in fact had. Contemporaries were well aware of this fact. It was a phenomenon common to all denominations and all areas of London. The minister of St Saviour's, Brixton Hill, in 1900 confessed that nine out of every ten in his congregation were women.[3] The pastor of the Kenyon Baptist Church on Acre Lane put a courageous front on it by claiming that a full quarter of his congregation was male.[4] Alfred Sargent of Brixton Hill Methodist Church put on a similarly brave face when he said 'there are more women than men at both services but the level of men is fairly high'.[5] St Matthew's, Brixton, offers a good example of a church which was proud of its successes with young men yet the Revd W.D. Springett was obliged to admit that 'women, of course, preponderate but not largely.'[6] St Frideswide's in Outer East London normally had a congregation in which women far outnumbered men and the Rector could scarcely contain himself one Easter Sunday when 'there were three more men than women'.[7]

In some cases the preponderance of women did not mean much in absolute terms, at St Gabriel's, Poplar, there were but fifty adults at the Sunday morning service and thirty of these were women – not exactly a full church. Contemporaries were well aware of the decline in the habit of churchgoing: 'families used to come' mourned the Rural Dean of Camberwell, adding wryly, 'Now the younger ones are off bicycling or go to another church; now they keep no servant, someone must stay at home and someone else besides to keep that someone company. Really only an excuse for carelessness.'[8] So we must not run away with the idea that the churches were necessarily succeeding in recruiting droves of women to active worship. What we can safely conclude is that they were more successful in persuading women to attend church than in persuading their menfolk. In this respect the Unitarians alone seem to have differed: 'The congregation is peculiar (but not for Unitarians) in that it is mostly composed of men' for there are 'a good many more men than women'.[9]

It seems that women did not attend all services. The Minister of the Baptist Chapel at Denmark Place told George Duckworth that women attended in greater numbers in the evening because they were then more 'able to get away from dinner'.[10] Very occasionally there are indications that women who regularly attended church shared in its organization. The Vicar of the Church of Epiphany, Stockwell, informed George Duckworth that the church council, an all-male consultative body, was at least elected by male and female communicants of eighteen and over.[11]

The congregation of the churches was not confined to those who came to Sunday services. Were women still in the huge majority at the Bible classes, prayer meetings and weekday services which were a feature of church and chapel life? The answer must be that their overwhelming presence was even more noticeable. Between three and four hundred people attended the Revd W.A. Mowle's Bible reading on Tuesday afternoons at Christ Church, North Brixton. Most of these were women 'getting on in years, but with a sprinkling of men, and with some young people'. This situation was echoed elsewhere.

So we can find descriptive evidence in the Booth archive of the preponderance of women in church congregations. But there is also evidence that this situation was not unproblematic. There has been a great temptation to explain the sex imbalance in church attendance and formal religious worship in terms of an alleged natural affinity which women have with religion. This is as may be, but certainly the ministers interviewed by Booth's associates identified other reasons. The 'social' aspects of churchgoing did not go unnoticed. 'It is a regular courting church' observed the Vicar of St Stephen's, North Bow, 'and the galleries are full of young couples' at evensong.[12] Sweetnam of St Martin's, Victoria Park, was more cautious: 'Though some come because it is respectable, and some of the young for courting, the majority certainly come from a genuine desire to worship.'[13] Another explanation lay in the idea that men were exhausted in the evenings after work and when Sunday came around.

Note the assumption that it was only the menfolk who did work of an exhausting kind! The women of Bromley might find it difficult to get away to the morning service because of family responsibilities but they were able and willing to turn out for evensong – swelling the congregation to between 80 and 180. The congregation almost entirely of males and children at 11.00 a.m. barely touched thirty.[14] Perhaps the significance of Carroll of St Frideswide's comment that 'There are more women than men but many of them are the wives of sailors' is that these women were able to attend because their husbands were at sea.[15]

Even more frequently identified was the difficulty which the churches had in making contact with the male population after the working life began. Carroll of St Frideswide's, for example, observed that the roll of communicants comprised 'mainly females of all ages and a good many lads', commenting that the boys drop off as they grow older.[16] Figures for attendance at Sunday Schools indicate rough equivalence between boy and girl pupils. The inference is that both sexes were part of the churches' congregation throughout childhood – then the girls were reasonably likely to remain but the boys left. A ratio of two teenage girls to one teenage boy involved in classes for older youth is sometimes mentioned. The Curate-in-Charge of St Gabriel's, Poplar, explained that the small number of communicants on the average Sunday was made up of 'females of all ages and a good many lads, among whom there is a serious leakage as they grow older'.[17] A ratio of three women to every one man attending church sounds conservative. Determined efforts were made by some ministers of all persuasions to reverse this trend but the fact remained that the normal means of encouraging a congregation by missionary effort tended to focus upon the women of the community, upon the home from which the working male was absent. Bible readings, Bible classes, prayer meetings and weekday services were held at times when working men could not attend. The church workers who were sent out to convert the laity, to establish them in their faith and to swell the church's congregation were themselves more often than not women. Women church workers talked to women – the visits made by these ladies occurred during the day when the menfolk were at work. There was 'Hardly a man in the parish' of St James, Camberwell, 'by midday'.[18] Sweetnam 'spoke with regret of the great difficulty in ever seeing the men'.[19] Vere Barly, who tried to visit every house in Bromley, had some shrewd comments to make about clerical relations with both women and men parishioners: 'I never feel I am proper [sic] terms with them if they take me into their best room and dust a chair; you should be able to walk into the kitchen and set down on a wash tub.' It was generally easier to converse with the women than with men for, if the man is in, he usually retires to the backyard when a person enters. 'Then I always follow him'. It was even more difficult to visit the upstairs people, who were often tenants of those downstairs, men or women.[20] Ministers and missioners met the menfolk only when they were ill.

Vere Barly, Curate of Bromley, put forward an interesting and idiosyncratic theory:

> When I came to London I said where are the men?; but the men are now increasing. Mr B has a theory that the men who attend church in London are almost without exception countrymen born and bred. It is certainly so in his district; in some cases they are men who have always kept up the church going habits of their youth, but much more frequently they are men who have lapsed and been won back. The social habits of the Londoner are all against church going. Mr B is very anxious that we should enquire this point.[21]

All of this might suggest that the preponderance of women in formal religious worship was due less to natural religiosity than to a set of circumstances which militated against male attendance at church and/or contact with church workers. It might also suggest that women, normally in the isolation of their own homes, felt a need for companionship and association which the church helped to satisfy, and which in men was satisfied by the workplace, the club and the pub. Women, kept in a subordinate position at home, perhaps welcomed the chance to escape male authority in the compass of an all-female club or class. This would be especially true of the 'respectable' working-class or middle-class woman to whom the 'pub' was closed.

Some clergy positively welcomed the imbalance as natural and set out to exploit it. Charles Brooke of St John the Divine, Kennington, made no bones about it:

> It sometimes seems as if more were being done for the women than the men, though I did hear that a lady had good humouredly remarked that 'of course everything must be given up to the men'. In St John's, in spite of our very large congregation of men, I have always felt that our men have not responded so quickly to the Church's effort as others have done. I have never been over disturbed by this, nor have I been in any way affected by the silly jibes one sometimes sees and hears about religion being an occupation for women and children. Influence for good or bad is the property of the women far more than of the man, and so the bringing up of women 'in the fear and nurture of the lord' is

infinitely the most important of the Church's duties to her children. Men are what the women make them: a good woman can influence most men for good; a bad woman can, alas, drag down and ruin even a good man. Hence the vast importance of helping women to attain to the virtues of sympathy, modesty and self-respect ...[22]

The women who attended church were not, however, poor women. 'Churchgoing is almost exclusively a matter of social standing', that a certain class 'will come to church unless you positively repel them' while another class 'cannot be induced to come at all'. 'Going to Church is entirely a matter of clothes' said another.[23] Ramsey of the Emmanuel Congregational Chapel in Dulwich perceived that the well-to women who did attend church were more than happy to exclude their poorer sisters: 'The fine lady in her silks will not mix with the lapsed masses.'[24] Some unfashionable parishes which did attract congregations of working women nevertheless found that the ability to dress respectably and fashionably tended to divide the attenders from the non-attenders. At St John's, Isle of Dogs, 'A fair sprinkling of poorly dressed people attend but not the very poorest. The women generally are very dressy, and now with the prevalence of flowery hats the Church looks rather like the flower beds in Park Lane'.[25]

The number of Catholic parishes in London was not large but Booth's team made every effort to elicit the views of, and collect information from, Catholic clergy. Their concerns were very different from those of the Protestant churches. Mixed marriages, which according to several of the clergy amounted to between a quarter and a third of all marriages in Catholic churches, were viewed as 'a great curse' by some and as a mixed blessing by others.[26] It was agreed that such marriages were allowed only by special dispensation and on condition that the children were brought up Catholics. There is a strong suggestion that most mixed marriages celebrated in the Catholic churches involved Catholic women and 'indifferent' men. In this lay the secret of the success which most noted in retaining the children for Catholicism. For it was known that it was the women who decided the religious upbringing of the children: husbands, whether indifferent or committed, acknowledged it; the clergy and ministers acknowledged it. 'Less bad when a woman is the Catholic because hers is the home influence.'[27] Thus a mixed marriage could bring converts to the church if the wife were Catholic; if the man were Catholic it caused leakage.[28] Therefore, it was recognized that it was essential to nurture the young women in the faith and offer them great encouragement – in a city where Catholics were in a minority and counter attractions potent, the chief defence of Catholicism lay in the rule that religious allegiance passed through the female line (informally, of course) and the strength of female commitment to Catholicism must be assured. It was not always to be: Father Lawless lamented that he knew of one case in which the 'woman does not come to him though the husband gives her every liberty to do so'. He went on to say that he had talked to the woman and 'finally preached against her publicly in church'.[29]

If such appeals to authority and public disgrace might be expected to bring Catholic women to heel, they were not likely to work with Protestants. The problem and the proffered solutions were different. Striking is the feeling of some ministers that the church was failing to tap properly even the pool of women. Anglicans were particularly vociferous on this point. The Reverend R. Appleton of the Trinity Mission in George's Parish, Camberwell, devoted a large part of his Trinity Mission Notes in June 1898 to describing the problem and his suggested solutions:

> I used to get to church when I had only two children, but now I have three it is impossible. The arithmetic may be personal, but the broad fact is general, and see what it means. The great mass of mothers in a poor district, where even 'gells' [i.e. female servants] are an unknown luxury, are almost as completely prisoners to their home as if they were tied with three chains to the kitchen grate ...
> In most well-ordered homes among us there are three children below school age and several above it. The mother is even harder worked than her husband or her daughter 'in business' and that is to say a great deal. The little daughters soon learn to do the shopping, and to drive pretty close bargains, I shrewdly suspect; and the mother becomes like one that we heard of, who lived in the sixth storey of the 'blocks' and was not known to have come down to the street for five months certain.[30]

Appleton shared with Brooke the conviction that it was with women that the moral standing of the nation rested. The woman was 'the religious safeguard of the home'. But he worried. The working-class woman was difficult to recruit. She could not safeguard the home if her own spiritual position was in decline. Material conditions hindered her participation in worship. 'Few women can make spiritual progress when they cannot receive the grace of Holy Communion, or even join in public worship, especially when work is driving seven days every week, and the husband stands by as a constant refrigerator of all devotional warmth.'[31] Some women of course did manage to escape and attend church, but for most domestic isolation was the order of the day.

How could the church penetrate this isolation? Appleton's remedies were fourfold. The first remedy was visiting. But he was a realist: many of the women were hard cases.

> Happily a woman can generally be seen at home. Not that she is often free for more than five minutes talk. I suppose if you, gentle reader, had to be mother and all her servants in one; to cook and set out the meals, do the washing up, dress and feed the children, wash the clothes, wage the fierce and losing war against London dirt, provide a dinner at one for a daughter, at two for a husband, at three for a son, take little Harry to school and go with an umbrella for him at four o'clock, carry on the perpetual campaign against the astute tradesman and often, alas, with resources sadly diminished by the public house, you would not always welcome effusively a visitor who came 'to keep you up to the mark'.

> ... but [he urged] a great deal can be done in five minutes to cheer and to brace up to some special effort. The short interview, the brief prayer in some time of special softening, the sympathy, the reminder of higher things, is truly a means of grace.[32]

The secret was not to be deterred by the difficulties encountered in gaining admission to private homes. 'Sometimes you have to imitate the school child's knock or rattling at the letter box before you can gain admission.'[33]

Second to visiting, he recommended the institution of the Mother's Meeting. Attendance there represented both a social bond and an opportunity for simple teaching and devotion. Next he urged special services for women in the Church. And finally, a guild or League of Mothers. I shall say a little more about these remedies now in a general context. The Booth papers indicate that churches of almost all denominations put themselves out to provide opportunities for women of all classes to participate in the church's life and worship. In almost all, women were segregated from men. Such opportunities fall into several broad categories: religious services and classes; charitable enterprises; social and leisure activities; charities.

The chief exception to this rule was the Catholic Church. 'As usual there are few strictly social agencies' commented Ernest Aves of the Catholic Church at St Peter's Square.[34] Catholic churches made provision for the young in religious but not social terms. There are occasional mentions of men's clubs. Booth's associates noted down the existence of confraternities. Branches of the Guild of Our Lady of

Ransome were common.[35] The Bow Mission had a club room where its 'Children of Mary' for the young women met.[36] On just one occasion an interviewer was told that 'plays for girls in Whitsun week are arranged for by the nuns so that they [the girls, not the nuns!] may not run loose during Bank Holiday'.[37]

What different opportunities were presented to women for participation in church or chapel life? The Young Women's Christian Association was active in the parish of St Matthew's, Brixton.[38] It ran an institute and a boarding house. The institute was open every day but Saturday and set out to cater for all sections of society. In addition to prayer meetings and Bible classes there were a number of clubs and courses – sewing, singing, music, a holiday club and a penny bank. The Girls' Friendly Society at St Matthew's boasted a membership of 107 and asked an annual fee of 1s.[39] The range of social, leisure and cultural societies in London's churches was great: in one parish the Girls' Friendly Society might be very large; in another a debating society or a sewing class. The Pastor of the Old Baptist Union Chapel in Stockwell was proud of the sewing classes held under its auspices.[40] At St Frideswide's in the East End, the Girls' Club run by the Clewer Sisters came in for especial note; membership was limited to 100 and they 'go in much for dumb-bells, drill etc'.[41] The Our Girls' Club at the Church of the Epiphany, Stockwell, attracted thirty girls and went in for musical and dramatic sketches. At the same church a club for twenty-five younger girls between twelve and sixteen years old taught drill and painting.[42] Less organized but equally common were women's gatherings. St Frideswide's held Mothers' Meetings which were 'very easy to manage: they can always talk scandal'.[43] At the Baptist Chapel in Denmark Place there was a Mothers' Meetings for about 100 mothers (not from the congregation) on Monday afternoons between 3.30 and 4.30 p.m.: 'they bring their work and babies, a lady reads a book to them or an address is given'.[44] That at Epiphany, Stockwell, was described by the vicar as 'a social chat over tea provided by his sister'.[45]

Occasionally there were co-educational institutes and societies. The Young People's Institute at Camberwell Green Congregationalist Church had a membership of 147 women and 101 men. It held Sunday Bible classes and the five teachers also held social evenings in turn. The church secretary said that it had its own cycling, football and debating clubs and that it was seen as a continuation of the Sunday School. It provided a link between young and old, childhood and adulthood. All the young women worked in the city. Women were trained to speak in the Young People's Christian Endeavour Society 'and now make their voices heard at the prayer meetings in Church ...

In the literary society women speak very occasionally except one who is very well read in Huxley and can hold her own with any one.'[46]

When looking at this evidence it is important to note that the membership of the various clubs and classes was often class specific and, moreover, that they were intended to appeal to different classes of women. A sewing class might be designed to teach a commercial skill to poor women and girls so that they could 'help themselves'. At St Saviour's, Camberwell, we are informed:

> The Girls' Friendly Society is of importance here where all girls are expecting to make an independent livelihood: none go to service except 2 or 3 from poor streets such as Wanless and Hardess but most expect to be Board School Teachers or go into the post office or theatrical or shop assistant work. About 100 belong of all ages from 14 upwards.[47]

Or there might be an attempt to provide the poor with paid work and, incidentally, a sense of self-respect. The Industrial Society at St Matthew's, Brixton, 'was formed for the relief of poor needlewomen by supplying them with work at their own homes, for which they were paid 1s per week'. 'Each subscriber receives work-tickets (to give away) in proportion to subscription. 179 women are thus employed.'[48]

The mothers' meeting at Camberwell Green Congregationalist Church drew an average attendance of eighty 'respectable mothers: all ages, with which is a clothing and coat club and blanket club'.[49] The membership of that at the Bromsgrove Mission of St Andrew's, Stockwell, was seemingly less desirable: 'The yearly treat for the mothers' meeting is a very trying day for the clergy; their men, though not invited, escort the party throughout the streets in their coster carts and make a day of it too.'[50]

Appleton of the Trinity Mission, Camberwell, saw services, mothers' meetings and guilds as ways of bringing poorer women out of their homes and into the church. His visitors invited all women in the parish of St George to 'a course of services, lasting one hour, 3.00 p.m. to 4.00 p.m. on Thursdays in Lent … Bright Services. Hymn Books provided'. The problem of what to do with the children was broached. 'Babies and young children may be brought into church or left in the choir vestry, where they will be taken care of by ladies.' The crèche provided opportunities for a little well-intentioned but ham-handed charity.

> The babies are managed with great skill. Noisy ones are eliminated with much tenderness into the vestry and there find themselves in a kind of paradise of devoted attention. Sometimes too, it is possible to do more than amuse them. We often laugh over the

picture presented one Thursday. A singularly dirty mother and baby appeared at the Vestry Door. The Mother went up into church for the service. The baby was confided to our Nursing Sister and one of our cleverest visitors. They looked at each other, hurried off to the Visitor's home near by, and while she looked out some of little Harold's cast-off clothes, sister washed the child downstairs. Soon they stole back to the vestry, and when the mother appeared to reclaim her baby at the end of the service, presented to her astonished view an altogether transformed child.[51]

This ploy to attract women to church was not entirely successful – unsurprising as the meetings coincided with school closing times. But the warden was comforted by the fact they reached a shifting population of about thirty women a week. To try to consolidate this minor achievement, Appleton founded a League of Mothers on the Feast of the Purification. 120 women had signed a promise as follows:

I will try by help of God,

1. To say my prayers regularly night and morning

2. To pray for my children and teach them to love God

3. To read a few verses of my Bible every day

4. To come to Church or Mission Hall at least once a week, or, if I cannot do this, to use some of the service in the Prayer Book on Sundays at home.

Signed

1898 [52]

A different type of women's association is represented by the Guild of Willing Helpers of St Matthew's, Brixton. The guild had sixty-nine members: twenty-six of these subscribed, eighteen sent in parcels of work and the remainder either worked up material supplied or paid some poor women in the parish to sew it for them. 'By means of this Guild, 341 useful Christmas presents have been provided. When it is remembered these have to be divided amongst 26 district visitors to give to their deserving poor, it will be understood there is not one too many.'[53]

It is clear that the clubs, associations, leagues and guilds maintained by the various denominations fell into different categories.

Some were opportunities for social contact with space for 'improvement' of one kind or another, either material or spiritual. Some were designed for worship alone. Some distributed largesse. Others received it.

Of course, counting and categorizing the women's clubs and classes does nothing to further our appreciation of the extent to which the female population as a whole became involved in them. The figures of membership and attendance furnished by the interview reports suggest that involvement was not large when compared with the number of women in a parish, and that it was not commensurate with the amount of time and energy expended upon recruitment by the clergy and visitors. This is not to say that the absolute numbers of women involved in church and chapel activities were small or insignificant – far from it. Substantial numbers of women – often from outside the church-going classes – participated at this level.

A further important point emerges from our study of women's clubs and classes. This is that the charitable and social efforts of the churches worked on the following principal: the reasonably well-to-do faithful associate and provide facilities of one kind or another designed to bring poorer women and girls into the fold and to give them practical assistance. Bands of Hope and sewing classes as well as industrial and maternity societies owed their origins to this system. So did many guilds and clubs. At Poplar 'there is a Dorcas society for the high nobility of the district. They spend their time in making clothing for the poor'.[54] At St Matthew's, Brixton, subscribers to a Maternity Society were actively recruited: £1.1s per annum would entitle the subscriber to recommend two pregnant women for relief; 10s 6d to recommend one woman. Between April 1898 and April 1899 sufficient had been subscribed to relieve seventeen women. More subscribers were desperately needed. The society loaned a box worth £5 to each expectant mother two months before her baby was due. The box contained all the necessary linens for the delivery, lying in period and the baby's early days. A gift was made when the mother returned the box in good order, when she was churched and when her baby was baptized.[55] The jumble sale was traditionally held in the late autumn at the South London Tabernacle, Peckham. The pastor alleged that it was 'crowded: old garments from church members sold, trousers worth 5/- sold for 2d or 3d', 'you can get 7/6 on them from the pawn shop immediately after buying; they are sold in order to let the poor have good clothing for the winter cheaply; the great difficulty is to keep out dealers, not many get in but he thinks some always do so'.[56] It was another way, and one which has persisted, of the well-to-do woman ridding her household of superfluous items and thus enabling the poor woman to clothe her family and make ends meet.

The internal working of the clubs and societies is more rarely opened to our gaze. Occasionally one can see that clubs and mothers' meetings might be a useful forum for 'social action' as well as talking scandal. At Bromley the mothers' meeting, which attracted an attendance of about sixty women, was run by the 'ladies' but the curate 'nearly always looks in, and talks to the mothers on microbes, vaccination, ventilation, sanitation etc.'. Once there also he 'Gets ladies to talk to them about the promiscuous sleeping arrangements of their children; have induced a good many to separate the sexes by at least a curtain'.[57]

What happened though if a parish had no reasonably well-to-do faithful and perhaps it was an unfashionable parish or chapel which drew no wealthy outsiders into its congregation? The short answer is, its efforts on behalf of the less well-to-do collapsed.

This was as true of the more strictly pastoral work of the church as it was of social and cultural activities and active charity. (I should point out here that a difference emerges between the Anglican and the other churches at this point. A clergyman of the Church of England has responsibility for the entire population, church-going or not of a given area, a parish, whereas a Methodist minister, say, was responsible to his congregation.) As Lawley of Hackney observed, visiting was the unique inheritance of the Church of England.[58] When ministers were questioned about their pastoral visiting it became clear that most house-to-house visiting depended upon the services of female district visitors. There was often no pretence of widespread visiting by the clergy. 'In Poplar parish ... the clergy have little time for visiting, which is done mainly by the District visitors.'[59]

St Matthew's Brixton had twenty-eight district visitors, all of them female and all but six spinsters.[60] Christ Church, North Brixton, had twenty-seven district visitors. Some churches in less well-to-do or fashionable neighbourhoods, had far smaller numbers. St Stephen's, North Bow, had six; Bromley, seven; St Gabriel's, Poplar, three.[61] District visitors were voluntary and unpaid.

The papers provide many details of the organization of the visiting system adopted in various parishes. The Vicar of St Andrew's, Bethnal Green, reported:

> At Bethnal Green the Parish was strictly divided up for visiting purposes, each curate and himself had a district allotted to them, under each curate there was a district visitor, all complaints passed in the first instance to the curate and then to himself as a court of appeal. Every Monday morning they met together and after a

prayer compared notes. Relief was allotted according to needs and means. Only one exception, whenever the district nurse recommended expensive foods for the sick they were always granted whatever the cost.[62]

At St Stephen's, North Bow, the parish was split into two halves, each under the supervision of a curate, but the responsibility for visiting itself lay with the six female district visitors who concentrated their efforts on 'special streets'.[63]

As the report of Appleton of the Trinity Mission, Camberwell, indicated, the visitors were ladies. These were drawn from an entirely different social class from the women they visited. Appleton wrote to young ladies who had to make a deliberate mental effort to imagine themselves into the position of impoverished, harassed housewives and mothers who had to do everything for their families without the assistance of servants or money.

The service of such ladies was often hard to come by – especially in a metropolis characterized by a shifting population. The well-to-do were the first to move on from the poor parishes of central London. Clergymen well appreciated the importance of female service to the church's pastoral effort and accepted the problems attached to it.

> This nucleus is the hub of the church life in a parish. Like a corporation it never dies and when once properly started is independent of a change of minister ... what he has to do is to see that those who are not so likely to leave as himself are the conducts of right thinking and right living to the congregation rather than the minister himself ... He admitted one great difficulty, i.e. that the church nucleus were the better men in a poor parish and for that very reason were more likely than not to move out of it as soon as they could afford to: but he was sure that the principle was the right one.[64]

Lawley could not, he said, understand why the dissenters did not visit.[65] At least in part it was because of their lack of available female helpers. A chapel with no middle-class members and with a part-time minister was often severely restricted in the pastoral care it could give. Of the Durand Gardens Baptist Chapel in Stockwell we are told, '... as is necessary in a church made up entirely of busy people with no leisured people on the staff, and no paid workers, everything goes on in the evening'.[66]

But the complaint almost everywhere was the shortage of available help – paid and unpaid. At St Gabriel's, Bromley, the mission lady and the three district visitors did little more than visit the sick; the parish paper was delivered to every home but there was no house visiting because 'there is not the staff for it'.[67] Adamson of Old Ford Parish Church explained that the lay reader and the mission woman visited each home once every eighteen months and that the sick were visited by the Bible nurse and the vicar. Nothing more was possible. The abbreviated comment on the report tells all: no district visitors obtainable; all too poor; no middle-class families.[68]

For many this plight was new. Allnutt of St Jude's, East Brixton, explained that the drift of the well-to-do out of the parish was responsible: 'It is getting harder to get voluntary workers ... (the presence of the less well-to-do class of people will eventually land the parish in considerable difficulties, on the scores alike of finance and of personal service).'[69]

Charles Brooke of Kennington thought the paid employment of young ladies to be responsible. 'This is as it should be, except in the case of wives and mothers whose place is surely at home, but it makes it very difficult to keep up our supply of district visitors.'[70]

The archive underlines the importance of middle-class female service to the churches. In huge parishes, the clergy could not hope to reach working-class women unless middle-class ladies did the work for them. The scarcity of such service was explained variously – Booth himself argued that parishes were being progressively stripped of their middle classes, and this was probably part of the reason. Or Brooke might have been correct. We must also entertain the possibility that ladies were ceasing to be attracted by the work of the church.

When a parish did not have a resident leisured class from which to draw willing lady helpers it seems that three routes were open to the paid ministry. It had to obtain voluntary help from elsewhere, pay workers or simply make the best of a very bad job.

At St Frideswide's – an East End parish popular with the intelligentsia – there were a 'large number of lady visitors from outside the parish'.[71] The Rector of Poplar had fourteen district visitors – five were 'residents who belong to the local aristocracy, daughters or wives of doctors etcetera' and nine were from other parts of London.[72] Paid mission women had often to be used as substitute visitors. Only a very few ministers found the services of working-class visitors satisfactory. One such was Cowan of St John's on the Isle of Dogs. He claimed that the thirty-five district visitors were excellent: 'The visitors have to cover their district weekly. These working women do the work very well and there is a good deal of rivalry among them in their work especially in collecting money for banks etc.'[73]

When voluntary workers were few and far between and often when they were not, ministers found in their wives willing workers.

Mr and Mrs Free of the St Cuthbert's Anglican Mission on the Isle of Dogs 'are setting about their work with the utmost earnestness and energy. Mrs Free I imagine will do almost as much as her husband; she is a bright, cheery, buxom woman, quite an ideal parson's wife'.[74] The position of the parson's wife in the Church of England was long established and acknowledged but perhaps even more important, the Booth papers suggest, was the ministry of the wife in the Nonconformist chapels. 'As Mrs Millwood was at home' at the Baptist Chapel, Durand Gardens, Stockwell, 'and had an intimate knowledge of the work, I had a conversation with her. She was a woman of about forty, very pleasant, bright and capable, clearly happy in her husband, her family and her work. She had been one of the small band of workers at the building of St Anne's Road, some twenty years ago, before her marriage, her future husband having been another of them, so she has had a long experience of "the cause".'[75] In some chapels where the minister was in part-time capacity, as with Mr Millwood who was engaged in business all day, it was the wife who provided day-to-day pastoral care and continuity. Of course, the wife did not always prove of much assistance. Mrs Smith of the Christian Mission on Sussex Road, Brixton declared that she never meddled with her husband's work and when she was asked whether she ever attended the services she replied, 'Not very often ... I generally go to Church with my daughters'.[76] And sometimes the work was of doubtful worth – Mrs Beale, wife of the part-time pastor of the East Dulwich Baptist Church, was described as 'uninteresting and uneducated. She is the President of the Ladies Christian Association of the chapel and we can probably measure something of its vitality by hers'.[77]

Daughters of the vicarage were also engaged in pastoral work. At Old Ford Parish Church the vicar's wife, son and three daughters were active workers.[78] At Poplar there was a night school 'for rough boys; conducted by Miss Chandler. This is attended by about twenty, most of whom have left school in low standards – only the three Rs are taught'.[79] R.J. Elliott, the genial and sunny vicar of St Stephen's, East India Dock Road, laid claim to a large number of helpers, especially his two daughters of whom he said 'they have been more to me than any curate ... Last year one of them was married, and the other is almost worn out with work.' In his parish although there was no house-to-house visiting, congregational visiting was frequent and thorough. There was an intimate knowledge of the circumstances and needs of each family for 'we know a great deal about our own people'. This was because 'the Mission woman spends a large part of each day visiting and the Clergy and Miss Elliott go about a good deal'. Cases of sickness were drawn to the attention of the nurse and the minister.

Money was found for fares to hospitals. Stays in convalescent homes were financed. Prescriptions were given. Relief was meted out to pregnant women or to the family without a breadwinner. Advice was rendered.[80] In the age before the welfare state, the role of the lady visitor could be all important. When even that lifeline was removed, the effect upon a poor family could be ruinous. Moreover, the church would lose all pretence of being in touch with the pulse of the parish.

The archive suggests that we should beware of assuming that the district visiting system worked well even when willing volunteers were plentiful. Walter Horne of St Saviour's, Brixton Hill, told Ernest Aves that relief is very largely in the hands of the district visitors, who report to the vicar what they have done. Tickets are used. The vicar claimed that great care was used, even too much 'and I have sometime to urge my visitors to give'. Even then he had difficulty in giving away more than £32 a year.[81] But at a time when parishes were enormous and paid ministers or workers relatively few, the system was probably better in operation than out.

Many London clergy were assisted by paid women helpers – deaconesses, sisters, nurses, mission women. The sisterhoods of the Church of England were in their pastoral aspects post-Crimean creations. The most well known were the Devonport Society (which incorporated that founded by Dr Pusey) and the Clewer Sisterhood founded by Canon Carter. In principle they met with a very mixed reception within the church. Although the value of their charitable and pastoral work was readily acknowledged there was much unease at the untrammelled authority within each community of the 'mother superior', and at the absence of any commission from the church itself. Priests of the Church of England certainly professed 'sisters' to the nun's vocation in solemn ceremonies – but these had no place in any statutory Book of Common Prayer. The work of some of the sisterhoods is recorded in Booth's notebooks. Notable is St Frideswide's. Here five Clewer Sisters ran a girls' club, a mothers' meeting, cooking classes and sewing classes for girls, taught in the large Sunday Schools and helped with the district visiting. 'The sisters and lady visitors visit every house about once a month.' One sister, Sister Constance, was 'evidently a person of great importance in the work' and she 'has the alms funds in her hands. She is the straitest sect of the Charity Organization Society and often refuses help.'[82] Brooke at St John the Divine, Kennington, was helped by eight sisters from a Wantage sisterhood.[83] Interestingly, other denominations sometimes attributed great influence to the Anglican 'Sisters'. Ernest Aves gathered from Canon Murname, Mission Priest of the Roman Catholic Church of the Sacred Heart, Knatchbull Road, that he 'found in the work of the Anglican Clergy and Sisters the chief explanation of the disappointing recognition and reception of the Catholic priests ... the sisters of the Anglican Church look like nuns'.[84]

But the presence of deaconesses was much more widespread. The office of deaconess had an ancient pedigree and when it was revived in 1861 (when the Bishop of London invested Catherine Ferard with the office) met with much less opposition from the low and broad church movements. There was a formal course of training at the London Diocesan Deaconess Institution. At St Martin's, Victoria Park, the Mildmay Mission supplied five spinster deaconesses. The deaconesses and the scripture reader systematically visited and covered the entire parish about once in every six weeks. The deaconesses also helped in the Sunday School.[85] Some clergy actively preferred a deaconess to any number of district visitors. Of James Roe of St Catherine's, Loughborough Park, it was said:

> He values the work of his deaconess, who has been with him for some years. She knows everybody, and people that want her know where to find her, and when they find her she knows how to deal with them for she is a trained worker. He professed to have no patience with district visitors, 'licensed impertinences' I call them, tactless, indiscreet.[86]

And the vicar of St Andrews, Stockwell Green, expressed the wish that he could replace his mission woman with 'a deaconess who would be more actively a religious agent'.[87] In this case at least, the mission women mainly collected money for the provident club.[88]

Paid women workers, then, did figure in the life of the late Victorian churches and chapels in London. But their importance was far outweighed by that of the myriad unpaid, voluntary helpers – the district visitors, the Sunday School teachers, the organizers of clubs and charities. This is true even if we take into account the few paid parish nurses and bible women, the mission women and factory workers.

As intimated, the Catholics presented a somewhat different case. Sisters, who had vowed to give their lives to God's work and who were unpaid, proved the mainstay of parochial work. Father Gordon Thompson of The Presbytery Bow Common Lane E told Charles Booth and George Duckworth that he had 'seven sisters working for him. These sisters are his only helpers. Sisters live at corner of Gale Street. Work for the love of God only and are not paid' and reported that they had wrought a remarkable change.[89] Thacker of the Bow Mission had three communities of nuns to help him, numbering over thirty-seven willing assistants, although he 'does not exactly order them about'.[90] The work of nuns and sisters was heavily concerned with education although it might involve a positive social element.

> His sisters are out each morning and dress and collect the children. Indifference on part of the parents. 'Oh yes Sister take them if you like.' No initiative on the part of the parents. Give breakfasts to 30 or 40 during winter, hot cocoa and bread and jam. Must give them something to warm them or you could never teach them anything. School fires lit between 5 and 6. Children come in at 7. Easier to get them up in winter than in summer it is so cold in bed man stays in bed while sister dresses children. Required some courage on the part of the sisters to get the children up under these circumstances but they do it.[91]

Aside from their school teaching, it was accepted that nuns and sisters would work with the groups of young girls and would help instruct female converts 'unless too intelligent'.[92]

The presentation of women in the Booth archive is, of its essence, a gendered one. These are women seen through clergymen's eyes. Only a very few women were interviewed and usually because their menfolk were unavailable to speak to Booth or his associates. But the archive does allow us a rare opportunity to do several things on a metropolis-wide scale: to see which roles were assigned to women by the male-dominated Christian churches; to begin to assess the contribution of women to organized religious life; to examine the attitude of the personnel of the various churches to women; to see to some extent the space which women created for themselves to occupy outside the domestic sphere. Of course, there are deficiencies in this documentation.[93] Some of the material is opinion and as such useful for attitudinal studies. Some of the material is statistical. Once these limitations are allowed for, however, the historian has at his or her disposal up to 1,800 separate records pertaining to the place of women in London religious life, which can and should be exploited. (Further possibilities include: local variation within London in the role of women; the statistical study of female involvement; closer study of the attitudes of ministers to women; study of the attitudes of the interviewers themselves; study of nursing provision; the approach of clergymen to the domestic lives and problems of their flocks.)

A sketch of the role of women in late Victorian religion has emerged which shows them to have been of crucial importance to the proper functioning of the churches. In no sense was their role peripheral or seen to be so. A currently fashionable explanation for the crisis of the early twentieth-century Christian churches has been that of Cox. He has explained the crisis in terms of the encroachment of the state upon the accepted social role of the churches.[94] An alternative thesis, it seems, might well be that the church entered a crisis when women ceased to support its efforts as effectively as traditionally they had. As urban parishes grew in size and the ratio of minister to flock worsened, any pretence which the churches could make to fulfil a truly pastoral role rested upon the work of women. The climax of the illness passed but the church, while it lingered, could not recover its former health. The state or someone else had to step in. The collapse had occurred before 1914.

Notes

1   See, for example, Prochaska, F.K. (1980), *Women and Philanthropy in 19th Century England*, Oxford University Press; Prochaska, Frank (1987), 'Body and Soul: Bible Nurses and the Poor in Victorian London', *Historical Research*, 60, pp.336–48 (makes no use of Booth); Field-Bibb, Jacqueline (1991), *Women Towards Priesthood*, Cambridge University Press, especially pp.10–162 and 201–18.

2   For a fuller discussion of the nature of the interview material see O'Day, R. (1989), 'Interviews and Investigations: Charles Booth and the Making of the Religious Influences Survey', *History*, 74.

3   BLPES, Booth Collection, B305 fo.201, Interview of Revd Walter Herne, Vicar of St Saviour's, Brixton Hill, by Ernest Aves, 6 November 1900.

4   B304 fos 5–6, Interview of Revd J. Douglas, MA, Pastor of the Kenyon Baptist Church, Solon Road, Acre Lane, by George Duckworth, 7 November 1900.

5   B304 fo.107, Interview of Revd Alfred Sargent, Minister of the Brixton Hill Wesleyan Church, by George Duckworth, 13 November 1900.

6   B305 fo.133, Interview of Revd W.D. Springett DD of St Matthew's Brixton by George Duckworth (?), 30 October 1900.

7   B175 fo.103, fo.105, Interview of Revd W.A. Carroll of St Frideswide's, 17 May 1897 (?)

8   B305 fo.103, Interview of Revd John Dixon, Vicar of St James Camberwell and Rural Dean, by George Duckworth, 30 October 1900.

9   B307 fo.125, Interview of Revd G. Carter of Unitarian Christian Church Peckham, by George Duckworth, 3 December 1900.

10   B307 fo.90, Interview of Mr W Woolgar, Deacon of Denmark Place Baptist Chapel, by George Duckworth, 4 December 1900; see also B175 fo.233.

11   B305 fo.87, Interview of Revd J.B. Sharp AKC, Vicar of Church of Epiphany, Stockwell by George Duckworth, 26 October 1900.

12   B175 fo.29, Interview of Revd H.Q. Mason, Vicar of St Stephen, North Bow, 12 and 13 May 1897; see also St Frideswide's Interview, fo.103.

13   B175 fo.85, Interview of Revd M. Sweetnam of St Martin's Victoria Park, 11 May 1897.

14   B175 fo.233, Interview with Revd C. Vere Barly, Curate to Mr Parry of Bromley, 18 June 1897 (?).

15   B175 St Frideswide's Interview, fo.103.

16   B175 St Frideswide's Interview, fo.105.

17   B175 fo.123, Interview of Revd A. Wentworth Bennett, Curate-in-Charge, St Gabriel's Poplar, 24 May 1897(?).

18   B305, Interview of Revd John Dixon Dyke, Vicar of St James, Camberwell and Rural Dean of Camberwell, by George Duckworth, 30 October 1900, fos 99–103.

19   Sweetnam Interview, fo.91.

20   Barly Interview, fo.243; see also B307 fos 109–10, Interview of Mr Pim, London City Missionary by George Arkell, 7 December 1900.

21   Barly of Bromley Interview, fo.233.

22   B305, see fos 1–28, *Letter to the Parishioners and Friends* of St John the Divine, Kennington, pp.10–11.

23   B169 fo.211, Interview of Revd Protheroe Alpe of St Peter's Limehouse, by Arthur Baxter(?), 1897.

24   B306 fo.5, Interview of Revd Adam Averell Ramsay, Minister of the Emmanuel Congregational Church, Barry Road, Dulwich, by George Arkell, 16 November 1900.

25   B169, fo.75, Interview of Revd D.G. Cowan, St John's, Isle of Dogs, 10 May 1897.

26   B180, Thacker Interview, fo.85; B180, Interview of Revd Father Egglemears of St Edmunds, Isle of Dogs, by George Duckworth, 18 May 1897, fo.67; B180, Interview of Father Highley by Charles Booth, *c*.May 1897, fos 5–15; Thompson Interview, fo.29.

27   B180, Thacker Interview, fo.87.

28   B180, Thompson Interview, fo.29.

29   B180, Interview of Revd Father Lawless of Poplar E. by George Duckworth and Ernest Aves, 19 May 1897, fo.67.

30   B281, fos 19–20, Interview of Revd R. Appleton of Trinity College Mission in St George's Parish, Camberwell, by Arthur Baxter (?), 31 January 1900.

31   B281 Appleton Interview, Trinity Parish Notes No.1 June 1898, p.7.

32   B281 Appleton Interview, *Trinity Parish Notes* No.1. June 1898, pp.7–8.

33   B281, Appleton Interview, p.17.

34   B180, Interview of Very Revd Major Howlett of St Peter's Beauvoir Square at the Presbytery, Tottenham Road, by Ernest Aves, *c*.June 1897, fo.179.

35   See Howlett Interview, fo.181.

36   B180, Interview of Revd Dr J.P. Thacker of the Bow Mission, 26 Cambell Road, by George Duckworth, 2 June 1897, fo.85.

37   B180, Thacker Interview, fo.87.

38   B305 fos 127–141, Interview of Revd W.D. Springett DD, St Matthew's Brixton, by George Duckworth, 30 October 1900, fo.31.

39   *Ibid.*, fo.32.

40   B304, fos 121–33, Interview of Mr Allen, Pastor of the Old Baptist Union, 5 Sidney Road, Stockwell, by Ernest Aves, 5 December 1900.

41   B175, Interview of Revd W.A. Carroll of St Frideswide's, 17 May 1897, fo.107.

42   B305, Interview of Revd J.B. Sharp, AKC, Vicar of Church of Epiphany, Stockwell, by George Duckworth, 26 October 1900, fo.89.

43   B175, Carroll Interview, fo.107.

44   B307, Interview of Mr W. Woolgar, Deacon of Denmark Place Baptist Chapel, by George Duckworth, 4 December 1900, fo.95.

45   B305, Sharp Interview, fo.91.

46   B307, Interview of Mr T.D. Bell, Church Secretary of Camberwell Green Congregationalist Church in Wren Road, by George Duckworth, 14 November 1900, and of Mr Stephens and Mr Bell on 19 November 1900, fos 61, 67, 69, 73.

47   B305, Interview of Revd J. Bayfield Clerk, MA, Vicar of St Saviour's, Herne Hill Road, Camberwell, by George Duckworth, 1 November 1900, fo.157.

48   B305, Springett Interview, Vicar's New Year Letter, p.44.

49   B307, Bell and Stephens Interview.

50   B305, fo.57, Interview of Revd J.H. Browne, Vicar of St Andrew's, Stockwell Green, by George Duckworth, 23 October 1900.

51   B281, Appleton Interview, Trinity Mission Notes, p.9.

52   *Ibid.*

53   B305, Springett Interview, Year Book p.33.

54   B169, Interview of Revd A. Chandler, Rector of Poplar, by Arthur Baxter, 4 May 1897, fo.21.

55   B305, Springett Interview, New Year's Letter, p.24.

56   B306, Interview of Pastor E. Roberts of South London Tabernacle, Peckham, by G.H. Duckworth, 12 November 1900, fo.55.

57   B175, Barly Interview, fo.241.

58   B350, Interview of Revd the Hon. A. Lawley, Rector of St John's, Hackney, and formerly Vicar of St Andrew's, Bethnal Green, by George Duckworth, 28 January 1898, fo.119.

59   B169, Interview of Revd A. Chandler Rector of Poplar, 4 May 1897, fos 5–7.

60   B305, Springett Interview, Year Book, p.21.

61   B175, fos 23, 51 and 119.

62   B350, Interview of Revd the Hon. A. Lawley, Rector of St John's, Hackney, and formerly Vicar of St Andrew's, Bethnal Green, by George Duckworth, 28 January 1898, fo.117.

63   B175, Interview of Revd H.Q. Mason, Vicar of St Stephen's, North Bow, 12 and 13 May 1897, fo.23.

64   B350, Lawley Interview, fo.125.

65   B350, Lawley Interview, fo.119.

66   B304, Interview with Mrs Milwood, wife of Pastor A.J. Milwood of the Baptist Chapel, Durand Gardens, Stockwell, by Ernest Aves, November 1900, fo.53.

67   B175, Interview of Revd A. Wentworth Bennett, Curate-in-Charge, 24 May 1897 (?), fo.129.

68   B175, Interview of Revd W. Adamson, Vicar of Old Ford Parish Church, *circa* 1898, fo.163.

69   B305, Interview of Revd M.R. Allnutt, Vicar of St Jude's, East Brixton, by Ernest Aves, 1 November 1900, fo.183.

70   B305, Brooke Interview, fos 1–27, Advent Letter, p.10.

71   B175, Interview of Revd W.A. Carroll of St Frideswide's, 17 May 1897, fo.101.

72   B169, Interview of Revd A. Chandler, Rector of Poplar, 4 May 1897, fos 5–15.

73   B169, Interview of Revd D.G. Cowan, St John's, Isle of Dogs, 10 May 1897, fo.81.

74   B170, Interview of Revd and Mrs Richard Free, St Cuthbert's Lodge, Millwall, 9 June 1897, fo.21.

75   B304, Millwood Interview, fo.51.

76   B304, Interview of Mrs Smith, Wife of the Superintendent of the Brixton Christian Mission, by Ernest Aves, 19 November 1900, fos 67–71.

77   B306, Interview of Mrs Beale, wife of Mr G.W. Beale, East Dulwich Baptist Church, Arnott Road, by Ernest Aves, 12 November 1900, fos 155–9.

78   B175, Adamson Interview, fo.165.

79   B169, Chandler Interview, fos 21–3.

80   See e.g. B169, Chandler Interview, fos 13–15; B169, Bedford Interview, fo.177; B305, Browne Interview, fo.59; and, most detailed of all, B305, Springett Interview, Year Book, pp.51–2.

81   B305, Interview of Revd Walter Horne, Vicar of St Saviour's, Brixton Hill, by Ernest Aves, 6 November 1900, fos 205–7.

82   B175, Carroll Interview, fo.101.

83   B305, Brooke Interview, fo.13.

84   B307, fo.3, Interview of Revd Canon Murname, Mission Priest of the Roman Catholic Church of the Sacred Heart, Knatchbull Road, by Ernest Aves, 15 November 1900.

85   B175, Sweetnam Interview, fos 89–91.

86   B305, Interview of Revd James Roe, Incumbent of St Catherine's, Loughborough Park, by Ernest Aves, 2 November 1900, fo.181.

87   B305, Browne Interview, fo.63.

88   *Ibid.*

89   B180, Interview of Father Gordon Thompson, The Presbytery, Bow Common Lane E., by Charles Booth and George Duckworth, fo.23.

90   B180, Thacker Interview, fo.81.

91   B180, Thompson Interview, fo.25.

92   B180, Interview of Revd Father Carey of the Church of the Sacred Heart of Jesus, Eden Grove, by Ernest Aves, c. November 1899, fo.223.

93   For this see especially, O'Day, 'Interviews and Investigations', *passim* and Mcleod, above.

94   Cox, Jeffrey (1982), *The English Churches in a Secular Society*, Oxford University Press.

13 Gambling, 'the fancy' and Booth's role and reputation as a social investigator

Mark Clapson

Charles Booth has been compared unfavourably with social investigators from different traditions of social enquiry, most notably Henry Mayhew, a journalist who was writing some forty years earlier. Although both men were seeking to inform public opinion on poverty, Mayhew was allegedly human and empathetic, providing both tragic and colourful descriptions of slum dwellers and street characters. Booth's classificatory approach, however, stands accused of a 'deliberate impersonality' and of treating the poor as 'objects of study'.[1] He has also been portrayed as 'a middle-class moralist who saw any departure from middle-class norms as social disorganisation or immorality'.[2] Thus one historian of popular culture has described Booth's attitude to, and descriptions of, gambling and 'the fancy' as 'less favourable' than Mayhews'.[3]

It can be objected that gambling was not a central concern of Booth, and reveals little that is substantive about the man and his method. Moreover, why not assess Booth's propensity to moralize on a greater social problem such as drink and intemperance? Yet the significance of gambling for Booth's approach lies in its secondary importance. Booth's undertaking was massive. He cast his nets wide, and carefully examined his trawl. We can see this both in the notebooks, the raw materials of his great survey, and in the published volumes of *Life and Labour*. What he found, and the ways in which he interpreted and presented his findings, tells us much about Booth the empirical investigator and Booth the so-called moralist.

Gambling and 'the fancy' in Victorian London

Many of today's popular sports and pastimes, such as greyhound racing, boxing and the love of pigeons, are tamer versions of the sports of the 'fancy'.[4] As Dr Johnson had defined the word, the 'fancy' was 'an opinion bred rather by the imagination than the reason', or 'an inclination, liking, fondness'.[5] Any dog or bird cultivated for its beauty, prowess or strength was a fancy animal.[6] Until the early nineteenth century, cock fighting, dog fighting, ratting and prize fighting were popular sports of the fancy. People would gather at cockpits and compounds in public houses, fields or fairgrounds to discuss the form and prospects of the competitors and wager among themselves on the basis of their information or inclination.

The nineteenth century eroded the rustic basis of the fancy. Urbanization cut off immediate access to the countryside for millions, and by-laws against cruel-sports from the earliest decades effectively reduced the brutality of the spectacle and altered the role of the animals. Dogs, for example, were increasingly bred for speed. Mayhew, during one of his forays into the street life of London, observed the relatively recent popularity of the 'Italian greyhound' as one of the wares of 'the street sellers of dogs'.[7] Some forty years later, when Booth was observing the fancy, animals were sold on the street for their appeal as racers and pets. Anywhere such as a back-yard big enough to rough-house a dog or hold a pigeon loft was suitable for this inexpensive hobby.

Booth's Poverty survey relied primarily on the local knowledge of the visitors for the London School Board. They carried out house-to-house visits. Their information on families with schoolchildren was recorded in notebooks by Booth or one of the interviewers who worked for him on the Poverty Series. Booth would follow up this information by a walk around the areas he was writing about, verifying or questioning the impressions in the notebooks. In 1887, the School Board Visitor (SBV) for Finsbury, Mr Lambert, described a 'dog fancier' living on the third floor at Number 31 Parker Street. This street was coloured black for the map. Its inhabitants were largely of 'the semi-criminal class, people who don't get an honest living'. As for the fancier:

> Sometimes keeps a dog or two here but probably has a place elsewhere – belongs to the betting class but hardly makes his living by this trade – dresses well – neglects his wife and family who seem very poor.[8]

Booth placed him in social class 'A', the lowest class of occasional labourers and street sellers, criminals and semi-criminals. Under the entry for Parker Street in Volume 2 of the Poverty Series, Booth elaborated on what he saw as the unsavoury and selfish side of this dog fancier:

> Martin was a dog fancier and dog doctor. On the landing there was generally a dog chained to its kennel. The dogs varied; sometimes of the smallest and sometimes of the largest kind. Cleanliness not being a strong point with Mrs. Martin, the smell may be imagined. The man looked after himself for food and drink, and the woman

seemed too ignorant to realise his unkind treatment or feel her poverty. She had scarcely anything to wear, and the little child of five years would run about the house in daytime almost naked, and frequently without food.[9]

Booth's concern for the economically vulnerable dependents of gamblers is not a specifically late Victorian one. It has been shared by many social investigators since.[10]

As for the dogs, they were raced in fields or wastelands in or near the working-class areas of the capital. Bow Running Ground, Hackney Marshes, and the marshes next to Woolwich Arsenal were the most prominent meeting places for whippet racing by 'the sporting set' at the end of the nineteenth century.[11] Many races were small informal affairs, organized between local dog fanciers for both sport and betting. But bookmakers and publicans, and other prominent characters in the leisure life of the working class, were increasingly involved in promoting dog racing. Bookmaker capital was central to the establishment of electric greyhound stadia on Hackney Marshes and other sites from 1926.[12]

Bird breeding and fancying was a widespread activity in working-class areas. It had long been popular with the Huguenot silk weavers since their settlement in Bethnal Green in the late seventeenth century. Mayhew described the love of birds among this community, and their gentle contentment which resulted from this pastime.[13] But, as Booth noted, the attraction of captive birds as a cheap domesticated form of the fancy had spread to the wider area of Bethnal Green, Spitalfields, Whitechapel, Hackney and Finsbury by the late nineteenth century. From the window of a railway carriage passing over a viaduct above 'two-storied London', one could see 'small rough-roofed erections' for the pigeons and other birds in the little backyards of the workers' cottages.[14] 'Bird fanciers', wrote Booth, 'are mostly to be found in the mixed streets which lie near Black districts.'[15] These were the streets which he coloured purple and light blue on his *Descriptive Maps of London Poverty*. These streets were made up of those in 'standard poverty', classes C and D, with a smattering of Bs, Ds and Fs. Booth noticed a distinction within the world of the 'fancy': the more domesticated hobby of bird keeping was less associated with the poorest or semi-criminal element than dog fancying or prize fighting. These observations stemmed from Booth's concern with the ecology of the city.[16] He tried to identify the social and economic processes which differentiated one area from another.

The Sunday morning bird fair or 'fancy market' of Sclater Street in Bethnal Green was the hub of the betting and fancying fraternity of the East End. Here, those whom Mayhew had termed 'the street sellers' of dogs and birds displayed their animals to the market crowd. As a well-known spot it was also useful for bookmakers and their agents to collect and pay-out bets. Booth gave a vivid impression of the bird fair. One Sunday morning in the late 1880s he alighted from an omnibus, looked at the animals, bought a racing tip from a tipster for 3d, and 'listened to the harangues of the bookmakers'. While he was mindful of the fancy markets' association with the 'doubtful characters' from the nearby slum around Old Nichol Street, he also emphasized the 'life and good humour' of this Sunday occasion. It had 'all the crowded geniality of a race meeting':

> The bird fair [is] attended from far and wide, but specially reflects the pleasures and habits of the neighbouring people of Bethnal Green, which turn largely on domestic pets, singing birds, rabbits and guinea pigs, fowls, pigeons, dogs and even goats, are dealt in, any kind of animal that can be kept in or on a house or in a back yard.[17]

This is hardly the language of a middle-class moralist with designs on lower-class recreation. Booth was more concerned with the role of the 'fancy' in the formation of community identity than with the individual and expressive role associated with bird keeping.

This general approach left a gap in the discussion of gambling and the fancy in *Life and Labour*. Its individual attraction as a hobby is only indirectly alluded to in the Poverty volumes and in the notebooks. For example, Hare Street, an extension of Sclater Street, was described by the SBV as a 'celebrated place for pigeons, quite some 70 "dormers" on the tops of the houses, and over 100 people keep pigeons in this street'.[18] (Hare Street was given as light blue in the notebooks but is coloured dark blue on the map.) New Square, Whitechapel, was also given as light blue in the notebook, consistent with Booths' comment on the locations of bird fanciers given above. The houses in the square had 'Nice little gardens. People [have] taken an interest in them and keep pigeons'.[19] This pride in the appearance of gardens was consistent with the individual care and creativity associated with the cultivation of birds. Later social surveys of London, which acknowledged their debt to Booth, took up where he left off. Ruth Bowley for the *New Survey of London Life and Labour*, 1935, was more concerned with the individual inclinations of 'Pigeon and Cage Bird Fancying'.[20]

Booth's concern with the subcultural network of the 'fancy' extended to his discussion of organized street betting with bookmakers. 'Street betting' was a colloquial term for off-the-course ready-money (or cash) betting on horses, which had been made illegal during an earlier moral campaign against lower-class gambling in 1853. A new concern with gambling arose during the 1880s: contemporaries of Booth were convinced that the country was in the grip of a gambling fever, which they saw as evidenced in the growth of bookmaking and the sporting and racing press. Hence the formation of the National Anti-Gambling League in 1889–90. Fears about gambling were related to the crisis in confidence in British economic performance, and seen as part of an immoral get-rich-quick attitude which was permeating society.[21]

The street betting network comprised the bookmaker and his agents (colloquially known as 'runners'), look-outs to watch for the police, and the punters. For his information on this during the Poverty survey, Booth drew upon the intelligence of the SBVs and his own observations. In the Religious survey, he again recorded what he saw, and he was also well served by his assistant Arthur Baxter's summary notes on gambling upon which the text of the last few editions of the Religious Influences Series, and Booths' concluding remarks in the final volume of *Life and Labour*, were based.

Baxter's notes were composed of little résumés of the testimonies of missionary workers and higher-ranking policemen. He pointed to the places where illicit ready money betting and bookmaking took place: street, alley, workplace, barber shop, coffee shop and clubs. In the East End, betting was especially common in those 'Proprietary' clubs who 'decline[d] to open their doors to strangers'.[22] The ease with which most bookmakers and their agents carried out their trade was a complaint from both religious and police spokesmen, although the police emphasized their problems in enacting the unpopular betting laws, while missionaries and anti-gambling campaigners lamented their manifest unwillingness to intervene:

> Fining bookmakers no good. Seabright only knows of three prominent bookmakers in the district (Chelsea); they are constantly being run in and fined. One of them summoned takes a cab, drives to the court, tells his cab to wait, is fined £5, gives another £5 to the Poor Box, and returns to his work.
>
> Bookies stand about to meet men coming from or going to work; police take no notice. The sudden life of a street after a great race and the newspapers' out. Boys on bicycles with pink reams [of papers] scorching along and tossing bundles to little boys at street corners – off with the boys shouting – doors and factory gates open, men tumble out, men bet with the bookmaker.[23]

As the central figure in off-course ready-money betting, the street bookmaker was an aggregator of a multitude of small stakes from which he laid odds, paid winnings, and pocketed the remaining cash, the unsuccessful bets, as profit. He was thus castigated by the National Anti-Gambling League, a coalition of Nonconformist churches, as both parasite and predator, living and profiting from the pickings of the poor. Booth appears to have supported this view, providing a number of gobbets from the testimonies of missionary workers or chapel ministers throughout *Life and Labour*. One Presbyterian minister, for example, using the insect metaphor, lamented that Putney was 'a great place for sporting men, and swarming with bookmakers'.[24]

The disreputable and illegal status of bookmakers made them firm candidates for Class 'A', the vicious and semi-criminal poor. In the Bethnal Green and Hackney notebooks, the first descriptions of bookmakers in Booths' survey are given. It is interesting to note the sporting, pseudo-genteel and business-like appearance of this struggling Hackney bookmaker. And like the dog fancier mentioned above, he is cast by the SBV as a selfish character, a drain on his family's economy:

> This man describes himself as a billiard marker and sometimes as a traveller. He goes out dressed up with gold albert, etc., while his wife and children are in rags. The children were locked up in a room and when summoned the man said they were in the country whereas he had them shut in the room as they were not fit to be seen.[25]

The SBVs were concerned with the vulnerability of these children to the vicissitudes of their fathers' occupation. It threw into sharp relief the indifference of bookmakers and betting men to the welfare of their class.[26]

For Booth, the working-class bookmaker was not to be confused with the 'bookmakers of good repute' who went to the respectable clubs of London.[27] The poorest bookmaker was an unprincipled opportunist in the street economy of the poor. He was one of the 'worst class of corner men ... who hang round the doors of public houses, the young men who spring forward on any chance to earn a copper ... They render no useful service, they create no wealth: more often they destroy it.'[28]

From this class came the loafers and 'street arabs', those youths who earned a precarious and often immoral living in the streets, and the bookmakers and their runners. Those who would not work were seen as a counterweight to the forces of individual self-help which created wealth and enabled civilization to progress both morally and materially. They were viewed as the unregenerate poor, 'the occasional labourers, street sellers, loafers, criminals and semi-criminals' whom Booth estimated to be 1.25 per cent of all Londoners. This self-perpetuating bedrock of the poor, he argued, would create for itself another Alsatia, the infamous refuge of rakes and scoundrels in seventeenth-century Whitefriars where villainy and vice were allegedly commonplace.[29]

Together, the bookmakers, punters, publicans and dog fanciers made up what Booth, in common with middle-class social reformers, referred to as an undifferentiated 'sporting set'. He was well aware of the camaraderie of the punters and bookies whom he described as 'a happy family'. They would have a '"whip round" to make up a purse for bail or anyone "in trouble"'.[30] Booth placed them the sporting set *en masse* into Class A. This also included prize fighters and race-course thieves.[31] The bookmakers and the active members of the fancy in a sense serviced the demand of the majority of people in Class B (the very poor, casual labourers and those in chronic want) for unedifying and unrespectable entertainments, and acted as a drag on its economic well-being. This was what Booth and other Edwardian social commentators termed the 'leisure class'. The 'ideal' of this non-productive group was 'to work when they like and play when they like'. They could not stand regularity and dullness, and found their excitement in the life of the streets or as 'participators in some highly coloured domestic scene'.[32]

Beatrice Potter shared Booth's view of the leisure class, but described it in a more forthright way. Of those who were mentally and physically unsuited to work, and who hung about the docks for the odd hour of work, she wrote:

> Their passion is gambling. Sections of them are hereditary casuals;
> a larger portion drift from other trades. They have a constitutional
> hatred of regularity and forethought, and a need for paltry
> excitement. They are late-risers, sharp-witted talkers, and [they]
> have that agreeable tolerance for their own and each other's vices
> which seems characteristic of a purely leisure class ...[33]

In short, socially they had a 'particular attractiveness'; economically and morally they were 'parasites eating the life out of the working class, demoralizing and discrediting it'.[34]

Potter further interpreted gambling as an attempt to realize the aspirations of the poor, specifically the Jewish community of East London.[35] Her discussion pointed to the role of Jewish social clubs – *chevras* – and card gaming clubs in the economic and social assimilation of a 'greener', an unskilled recent immigrant. In her eyes gambling and petty capitalism were two sides of the same coin of self-help in an uncertain economy of the poor. While the more simple-minded might fall victim to 'the Jewish passion for gambling', other recent immigrants were attracted by gambling and the fancy as an expression of their Anglicization and as a way to make money. The successful 'tiny capitalist' bedecked his parlour with, among other things, prints of prize fighters and race horses.[36] Oral history for other parts of England illustrates the attraction of horse racing and betting for both casual and more established Jewish traders, and its role in their adoption of an 'English' recreational culture which was compatible with the defence of ethnic identity.[37] Jewish bookmakers reflected perhaps the most successful workers in this connection. Joe Coral, for example, came to London from Poland with his widowed mother and three brothers in 1912. He realized soon enough that 'the English will always back their fancy' and that the stake money usually stopped with the bookies. After a short spell as a bookies' runner in Dalston, he started his own ready-money business and had soon spread to Hackney and Stoke Newington. By the 1960s his betting shops were all over London.[38]

Potter's contribution to the Poverty Series was based on observations made when visiting with the Charity Organization Society, during a 'short spell of rent collecting' in the low-class dwellings of the East End, and from a lengthy inquiry into the sweating system of the Jewish tailoring trade.[39] She perhaps accepted too easily that Jews were more fond of a gamble than other groups,[40] but her observations were necessarily more focused than in Booth's general co-ordinating approach. In this, her method had more in common with the social observation of discrete working-class communities both in the Edwardian years, and since.[41] Such studies provide more detail on recreation at close quarters, and thus tell us more about the personal appeal of gambling for regular gamblers.

Like Potter, Booth noted the psychological traits of the 'leisure class': as a result of 'shiftlessness, helplessness, idleness or drink', they were 'inevitably poor'.[42] But he pointed to hard realities which circumscribed the existence of Class B and moulded their outlook. The recreation of this group was 'bounded very closely by the pressure of want' and 'habitual to the extent of second nature'.[43] Here, an important point can be made. Booth primarily interpreted gambling among the 'A's and 'B's as a symptom rather than a cause of the tenacity of poverty. It was one of many low-life activities transmitted from generation to generation in economically disadvantaged areas. This has since been termed 'the culture of poverty'. Thus Shelton

Street near Covent Garden, for example, a street coloured black for the Descriptive Map of London Poverty, was inhabited mainly by Irish costers. Street betting, drunkenness, dirt and bad language prevailed: 'Add to this a group of fifteen or twenty young men gambling in the middle of the street and you complete the general picture.'[44]

Booth presented a similar picture of the 'Fenian Barracks' off Limehouse Cut in East London, where the 'general appearance of the street' bore out its unrespectable character. Drunken women, women 'without hats or bonnets', truanting children and children playing pitch and toss were 'the usual signs of semi-vicious poverty'.[45]

As E.P. Hennock and Susanne MacGregor have noted, one of the early criticisms of Booth from Professor Leone Levi of the Royal Statistical Society was that he did not blame gambling as a cause of individual poverty.[46] B.S. Rowntree, like Booth a businessman and a social investigator, was a prominent anti-gambling campaigner. He argued that gambling was a cause of 'secondary' poverty, which meant that money which was otherwise sufficient to maintain physical efficiency was gambled away.[47] (Primary poverty was caused by insufficient money in the first place.) Booth was never as explicit as Rowntree in this.

Yet Booth was alert to the social implications of gambling. This comes out most clearly in the Religious Influences Series. (There seems to be nothing on gambling in the Industry Series). In the Poverty Series, Booth's primary aim was to quantify poverty and relate its incidence to changes in the labour market. He stratified households, streets and areas according to levels of income, and provided information for social policies designed to alleviate the problems of the poor and run-down areas of the capital. In the survey of religion, however, he eschewed such a systematic and statistically-oriented approach in order to test the waters of religiosity. The methodology of the Religious Influences work reflected the greater personal involvement of Booth within the process of primary observation, and in recording the views of ministers and missionaries. There were fifteen research assistants on the Poverty Series compared to five on Religious Influences, and Booth wrote up almost all of the volumes with little help from others.[48]

In the first volume of the Religious Influences Series Booth stated his aim of describing 'things as they are' and adopted 'a sympathetic rather than critical attitude' to the religious life of the capital. Despite this, as Hugh McLeod has written, Booth too readily pointed to the 'failure' of organized religion.[49] In Religious Influences gambling is thus mainly identified as an impediment to evangelical and philanthropic effort in the capital. For example, Booth lamented the failure of religious and political social clubs in East London to 'create a great fellowship of men drawn from its own neighbourhood', and in so doing he blamed the early victory of the working-class taste for beer and betting over the rational designs of the Clubs and Institutes Union, an organization designed to foster a spirit of providence and sobriety in working-class recreation. Drink and betting were soon common in such establishments, and viewed by Booth as the two most prominent evils, 'ruining so many of the great social and political working mens' clubs, and causing them to be regarded as curses to the community'.[50]

Yet Booth was aware of the problem in trying to convert gamblers into more restrained pastimes. The Religious Influences notebooks contain a fascinating episode in Notting Dale concerning a policeman and 'an exceptional London City Missionary', Mr Campbell Morgan, in May 1899:

> As we walked from [Mary Place] to Walmer Road at the corner just opposite the Rugby Club we came upon six hulking lads playing pitch-and-toss. Mr. M. took the opportunity for another denunciation and turning to me said 'I hope, Sir, when you get back to Scotland Yard you will report as to the way in which the lads in this district spend their time'. The lads rather quailed at the suggestion that I was a tec [detective] but for Mr. M. and his thunders they evidently cared not at all, they in common with others rather tending to resent his interference with what they clearly felt was no business of his ... Further on we came upon another similar group, and the missionary, jumping into the gang, seized a penny which was on the ground. This led to a scene. The owner, trembling and pallid, with mingled fear and rage, removed his coat and squared up, using horrid language. He was, however, afraid to strike, and after some parley his penny was returned, and his game resumed as we passed on.[51]

These 'hulking' youths were more widely known in Edwardian society as 'street arabs' and 'loafers'. These terms, which are peppered throughout the text of *Life and Labour*, were common phrases which belied a view of young lads adrift from the world of work and religion.

Gambling was seen as evidence of irreligion all over London, including middle-class areas.[52] Yet Booth's concern was focused mostly on the poorest areas. He lamented that religious endeavours 'amongst the rough population of the Nichol' were 'very largely failures'. The out-of-doors preaching at the bird fair every Sunday fell on deaf ears. Successful missionary work was 'carried on mainly amongst a class very much above the lowest' but among the very poor, 'the people for whose sake especially the mission was established', there was 'little effect'.[53]

Booth appears to have accepted the growing number of unscientific and exaggerated claims about the extent of gambling in late Victorian Britain. But most of his contemporaries or near-contemporaries did so.[54] Yet it was an important consequence of prohibition that bookmakers, being illegal, could not register their occupation and were not inclined to record their betting transactions, which could have been used as evidence against them in a court of law. It was thus impossible to assess their numbers and the extent of their operations beyond impressionistic guesswork. Here the alarmist or partisan propaganda of the authorities and the anti-gambling lobby held sway. Arthur Baxter's notes reflect this, portraying gambling as 'increasing beyond imagination', as 'increasing by leaps out of all proportion to other forms of vice', and viewing gambling among women 'as an invention of the last two years: comes of greater freedom and saving power'.[55]

Booth's concluding comments on organized illegal betting drew upon his impressions of London's streets with missionaries and ministers, and reiterated much of the summary notes. He was well aware of the internal organization of street betting, understanding of the difficulties facing the police in dealing with it, especially clubs, and felt that the problem was growing rapidly as a result of the sporting press. But ultimately, Booth held back from the fearful pronouncement on gambling that Rowntree made. The subject, he wrote, 'needs special study, as do some of the others treated in this volume'.[56]

Conclusion

Thus Booth openly acknowledged his general rather than close-up approach to a pressing problem of his time. Perhaps by 1903 he was mindful of the criticisms of Arthur Sherwell, a contemporary social investigator in London. In his *Life in West London*, he criticized Booth not just for a scant treatment of West London, but for failing to investigate locally distinct areas of the capital more microscopically. Thus 'the scope of his enquiry', wrote Sherwell, 'prevented him from giving, at any time, more than a casual and indirect clue to the moral and religious conditions of the districts which he investigated'.[57]

Over half a century later, however, the sociologist Ruth Glass turned this criticism on its head. She lamented the divorce of social enquiry from social policy, blaming the rise of micro-sociologies of working-class life, conducted by vague researchers 'in search of a theme', in place of 'the Booth tradition'.[58]

In losing out to the general trend away from the ecological survey, Booth fell victim to the picaresque tradition of social journalism embodied by Mayhew. This is perhaps because both community studies and the Mayhew approach have better served the interests of the romantic strain of cultural studies since the war. Yet the piecemeal nature of Booth's legacy is caused by reasons which go much deeper than this.

He was also a victim of what Hobsbawm calls the *nouvelle couche sociale*, or the politico-administrative professionals.[59] They sought knowledge for social policy, and used social policy for political ends. The Royal Commission on the Poor Laws, which reported twice in 1909, was the early debate which exposed this clash. Booth emerges as a key figure and honest broker in the early phases of the Commission's work, but he was to be elbowed out by the wranglings between the Bosanquets and the Webbs, who occupied key positions as both 'experts' on social policy and as political lobbyists.[60] This was the start of the process by which Booth's reputation and achievement has been progressively denigrated or ignored until recent years.

From a closer reading of *Life and Labour*, both the 'unknown Booth' of the notebooks, and the published volumes, Booth can be rescued from the condescension of those who refrained from engaging with the complexities of his views and his work. A discussion of gambling in *Life and Labour* does not give an impression that Booth's moral side got the better of his concern for objectivity. *Life and Labour* was both a product of its age and a significant advance in the scientific study of urban life. At a time when a great moral campaign was being waged against gambling, the analysis, which reflected perennial concerns about the problem, was careful and qualified. It was one small but revealing part in Booth's catholic approach to the interrelationship of all aspects of city life.[61]

(I am grateful to Mary Carter and John Mason for their comments on an earlier draft of this essay.)

Notes

1   Williams, Raymond (1973), *The Country and the City*, Palladin, pp.221–2.

2   Yeo, Eileen (1973), 'Mayhew as a Social Investigator', in Thompson, E.P. and Yeo, Eileen (eds) (1973), *The Unknown Mayhew: Selections from the Morning Chronicle*, Penguin, p.93.

3   Mott, James (1973), 'Miners, Weavers and Pigeon Racing', in Smith, Michael, Parker, Stanley and Smith, Cyril (eds) *Leisure and Society*, pp.88–9.

4   Mott, *ibid*. See also his (1975), 'Popular Gambling from the State Lotteries to the Rise of the Football Pools' for the Society for the Study of Labour History conference on *The Working Class and Leisure*.

5   Johnson, Samuel (1755), *Dictionary of the English Language*.

6   Mott, 'Pigeon Racing', pp.86–7.

7   Mayhew, Henry (1967), *London Labour and the London Poor*, 2, p.53.

8   BLPES, Booth Collection, B54, pp.25–6.

9   Booth, Charles (1891), *Life and Labour of the People in London*, First Series; *Poverty*, 2, p.74.

10   For example Spring Rice, Marjorie (1981), *Working-Class Wives*, pp.115–27. Campbell, Beatrice (1984), *Wigan Pier Revisited*, Virago, p.106.

11   *Religious Influences*, 1, p.252; 5, p.126.

12   On greyhound racing in London between the wars see Smith, H. Llewellyn (1935), *New Survey of London of London Life and Labour*, 9, P.S. King, pp.54–5.

13   Mayhew, *London Labour*, pp.63–4.

14   *Poverty*, 1, p.31.

15   *Poverty*, 2, p.83.

16   Glass, Ruth (1955), 'Urban Sociology: A Trend Report', *Current Sociology*, 4, pp.10–12. See also Marsden, W.E. in this volume.

17   *Religious Influences*, 2, p.246.

18   B47, p.155.

19   B28, p.24.

20   Bowley, Ruth 'Pigeon and Cage Bird Fancying', in Smith, H. Llewellyn (ed.) *New Survey of London Life and Labour*, 9, pp.70–1.

21   McKibbin, Ross (1979) 'Working-Class Gambling in Britain, 1880–1939,' *Past and Present*, 82, pp.148–50.

22   *Poverty*, 1, p.94.

23   Baxter, Arthur 'Drink, Gambling, Housing', ULL, Booth Correspondence, MS 797/2/32/4.

24   *Religious Influences,* 5, p.212.

25   B50, p.160.

26   Thus in B57, p.48, a Westminster SBV, Mr Mason, pointed to a 'Betting Man – so called 'Comm. Agent' living in Bear Yard. His class was given as C28, so he fared better than many on this score. His earnings were 'unknown', however, and his family was 'very poor and neglected'.

27   *Poverty,* 1, p.94.

28   *Ibid.,* p.38.

29   *Ibid.,* p.594. On 'Alsatia' see Weinreb, Ben and Hibbert, Christopher (1983), *The London Encyclopedia,* Macmillan, p.20.

30   *Religious Influences,* 2, p.98.

31   B47, p.209; B41, p.69.

32   *Poverty,* 1, p.43; Potter, Beatrice, 'The Docks'*, Poverty,* 4, pp.31–3.

33   Potter, 'The Docks', pp.31–2. Like Potter, Octavia Hill of the Charity Organization Society saw gambling as a predilection of those who would undermine their own lives and spoil things for those who worked to maintain their self-respect. In her discussion on the influence on character of model dwellings she attacked gambling on the stairs as a habit of the vicious and drunken people who degraded tenement blocks, and made intolerable the life of 'decent, hard working' families. *Poverty,* 2, p.266.

34   Potter, *ibid.*

35   Potter, Beatrice, 'The Jewish Community', in *Poverty,* pp.567–9; 583–4.

36   *Ibid.*

37   The Manchester Studies Jewish History Tape Collection, held at the Jewish Museum, Cheetham Hill. See, for example, the recollections of his father by Ben Weingard, Tape J253.

38   *The Licensed Bookmaker,* October 1962, pp.12–14.

39   Webb, Beatrice (1979), *My Apprenticeship,* Cambridge University Press, pp.32–3. But see O'Day, Rosemary (1993), 'Before the Webbs: Beatrice Potter's Early Investigations for Charles Booth's Inquiry', *History,* 78, pp.236–7 for detail of her information on gambling.

40   Englander, David (1989) 'Booth's Jews: The Presentation of Jews and Judaism in *Life and Labour of the People in London*', *Victorian Studies*, 32, (4), p. 557.

41   For discussions on the punters' rationale in such studies, see for example, (Lady) Bell, Florence (1985), *At the Works*, Virago; Mays, J.B. (1964), *Growing Up in the City*, p.101 and Appendix.

42   Booth, *ibid.*, p.43.

43   Booth, *ibid.*

44   *Poverty*, 2, p.8.

45   *Ibid.*, p.116

46   Hennock, E.P (1976), 'Poverty and Social Theory in England: the Experience of the Eighteen-Eighties', *Social History*, 1, p.83. MacGregor, Susanne (1981), *The Politics of Poverty*, p.63.

47   Rowntree, B.S (1980), *Poverty, A Study of Town Life*, p.144. See also Rowntree, B.S. (ed.) (1905), *Betting and Gambling: A National Evil*, Macmillan.

48   Simey, T.S. and Simey, M.B. (1960), *Charles Booth: Social Scientist,* Oxford University Press, p.220.

49   McLeod, Hugh, 'Working-Class Religion in Late Victorian London: Booth's 'Religious Influences' Revisited', in this volume.

50   *Poverty*, 2, p.88. See also 1, pp.89–90 and 5, p.164.

51   B262, pp.201, 206–7.

52   *Religious Influences*, 3, pp.147–8, Kensington; pp.194–5, Notting Dale. Vol.5, pp.125–6, Woolwich; p.154, Battersea; pp.202–06, and p.212, Putney. In Putney both the Wesleyan and Presbyterian churches complained of gambling and an atmosphere of pleasure seeking generally. The Presbyterian Minister told Booth: 'The churches do not prosper. The middle class here are as indifferent to religious observances as the poor elsewhere.' *Ibid*, p.212.

53   *Religious Influences,* 2, pp.72–4.

54   Rowntree B.S, 1905, *passim*; see also Lady Florence Bell.

55   Arthur Baxter, 'Drink'.

56   *Religious Influences*, 17, p.58.

57   Sherwell, Arthur (1901), *Life in West London,* p.1. See Chapter 2, 'Gambling and Intemperance', pp.126–32, and Chapter 3, 'Clubs and Saloons' pp.137–40 for Sherwell's observations on betting and gaming. Sherwell's criticism was in one respect premature. Booth's

survey of West London was undertaken in 1898 and published in 1902.

58   Glass, 'A Trend', p.8

59   Hobsbawm, E.J. (1979 edition), 'The Fabians Reconsidered', in *Labouring Men*, Weidenfeld and Nicholson, pp.267–8.

60   McBriar, A.M. (1987), *An Edwardian Mixed Doubles: The Bosanquets Versus the Webbs. A Study in British Social Policy*, Clarendon Press, *passim*, but especially, pp.188–9, pp.207–8.

61   Glass, 'A Trend', p.11. See also Wirth, Louis 'A Bibliography of the Urban Community', (1968), in Park, Robert and Burgess, Ernest W., *The City*, University of Chicago Press, p.188.

Select bibliography

This does not pretend to be an exhaustive bibliography. Rather, it is designed to assist those readers who wish to pursue the study of social investigation and social history further.

Manuscript collections

British Library of Political and Economic Science, London School of Economics:
    Booth Collection
    Passfield Papers
    Schloss Collection – Miscellaneous Collections
    Inhabitants of Katharine's Buildings, 1885–90 – Miscellaneous Collections
    New Survey of London Mss
    Courtney Papers – Kate Courtney's Diaries
    Beveridge Collection

Greater London Record Office
    Toynbee Hall Minute Books and Correspondence

Jewish Museum, Cheetham Hill
    The Manchester Studies Jewish History Tape Collection

Royal Statistical Society Library
    Minute Books, 1875–90, 1890–1909

University of London Library, Senate House
    Booth Correspondence, MS 797

University of Liverpool Library
    Booth Papers

University of Warwick, Modern Records Centre
    Collet MSS

Printed Primary Sources

    Parliamentary Papers

    PP.1842, XXVI: Edwin Chadwick, *Report on the Sanitary Condition of the Labouring Population of Great Britain.*
    PP.1856, XVII: *Second Report of the Select Committee of the House of Commons on Transportation.*
    PP.1881, VII; 1882, VII: *Select Committee on Artisans' and Labourers' Dwellings' Improvement.*

PP.1884–5, XXX: *Royal Commission on the Housing of the Working Classes.*

PP.1887, LXXXIX: John Burnett, *Report to the Board of Trade on the Sweating System of the East End of London.*

PP.1888, XX, XXI: 1890. XVII, *Select Committee on Sweating.*

PP.1892, XXIV, XXXV, XXXVI; 1893–4, XXXIII, XXXIV, XXXV, XXXVII, XXXVIII, XXXIX; 1894, XXXV: *Royal Commissions on Labour.*

PP.1895, VIII, IX: *Select Committee on Distress From Want of Employment.*

PP.1904, XXXII: *Inter-Departmental Committee on Physical Deterioration.*

PP.1909, XLII, XLIII, XLIV; 1910, XLIV, LIII: *Royal Commission on the Poor Laws and the Relief of Distress* (Special Reports).

Periodicals and newspapers consulted:

The Athenaeum
The Bookman
Charity Organization Review
Church Quarterly Review
The Colony (7 vols, 1866–71)
Contemporary Review
Economic Journal
Gunton's Magazine
Journal of the Royal Statistical Society
Literary World
London Quarterly Review
National Review
Nineteenth Century
Pall Mall Gazette
Philosophical Transactions of the Royal Society
Political Science Quarterly
Positivist Review
Quarterly Journal of Economics
Quarterly Review
Saturday Review
School Board Chronicle
Social Services Review
The Times
The Times Literary Supplement
Toynbee Record

Transactions of the British Association for the Advancement of Science.
Yale Review

Books, theses and articles

Abel, Emily Klein, 'Canon Barnett and the First Thirty Years of Toynbee Hall' (Unpublished University of London Ph.D. Thesis, 1969).

Abrams, Philip, *The Origins of British Sociology* (Chicago, 1968).

Acorn, George, *One of the Multitude* (London, 1911).

Adler, Henrietta, 'Jewish Life and Labour in East London' in Vol.6 of H.L. Smith (ed.), *The New Survey of London Life and Labour* (London, 1930–35).

Allen, V.L., 'Valuations and Historical Interpretations', *The Sociology of Industrial Relations* (London, 1971).

Annan, Noel, 'The Intellectual Aristocracy', in J.H. Plumb (ed.), *Studies in Social History* (London, 1955).

Anon., 'East London', *Literary World*, xx (1889).

Anon., 'Life and Labour in East London', *London Quarterly Review*, lxxiv (1890).

Ashley, W.J. 'Booth's East London', *Political Science Quarterly*, v (1891).

Ashton, T.S. *Economic and Social Investigations in Manchester, 1833–1933* (Hassocks, Sussex, 1977, reprint of 1934 book).

Atkinson, A.B., Corlyon, J., Maynard, A.K., Sutherland, H. and Trinder, C.G. 'Poverty in York: a true analysis of Rowntree's 1950 survey', *Bulletin of Economic Research*, 33 (1981).

Aves, Ernest, 'Obituary: Ernest Aves' by G.T.R., *Economic Journal*, xxvii (1917).

Bales, Kevin, 'Reclaiming Antique Data: Charles Booth's Poverty Survey', *Urban History Yearbook* (Leicester, 1986).

Barker, P. (ed.), *Founders of the Welfare State* (London, 1984).

Barker, Rodney, *Political Ideas in Modern Britain* (London, 1978).

Barnett, Henrietta, *Canon Barnett: His Life, Work and Friends* (London, 1921, 3rd edn).

Bartlett, Alan, 'The Church in Bermondsey, 1880–1939' (Unpublished University of Birmingham PhD Thesis, 1987).

Besant, W., *London North of the Thames* (London, 1911).

Beveridge, W.H., 'The Problem of the Unemployed', *Sociological Papers*, 3 (1906).

Black, Clementina, 'Labour and Life in London', *Contemporary Review*, 40 (1891).

Booth, Mary, *Charles Booth: A Memoir* (London, 1918).

Booth, William, *In Darkest England and the Way Out* (London, 1890).

Bosanquet, Bernard, (ed.) *Aspects of the Social Problem* (London, 1895).
'The Majority Report', *Sociological Review*, 2 (1909).
The Philosophical Theory of the State (London, 1899).

Bosanquet, Helen, *The Family* (London, 1906).
The Standard of Life (London, 1897).
The Strength of the People: A Study in Social Economics (London, 1903, 2nd edition).
'The Historical Basis of English Poor Law Policy', *Economic Journal,* 20 (June 1910).
'Physical Degeneration and the Poverty Line', *Contemporary Review*, lxxxv (1904).

Bowley, A.L. and Burnett-Hurst, *Livelihood and Poverty: A Study in the Economic and Social Conditions of Working-Class Households in Northampton, Warrington, Stanley, Reading (and Bolton)* (London, 1915).

Bowley, A.L. and Hogg, M.H., *Has Poverty Diminished?* (London, 1925).

Briggs, A., *Social Thought and Social Action: A Study of the Work of Seebohm Rowntree* (London, 1961).

Briggs, Asa and Anne Macartney, *Toynbee Hall: The First Hundred Years* (London, 1984).

Brown, John, 'Charles Booth and Labour Colonies, 1889–1905', *Economic History Review*, 2nd series, xxi (1968).

Brown, K.D., *A Social History of the Nonconformist Ministry* (Oxford, 1989).

Brown, M., *Introduction to Social Administration in Britain* (London, 1982).

Brown, M. and Madge, N., *Despite the Welfare State* (London, 1982).

Bruce, Maurice, *The Coming of the Welfare State* (London, 1961).

Bryce, James, *The American Commonwealth* (London, 1888).

Bulmer, M., (ed.), *Essays on the History of British Sociological Research* (Cambridge, 1985).

Bulmer, M., Lewis, J. and Rachaud, D. (eds), *The Goals of Social Policy* (London, 1989).

Bulmer, M., *The Social Survey in Historical Perspective* (Cambridge, 1991).

Caine, Barbara, *Destined to be Wives: The Sisters of Beatrice Webb* (Oxford, 1986).

Carpenter, N., 'Social Surveys' E.R.A. Seligman (ed.), *Encyclopaedia of the Social Sciences*, xv vols (New York, 1930–35), xiv.

Clegg, H.A., Fox, Alan and Thompson, A.F., *A History of British Trade Unions Since 1889* (Oxford,1964).

Cole, Margaret, *Beatrice Webb* (London, 1945).

Collet, Clara, Two Obituaries of Clara Collet, *Journal of the Royal Statistical Society*, Series A, cxi (1948).

Collini, Stefan, *Liberalism and Sociology: L.T. Hobhouse and Political Argument in England 1880–1914* (Cambridge, 1979). *Public Moralists, Political Thought and Intellectual Life in Britain, 1850–1930* (Oxford, 1991).
'The Idea of "Character" in Victorian Political Thought', *Transactions of the Royal Historical Society*, 35 (1985).

Collins, Doreen, 'The Introduction of Old-age Pensions in Great Britain', *Historical Journal*, 8 (1965).

Cox, Jeffrey, *The English Churches in a Secular Society* (Oxford, 1982).

Cripps, Alfred see Parmoor, Lord.

Crompton, Henry, *Industrial Conciliation* (London, 1876). *Letters on Social and Political Subjects Reprinted from the Sheffield Independent* (London, 1870).

Cullen, Michael J., *The Statistical Movement in Early Victorian Britain, The Foundations of Empirical Social Research* (Hassocks, Sussex, 1975).
'Charles Booth's Poverty Survey: some new approaches' in T.C. Smout (ed.), *The Search for Wealth and Stability. Essays in Economic and Social History* (London, 1979).

Dana, M. McG.,'Charles Booth and His Work', *Gunton's Magazine*, x (1896).

Davidson, Roger, *Whitehall and the Labour Problem in Late Victorian and Edwardian Britain* (London, 1985).

Davies, W.K.D., 'Charles Booth and the Measurement of Social Character', *Area*, 10 (1978).

Davis, John, 'Slums and the Vote, 1867–90', *Historical Research*, 64 (1991).

Dendy, H. (subsequently Bosanquet, Helen), 'The Industrial Residuum' in Bernard Bosanquet (ed.), *Aspects of the Social Problem* (London, 1895).
'Thorough Charity', *Charity Organization Review* (June 1893).

Dodd, George, *Days at the Factories* (London, 1843).

Drage, Geoffrey, *The Problem of the Aged Poor* (London, 1895).

Drinkwater, R.W., 'Seebohm Rowntree's Contribution to the Study of Poverty', *Advancement of Science*, 16 (1960).

DeSalvo, Louise, *Virginia Woolf: The Impact of Childhood Sexual Abuse on Her Life and Work* (London, 1989).

Dyos, H.G., 'The Slums of Victorian London', *Victorian Studies*, 11 (1967).

Elesh, David, 'The Manchester Statistical Society: A Case Study of Discontinuity in the History of Empirical Social Research' in OBERSCHALL (1972).

Endelman, Todd, 'Communal Solidarity and Family Loyalty among the Jewish Elite of Victorian London', *Victorian Studies*, 28 (1985).
Radical Assimilation in English Jewish History 1656–1945 (Bloomington, Indiana, 1990).

Englander, David, 'Booth's Jews: The Presentation of Jews and Judaism in *Life and Labour of the People in London'*, *Victorian Studies*, xxxii (1989).
A Documetary History of Jewish Immigrants in Britain, 1840–1920 (Leicester, 1994).
Landlord and Tenant in Urban Britian 1838–1918 (Oxford, 1983).
'Anglicised not Anglican: Jews and Judaism in Victorian Britain' in vol.I of G. Parsons (ed.), *Religion in Victorian Britain* (Manchester, 1988).
'Stille Huppah (Quiet Marriage) Among Jewish Immigrants in Britain', *The Jewish Journal of Sociology*, 34 (1992).

Epstein-Nord, Deborah, *The Apprenticeship of Beatrice Webb* (London, 1985).

Evans, E.J., (ed.) *Social Policy, 1830–1914* (London, 1978).

Feldman, David, *Englishmen and the Jews: Social Relations and Political Culture, 1840–1914* (London, 1994).

Field-Bibb, Jacqueline, *Women Towards Priesthood* (Cambridge, 1991).

Fishman, W.J., *East End Jewish Radicals 1870–1914* (London, 1975).

Forrest, Noah, 'The Chain and Tracemakers of Cradley Heath', *Transactions of the National Association for the Promotion of Social Science* (1859).

Freeden, Michael, *The New Liberalism: An Ideology of Social Reform* (Oxford, 1978).

Fried, A. and R. Eldman (eds), *Charles Booth's London* (Harmondsworth, 1971).

Gainer, Bernard, *The Alien Invasion, The Origins of the Aliens Act of 1905* (London, 1972).

Galton, F., 'Investigating with the Webbs' in Margaret Cole (ed.), *The Webbs and their Work* (London, 1949).

Gardiner, A.G., *Pillars of Society* (London, 1916).

Gartner, Lloyd P., *The Jewish Immigrant in England 1870–1914* (London, 2nd edn 1973).

Gaskell, G.A., *The Futility of Pecuniary Thrift as a means of General Wellbeing* (London, 1890).

Gautrey, T., *'Lux Mihi Laus': School Board Memories* (1937).

Gide, Charles and Charles Rist, *A History of Economic Doctrines: From the Time of the Physiocrats to the Present Day* (London, 2nd edn,1948).

Gilbert, A.D., *Religion and Society in Industrial England: Church, Chapel and Social Change 1740–1911* (London, 1976).

Gilbert, Bentley B., *The Evolution of National Insurance in Great Britain. The Origins of the Welfare State* (London, 1966).

Glass, Ruth, 'Urban Sociology in Great Britain', *Current Sociology*, 4 (1955).

Goldmann, Lawrence, 'The Social Science Association and the Absence of Sociology in Nineteenth-Century Britain', *Past and Present*, cxiv (1987).

Goldsmith, M.M., *Private Vices, Public Benefits* (Cambridge, 1985).

Green, David, 'The Poverty of an English Town', *Yale Review* (1903).

Harris, José, *Beatrice Webb, The Ambivalent Feminist*, London
School of Economics Lecture (London, 1984).
'The Webbs, the COS and the Ratan Tata Foundation: social
policy from the perspective of 1912', in Bulmer, M. (1989).
William Beveridge: A Biography (Oxford, 1977).

Harrison, Brian, 'The Pub and the People', in H.G. Dyos and M.
Wolff (eds), *The Victorian City: Images and Realities* (London,
1973).
Peaceable Kingdom: Stability and Change in Modern Britain
(Oxford, 1982).

Harrison, Royden, *Before the Socialists: Studies in Labour and
Politics, 1861–1881* (London, 1965).
'The Webbs as Historians of Trades Unionism', in Raphael
Samuel (ed.), *People's History and Socialist Theory* (London,
1981).

Harrison, Royden and Jonathan Zeitlin (eds), *Divisions of Labour:
Skilled Workers and Technological Change in Nineteenth-
Century England* (Brighton, 1985).

Harvie, Christopher, *The Lights of Liberalism: University Liberals and
the Challenge of Democracy 1860–1886* (London, 1976).

Hennock, E.P., 'Poverty and Social Theory in England: The
Experience of the Eighteen-Eighties', *Social History*, i (1976).
'The Measurement of Urban Poverty: From the Metropolis to the
Nation, 1880–1920', *Economic History Review,* 2nd series, xi
(1987).
'Concepts of Poverty in the British Social Surveys from Charles
Booth to Arthur Bowley', M. Bulmer et al. (eds), *The Social
Survey in Historical Perspective, 1880–1940* (Cambridge, 1992).

Herbert, Christopher, *Culture and Anomie: Ethnographic Imagination
in the Nineteenth Century* (Chicago and London, 1991).

Hill, Octavia, *Homes of the London Poor* (London, 1975).
Letter to My Fellow Workers (London, 1889).

Himmelfarb, Gertrude, 'Bentham's Utopia: The National Charity
Company', *Journal of British Studies* (1970).
The Idea of Poverty: England in the Early Industrial Age
(London, 1985).
*Poverty and Compassion: The Moral Imagination of the Late
Victorians* (New York, 1991).

Hobsbawm, E.J., *Labouring Men* (London, 1964).

Hobson, J.A., *Capitalism. A Study of Machine Production* (London, 1894).

Hollingsworth, T.H., *Historical Demography* (London, 1969).

Holmes, Colin, *Anti-Semitism in British Society 1876–1939* (London, 1979).

Humpherys, Anne, *Travels into the Poor Man's Country: The Works of Henry Mayhew* (Athens, Georgia, 1977).
(ed.) *Voices of the Poor; Selections from Mayhew's Morning Chronicle Letters* (London, 1971).

Hunt, E.H., *British Labour History, 1815–1914* (London, 1981).

Hutchinson, T.W., *A Review of Economic Doctrines, 1870–1929* (Oxford, 1960).

Huxley, T.H., *Evolution, Ethics and Other Essays* (London, 1894).

Hyde, R., *Printed Maps of Victorian London, 1851–1900* (Folkestone, 1975).

Hyman, Herbert H., *Interviewing in Social Research* (Chicago, 1954).

Hyndman, H.M., *Commercial Crises of the Nineteenth Century* (London, 1892).
Record of an Adventurous Life (London, 1911).

Ikin, J.J., 'On the Prevalent Causes of Rejection of Recruits, Enlisted in the West Riding and Northern Districts' *NAPSS Transactions* (1864).

Jay, Osborne, *The Social Problem: Its Possible Solution* (London, 1893).

Jones, Gareth Stedman., *Languages of Class: Studies in English Working Class History, 1832–1982* (Cambridge, 1983).
Outcast London: A Study in the Relationship between Classes in Victorian Society (Oxford, 1971).
'The Labours of Henry Mayhew, "Metropolitan Correspondent"', *London Journal*, 10 (1984).

Jones, Greta, *Social Darwinism and English Thought. The Interaction between Biological and Social Theory* (Brighton, 1980).

Kadish, Alon, *The Oxford Economists* (Oxford, 1982).
Apostle Arnold. The Life and Death of Arnold Toynbee 1852–1883 (Durham, North Carolina, 1986).

Kaplan, Stanley, 'The Anglicization of the East European Jewish Immigrant as Seen by the London *Jewish Chronicle*, 1870–1897', *YIVO Annual for Jewish Social Science*, 10 (1955).

Keating, P.J., *The Working Classes in Victorian Fiction* (London, 1971).
Into Unknown England, 1866–1913 (Glasgow and Manchester, 1976).

Kent, Raymond, *A History of Empirical Sociology* (Aldershot, 1981).

Kershen, Anne J., 'Henry Mayhew and Charles Booth: Men of their Times?' in Alderman G. and Holmes, C. (eds), *Outsiders and Outcasts: Essays in Honour of William J. Fishman* (London, 1993).

Lazarfeld, Paul F., 'Notes on the History of Quantification in Sociology – Trends, Sources and Problems', *Isis*, lii (1961).

Lees, Lynn H., *Exiles of Erin: Irish Migrants in Victorian London* (Manchester, 1979).

Levy, Carl (ed.), *Socialism and the Intelligentsia, 1880–1914* (London,1987).

Lewis, Jane, 'Parents, Children, School Fees and the London School Board 1870–1890', *History of Education*, xi (1982).
Women and Social Action in Victorian and Edwardian England (Aldershot, 1991).

Lipman, V.D., *A Social History of the Jews in England, 1850–1950* (London, 1954).
'The Rise of Jewish Suburbia', *Transactions of the Jewish Historical Society of England*, 21 (1926–7).

Loch, C.S., 'Charity Organisation and the Feeble-Minded', *Charity Organization Review*, 33 (1913).

Loewe, L.L., *Basil Henriques: A Portrait* (London, 1976).

Lovell, John, *Stevedores and Dockers* (London, 1969).

Lummis, Trevor, 'Charles Booth: Moralist or Social Scientist', *Economic History Review*, 2nd series xxiv (1971).

McBriar, A.M., *Fabian Socialism and English Politics, 1884–1918* (Cambridge, 1966).
An Edwardian Mixed Doubles: the Bosanquets versus the Webbs. A study in British social policy (Oxford, 1987).

McClachlan, H.V., 'Townsend and the Concept of "Poverty"', *Social Policy and Administration*, 17 (1983).

McCormack, Dr Henry, 'A Few Particulars relative to our Town-Poor, especially the Irish Town-Poor, *NAPSS Transactions* (1861).

McGee, J.E., *A Crusade for Humanity: The History of Organized Positivism in England* (London, 1931).

McIlhinney, D.B., 'A Gentleman in Every Slum: Church of England Missions in East London 1837–1914' (Unpublished Princeton University PhD Thesis, 1977).

McKibbin, R.I., 'Social Class and Social Observation in Edwardian England', *Transactions of the Royal Historical Society* (1978). *The Ideologies of Class. Social Relations in England 1880–1950* (Oxford, 1990).
'Working-Class Gambling in Britain, 1880–1939', *Past and Present*, 82 (1979).

McLeod, Hugh, *Class and Religion in the Late Victorian City* (London, 1974).
'The Culture of Popular Catholicism in New York City in the Later Nineteenth and Early Twentieth Centuries', in Heerma van Voss, Lex (ed.), *Working Class and Popular Culture* (Amsterdam, 1988).

Macgregor, D.H., 'The Poverty Figures', *Economic Journal*, xx (1910).

Mackenzie, Norman (ed.), *The Letters of Sidney and Beatrice Webb*, 3 vols (London and Cambridge, 1978).

Mackenzie, Norman and Jeanne, *The Diary of Beatrice Webb,* 4 vols (London, 1982–86).

Macnicol, John, 'In Pursuit of the Underclass,' *Journal of Social Policy,* 16 (1987).

Madge, John, *The Origins of Scientific Sociology* (London, 1963).
The Tools of Social Science (London, 1967).

Maloney, John, *Marshall, Orthodoxy and the Professionalisation of Economics* (Cambridge, 1985).

Marchant, C., 'Interaction of Church and Society in an East London Borough (West Ham)' (Unpublished University of London PhD Thesis, 1979).

Marsden, W.E., *Educating the Respectable: A Study of Fleet Road Board School, 1879–1903* (1990).
'Education and the Social Geography of Nineteenth-Century Towns and Cities' in D. Reeder, (1977).

'Residential Segregation and the Hierarchy of Elementary
Schooling from Charles Booth's London Surveys', *The London
Journal*, xi (1985).

Marshall, Alfred, *Principles of Economics* (London, 1930).

Marshall, T.H., *The Right to Welfare and Other Essays* (London,
1981).
'Poverty or Deprivation?', *Journal of Social Policy*, 10 (1981).

Masterman, C.F.G., 'The Social Abyss', *Contemporary Review*, lxxxi
(1902).

Maurice, C. Edmund, *Life of Octavia Hill* (London, 1913).

Maurice, Emily, *Octavia Hill, Early Ideals* (London, 1928).

Maus, Heinz, *A Short History of Sociology* (London, 1962).

Mayhew, Henry, *The Morning Chronicle Survey of Labour and the
Poor*, Peter Razell (ed.), 6 vols. (Caliban, 1980).
London Labour and the London Poor, 4 vols (London, 1861–62).
London Labour and the London Poor, 3 vols (London, 1851–52)
BL Pressmark 8276c.55. (Contains bound wrappers with Answers
to Correspondents).
Low Wages: Their Causes, Consequences and Remedies (London,
1851).
German Life and Manners, 2 vols (London, 1864).
'What is the Cause of Surprise? and What Connection has it with
Suggestion?', *Douglas Jerrold's Shilling Magazine*, 6 (1847).

Mayhew, Henry and Binny, John, *The Criminal Prisons of London*
(London, 1862).

Meacham, Standish, *Toynbee Hall and Social Reform 1880–1914*
(New Haven, 1987).

Mencher, S., 'The Problem of Measuring Poverty', *British Journal of
Sociology*, 18 (1967).

Mill, J.S., *Principles of Political Economy,* W.J. Ashley (ed.)
(London, 1909).

Miller, Jane, *Seductions* (London, 1990).

Moore, Robert, *Pit-men, Politics and Preachers* (London, 1974).

More, Charles, *Skill and the English Working Class, 1870–1914*
(London, 1980).

Morris, J.N. 'Religion and Urban Change in Victorian England: A
Case-Study of the Borough of Croydon, 1840–1914'
(Unpublished University of Oxford D.Phil. Thesis, 1986).

Moser, C.A., *Survey Methods in Social Investigation* (London, 1958).

Mudie-Smith, Richard, *The Religious Life of London* (London, 1904).

Munroe, J.P., *A Life of Francis Amasa Walker* (New York, 1923).

National Birth Rate Commission, *The Declining Birth Rate. Its Causes and Effects* (London, 1916).

Nevinson, Margaret Wynne, *Life's Fitful Fever: A Volume of Memories* (London, 1926).

Newman, Aubrey (ed.), *The Jewish East End 1840–1939* (London, 1981).

Newman, George, *The Nation's Health* (London, 1908).

Newton, Bernard, *The Economics of Francis Amasa Walker: American Economics in Transition* (New York, 1968).

Nord, Deborah Epstein, *The Apprenticeship of Beatrice Webb* (London, 1985).

Norman-Butler, Belinda, *Victorian Aspirations: The Life and Labour of Charles and Mary Booth* (London, 1972).

O'Day, Rosemary, 'Interviews and Investigations: Charles Booth and the Making of the Religious Influences Series', *History*, lxxiv (1989).
'The Men from the Ministry', in Gerald Parsons (ed.) *Religion in Victorian Britain*, 4 vols, ii, (Manchester, 1988).
'Before the Webbs: Beatrice Potter's Early Investigations for Charles Booth's Inquiry', *History*, lxxviii (1993).
'How Families Lived Then: Katharine Buildings, East Smithfield, 1885–1890', in R. Finnegan and M. Drake (eds), *From Family Tree to Family History* (Cambridge, 1994), pp.129,166.

O'Day, Rosemary and Englander, David, *Mr Charles Booth's Inquiry: Life and Labour of the People in London Reconsidered* (London, 1993).

Oberschall, Anthony (ed.) *The Establishment of Empirical Sociology, Studies in Continuity, Discontinuity, and Institutionalization* (New York, 1972).

Percivall, T. 'Observations on the State of Population in Manchester and other adjacent places', *Philosophical Transactions of the Royal Society*, 64–6, (1774, 1775, 1776).

Pfautz, Harold W. (ed.), *Charles Booth and the City* (Chicago and London, 1973 edn).

Phillips, Gordon and Noel Whiteside, *Casual Labour: The Unemployment Question in the Port Transport Industry, 1880–1970* (Oxford, 1985).

Pick, D., *Faces of Degeneration* (Cambridge, 1989).

Pimlott, J.R., *Toynbee Hall* (London, 1935).

Prochaska, F.K., 'Body and Soul: Bible Nurses and the Poor in Victorian London', *Historical Research*, 60 (1987).
Women and Philanthropy in 19th Century England (Oxford, 1980).

Reeder, David (ed.) *Urban Education in the Nineteenth Century* (London, 1977).

Reisman, David, *Alfred Marshall. Progress and Politics* (London, 1987).

Reynolds, Stephen, *Seems So! A Working-Class View of Politics* (London, 1913).

Ricci, D.M., 'Fabian Socialism: The Theory of Rent as Exploitation', *Journal of British Studies*, ix (1969).

Richman, Geoff, *Fly a Flag for Poplar* (London, 1976).

Robertson, J.M., *The Fallacy of Saving. A Study in Economics* (London, 1892).

Rogers, Frederick, *Labour Life and Literature: Some Memories of Sixty Years* (London, 1913).

Ross, Ellen, '"Fierce Questions and Taunts": Married Life in Working-Class London, 1870–1914', *Feminist Studies*, 8 (1982).
'Survival Networks: Women's Neighbourhood Sharing in London Before World War I', *History Workshop Journal*, 15 (1983).
'Hungry Children: Housewives and London Charity, 1870–1918' in Peter Mandler (ed.), *The Uses of Charity: The Poor on Relief in the Nineteenth Century Metropolis* (Philadelphia, 1990).
Love and Toil. Motherhood in Outcast London (Oxford, 1994).

Rowe, J.W.F., *Wages in Practice and Theory* (London, 1928).

Royle, Edward, *Modern Britain: A Social History, 1750–1985* (London, 1986).

Rubinstein, David, 'Booth and Hyndman', *Bulletin of the Society for the Study of Labour History*, xvi (1968).
School Attendance in London, 1870–1906: A Social History, Occasional Papers in Economic and Social History, i (Hull, 1969).

Russell, Charles and Lewis, H.S., *The Jew in London. A Study of Racial Character and Present-day Conditions* (London, 1900).

Samuel, Raphael, 'Comers and Goers' in H.G. Dyos and M.Wolff (eds), *The Victorian City: Images and Realities*, 2 vols (London, 1973).
'Mayhew and Labour Historians', *Bulletin of the Society for the Study of Labour History*, 26 (1973).
East End Underworld: Chapters in the Life of Arthur Harding (London, 1981).

Scannell, Dolly, *Mother Knew Best* (London, 1975).

Schmiechen, James A., *Sweated Industries and Sweated Labour. The London Clothing Trades, 1860–1914* (London, 1984).

Schumpeter, Joseph, *A History of Economic Analysis* (London, 1954).

Selvin, H.C., 'Durkheim, Booth and Yule: The Non-Diffusion of an Intellectual Innovation', *European Journal of Sociology*, xvii (1976).

Sharot, Stephen, 'Religious Change in Native Orthodoxy in London 1870–1914: Rabbinate and Clergy', *Jewish Journal of Sociology*, 15 (1973).

Shaw, Christopher, 'Eliminating the Yahoo. Eugenics, Social Darwinism and Five Fabians', *History of Political Thought*, 8 (1987).

Sherwell, Arthur, *Life in West London* (London, 1901).

Shipley, Stan, *Club Life and Socialism in Mid-Victorian London* (Oxford, 1971).

Sills, David, (ed.) *International Encyclopaedia of Social Sciences*, 18 vols. (New York, 1968–9).

Simey, T.S., 'The Contribution of Sidney and Beatrice Webb to Sociology', *British Journal of Sociology*, xii (1960).

Simey, T.S. and Simey, M.B., *Charles Booth, Social Scientist* (Oxford, 1960).

Smith, F.B., 'Mayhew's Convict', *Victorian Studies*, 22 (1979).

Smith, Michael, Parker, Stanley and Smith, Cyril (eds), *Leisure and Society* (London, 1973).

Soffer, Reba N., *Ethics and Society in England: The Revolution in the Social Sciences, 1870–1914* (Berkeley, 1978).

Spotts, Frederic (ed.), *Letters of Leonard Woolf* (London, 1989).

Sprott, W.J., 'Sociology in Britain: Preoccupations', in Howard
    Becker and Alvin Boskoff (eds), *Modern Sociological Theory in
    Continuity and Change* (New York, 1957).

Swift, Roger and Gilley, Sheridan (eds), *The Irish in the Victorian
    City* (London, 1985).

Swinny, S.H., 'Charles Booth', *Positivist Review*, xxvii (1919).

Tarn, J.N., *Five Per Cent Philanthropy* (Cambridge, 1974).

Thane, P., *The Foundations of the Welfare State* (London, 1982).

Thompson, E.P., 'The Political Education of Henry Mayhew',
    Victorian Studies, 11 (1967).

Thompson, E.P. and Yeo, Eileen (eds), *The Unknown Mayhew*
    (Harmondsworth, 1973).

Thompson, F.M.L., *Hampstead: Building a Borough, 1650–1964*
    (London, 1974).

Thompson, Paul, *The Edwardians* (London, 1977).
    *Socialists, Liberals and Labour in the Struggle for London, 1885–
    1914* (London, 1967).

Titmuss, R.M., *Essays on the Welfare State* (London, 1958).

Topalov, Christian, 'La Ville "Terre Inconnue". L'Enquete de Charles
    Booth et le Peuple de Londres 1886–1891', *Geneses*, v (1991).

Townsend, P., 'Measuring Poverty', *British Journal of Sociology*
    (1954).
    Poverty in the United Kingdom (Harmondsworth, 1979).
    (ed.), *The Concept of Poverty* (London, 1970).

Treble, J.H., *Urban Poverty in Britain* (London, 1979).

Veit-Wilson, J.H., 'Consensual Approaches to Poverty Lines and
    Social Security', *Journal of Social Policy*, 16 (1987).
    'Paradigms of Poverty: A Rehabilitation of B. S. Rowntree',
    Journal of Social Policy, xv (1986).

Vicinus, Martha, *Independent Women: Work and Community for
    Single Women, 1850–1920* (London, 1985).

Vincent, A.W., 'The Poor Law Reports of 1909 and the Social Theory
    of the COS', *Victorian Studies*, 27 (1984).

Vincent, Andrew and Plant, Raymond, *Philosophy, Politics and
    Citizenship. The Life and Thought of the British Idealists* (Oxford,
    1984).

Walker, Francis Amasa, *Political Economy* (London, 1883).

The Wages Question: A Treatise on Wages and the Wages Class (London, 1876).

Wells, A.F., *The Local Social Survey in Great Britain* (London, 1935).

Wells, David, 'The Great Depression of Trade. A Study of Its Economic Causes, Part I', *The Contemporary Review*, 52 (August 1887).

White, Jerry, 'Jewish Landlords, Jewish Tenants: An Aspect of Class Struggle within the Jewish East End, 1881–1914' in Newman, 1981.

Williams, Gertrude, *The State and the Standard of Living* (London, 1936).

Williams, K., *From Pauperism to Poverty* (London, 1981).

Williams, Raymond, *The Country and the City* (London, 1973).

Wilson, Charles, *England's Apprenticeship* (London, 1965).

Wolfe, Willard, *From Radicalism to Socialism: Men and Ideas in the Formation of Fabian Socialist Doctrines, 1881–1889* (New Haven and London, 1975).

Woodward, Eileen, *Jipping Street* (London, 1928).

Wright, Thomas, *Our New Masters* (London, 1873).

Wright, T.R., *The Religion of Humanity. The Impact of Comtean Positivism on Victorian Britain* (Cambridge, 1986).

Yeo, Eileen, 'The Social Survey in Historical Perspective, 1830–1930' in Martin Bulmer et al., (1991).

The principal works of Henry Mayhew

The Morning Chronicle Survey of Labour and the Poor, Peter Razell (ed.), 6 vols. (Caliban, 1980).
London Labour and the London Poor, 4 vols (London, 1861–62).
London Labour and the London Poor, 3 vols (London, 1851–52) BL Pressmark. (Contains bound wrappers with Answers to Correspondents.)
Low Wages: Their Causes, Consequences and Remedies (London, 1851).
German Life and Manners, 2 vols (London, 1864).
'What is the Cause of Surprise? and What Connection has it with Suggestion?', *Douglas Jerrold's Shilling Magazine*, 6 (1847).

Mayhew, Henry and Binny, John, *The Criminal Prisons of London*
(London, 1862).

The principal works by Charles Booth and his team
(including H.L. Smith and Beatrice Potter)

Booth, Charles
'Occupations of the People of the United Kingdom, 1801–81',
Journal of the Royal Statistical Society, xlix (1886).
England and Ireland: A Counter Proposal (London, 1886).
'The Inhabitants of Tower Hamlets (School Board Division), their
Condition and Occupations', *Journal of the Royal Statistical
Society*, l (1887).
'The Condition and Occupations of the People of East London
and Hackney, 1887', *Journal of the Royal Statistical Society*, li
(1888).
Life and Labour of the People, 2 vols (London, 1889).
'Enumeration and Classification of Paupers, and State Pensions
for the Aged', *Journal of the Royal Statistical Society,* liv (1891).
Pauperism: a Picture.The Endowment of Old Age: an Argument
(London, 1892).
Presidential Address on Dock and Wharf Labour, *Journal of the
Royal Statistical Society*, lv (1892).
Presidential Address: 'Life and Labour of the People in London:
first results of an Inquiry based on the 1891 Census', *Journal of
the Royal Statistical Society*, lvi (1893).
Life and Labour of the People in London, 10 vols (London, 1892–
97) The last volume contains maps.
'Statistics of Pauperism in Old Age', *Journal of the Royal
Statistical Society*, lvii (1894).
The Aged Poor in England and Wales: Condition (London, 1894).
Old Age Pensions and the Aged Poor: a Proposal (London,
1899).
*Improved Means of Locomotion as a First Step Towards the Cure
for the Housing Difficulties of London* (London, 1901).
Life and Labour of the People in London, xvii vols, (London,
1902–03).
'Fiscal Reform', *National Review* (1904).
Poor Law Reform (London, 1910).
*Reform of the Poor Law by the Adaptation of the Existing Poor
Law Areas, and their Administration* (London, 1910).

Comments on Proposals for the Reform of the Poor Laws
(London, 1911).
Industrial Unrest and Trade Union Policy (London,1913).

Booth, Charles, Ernest Aves and Henry Higgs, *Family Budgets: Being
the Income and Expenses of Twenty-Eight British Households,
1891–1894* (London, 1896).

Aves, Ernest, 'Some Recent Labour Disputes', *Economic Journal*
(1897).
'Labour Notes', *Economic Journal* (1898–1906).
Co-operative Industry (London, 1907).

Booth, Mary, *Charles Booth: A Memoir* (London, 1918).

Collet, Clara, *The Economic Position of Educated Working Women*
(London, 1902).
Women in Industry (London, 1911).
The History of the Collet Family (London, 1935).
'Some Recollections of Charles Booth', *Social Services Review*
(1927).

Cripps, Alfred (Lord Parmoor) Parmoor, Lord, *A Retrospect* (London,
1936).

Duckworth, G.H., 'The Making, Prevention and Unmaking of a
Slum', *Journal of the Institute of British Architects*, xxxiii (1926).
'The Work of the Select Committee of the House of Commons on
Distress from Want of Employment', *Economic Journal*, vi
(1896).

Fox, Stephen N., 'The Factories and Workshops Bill', *Economic
Journal*, x (1900).

Higgs, Henry, 'Workmen's Budgets', *Journal of the Royal Statistical
Society*, lvi (1893).

Howard, Esmé, *Theatre of Life*, 2 vols (London, 1935).

Nevinson, Henry Woodd (sic), *Last Changes, Last Chances* (London,
1928).

Parmoor, Lord, *A Retrospect* (London, 1936).

Schloss, David, *Insurance Against Unemployment* (London, 1909).
Methods of Industrial Remuneration (London, 1892).
'The Reorganisation of our Labour Department', *Journal of the
Royal Statistical Society*, lvi (1893).
'Sweating System', *Encyclopaedia Britannica*, 11th edn (1910).

Smith, Hubert Llewellyn, *The Story of the Dockers' Strike* (with
Vaughan Nash) (London, 1890).

The Board of Trade (London, 1928).
History of East London (London, 1939).
New Survey of London Life and Labour (London, 1928–35).

Webb, Beatrice (including work while she was Beatrice Potter)
My Apprenticeship (Harmondsworth, 1971 edn).
Our Partnership B. Drake and M. Cole (eds) (London, 1948).
'The Dock Life of East London', *Nineteenth Century*, xxii (1887).
The Co-operative Movement in Great Britain (London, 1891).
Women and the Factory Acts, Fabian Tract no.67 (1896).

Webb, Sidney and Beatrice
The History of Trade Unionism (London, 1894).
Industrial Democracy (London, 1897).
English Local Government (London, 1906–22).
English Poor Law History (London, 1927–29).
Methods of Social Study (London, 1932).
Soviet Communism: A New Civilization? (London, 1935).

The works of B.S. Rowntree

Poverty: A Study of Town Life (London, 1901).
The Poverty Line: A Reply (London, 1904).
Betting and Gambling: A National Evil (London, 1905).
Poverty and Progress (London, 1941).
The Human Needs of Labour (London, 1937).

Rowntree, B.S. and Kendall, M., *How the Labourer Lives* (London, 1913).

Other works of social inquiry

Besant, W., *London North of the Thames* (London, 1911).

Bosanquet, Bernard (ed.) *Aspects of the Social Problem* (London, 1895).
'The Majority Report', *Sociological Review*, 2 (1909).
The Philosophical Theory of the State (London, 1899).

Bosanquet, Helen, *The Family* (London, 1906).
The Standard of Life (London, 1897).
The Strength of the People: A Study in Social Economics (London, 2nd edition, 1903).
'The Historical Basis of English Poor Law Policy', *Economic Journal*, 20 (June 1910).

'Physical Degeneration and the Poverty Line', *Contemporary Review*, lxxxv (1904).

Bowley, A.L. and Burnett-Hurst, *Livelihood and Poverty: A Study in the Economic and Social Conditions of Working-Class Households in Northampton, Warrington, Stanley, Reading (and Bolton)* (London, 1915).

Dendy, H. (subsequently Bosanquet, Helen), 'The Industrial Residuum' in Bernard Bosanquet (ed.), *Aspects of the Social Problem* (London, 1895).
'Thorough Charity', *Charity Organization Review* (June 1893).

Howarth, E. G. and Wilson, Mona, *West Ham, A Study in Social and Industrial Problems* (London, 1907).

Russell, Charles and Lewis, H.S., *The Jew in London. A Study of Racial Character and Present-day Conditions* (London, 1900).

Sherwell, Arthur, *Life in West London* (London, 1901).

Index

For reasons of space, this index is restricted in the main to proper names of persons and places. A limited number of other topics are also indexed. Because there is scarcely a page without mention of Charles Booth, the reader will not find all references to this name in the index.

Aarons, Joseph, 190
Acland, A.H.D., 22, 24
Acorn, George, 280
Adams, Mr W.B., 255–6
Adamson, Revd W., 153, 155, 353
Adelphi Terrace, 24, 27, 149
admissions registers, 243
agnostic, 271
All Hallows, Bromley, 153, 155
All Hallows Church, 281
All Hallows, East India Docks, 151–2
All Saints, Poplar, 150
Allen, Percival Burt, 21
Allnutt, Revd M.R., 353
Amalgamated Stevedores' Society, 183
Ammon, Charles, 282
amusements, 324
Anglican (and derivatives), 267, 271–3, 279, 281
Anglo-Catholics, 266, 273
Annales d'hygiène publique, 110
Annan, Noel, 26
anthropology, 117
anti-clericalism, 273
anti-semitism, 107
appearance, 327
Appleton, Revd R., 345, 348, 349, 352
Argyle, Jesse, 22, 24, 27, 38, 146, 182, 186, 257, 271

Arkell, George, 22, 27–9, 38, 146, 150, 186–8, 192–3, 265, 271
army personnel, 326
Aronson, N., 204, 227, 233, 237
artisan (and derivatives), 109, 113–14, 116, 130, 255, 259, 333
Ashby-de-la-Zouche workhouse, 176
Ashton, T.S., 7, 9
assistant teachers, 256, 259
associates, Booth's, 19, 21–2, 24–8, 126, 132–3, 166, 266, 329, 346, 357
Association of Assistant Schoolmistresses, 167, 178
Association of Medical Officers of Health, 69
attendance, church (see also church going), 5–6, 270, 339, 341–2, 344, 346
attendance, school, 242, 247, 260
attitudes, 273, 327
authority, 343, 345
autobiography, 52–4, 165–200, 276
Aveling, Ernest, 176
Aves, Ernest, 21–2, 25, 26, 29–30, 38, 146, 150, 155, 156, 186–7, 190, 265, 271, 273, 274, 278, 346, 355

Babbage, Charles, 6, 115
Balfour, Graham, 24, 28, 176,
    191
Bands of Hope, 249, 350
Bangor Street, Notting Dale, 331
Bank Holiday, 347
bankruptcy (and derivatives),
    107–8
baptism, 350
Baptist, 275, 282, 340
Baptist Chapel, Denmark Place,
    341, 347
Baptist Chapel, Durand Gardens,
    Stockwell, 354
Barly, Revd Vere, 151, 341, 343
Barnett, Samuel Augustus, 15, 21,
    31–2, 54, 181, 187
barriers, physical, 330
Barrow Hill Road Board School,
    257
Bartlett, Alan, 37, 268–71, 275–7,
    299
Battersea, 24, 176, 191, 329
Battersea School, 259
Baxter, Arthur Lionel, 31, 38,
    146, 151–2, 155 265, 271–5,
    369
Beale, G.W., 156
Beale, Mrs, 354
Beck, Mr, 183
Beckett, Gilbert, 108
Bedford College, London, 167,
    172
Bedford, Revd A.W., 151–2
bedrooms, 327
beer, 267
beggars, 110, 268
behaviour, 333
beliefs, 114
Bell, Lady Florence, 79
Bell, T.D., 151
Belvedere Place Board School,
    259

Bennett, A. Wentworth, 155
Bentham, Jeremy, 73
Benthamism, 118
Benthamite social analysis, 5, 119
Berlin, 282
Bermondsey, 127–8, 246, 248,
    268, 270–1, 275, 280, 332
Bermondsey New Road, 332
Berner Street, 252
Berthoud, R. and Brown, J., 203,
    232
Besant, Walter, 105, 255
bet, 267
Bethnal Green, 77, 246, 257, 275,
    280–1, 332, 367, 370
betting, street, 368–9
Betts Street, 252
Beveridge, William, 21, 60, 69,
    72, 78, 81, 228, 229
bias, 112, 118, 127, 326
Bible, 9, 349
Bible classes, 281, 341–2, 347
Bible nurse, 353
Bible reading, 341–2
Bible women, 356
bicycling, 341
billiards, 267
Bink's Row, 252
bird breeding and fancying, 367–8
bird fair, Sclater Street, Bethnal
    Green, 368
Birmingham, 5
black and blue localities, 331–2
Black, Clementina, 169, 177
Blakesley Street, 252
block dwellings, 333
blue book, 5, 109–10
Board of Education, 70
Board of Statistical Inquiry
    (Research), 181, 323
Board of Trade, 8, 10, 18, 24–5,
    72, 167, 177–8, 187, 193

Board school catchment zones, 253
Board school teachers, 348
Board schools, 247, 252, 259–60, 274
    penny, 248
boarding house, 347
Bolton, 4
Bonar, James, 22
book binders, 130
Book of Common Prayer, 355
book trade, 129
bookmakers, 368–72
boot and shoe trade, 21, 28, 186
boot makers, 109, 186
Booth, Charles
    background, 12
    comparison with Henry Mayhew, 105–42
    economist, under-consumptionist, 89–102
    interest in social action, 14
    interest in social problems, 12
    sense of personal responsibility, 13
    social investigator, role and reputation, 365–80
    symposium with socialists, 15–21
Booth Collection, 265–6, 268, 270–1, 275–6
Booth, General William, 69, 72
Booth, Mary, 14–15, 23, 25–6, 28, 31, 36, 49, 54, 181–2
Borough Road, 259
Bosanquet, Bernard, 49, 57, 61–2
Bosanquet, Helen (Dendy), 49–53, 56–7, 59–61, 63, 71–3, 77, 79, 81–2, 213–4, 217
Bouchier, Revd Walter, 158, 298
Bow, 146, 153
Bow Mission, 347, 356
Bow Running Ground, 367

Bowley, A.L., 212–13, 234
Bowley, Ruth, 368
Bradford, 23
brawling, 331–2
Bray, Mr T.C., 260
brewery horseman, 279
Brewhouse Lane, 252
bribing, 268
bricklayers, children of, 255
Bridge, Revd S.F., 150, 155
Briggs, A::, 216–17, 225, 235
Bright, John, 71, 74, 79, 81–2
Bright, Mr, 183
Brinsmead's piano makers, 255
Brinson, Bill, 281
Bristol, 5
British Association for the Advancement of Science (BAAS), 6
British Museum, 26, 182
British Weekly, 5
Brixton Hill Methodist Church, 340
Bromley, 146, 151, 153
Brompton, 328
Bromsgrove Mission, St Andrew's Stockwell, 348
Brooke, Revd Charles, 343, 353, 355
Brooks, E.W., 21–2
Brown, John, 124
Brown, Sir James Crichton, 70
Bryce, James, 76
buildings, 266
burglar, the Hoxton, 332
Burnett, John, 26, 187
Bury, 9
Buss, Miss, 169, 173
Byrum Street, Deptford, 331

cabinet-maker/s, 109, 280
Cable Street, 252
Cadbury, George, 5

cadgers, 332
Camberwell, 257, 266, 282, 331
Camberwell Green
    Congregationalist Church,
    151, 347–8
Cambridge, 6
capital punishment, 118–19
cards, 267
carpenters, 109
Carroll, Revd W.A., 157, 342
casework, 56, 59, 62, 80, 82, 180
casual labour, 67, 70, 78–80, 83,
    130, 251
casual loafer, 331
casual workers, 122
catchment areas, 243, 255–7
catechisms, 120
Catholic priests, 356
Catholic schools, 247
Catholicism, 271, 278, 282, 345
Catholics, Roman, 37, 340, 344–6
causality, 55
census, 3–4, 6, 11, 24–5, 144
Census (1881), 191
Census (1891), 144, 246, 251,
    257
Census (1901), 206
census enumerators, 118
census enumerators' books, 275
censuses, religious, 3–6, 10
centrifugal tendency, 329
Chadwick, Edwin, 5, 118–19
Chalmers, 115–16
chamber or piece-master, 111
Chamberlain, Joseph, 81, 180–1
Champion, Mr, 154
Chandler, Miss, 354
Chandler, Revd A., 150
change, concept of, 329
change, theory of urban, 328
changes in labour, shopfloor
    responses to, 130
chapel/s, 266, 340, 341, 354

character, 51, 54, 56–9, 61–3, 70,
    75, 80–2, 247, 273, 307, 332
charity, 78, 262, 266, 268–9, 270,
    276, 278, 281, 297, 301–2
    scientific, 53, 59
Charity Organization Society,
    12–15, 21, 25, 33, 49, 52,
    68–9, 70, 73, 107, 151, 180,
    213, 265–6, 273, 278, 355,
    372
Charles Booth Research Centre, 1
Charles Booth – Social Scientist,
    211
Chartism, 114, 122
chauvinism, 107
chauvinist, male, 275
Chelsea, 246–7, 257
Chetham Society, 7
Chicago school, 324
Chicksand Street, Whitechapel,
    252
Chief Rabbi, 297, 311
Children of Mary, 347
children, school-age, 241–64,
    306, 333
children, under-representation of,
    126
cholera, 110, 122
Christ Church, North Brixton,
    341, 351
Christ Church, Watney Street,
    302
christenings, 270
Christian Mission, Sussex Road,
    Brixton, 354
Christian Street, 252
Christianity, 12, 274
Christmas presents, 349
church attendance, 6, 270, 339,
    341–2, 344, 346
church council, 341
church courting, 341
Church Crescent, Hackney, 272

church going, 267, 276–7, 279,
    281, 340–1, 343–4
Church of England, 351, 354–5
Church of Epiphany, Stockwell,
    341, 347
churches, 243, 260–2, 267, 269,
    274, 276, 278
churchings, 270
citizens/hip, 72, 77, 81–3, 135
City of London, 246–7, 251,
    256–7
City Temple, 271–2
civic virtue, 82
Clapham, 328
Clapson, Mark, 38–9
Clapton, 308
Clare Market, 333
class, 19–20, 68, 83, 122, 128,
    330, 344, 346, 353
    lower middle, 247, 256–7,
        272, 281
    middle, 107–10, 116, 121–2,
        124, 131, 268, 270, 275, 280
    poor rough, 333
    servant-keeping, 241, 257
    under, 68
class,
    church-going and, 37–8, 341
    fears, 131
    feeling, 20, 267
    and the Jews, 307–9
    leisure, 371
    prejudice, 133
    and religion, 268
    residential succession, 329
    structure, 333
classes, 109, 117
    A, 59, 123, 249, 331, 333,
        367, 370, 371–2
    B, 59, 61, 78, 123–4, 249,
        331–3, 367, 371–2
    Booth's social, 326, 329
    C, 39, 123–4, 249, 367

D, 39, 123–4, 249, 367
E, 123, 249
F, 123, 249, 367
classes,
    dangerous, 110, 116, 119,
        121,122
    economic, 123
    fluid boundaries between, 123
    labouring, 119, 121–2, 125
    Mayhew as intermediary
        between, 110
    professional, 14
    reconciliation of the, 115
    religious, 346
    social, 267
    submerged, 125
classical economics/sts, 80, 115
classification, 124–5, 131, 133,
    290, 323, 326
    of schools, 247
cleanliness, 261–2, 306–7
clergy, 21, 125, 147, 151, 155,
    260, 265–6, 270, 273–5, 278,
    281, 297–9, 302, 304, 308,
    310, 326–7, 333, 339–63
clerical attitudes, 339
Clerkenwell, 130
clerks, 256
clerks, Mayhew's, 111
Clewer Sisters, 347, 355
clubs, 38, 267, 307, 340, 343
    347–8, 369–70
    Catholic men's, 346
    football, 347
    girls', 347, 355
    holiday, 347
    provident, 356
    youth, 270, 277
Clubs and Institutes Union, 374
co-educational institutes and
    societies, 347
Coates, K. and Siburn, R., 203,
    232

Coldwell, Revd C.S., 155
Coleman, Mr, 183
Coleridge, S.T., 121
Collet, Clara, 22, 24, 25–6, 28,
    35, 165–200
    cultural interests of, 170–1
    social life and pastimes of,
    171–5
    romantic life of, 173–5
Collet, Collet Dobson, 168–9
collectivism, 17–19, 33, 63, 82
Collini, Stefan, 81
colonies, 61
colour, 57, 307, 323, 327, 333
Commercial Road, 252, 310
Commercial Road Baptist Church,
    298
common lodging houses, 295
communicants, 342
competition, 71, 130
compositors, 130
condition of England question,
    109
confraternities, 346
congregation/s, 265, 340–4, 347,
    351–2
Congregational Church, 272
Congregationalists, 272
conjugal roles among Jews, 311
Cons, Emma, 53
constables, 114
convalescent homes, 355
converts, female, 357
convicts, 110
cook, 279
cooking classes, 355
cooperage company, 128
co-operation, 17, 26
correspondence, 108
costermongers, 114, 331, 333
countrymen, 343
countryside, 366
courses, 347

Courtney, Leonard, 23, 26
Cowan, Revd D.G., 353
Cox, Jeffrey, 37, 268–71, 273–8,
    357
Cox, Mr, 183, 185
craft societies, 129
crafts, 16, 114, 129–30
crèche, 348
Creighton, Mandell, 146
cricket, 249
crime, 6, 110, 119, 121–2, 304–5
criminal classes, 116–7, 119, 305
criminality, 8, 10, 110, 119
criminals, 135, 332, 371, 305–6
criminals, semi-, 123, 331, 371
Cripps, Alfred (later Lord
    Parmoor), 14–21, 24, 26
Crompton, Albert, 12, 13
Crompton, Caroline, 12
Crompton, Henry, 12
Cross Commission on Elementary
    Education, 255
Croydon, 328
Cruikshank, William, 134
Cullen, Michael, 11, 109
culture, 114, 118, 129–31, 326,
    328, 333
    Jewish, 290, 306, 309, 312
    popular (see also gambling
    and individual sports and
    pastimes), 38–9, 282, 365–80
    working-class sub, 126, 129,
    133, 269
    fancy sub, 365–80
culture of poverty, 372
curriculum, 121
curtains, 306
custom, 126
Cutler Street warehouse, 183
cycling clubs, 347

Daily News, 5
Dalston, 308, 372

D'Arcet, 110
Dare, Mr H.J., 257
Davenant, Charles, 4
Davenport, Revd George, 158, 302
Davies, Revd W.H., 301
Davis, John, 77
day work, 112
De la prostitution dans la ville de Paris (1836), 110
deaconess/es, 355–6
Deansgate, 9
death rate, 251
debating, 347
degeneracy (and associated terms), 61, 67–87, 122, 134
demand and supply, law of, 115
Democratic Federation, 15
Denison Club, 25
Denmark Place Baptist Church, 154
denomination/s, 266, 267, 271
dependence/y, 67–8, 73, 75
depravity (and derivatives), 119, 122
depression of 1892–95, 130
Descriptive Map of London Poverty, 1889, 324, 367, 373
destitution, 122
Devonport Society, 355
diaries, 165–200
Dickens, Charles, 108
diet, Jewish, 296
Diocesan Visitation Returns, 270
Dimsdale, Revd H.C., 302
Diplomatic Review, 168
discipline, 121, 261–2
distribution, 17, 26, 125
dock labour, descasualization of, 135
dock labourer, 80, 109, 184
dock missionary, 183
dock strike, 130, 135

dock strike (1912), 281
dock workers, 185, 331
docker, 282
dockers' wives, 185
dockland (see also waterside), 246, 371
'The Docks', 183–85
Docks, 21, 28
   Albert, 183
   East India, 183
   Millwall, 183
   St Catherine, 183
   Tilbury, 183
   Victoria, 183
   West India, 183
Dogberry Club, 170
dogs, 366, 367
domestic service, 109
Donald Street, Bromley, 279–80
Dorcas Society, 350
dosser, Spitalfields, 332
Douglas, Mr, 154
Downes, Arthur, 62
Dracup, Mr, 154
drama, 347
Draper, Revd John, 301, 303
drapery establishment, 271
drawings, 127
dress, 13, 126, 129, 266, 279
Drew, Inspector, 306–7
drill, 347
drinking (see also drunkenness), 68, 281, 251, 327, 332–3
Drinkwater, John Elliot, 6
Drinkwater, R.W., 204, 233, 226
Drummond Road Baptist Chapel, 275
drunken/ness, 260, 268, 274, 304, 306, 332–3, 373
Duckworth, George Herbert, 22, 26, 30, 38, 127–9, 146, 151, 153–4, 158, 271, 291, 302,

304, 307–8, 311, 326–31, 341, 356
Duke Street, 305
Dukinfield, 9
Duppa, B.F., 11
Durand Gardens Baptist Chapel, Stockwell, 352
Durham Methodists, 279
Dusthole, Woolwich, 331

earnings, 17, 20, 108, 111, 113, 122–3, 184, 206, 227, 290, 332
East Dulwich Baptist Church, 354
East Dulwich Church, Arnott Road, 156
East End (of London), 14, 19–23, 27, 29, 122, 131, 133, 186, 246, 257, 273, 279, 280, 282, 289–90, 292, 297, 299–300, 302, 304, 308, 311, 323, 325, 367, 369
Easter Sunday, 340
Ebenezer Congregationalist Chapel, Watney Street, 299
economic analysis, Mayhew's, 116
economics, Booth's under-consumptionist, 89–102
economics, neo-classical, 73
economics, replacement of classical, 135
Economy of Machinery and Manufacturers (1832), 115
economy, transformation of urban, 113
Edey, John, 127
Edgeworth, Maria, 134
Edgeworth, Professor, 26
Edinburgh, 4
education, 8–10, 12–13, 17, 19, 28, 121, 242–64, 266, 269, 274, 290, 297, 325, 357

Education Act 1870, 246–7
Education Department, 248–9
education, social geography of, 36–7, 241–64
educational work of the churches, 266
Edwards, Clem, 21
effeminacy, 273
Eichholz, Alfred, 70, 83
eight-hours movement, 130
Elesh David, 10
élite, 269
Elliott, Miss, 354
Elliott, Revd R.J., 354
Elm Park, 327
Eltham, 146
embourgeoisement, 308
emigration, 17, 116
Emmanuel Congregational Chapel, Dulwich, 344
Emmanuel Congregational Church, Barry Road, Dulwich, 150
empirical, 2, 4, 10–12, 106, 113, 119–20, 124, 133–4
empiricism, 118, 124
employer/s, 16–18, 125, 128–30
employment, 4, 13, 16, 17, 109, 115, 121–2, 124, 131, 280, 328, 353
endowment, 298–9
Engels, Friedrich, 170
engine drivers, 256
engineering trade, 17, 109
Englander, David, 32, 38, 333
entertainer, 272
entertainments, 267
environment, 70–2, 79, 83, 121, 326, 328, 332
environmental influences, 69, 122
ethical movement, 82
ethnicity, 129, 289
ethnography, 117

ethnology, 117
eugenics (and derivatives), 70, 72, 83
evaluation, 119, 126, 310–11
Evangelical (and derivatives), 72, 120, 153
evangelicalism, 272
Evans, E.J., 203, 232
evening,
    chapel activities in the, 352
    services, 277
evensong, 341–2
evolutionism, 67–87
evolutionist assumptions, 117, 332
expenditure, 13, 115, 126
expertise, 133
explanation, 113, 309
exploitation, 114

Fabians, 69
factories, 8, 125
factory
    inspectorate, 297
    prison as a, 114
facts, 15, 54, 56–8, 60, 63, 118, 290
    social, 4, 49, 51, 56–7, 59, 110, 116
family/ies, 24, 26, 51, 53, 56, 58, 61–2, 121, 125–6, 205–6, 217–18, 227, 242, 260, 280–1, 295, 301, 330, 333, 340, 351–5
family budgets, 26
family reputation, 277
family responsibilities, 342
family strategies for survival, 278
fancy, 327, 365–80
Farr, William, 5, 11
fees, school, 247–9
Feldman, David, 309, 311
female, 341

environment of the home, 278
    perspective, 277
    respondents, 128
Fenian Barracks, 331, 333, 373
Fenn, Mary Ann, 107
Ferard, Catherine, 356
Field, Frank, 203, 232
Figaro in London, 108
Finsbury, 246, 366
firemen, 17
Fisher, Arabella, 180
Fishman, W.J., 311
Fleet Road School, 255–7
Fletcher, Joseph, 11
flower girls, 333
food, 13–14, 17, 129, 268, 277, 296
football clubs, 249
foreman/men, 16, 126–7, 130
Forest Gate, 259
Fox, Stephen, 28–9, 308
Foxwell, Professor H.S., 22, 25
free dispensary, Jewish, 303
Free, Mrs, 354
Free, Revd R., 354
french polisher, 282
Fulham, 146, 257, 332
fur trade, 292
furniture trade, 309

Gale Street, 356
gambling, 294, 305, 327, 333, 366–80
gardens, 327, 368
garment trade, 292
gas works, 330
gender, 83, 128–9
generalization, 132
gentiles, 300–1, 307, 310
George V, 203, 232
ghetto, 289, 296, 305, 307, 310, 311
ghetto, garb of the, 307

Gibbs, Mr, 183
Gibraltar Walk, 281
Giffin, Robert, 71
girls, schooling of, 247
Girls' Friendly Society, 347–8
Gissing, George, 166
Glasgow, 5
Glass, Ruth, 375
Globe Street, 252
Gloversville, 14
Gluckstein, Mr (and Posner), 292
Golding, Mr (SBV), 296
Gospel Oak, 255–6
goy, 305
Grace Alley, Whitechapel, 296
Graunt, John, 4
Great World of London, 108
Green, Alice, 165, 176, 191
Green, Revd J.R., 191
Greenwich, 246, 257, 260
Greenwood, James, 73, 105
Gregg, Samuel, 7
Gregg, William Rathbone, 7, 9
Grey, E.C., 28
Grosvenor, Norman, 24, 26
Grub Street, 169
Guild of Our Lady of Ransome, 347
Guild of Willing Helpers, 349
guilds, 348
Gun Street, 305
gunov (see crime), 305

H (Whitechapel) Division of the Metropolitan Police, 306
habits, 51, 59, 62–3, 78–9, 114, 121, 124, 261, 304, 307, 326, 331, 343
    sexual, 266
Hackney, 146, 257, 267, 272, 273, 308, 329, 367, 370, 372
Hackney Marshes, 367
Hackney Wick, 267

Hagenbuch, W., 203, 232
Hallam, Henry, 11
Hammersmith, 146
Hampstead, 146, 251, 254–5, 257, 308
handloom weavers, 8
Hardess Street, 348
Harding, Arthur, 281
Hare Street, 368
Harkness, Margaret (Maggie), 191
Harney, G.J., 105
Harris, José, 135, 228
Harrison, Frederick, 26
Harvest Festivals, 270
hats, 333
hatters, 109
hawkers, 331
headmasters, 249, 255–7, 259–60, 265, 273
health-care, 4, 11, 270
Hebrew Cabinetmakers' Association, 310
Hebrew Guild of the East End Mission to the Jews, 301
hedonism, 119, 134
Henderson, Mr, 8–9
Hennock, Peter, 35, 50, 59–60, 124, 373
Herklots, Revd G.A., 299
Hewlett, Perse, 151
Heywood, Benjamin, 7–9
Heywood, James, 7–9
Higgs, Henry, 21, 25–6, 176–7
Highbury New Park, 308
Hill, Octavia, 15, 18, 25, 28–9, 33, 49–51, 53, 55–6, 61–3, 80, 82
Himmelfarb, Gertrude, 32, 73, 124–5
Hobhouse, L.T., 71
Hobsbawm, Eric, 277
Hoffman, Mr, 185

Holborn, 257
Holman, R., 203, 232
Holy Communion, 345
Holy Trinity, Shoreditch, 266
home/s, 113, 125–6, 250, 261,
    278, 329, 333, 341–3, 345–6,
    348–9, 352
Hope Mission, Camberwell, 154
Horne, Revd Walter, 355
hospitals, 355
host-minority relations, 309–10,
    312
hours, 17, 18
household (and associated terms),
    4, 24, 72, 76, 206, 219, 227,
    270, 277, 278, 295, 326
houses, 16, 266, 327–30
housing, 11, 14, 18–19, 29, 274,
    330–1
How the Labourer Lives, 216
Howard, Esmé, 26, 30–1
Hull, 9
Humpherys, Anne, 111, 132
Humphreys, N.A., 23
Huxley, T.H., 71, 348
Hyndman, H.M., 15–16, 18–20

idealist (and derivatives), 56, 82,
    135
immigrant trades, 290, 308
immigrants, 295, 307–10, 371–2
immigration, 38, 252, 289–91,
    310, 312
Imperialism, 325
income, 13, 14, 18, 53, 58, 112,
    114, 123–4, 126, 290
independence, 62, 75, 81–2, 114,
    122–3, 125, 262
individualism (and derivatives),
    12, 18–19, 33, 50, 63, 70, 72,
    82, 293
Industrial Democracy, 25, 178
industrial relations, 20, 126–7

Industrial Society, 348
industries, 125
industry, 8, 22, 112, 119, 121,
    328–30
Industry Series, 19, 24, 28,
    125–8, 130, 243
influences, non-material, 123
inheritance, 70–1, 80
inner ring, 328
inquiry, 8, 10, 21, 24–7, 110,
    131–2
Inquiry, milieu of the, 21–6
insecurity, 280
intellectual aristocracy, 26
Interdepartmental Committee on
    Physical Deterioration (1904),
    69
interviews and interviewing, 27,
    28, 29, 56–8, 110–12, 125–8,
    133, 143–64, 186–8, 259,
    265–6, 271–3, 275–6, 279,
    297, 304, 310, 326–7, 339,
    346, 357
    (see also social investigation
    and methodology)
Irish, 251–2, 280, 289–90, 305,
    331, 333
Irish home rule, 76
irreligion, 269
Irving, Henry, 170
Isle of Dogs, 146, 155, 281
Islington, 146, 272

Jackson, D., 203, 232
Jago, 305
Jamaica Road, 271
Jay, Revd Osborne, 266
Jeffrey, William, 127
Jerrold, Douglas, 108
Jerrold, Jane (Mayhew), 108
Jevons, W.S., 69, 105, 176
Jew, the Whitechapel, 332

Jewish Anti-Conversionist
   Society, 303
Jewish Board of Guardians, The,
   189, 294–7
Jewish Chronicle, 189, 297
Jewish clergy, 311
Jewish community, the, 189–91
Jewish Mothers' Meeting, 301
Jewish Trade Unionists, 293–4
Jewish worker, 309, 312
Jews, 35, 38, 251–2, 268,
   289–322, 333, 371–2
Jews and gambling, 370–2
Jews, converted, 158, 300–4
joiners, 109
Jones, Benjamin, 165, 191
Jones, Gareth Stedman, 68, 116,
   131, 277
Jones, Greta, 68
Jones, Richard, 6
journalism/ist/s, 105–9, 134
Judaism, 282, 290–1, 293, 299,
   304, 310–12
jumble sale, 350
Junior Economic Club, 22, 25–6,
   178
juvenile delinquency, 333
juveniles, 114

Kadish, Alon, 14, 33
Katharine Buildings, 21, 53, 180,
   184–5, 189, 292
Kay-Shuttleworth, Sir James, 7, 8,
   10, 75
Kensal Green, 332
Kensington, 77, 308
Kentish Town, 255
Kenyon Baptist Church, Acre
   Lane, 340
Kenyon Baptist Church, Clapham,
   153–4
Kerrigan, Mr (SBV), 183–4
Kidd, Benjamin, 71

Kincaid, J.C., 203, 233
King, Gregory, 4
kinship, 129
Knott Mill, 9
knowledge, 121

labour, 16–17, 20–1, 54, 61, 119,
   121, 124–5
   casual, 61
   colonies, 61, 68, 78, 82, 135
   degradation of, 113
   department of the Board of
      Trade, 24, 177–8
   division of, 113, 130
   force, 128
   market, 61, 78, 113, 122,
      124–5, 135
   migrant, 54
   process, 127
   question, 115, 120, 308
   sexual division of, 277–8
   skills, 112, 114, 122, 129, 133
   supply, 125
   surplus, 115–16
   sweated, 59
   training, 120, 125
Labour and Life of the People,
   243
Labour Party, 157, 281
labouring poor, 32, 255
Ladies' Christian Association,
   354
ladies, middle-class, 353
laissez-faire, 69–70
Lakeman, John, 187, 192
Lamarckianism, 312
Lambert, Mr, 366
Lambeth, 268, 270
Lancashire, 275
landlord, 11, 16
Langton, William, 7, 8
language, 111, 129, 132, 259,
   272, 280, 307, 310, 333, 374

Lansbury, George, 282
laundries, 255
Lawless, Father, 345
Lawley, Revd, 351–2
Lawson, Robert, 23
lay reader, 353
lay witnesses, 273
lay workers, 340
laymen, 274
League of Mothers, 346, 349
leather trade, 127–9
lectures, 267
Leeds, 5
Lefroy, W.C., 28
legislator, 120
Leicester, 170–5
Levi, Professor Leone, 23–4, 373
Levy family, 188
Lewis, 117
Lewis, Harry, 21
Lewis, Jane, 33, 34
Lewis, Revd Dolfan, 298–9
Lewisham, 257
liberalism, 51, 116, 135, 291–4, 312
libraries, 249
Life and Labour of the People in London, 2, 32–4, 78–9, 82, 133, 143–4, 166, 176, 180, 241, 243, 272, 289, 291, 309, 311, 323
light blue streets, 307, 329
Limehouse, 259
Linnecar, Mr, 154
linotype machine, 130
Lissagary, 169
literary society, 348
Liverpool, 4, 5, 9, 12–13, 271, 282
living conditions, 261, 332
living rooms, 327
living standards, 67, 109, 123, 289

Llewellyn Smith, Hubert, 21, 22, 25, 26, 29–30, 178, 190
Lloyd George, David, 218
loafers, 122–3, 370–1, 374
Loane, Margery, 58
Loch, C.S., 25, 70, 181
London, 10, 11, 15, 19, 23, 78, 107–8, 110, 125, 127, 132, 251, 267, 276, 289, 291, 304, 323, 325, 327–8, 343
    central, 28, 325, 352
    north, 28
    outer south, 328
    religion in, 277, 282
    socialism in, 281
    south, 328, 330
    south-west, 328
    west, 328–9
    west central, 308
    working class, 276, 279
London City Missionaries, 276, 298, 302, 374
    Mayhew's help from, 111
London Diocesan Deaconess Institution, 356
London Docks, 252
London Ethical Society, 82
London Hospital, 27, 292
London Labour and the London Poor, 1, 32, 105–8, 110, 117, 131, 134, 185
London School Board, 242, 246, 248–50, 252, 255, 259–60, 295, 366
London School of Economics, 265, 291
London, Survey of, 68
London University, 25
Lordship Lane Roman Catholic Church, 156
low life/ves, 105, 135, 331–2
Low Wages, 108, 116
Lower Chapman Street, 252

lumpen proletariat, 74

Macaulay, Charles Zachary, 14
Macaulay, Thomas Babington, 14
McBriar, A., 49
McCulloch, 115
Macdonald, James, 15–21, 28, 29
MacGregor, Susanne, 373
Mackenzie, Holt, 10
Mackenzie, Revd E.C., 155
McKibbin, Ross, 58
McLachlan, H.V., 227, 237
McLeod, Hugh, 37, 373
Maddison, Fred, 21
Madge, John, 311
Maida Vale, 146
Maitland, Eva, 26
Maitlands, the, 169
Majority Report of the Royal
    Commission on the Poor Laws,
    61–3
Mahomed, Revd J., 292
male, 341
male environment, 278
male perspective, 268, 277
male population, small contact of
    church with, 342
Malthus, Thomas, 6, 69
Malthusian assumptions and
    theories, 14, 113, 122, 135
management, 130
Manby Smith, Charles, 131
Manchester, 4, 8, 9, 282
Manchester Statistical Society
    (MSS), 5, 7–10
Mandeville, Bernard de, 119–20
manners and morals of the poor,
    243, 259–60
Mansfield Road, 256
Mansion House Inquiry, 27
Mansion House Mission,
    Camberwell, 154
manual occupations, 275, 310

manufacture, 9, 20, 108, 113–14,
    130
maps, 242, 247, 279, 304–7,
    321–38,
margins, life at the, 128
marital conflict, 277–8
market (see also labour), 115,
    120, 125, 130
market porters, 333
marriage, 6, 26, 68, 79, 277, 354
marriage registers, 275
marriages, mixed, 344
Marsden, William, 36
Marshall, Alfred, 22, 24–6, 69,
    77–9, 81, 191, 227
Marshall, T.H., 57–8, 211, 231,
    234, 237
Martley, W.G., 151
Marx, Eleanor (Tussy), 169–71,
    176
Marx, Karl, 15, 74, 106, 113,
    169–70, 311
Mary Place, 374
Marylebone, 246–7
Mason, Revd H.Q., 152–3
masses, 344
master/s, 16, 119, 129–30, 297
Masterman, Charles, 325
materialist, 1, 12, 266
Maternity Society, 350
Maulty, Mr, 183
Maus, Heinz, 311
Mayhew, Athol, 105
Mayhew, Augustus, 108, 111
Mayhew, Henry, 2, 27, 32–4, 73,
    105–42, 184–5, 289
Mayhew, Joshua, 107
Mayhew, Thomas, 107
Meade, J.E., 203, 233
measurement, 123
mechanics, children of, 259
Medical Mission for the Jews,
    303

Medical Relief (Disqualification
    Removal) Act, 1885, 76
Meinertzhagen, Daniel, 183
Memoir, 49
men, 114, 275, 277–8, 339–43
Men's Owns, 265
Mental Deficiency Act (1913), 72
meritocracy, 256
Messer, Fred, 282
metal trade, 109
method, 311, 323–4, 326
    comparative, 291, 311
    research, 57
    scientific, 52
Methodist, 340
methodology, 24, 32–4, 56–9, 62,
    105–42, 143–63, 164–200,
    201–38, 311, 323–4, 326
methods, 2
    deductive, 55
    inductive, 4, 55, 118
    qualitative, 49
    quantitative, 49
    social research, 15
metropolis, 2, 329
Metropolitan Commissioner, 116
migration, 280, 328
migration, general law of
    successive, 329
Mildmay Mission, 356
Mile End New Town, 298
Miles Platting, 9
Mill, John Stuart, 1, 114–16
Millwood, Mrs, 354
Milner, Alfred, 22
minister, part-time, 352, 354
ministers, 148–9, 151, 339–41,
    343, 375
ministry, women's, 339
Minority Report, 60–1
Mission Hall, 349
mission women, 352, 353–6
missionary effort, 298, 342, 374

missioners, 300, 339, 343, 373–5
missions, undenominational, 279
model dwellings, 27–8
Modern Records Centre, Warwick
    University, 174
Monday afternoon, 277
Monmow Road, 248
Montague, Samuel, 190
Montgomery, Revd Robert, 105
Morgan, Revd Campbell, 374
Morning Chronicle, 106–10, 117,
    120, 124
morning service, 342
Moses, Mrs (of Oxford Street,
    Whitechapel), 188
Mothers' Meeting, 269, 270,
    346–8, 351, 355
Mowle, Revd W.A., 341
Mr Charles Booth's Inquiry, 27
*Mr Mayhew's Spelling Book for
    the Working Classes*, 134
Mudie-Smith, Richard, 5
Mulvaney, Superintendent, 306
Mundella, A.J., 176
Municipal Registration Act
    (1878), 76
murder, 333
Murname, Canon (Mission
    Priest), 355
music, 256, 347
My Apprenticeship, 165–6, 175,
    182–3, 187

Nash, R., 211
National Anti-Gambling League,
    1889/90, 369
National Association for the
    Promotion of Social Science
    (NAPSS), 11–12, 73
National Commission on the Birth
    Rate (1912–16), 70
natural law, 80, 329
natural selection, 17, 67–9, 71, 81

needlewomen, 348
Neil, Mr, 151
Nelson, George, 151, 155
Nelson Street, 331
Neugewitz, Mr, 302
Nevinson, Henry Woodd [sic], 21
New Cross, 8
New Poor Law, 82
New Square, Whitechapel, 368
*New Survey of London Life and
    Labour,* 178, 312, 368
New Unionism, 130
New York, 282
Newland, Miss, 259
Nicol, the, 5, 333, 374
Nicol, Old, 77, 305
Nicoll, William Robertson, 5
night school, 301, 354
Nineteenth Century, 188
Nonconformist, 271–3, 275, 279,
    280–1, 292, 354, 370
North Brixton, 328
North London Collegiate School,
    168, 173–4
North London line, 256
North Place, Mile End New
    Town, 279
notebooks, interview and police,
    24, 27, 125, 127–31, 133,
    147–9, 265, 295, 300, 307,
    327–8, 339, 355, 365, 374
Notting Dale, 331–2, 374
Noyes, Revd J.P., 153, 155
nurse, 354–6
    Bible, 353
    district, 352
nursing sister, 349

observation, field, 110, 115, 126,
    133, 304, 326–7
occupation/s, 9, 19, 53, 59, 242,
    290, 326
O'Day, Rosemary, 21, 34, 38, 296

office jobs, 279
oilman, 327
old age, 14, 61
old age pensions, 25, 33, 50, 55,
    61,135
Old Baptist Union Chapel,
    Stockwell, 347
Old Ford Parish Church, 153,
    155, 353–4
Oliver, George, 127
open spaces, 324
opinions, 10, 123, 127, 271, 326
opium eater, the case of the, 52
oral history, 270, 275–6, 279
orders, 340
organic language, 69
Origin of Species, 69, 80
Our Girls' Club, 347
Outcast London, 68
*Outline of a Work Entitled Pauper
    Management Improvement,* 73
overcrowding, 122, 246, 248, 251,
    330, 333
Owen's College, Manchester, 7
Oxford, 6

painting, 347
Paley, Mary, 26
Pall Mall Gazette, 241, 325
Palmer, Mr, 128
Parent-Duchâtelet, Alexander,
    110
Paris, 110
parishioners, 266
Parker, Revd Joseph, 272
Parker Street, 366
parliamentary inquiries, Mayhew
    and, 109
Parry, Revd J., 151, 156
parson's wife, 354
parsons, 120, 275
pastoral work, 351, 355

Patent Leather Dressers' Society, 127
Paul, Maurice Eden, 27, 182
pauper line, 181
pauper population, 60
pauperism, 25, 67, 75, 82, 116, 122
pauperization, 121, 268
payments systems, 128
Peabody's dwellings, 184
Pearson, Karl, 69
Peckham Rye, 265
penal system, 114, 119
Pendleton, 9
Penny Bank, 249, 347
personal influences, 122
'Personal Observation and Statistical Inquiry', 56
perspectives
    female, 38
    male, 37–8
Peter Street, 9
Petty, William, 4, 6
pew rents, 298–9
philanthropy (and derivatives), 11, 12, 14, 21, 27, 33, 52–3, 58, 62, 74, 105, 120–2, 176, 272, 274, 339
Philosophy of Manufacturers (1835), 115
phrenologists, 117
piano craftsmen, 255–6
Pick, Daniel, 68
piece or day work, 112, 128
piety, 268, 310
pitch and toss, 294, 333, 374
Plant, Raymond, 49, 58
Pleasant Sunday Afternoons, 265
pleasure, 119
Plough Buildings, 296
pogroms, 289
Pointer, Mr (SBV), 296
Poles, 289

police/men, 123, 134, 280, 297, 304–10, 326–7, 332–3
    ex-, 295
police notes, 324, 330–3
political activism, 281
political arithmetic, 4, 5, 6
political economy, 6, 10, 33, 55, 72, 106, 108, 114, 116–17, 122, 134, 166, 176
Political Economy Club, 20
poor, 8, 11, 13–15, 17–21, 28, 33–4, 49, 51, 53, 58–60, 63, 67–8, 73–4, 77, 79–80, 83, 109–10, 117–19, 121, 123–5, 135, 201, 203, 207–9, 217–18, 225, 246, 268–9, 290, 307, 310, 327, 330–3, 339, 348, 353
    deserving, 119, 122, 349
    labouring, 32, 133
    outcast, 124, 134
    respectable, 50, 61
    undeserving, 52, 122, 295
    very, 72, 76–8, 81–2, 307
Poor Law, 60–2, 73, 134
Poor Law (1834), 50, 55, 61
Poor Law records, 276
Poor Law reform, 62
Poor Law Unions, 176, 191
Poor Man's Guardian, 107
Poplar, 146, 281, 351, 353–4
popular beliefs, 278
population, 4, 22, 108, 115, 123–4, 126, 210, 222, 243, 255, 275, 324, 331
port labour, 13
Porter, George Richardson, 10, 11
Portman Place Board School, 260
portraits, pen, 327
Positivism, 2, 14, 81–2, 124, 135, 271, 273, 291
Posner, Mr (and Gluckstein), 292
postman, 282

Potter, Beatrice, 14, 15, 20–1, 23, 25, 26, 28, 35, 52, 53, 56, 63, 80, 133, 165–200, 291–4, 296, 308–10, 312, 371–3
Potter, Kate (Courtney), 14
Potter, Mary, 14
Potter, Richard, 14
Potter, Teresa (Cripps), 14
poverty, 1, 2, 4, 10, 14, 19, 20, 25, 28, 33–4, 70–2, 74, 80, 82–3, 110, 115, 119, 122, 124–5, 242, 246–7, 251–2, 255, 257, 269, 290, 304, 310–11, 323, 325, 329–33, 340
Poverty in the United Kingdom, 209
  causes of, 59, 61, 67
  primary, 35–6, 201–3, 206–9, 212, 214–16, 218, 222–4, 373
  problem of, 19, 59–60, 62–3
  relativistic concept of, 35–6, 201–2, 204, 207–9, 212, 217, 220, 222–7, 229
  secondary, 35–6, 202–4, 206–9, 212, 214, 222–5, 373
  variable definition of, 204, 220, 224
  vicious, semi-, 373
poverty line, 14, 35, 58, 77, 123–4, 203–4, 207, 211, 213, 215–16, 218, 219, 223–5, 227–9
poverty map, 324
Poverty Series, 2, 19, 20, 25, 27, 28, 125, 144, 295, 323, 325, 329, 366
prayer, 272, 277, 346, 349, 352
prayer meetings, 341–2, 347
precision manufactures, 109
prejudice, 118, 129, 132, 295, 303, 306, 309, 333
prescriptions, 355

prices, 18, 112, 130
Primitive Methodist Chapel, Crystal Palace Road, 154
Principles of Economics, 227
Principles of Political Economy, 115
Principles of Sociology, 80
priests, 332, 355
printing, 109
prison/s/ers, 108, 114
Pritchard, 117
private property, 116
production, 18, 26, 113–6, 125–30
progress, 124, 135
proletariat, 34, 76, 106
property, 75, 119, 125, 132, 134, 330
prostitution, 119, 327, 331
protectionists, 20, 134
Protestant/s/ism, 153, 248, 282, 290, 343, 346
public hygienists, 11, 110
public inquiry, 110
public meeting/s, 110, 128
public opinion, 267, 302
publicans, police relations with, 327
Punch, 108, 119
purple streets, 307, 329
Putney, 328, 330
Pycroft, Ella, 182

questionnaire (see also schedules) 10, 126, 128, 297
Quetelet, Adolphe 6, 11

race, 53
Radcliffe Highway, 331
Radford, Ernest, 169
Ragged School Union, 120
railway guards, 110

railways, 18, 125, 255–6, 328, 330–1
Ramsay, Mr, 150
Ramsey, Revd, 150, 344
Rawson, Rawson, 10
reasoning
    deductive, 58
record keeping, 53, 113
recreation, 129, 269–70
Red Republican, 105
Reeder, David, 38–9
reformatories, 114
regeneration, 274
Regent's Canal, 306
Registrar General, 24–5
rehabilitation, 118, 121
Reid, Inspector, 306–7
Rein, M., 203, 232
relief, poor, 52, 55, 61, 115, 269, 270, 273, 303, 352, 355
religion, 10, 53, 129, 143–63, 262, 265–88, 325, 339–68,
    alleged affinity of women for, 341
    Jews and Judaism, 289–322
    paradoxical position of women in, 340
    women in Victorian, 339–65
    working-class, 265–88
religiosity, 38, 268–70, 343
religious backgrounds of Labour MPs, 281
religious belief, changes in, 274
religious debate, 277
religious festivals (see also individual festivals), 278
religious indifference, 268
Religious Influences Series, 6, 19, 34, 37, 143–63, 243, 260–1, 265–88, 290–1, 297, 311, 324, 327, 329, 339–68, 373–4
religious life of women, 270, 340

religious meetings, segregated 277
religious observance, 270
religious services, 346
religious upbringing, 344
religious worship, 343
rent/s, 11, 76, 112, 126, 295, 305, 326–8
rent of ability, 20
rent collection, 53, 61
rent collectors, 51
Report on the Constabulary, 1839, 118
residential segregation, 243
residuum, 34, 61–2, 67–87, 122, 134, 246, 333
residuum, political, 82
respectable (and derivatives), 68, 75, 119–20, 122, 275–6, 279–80, 306–7, 341, 343, 348
Ricardo, David, 72, 115
Rickman, J., 4
rites of passage, 278
Ritualism, 266
rituals, 277
riverside, poverty and, 330
Robinson, Mr, 185
Rochester, Bishop of, 146
Rodgers, B., 203, 233
Roe, James, 356
Roehampton, 146
Roman Catholic Church of the Sacred Heart, Knatchbull Road, 355
Roman Catholic churches, 280
Ropeyard Rails, the Dusthole, 331
Rose, Edward, 169
Rose, M.E., 203, 233
Rosenthal, Revd Michael, 303
Ross, Ellen, 276–8
Rotherhithe, 271
Rothschilds, 293
rough, 122, 279, 305–7, 331–3

rough boys, 354
rowdyism, 274
Rowntree, Seebohm, 1, 2, 27,
    34–5, 36, 58, 201–32, 373
Royal Commission on the Care
    and Control of the Feeble
    Minded, 70
Royal Commission on Handloom
    Weavers, 11
Royal Commission on the
    Housing of the Working
    Classes, 53, 69, 82
Royal Commission on Labour,
    131, 176, 191–2
Royal Commission on the Poor
    Laws, 49, 50, 60, 69, 376
Royal Commission on Venereal
    Disease, 70
Royal Commissions, 10, 109, 147
Royal Economic Society, 21, 25,
    26, 178
Royal Statistical Society (also
    London Statistical Society), 2,
    5–7, 10–11, 21, 23–6, 28, 78,
    178, 241, 295
Rugby Club, 374
Rural Dean of Camberwell, 340
Ruskin, John, 52
Russell, Clark, 105
Rutland, 9
Rutland Street, 252

Saffron Hill, 259
sailmakers, 130
sailor's wife, 331
St Andrew's, Bethnal Green, 351
St Andrew's, Stockwell Green,
    356
St Anne's, Underwood Street, 146
St Anne's Road, Stockwell, 354
St Catherine's, Loughborough
    Park, 356

St Cuthbert's Anglican Mission,
    Isle of Dogs, 354
St Frideswide's, 157, 340, 347,
    353, 355
St Gabriel's, Bromley, 155, 352
St George, 348
St George's Street, 252
St George's-in-the-East, 11, 246,
    251–3
St George's Yard, 184
St James, Camberwell, 342
St John the Divine, Kennington,
    343, 353, 355
St John's Wood, 257
St John's, Commercial Road, 298
St John's, Isle of Dogs, 344, 353
St John's, Westminster, 11
St Jude's, East Brixton, 353
St Jude's, Whitechapel, 22, 300
St Luke's, Millwall, 151
St Margaret's, Westminster, 11
St Mark's, Dalston, 299
St Mark's, Maida Vale, 299
St Mark's, Whitechapel, 157,
    300, 302
St Martin's, Victoria Park, 341,
    356
St Mary, 300
St Mary's Kilburn, 299
St Mary's, Spitalfields, 301
St Mary's, Whitechapel, 301
St Matthew's, Bethnal Green, 281
St Matthew's, Brixton, 340,
    347–51
St Matthias, Poplar, 151
St Michael's, 8
St Michael's, South Bromley, 155
St Olave's, Hanbury Street, 298–9
St Olave's, Southwark, 257
St Pancras, 146
St Paul's, Bethnal Green, 281
St Paul's, Herne Hill, 150, 155
St Paul's, Whitechapel, 158

St Peter's Square Catholic
    Church, 346
St Saviour's, Brixton Hill, 340,
    355
St Saviour's, Camberwell, 348
St Saviour's, South Hampstead,
    299
St Saviour's, Southwark, 257
St Stephen's, East India Dock
    Road, 354
St Stephen's, North Bow, 152,
    341, 351–2
St Stephen's, Spitalfields, 300
Sala, Augustus, 131
Salford, 4, 9
Salisbury, Lord, 77
Salvation Army, 69
Samuel, Raphael, 265, 276, 279,
    281
Sandringham Road, 308
sanitation, 55, 110, 351
Sargent, Revd Alfred, 340
Saturday Review, 131
savages/ry, 117, 274
savings banks, 10, 270
Savoy Hotel, 29
Schapira, Revd A.W., 301
schedules, 10, 149, 151–2
scheduling, 242
Schloss, David, 21, 24, 26, 28,
    185, 187, 291, 294, 310
school age, 345
School Board Chronicle, 241
School Board Division, 243, 247
School Board Visitors, 24, 27, 28,
    58, 123, 126, 147–8, 181, 183,
    242, 257, 259, 295–7, 310,
    326, 366, 368–70
School Boards, 36
school buildings, 252, 260–1
school concerts, 256
school teachers (see teachers)
schools, 243, 247–9, 250, 252

Scotland, central, 275
Scott Holland, Revd Henry, 157
scripture reader, 300, 356
Scurr, John, 282
Second Reform Act 1867, 74
secretaries (see also associates),
    21, 27, 265
secular agencies, 273–5, 281
secularism (and derivatives), 269,
    276–7, 282
Select Committee on Distress
    from Want of Employment
    (1894–96), 69, 80
self-employed, 127, 294
self-help, 68, 80, 122
self-respect, 261, 348
servant/s (see also class), 24, 206,
    220, 290, 308, 341, 345–6,
    352
services, 266, 340–1, 348, 354
sewing, 347, 355
    machine, 281, 296–7
sex imbalance, 341
sex lives of the poor, 266
Shackewell Lane, 308
Shaw, Christopher, 68
Shelton Street, 333, 373
Shepherd Street, 305
Sherwell, Arthur, 375
shoemakers, 109
shop clubs, 129
shopkeepers, 255, 259
shopping, 345
shops, 125
shopworkers, 22
Shoreditch, 257, 274
sick, 280, 352–4
silk weavers, 28, 114
Sim, Stephen, 183, 185
Simey, T.S. and M., 211, 265,
    323
Sims, George, 105, 131

Singer Sewing Machine
   Collectors, 187
singing, 347
Sister Constance, 355
sisterhoods, Church of England,
   355–7
Skinner, Marian, 170
slate clubs, 129
sleeping arrangements, 351
slop-clothing workers, 109
slums, 12, 70, 76, 122, 242,
   249–51, 260, 294, 331
smallpox hospital, 255
Smith, Adam, 72, 115
Smith, Goldwin, 77
Smith, Mrs, 354
snapshot, 55, 57
snob/bery, 271, 281
Snow, Father Benedict, 156
sobriety, 8, 112, 123
sociability, patterns of, 129
social action, 1, 4, 14–15, 50, 54,
   56, 63, 118, 122, 125, 135,
   351
social area differentiation in the
   1890s, 253
social catchment, 256
social class (see class)
Social Darwinism, 67–87
Social Democratic Federation,
   68–9
Social Democratic Party, 282
'Social Diagnosis', 15, 54, 56
social evenings, 347
social history of education,
   241–64
social imperialists, 71–2
social inquiry, traditions of, 2–12,
   134–5
social investigation, 1, 2, 4, 8, 9,
   11, 22, 27–8, 49–52, 54–7,
   59–60, 63, 177–8, 290–1, 323

social investigation, the data of,
   55–63, 109, 125–6, 128–9,
   132
social investigation as
   team work, 27–31
   women's work, 35, 165–200
social investigator/s, 3, 12, 28
   Booth as, 105–42, 365–380
   Mayhew as, 105–42
   women as, 165–200
social mapping, 39, 122–40,
   323–38
social mobility, 294, 308–9
social problem, 2, 14–16, 49, 50,
   69, 81, 274, 124, 125, 131
   administrative solutions to,
      59–60, 62–3, 68
   casework approach to the, 56,
      59, 62
social reform, 10, 80, 107, 109,
   120–1
social research, 110, 119, 323
social role of the churches, 271,
   358
social science, 7, 67, 80, 110,
   122, 132, 290, 312, 323
Social Science Congress, 75
social survey, 1, 50, 57
social theory, 1, 2, 49–66, 67–87,
   106, 135, 312
social topography, 328
social work, 15, 49–53, 59, 61–3,
   123, 266, 269, 292, 297, 326
socialism, 15, 16, 18–21, 33, 72,
   82, 125, 134, 281, 305, 311
societies, 114, 347
Sociological Society, 72
sociology, 1, 71
   British, 49, 118, 311
   empirical, 49, 106, 113, 119,
      120, 133, 134, 366
   urban, 324
soldiers, 295

Somers Town, 278
soup kitchen, 281
South Kensington, 15
South Lambeth, 246
South London Tabernacle,
    Peckham, 350
Southwark, 246, 328, 332
Southwark Park, 267
Spanish and Morocco Leather
    Dressers, 129
special streets, 352
special subject inquiries, 28
Spencer, Herbert, 54, 57–8, 69,
    80, 180–1
Spitalfields, 109, 114, 268, 300,
    367
Spitalfields Parish Church, 301
Spring Gardens, 305
Springett, Revd W.D., 340
Spurgeon, 272
Stalybridge, 9
Stanley, Edward, 9
standard of living, 261, 310
Standards I–VI, 249–50
state, 62–3, 73, 78, 135
station masters, 256
statistical framework, 123
statistical movement, 5–12, 109
statistical societies (see also
    Royal Statistical Society and
    Manchester Statistical
    Society), 5, 7
statistics, 4, 5, 10, 11, 24, 54–8,
    111, 123, 295, 312
Stephens, Mr, 151
Stepney, 251, 289, 292, 311
Stepney Green, 306
stereotypes, 37, 268–9, 276, 279,
    289, 294, 333
Stern, Revd, 311
Stockwell, 328
Stoke Newington, 308, 372
Stone, Revd, 299

street trades, 108, 117, 120, 123
street walkers, 110
streets, life on the, 333
suburbs, 272, 280–1, 289, 308,
    328–30, 333
suffrage extension, 74
Sultan Street, 331
Summerford Street School,
    Bethnal Green, 259
Sunday, 266, 270, 277, 280,
    341–2
Sunday School/s, 260, 278, 301,
    342, 347, 356
Sunday walks, Charles Booth's,
    265
superstition, 266, 273
Surrey Docks, 257
survey (and associated terms), 9,
    11, 16, 68, 111, 113, 116,
    121–3, 126, 129, 133–4,
    289–90, 294, 303–4, 308–12,
    324, 326, 329, 331, 333
survey methods, 205–8, 211–14,
    219–20, 228, 291, 312
sweated trades, 61, 113, 122–3,
    131
sweating, 185–6
sweating system, 21, 188–9, 294,
    296–7, 312
Swedish drill, 249
sweet shop, 249
Sweetnam, Revd, 153, 342
Sykes, W.H., 6
symposium, 15, 19
Synagogue, Cannon Street Road,
    298

Tabor, Mary, 28–9, 165, 249
Tailoring Trade, the, 186–9
tailors, 15, 17, 22, 28, 109, 113,
    186, 296, 308
Talbot, Bishop of Rochester, 270
Talbot Court, 2, 24

Talbot Square, 2, 27
tanneries, 248
teachers, 242–3, 247, 256–7, 259–60
teaching, 125, 346
team (see also associates, secretaries), 27, 266, 275
temperance campaigning, 274
tenement dwellers, 82
tenements, 330
Thacker, 356
Thackeray, W.M., 33, 34, 108
Thames, the, 329
The Criminal Prisons of London, 108, 114
'The Diary of a Young Assistant Mistress', 175
The Human Needs of Labour, 216, 219, 228
The Presbytery, Bow Common Lane, 356
The Referee, 266
theatrical work, 348
theft, 119
Thenard, M., 110
theology, liberal, 272
Third Reform Act, 76
Thomas, Mr, 183
Thompson, E.P., 32, 106
Thompson, Father Gordon, 356
Thompson, Paul, 75–6, 279
Thompson, Poulett, 5, 8
thrift (and derivatives), 17, 119, 123, 260, 279
ticket-of-leave men, 114
tickets, 355
Tillard, Margaret, 28, 165
time rates, 128
Times, The, 294
Titmuss, R.M., 227, 237
tobacco workers, 308
Tottenham, 282

Tower Hamlets, 16, 21, 27, 295, 298
Townsend, Peter, 36, 202–3, 209, 222, 224, 226–8, 229–31
Toynbee Economic Club, 22, 26, 28
Toynbee Hall Settlement, 21–4, 27, 29, 54, 158, 176–7,193, 291
Trade Boards, 178
trade unions, 13, 19, 24, 55, 110, 116, 125–9, 131, 135
tradition
    Booth, 375–6
    Mayhew, 376
traditions, 14
Trafalgar Square riots, 1886–7, 77
tram routes, 255
tramp, the Notting Dale, 332
tramps, 331
transportation, 135, 328
Trench, Sergeant, 306–7
Trevelyan, Sir Charles, 14
Trinity Congregational Street, Hanbury Street, 299
Trinity Mission, Camberwell, 345, 348, 352
Trinity Mission Notes, 345
trouserhand, Beatrice Potter as, 133
Truman's Brewery, 280

Ulster, 5
underclass, 68
under-consumption, 14, 115
unemployment, 15, 27, 60, 67, 78, 80, 281
Unitarians, 12, 172, 176, 271, 273, 341
University College, London, 25
University Settlements, 26
university teachers, 26

unskilled occupations, 109, 114, 126, 275
upstairs people, 343
urban parishes, size of, 358
urban survey, 324
Ure, Adam, 115
utilitarian/ism, 118–19, 121–2, 134

vaccination, 351
vagabond/s/age, 118, 122
Valpy, R.A., 24, 28
Vaughan, Herbert, Cardinal, 146
Veit-Wilson, John, 36
Vellum Binders' Society, 130
ventilation, 351
verification, 56–7, 127
vestry, 348–9
vice, 304
vicious, 331–2
    semi-, 333
Victoria Park, 153, 184, 308
Vigne, Thea, 275–6, 279
villas, 256
Vincent, A.L., 49, 58, 62
violence, 304, 331, 333
violin, 279, 330
visiting, 7, 53, 72, 242, 342, 346, 348–9, 351, 353, 355
    district, 355
visitors
    district, 269, 349, 351–3, 356
    lady, 51
vital statistics, 10, 11, 25
voluntary schools, 247, 256

wage fund theory, 114
wages, 67–8, 111, 113–16, 122–3, 127–8, 130, 206, 219, 227, 262, 289, 295, 309, 326
Walker, F.A., 20, 176
Walmer Lane, 374
Walters, Father, 146–7

Walthamstow, 28
Walworth, 328
Wandsworth, 257, 328
Wanless Street, 348
Wantage sisterhood, 355
Wapping, 252
washerwomen, 332
watch makers, 130
Watch Night, 270, 278
waterside trades, 114, 131, 331
wealth, 12–14, 340
weavers, 109
Webb, Beatrice, 49–51, 58–63, 69, 105, 147, 323
Webb, Sidney, 25, 26, 181, 292
Webbs, the, 78
weekday services, 341–2
Wesleyan/s, 268, 282, 299
Wesleyan Chapel, Cannon Street Road, 298
West End, 246
West Kentish Town, 255
Westminster, 246–7, 257
White, Arnold, 69
Whitechapel, 14, 251–2, 289–300, 302, 308, 310, 367
Whitechapel Road, 292
white-collar occupations, 127, 275
White Cross League, 69
Whitsun, 347
wife beating and desertion among Jews, 306, 311
Willesden, 308
Williams, John 'Jack', 15–21
Williams, Judge Montague, 306
Willink, H.G., 28
windows, 306, 327
wives, 266, 275, 277, 332
wives of ministers, 353
wives of sailors, 342
women, 28, 53, 57, 114, 126, 128, 165–200, 257, 268, 270,

276–8, 296, 306–7, 328,
331–2, 339–65
professional, 178–80
workers, 35, 38, 186–7
Women's Work, 191–3
Woolf, Leonard, 60
Woolwich Arsenal, 367
work, 1, 13, 16–20, 73, 79,
113–14, 119, 121, 124–7, 129,
262
women's, 22, 28, 191–3
workhouse, 15, 48
work tickets, 348
workers, 9, 12, 13, 17, 21, 53,
111, 115, 125–6, 129, 297
factory, 356
working class, 11, 16, 53, 67–8,
70, 73–4, 78, 80, 122–5, 131,
134, 219, 255, 260–2, 266,
268–9, 270–7, 295, 309, 326,
328, 330, 333
working-class life, 10, 14, 18–19,
58, 274
working-class religion, 268, 270,
275–6, 280
working-class woman, spiritual
position of, 270, 276, 345

working men, 19, 268, 270, 342
working women, 344
workplace, 19, 113, 126, 129–30,
343
workshop (and derivatives), 267,
277–8
workshop trades, 309
worship, 282, 310, 341, 345
Wright, Mr, 183
Wright, Thomas, 73
Wyggeston Girls' School,
Leicester, 171

Yeo, Eileen, 32, 106, 111
Yiddish, 300–1, 307, 310
York, 58, 201–2, 205, 207–9,
218, 220, 222, 223
Yorkshire, 275
young men, 340
young people, 341
Young People's Christian
Endeavour Society, 347
Young People's Institute, 347
Young Women's Christian
Association, 347
youth clubs, 270, 277